Conscious

Awakening

A JOURNEY OF ASCENTION
To seek the truth of who we really are, where we have been, why we are here, and to discover our true mission

A Research Compendium

Arlene Lanman

ABOUT THE AUTHOR – ARLENE LANMAN

John 8:32: 'Then you will know the truth and the truth will make you free.'

Even as a child Arlene Lanman knew she came from the stars. She's experienced some very strange things, such as signs and symbols, with the universe guiding her on a certain path that started as a near-daily dream, a childhood nightmare of running in pitch blackness, as if running away from the boogeyman. The dream changed over time. Eventually, Arlene could see that the path extended through the Murky Woods (as described within The Hobbit by J.R.R Tolkien), and there, a voice boldly directed her to "stay on the path."

The path led to a Degree in Architectural Design and Engineering, marriage, children and eventually becoming an Engineering Manager. At the age of 49, the path ended at an ancient gate at the edge of the forest, with a beautiful mountain meadow beyond that had no pathway. Free to explore the universe on her own, she has experienced much that cannot be explained, always aware that true reality is beyond what we see, taste, touch, feel and hear.

Three years ago Lanman developed the urge to find out who she really was. This led to recording the research results of her enlightenment within this compendium in the hope that others can discover the roots of their own journey to reveal who they really are and their mission in life.

BookBaby
7905 N Crescent Blvd
Pennsauken, NY 08110

Copyright @ 2019 by Arlene Lanman

All rights reserved. No part of the Compendium may be reproduced or utilized in any form or by any means, electronic or mechanical, including photocopying, recording, or by any information storage and retrieval system, without permission from the author.

Library of Congress Cataloging-in-Publication Data
Names: Lanman, Arlene, 1946-
Title: Conscious Awakening: The Journey of Ascension into the 5th Dimension / Arlene Lanman.
Description: Pennsauken, New York: BookBaby, 2019 | Includes chapter references and preface.
Identifiers: IISBN 978-1-54397-219-1
Subjects: LCSH: Spirit, Soul, Mind, Body | Why we Were Created | The Earth Experiment | Earth Life Preparation | Alternate History of the Universe & Earth | We Are at War | Supplement – Gnostic Creation of Man | Many Species Throughout the Universe | Life Lessons for the Soul - The Journey to "I Am We Are" – Why We Are Here | The Lesson of Love – What I Have Discovered | 5th World, Rising Earth Frequency, Change in Density | Raising the Frequency of the Soul | Connecting With the Universe, Be Grounded, Remove the Blockage Between Left & Right Brain, Raising Your Antenna | False 2nd Coming /Death, Reincarnation | Being an Old Soul in a Young Soul World, Challenges Before Entering the 4th Density | Human Energy Field (Aura), Levels of Consciousness, Densities, Vibrational Frequencies, Quality of Our Spiritual Light | Guide to the 13 Dimensions & Observed Fields | Are You A Wanderer?? | Spiritual Protection (Self-defense) | Description of the Universe | Glimpses Into Enlightenment | The Five Stages of Awakening | Spiritual Emergence Symptoms | Nine Types of Lightworkers | Disclosure Revelations, Earth Frequency Changes, Changes Due to Entering the Photon Belt, Change in Earth Density, Paradox of Time | Life and Death of Earth's Civilizations, Caveman is a Myth | What UFO Sightings, Alien & Ancient Civilizations | Are Trying to Tell Us | Where Are We & What Are We Today, Realm is Shifting, Reclaim Your Power, A New Paradigm, Evoking I Am We Are, Dance of the Polarities | My Story and Past Lives Reflections | Why I Know I am a Lyran | My Aura and Frequency | Angel Numbers | Dreams – Imagination, Memory or Intuition? | My Cat as Spiritual Guide, Guardian and Companion

Printed and Bound in the United States by BookBaby.

This Compendium was typeset in Times New Roman

Cover background by potitus lanarm | Shuterstock.

To send correspondence to the author of this compendium, mail a first-class letter to the author c/o BookBaby, and we will forward the communication, or contact the author directly at www.arlenelanman.net.

The great Masters, Socrates, Moses, Jesus, Muhammad, Buddha and others of the indigenous Peoples, have pointed out to us that which must be sacrificed, emptied and given up, before a new quality of being can appear. A cup already full, cannot accept new material. Ultimately, our life teaches us our part – often most painfully. Our immediate labor is to ready the ground within ourselves so that the seeds of truth can find fertile soil in which we can grow.

Paraphrase and rewrite of quote by Margaret Becker

CONTENTS

	Preface – The Journey to Self	1
1	Spirit, Soul, Mind, Body	9
2	Why we Were Created, The Earth Experiment, Earth Life Preparation	23
3	Alternate History of the Universe & Earth, We Are at War Supplement – Gnostic Creation of Man	35
4	Many Species Throughout the Universe	113
5	Life Lessons for the Soul - The Journey to "I Am We Are" – Why We Are Here	175
6	The Lesson of Love – What I Have Discovered	185
7	5th World, Rising Earth Frequency, Change in Density	195
8	Raising the Frequency of the Soul	205
9	Connecting With the Universe, Be Grounded, Remove the Blockage Between Left & Right Brain, Raising Your Antenna	215
10	False 2nd Coming /Death, Reincarnation	233
11	Being an Old Soul in a Young Soul World, Challenges Before Entering the 4th Density	243
12	Human Energy Field (Aura), Levels of Consciousness, Densities, Vibrational Frequencies, Quality of Our Spiritual Light	263

13	Guide to the 13 Dimensions & Observed Fields	279
14	Are You A Wanderer??	291
15	Spiritual Protection (Self-defense)	297
16	Description of the Universe	311
17	Glimpses Into Enlightenment	331
18	The Five Stages of Awakening	359
19	Spiritual Emergence Symptoms	373
20	Nine Types of Lightworkers	391
21	Disclosure Revelations, Earth Frequency Changes, Changes Due to Entering the Photon Belt, Change in Earth Density, Paradox of Time	397
22	Life and Death of Earth's Civilizations, Caveman is a Myth	429
23	What UFO Sightings, Alien & Ancient Civilizations Are Trying to Tell Us	469
24	Where Are We & What Are We Today, Realm is Shifting, Reclaim Your Power, A New Paradigm, Evoking I Am We Are, Dance of the Polarities	501
	FINAL THOUGHT	583

APPENDIX

1 My Story and Past Lives Reflections   535

2 Why I Know I am a Lyran   545

3 My Aura and Frequency   551

4 Angel Numbers   557

5 Dreams – Imagination, Memory or Intuition?   563

6 My Cat as Spiritual Guide, Guardian and Companion   579

PREFACE

All truth passes through three stages: first, it is ridiculed. Second, it is violently opposed. Third, it is accepted as self-evident. (Arthur Schopenhauer).

THE JOURNEY TO SELF

Have you been seeing 11:11 everywhere, such as on clocks, receipts, license plates, game scores? It is the Universe trying to contact you to tell you to WAKE UP to learn Old Souls mission in life, to find your true self, and to "Re-Member" who you really are and remember things that you have long forgotten. When you came into this life, you were "dummied-down" so that you would not remember past lives or even the mission you agreed to complete during this life.

For the New and Returning Soul – Most people on Earth are returnees. They have been here before, and they'll return another time. The term for this recycling of lifetimes is the wheel of reincarnation. Karma, people's action and reaction in life, is the motor. The cycle goes on – lifetime after lifetime, until you WAKE UP to the reality that you are a free-spirit that is uncontrolled by anyone or anything.

THIS COMPENDIUM WILL HELP YOU ESCAPE THE REINCARNATION TRAP

After a person recycles through many successive lives, a feeling comes that something is amiss with this scene, that something is wrong with the script. A thought creeps in and the soul begins to grope for the truth.

Each Soul begins each lifetime with a clean slate. Memory is erased of an individual's old missions and past lives, which allows for a fresh start. This kindness sidesteps a dead end. It avoids the error of someone taking up a new life and wasting it on past-life problems like revenge for a lost love, property, or social position.

Such memory loss is thus of benefit to the Soul's progress. Yet, somewhere along the line, Divine Spirit sends a spiritual wake-up call through one means or another, such as seeing 11:11 everywhere. The message is, "OK, it's time to remember why you came to Earth."

Before we came to Earth this time, we made an agreement with Self to reach some goal and thus make headway in spiritual unfoldment. However, we go through years of doubt and uncertainty. We sample one religion or another, tripping from area to area in the occult field, or shifting from philosophy to psychology, even to mathematics. It's all in pursuit of the key to life and truth.

Sometimes a seeker makes a few apparent gains, but at some point says, "There's got to be more than this" since some inner nudge leaves him/her unhappy with the knowledge so far gained. Some hidden impulse of the heart drives him/her on in unending pursuit of God and truth.

This Compendium will help you understand the truth in order for you to complete your mission.

For the Old Soul – the Wanderer/ Traveler: This Compendium is to help Old Souls remember what Old Souls once knew and to remind Old Souls of their mission to help the Earth to transition into the 4th Density (Revelation 21 Then I saw "a new heaven and a new Earth, for the first heaven and the first Earth had passed away....").

For most people, their human bodies exist in the third density, and their spirit bodies are of a similar progressional level. However a Wanderer is much, much older and far more spiritually advanced. These souls wander between densities of existence (dimensions of a sort) seeking further enlightenment - hence the name 'Wanderer.' A Wanderer originates from any fourth, fifth or sixth density planet (higher dimensions of evolutionary existence than ours) and may choose to regress to a third density existence, such as Earth, for the purpose of raising its frequency, through both service to others, and through their own learning and experience.

Getting the chance at a lifetime on Earth, at this time of change, is a special opportunity and the Wanderer can fast track their own soul's progression. The dysfunctional nature and confusion within this earthly illusion offers many opportunities for expression of love, light and wisdom.

It is potentially dangerous for a Wanderer to incarnate within this third density planet in case the Wanderer does not at least partially remember it's reason for incarnating here in the first place. If the Wanderer should become enthralled in materialism, that's constant acquisition of goods to satisfy the self at the detriment of spirituality, or negatively polarized behaviors such as greed, acquisition of power and control - then the Wanderer would then be required to repeat the cycle (a new lifetime) or further cycles until they have regained their original state of positive progression. In other words, if a Wanderer only visits Earth for one lifetime and becomes negatively polarized, then they wouldn't be able to return home afterward.

THIS COMPENDIUM IS INTENDED TO HELP THE WANDERER TO "GET UP TO SPEED" of one's forgotten knowledge and remember how to raise the Earth's frequency to make its transition and to help those inhabitants who are lagging behind in their vibratory frequency.

Earth Shifting to a New Energy Level (from 3rd Density of the 4th world to the 4th Density of the 5th World) - According to ascension teachings, the Earth and all beings living on the Earth are in the process of shifting into a whole new level of reality in which a consciousness of love, compassion, peace and spiritual wisdom prevails. This has been called the Fifth Dimension.

Some say this shift will probably be complete within the next couple of decades; others give no date. But all seem to agree it will be complete sometime in the near future, although individuals will be each moving into the Fourth Density at their own rate when their frequency is high enough to match the vibration of the higher density.

Most teachings state that the shift the Earth and humanity are taking into the Fourth Density has been "planned" for eons. Also that it has already been happening in the last few decades. However, we have learned that the frequency of the Earth has been increasing at a faster rate than the frequency increase in the people on the Earth. This delay is caused in part by fear of the change by not knowing:

- Why am I here
- What is my purpose
- Why were we created
- What is the connection between my Spirit, Soul, Mind and Body
- What is the truth
- Who is God
- Who am I
- Where did I come from
- Am I a Universal Being or Human Being
- What is my history before here
- What occurs during and after ascension

Of these, "Who am I" is the primary question. All else is a Mind exercise to seek the truth, to only find that it lies within the Heart.

It is the intent of this Compendium to answer many of these questions.

Can ascension to the 4th Density happen within the next couple of decades? How can this world turnaround from where it is today and become this utopian kind of world? There is still so much darkness on the planet—wars, hatred, prejudice and injustice.

Preface

The answer is two-fold: First, thousands of people on the planet are now experiencing an awakening of the heart at an unprecedented rate—and this awakening appears to be speeding up, as time goes by. At some point, the hundredth monkey phenomenon will inevitably take hold.

And secondly, not everyone on the planet at this time is making the choice (consciously or unconsciously) to make the shift into the Fourth Density that some refer to as the Fifth Dimension (5D).

All souls have the choice to enter 4D (Density), given they have assimilated sufficient light to hold the energy levels that exist in that higher vibration. Earth is a multi-density planet since all souls on Earth have free to select among the various polarities.

While you are on this planet of duality, one will need to have increased skepticism and finely tuned discernment. One must be able to apply intuition that you receive, and ask yourself "what is the agenda here?" There is indeed a very large multi-dimensional "conspiracy" at work on this planet, and draws power from us by pushing us into one spectrum of one polarity or another. There are two forces at work, but they are not what you think. The polarity is between Divine Light and False Light/ Dark Side. Yes, False Light and Dark Side are two halves of the same coin that is controlled by the corrupt Demagogic Side of humanity.

The Forces of True Divine Light that exist outside of the corrupt demiurge are not bound by the left-brain right-brain dynamics and dark-light polarities that define the demiurgic sub-universe. This means that they do NOT sound like a voice in your head! Instead, they use "soul telepathy" to emanate feelings, archetypal expressions, and an extremely pure quality of light that speaks directly to your soul.

The difference between a being of the True Divine Light and one of the false light spiritual liar-archy beings is that the former's light is warm, enveloping, pure and unconditionally loving, whereas the latter's light is cool, piercing in an uncomfortable way, dominant and often overly-masculine. The spiritual liar-archy is a male-dominated group and even the females within their power structure have a very masculine energy. This male-domination is, of course, why the religious structures that the liar-archy enabled all to have a domineering male god, and no mention of an all-encompassing, feminine creator.

Another major difference between false light beings within the demiurge and beings of True Divine Light who are aligned with Infinite Source is that the Divine Light is not controlling, manipulative, bossy or judgmental in any way. Infinite Source will NOT impose an agenda upon you, although it will support you in your chosen mission to help dismantle the corrupt demiurge. You won't be given "marching orders" by Infinite Source or beings of True Divine Light who operate outside of the demiurge. They won't send you endless, energy-draining missions in your dream-time, and they won't ask you to do something that will result in loss of your soul energy, unlike the imposters in the false-light spiritual liar-archy.

The beings of True Divine Light are supportive, loving, nurturing, and they care about you as an individual. You are not just a cog in a machine to them, for they understand that you are a vitally important aspect of an intricately interconnected creation. They have the utmost respect for those of us who volunteered to incarnate into the "beast system" of the corrupt demiurge in order to help dismantle it from the inside. Indeed, there must be Divine Agents working both from within and outside of the corrupt demiurge in order to dismantle it.

THIS DISSERTATION - This dissertation, a compiling of multiple references, begins with Why we are here, and The Hidden/ Alternative History of where it started, eons, even millennia, to the present. Our Journey and how we prepared for it before we were born, Where did we originate - This is the reason we look to the stars. The universe is full of beings, both Divine Light/ One Source (Universe Creator) and False Light/ Dark Side, which are part of this reality. This research will lead to a brief review of my discoveries as to our aura, why the False Light/ Dark Side is consistently seeking separation and to the Lessons we are to learn as Spirits, in past lives, this life and, perhaps, in lives to come, both here on Earth or elsewhere in the universe, knowing that time is but one dimension and that it is not linear. In addition there are other discoveries that may help you to know who and whose you are.

I Am Thankful to Others Who Helped Me On My Path
I thank the spiritualist who visited me, in June 2016, to help me get past the Lesson that the Past Means Nothing and for the Meditation Exercises presented in this research dissertation, the encouragement provided to me by fellow Spiritual Wanderers/ Travelers, and the many extra-dimensional guides for keeping me on my Path and for pointing me, through various dreams, to make my research that showed me how simple the answer is.

Summarizing or even copying from many sources is called research. Copying from one source is called plagiarism. This is a research/ reference paper. The references/sources have been edited, abridged, condensed and/or sampled for inclusion in this Compendium, along with personal comments and additions. I have tried to list the key sources for a given topic at the end of each Section in order for you to begin your own research to solidify and expand your own spiritual path.

ONE QUESTION REMAINS
I leave you with a question that is posed in the lyrics of "The Happening" performed by the Supremes and written by Frank De Vol, 1967: "Hey! Life look at me, I can see reality…Now I see Life for what it is…is it real, is it fake, is the game of life a mistake…Suddenly I WOKE UP (to The Happening)."

I am hopeful for this Compendium will help you to WAKE UP and answer the question for yourself.

CHAPTER 1

Spirit, Soul, Mind, Body

Restoration – The soul controls the whole person so that one lives in ones IDEAS or ones EXCITEMENT. The lust and desires of the body bring the soul into subjection (judgment).

Health, Sickness, Pain, Happiness, and Suffering can be explained by the relationships that exist between Body (Mind, Heart), Soul and Spirit.

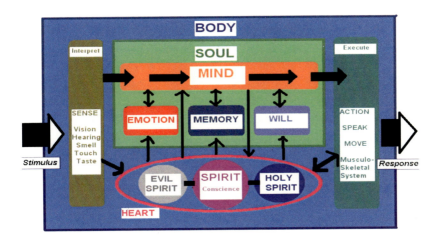

Spirit
- God (First Source) –The giver of Life and Creator of the Universe.
- Pure (given to us by First Source God – Spirit is part of First Source God).
- Communicates with First Source God and Has a direct relationship with First Source God.
- First Source God dwells in the Spirit (out "Temple").
- 3 Functions of the Spirit:
    o Consciousness - the discernment of right and wrong

- - Intuition – the direct consciousness not dependent on anything else
  - Fellowship – our service to First Source God
- Communicates with the Spiritual Realm - only the spirit can receive revelation from First Source God, who is spirit.
- The Spirit communicates with the Soul, but the Soul does not communicate with the Spirit. The Spirit remains pure.
- Gifts of the Spirit: There is some controversy as to the precise nature of each of the gifts of the Spirit listed in 1 Corinthians 12:8-10, but here is a list of spiritual gifts and their basic definitions. First Source God will always equip us with whatever gifts of the Spirit we need.
  - The gift of wisdom is the ability to make decisions and give guidance that is according to First Source God's will.
  - The gift of knowledge is the ability to have an in-depth understanding of a spiritual issue or situation.
  - The gift of faith is being able to trust First Source God and encourage others to trust First Source God, no matter the circumstances.
  - The gift of healing is the miraculous ability to use First Source God's healing power to restore a person who is sick, injured, or suffering.
  - The gift of miracles is being able to perform signs and wonders that give authenticity to First Source God's Word.
  - The gift of prophecy is being able to proclaim a message from First Source God.
  - The gift of discerning spirits is the ability to determine whether or not a message, person, or event is truly from First Source God.
  - The gift of tongues is the ability to speak in a foreign language that you do not have knowledge of, in order to communicate with someone who speaks that language.
  - The gift of interpreting tongues is the ability to translate the tongues speaking and communicate it back to others in your own language.
  - The gift of administration is being able to keep things organized and in accordance with First Source God's principles.

- The gift of helps is always having the desire and ability to help others, to do whatever it takes to get a task accomplished.
- Natural Senses: Sight, Hear, Touch.
- Spirit is the seat of our divine, spiritual emotions and impulses.
- SPIRIT CAN LEAVE: The Spirit often leaves us, and when it is away, the soul is lonely and feels abandoned. But when the Spirit comes home again, it brings with it an abundance of inspiration and light.
- SPIRIT and SOUL CAN LEAVE: when the soul and spirit leave "home" together, the heart and mind cannot wait to commit every possible kind of folly in the company of other foolish minds and hearts.

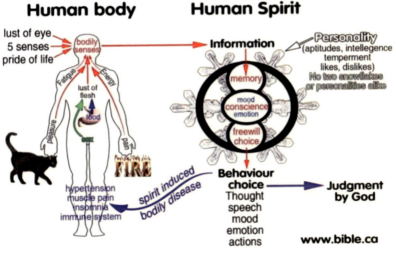

Restoration
- Romans 6:5: If we have been united with HIM in HIS Earth, we will certainly be united with Him in His resurrection.
- Ezekiel 36:26 I will give you a new heart and put a new spirit in you; I will remove from you your Souls heart of stone and give you a heart of flesh.
- John 3:16: The eternal life mentioned in John 3:16 is the life God puts into a man's spirit by the Holy Spirit. Because

this First Source God's Life, which can never die, all who have been regenerated have this life and are said to have eternal life.

Your choice will be to NOT FOLLOW THE LIGHT and be a free spirit in the universe or FOLLOW THE LIGHT and be recycled back to Earth as part of the Master-Slave environment established by Anunnaki, eons ago, until, after many recycles, you learn you are a free spirit and will make your own choices. There is a difference between the "God" given to you by the Anunnaki (God of the Bible and follows service to self) and Creator God who provided us with Free Will to follow the spirit of the heart (service to others).

Body
- Ground/dust. Dust of the ground
- World – what we see, touch, feel and smell
- Physical body to communicate to the physical world
- Senses dwell in the body
- 5 senses or organs:
  - Eyes (see)
  - Ears (hear)
  - Nose (smell)
  - Mouth/tongue (taste)
  - Hand (feel/touch)
  - Communicates with the physical world

Mind – Is the mental/emotional aspect of the human being. The mind is the generator of thoughts, feelings, and emotions. The mind processes thoughts and ideas as well as feelings and emotions. The mind is consciousness and imagination. The Mind is a chemical factory full of neurotransmitters that affect how and what we think and feel including pain.

The mind is the interactive mechanism between the body and soul. The mind registers and filters emotion (the language of the soul) and registers nerve impulses generated by the body. The degree of communication between the body and mind, and soul and mind depends on your ability to manipulate your mind to work for you. When the mind is functioning as intended, it is self-aware, focused and quiet as required. So the mind has two choices: to block out sensation or to listen to it. If the mind is smart, it listens.

Soul – Our consciousness of our own existence because of the activity of the soul. Our personality resides in our soul. As a soul, you are a vast, powerful entity, created directly from the same "stuff" as this Supreme Creator (First Source), and you possess all its powers. As soul, You spend eternities on frequency bands higher than the Earth plane, exploring, creating and loving, where experiencing anything other than unconditional love is impossible. Because of this soul plane limitation, the Creator and its hierarchy of souls established a "quarantine zone" of a lower frequency, to which a fragment of your soul's energy can incarnate and experience fear, which blocks the flow of unconditional love. The Earth plane is of such low frequency that much of what you as soul know is lost when your fragment descends here, so each incarnation starts with a "clean slate."

- Consummation of the body and spirit (Soul is not Spirit)
- Self – conscious
- Intellect which makes our existence possible
- Fruits of the Spirit (Gifts of the Spirit are "materialized" in the Soul). Galatians 5:22-23 (New International Version): [22] But the fruit of the Spirit is love, joy, peace, forbearance, kindness, goodness, faithfulness, [23] gentleness and self-control. Against such things there is no law.
- Has been given the power of Freewill (by First Source God)
- Self dwells in the soul
- Without Body or Spirit, Soul would only be conscious of Self
- 3 elements of personality:
  o Will (setting, choosing, judgment). This is where the power of judgment lies.
  o Mind (knowledge, imagination, memory) –thought, reason, intellect, knowledge and mental capacity reside. The mind is the seat of our ordinary, everyday thoughts and reasoning which concern only the satisfaction of our personal interests and our most material needs.

- Heart is the seat of our ordinary, Earthly emotions (desire to love, hatred, sensation, feelings of being affected) – love, desire, hatred and sentiments reside in the soul.

- **5 Different Types of Souls:**
  - **Vital Soul**, is purely vegetative enters and animates the embryo while it is still in the womb.
  - **Animal Soul:** At the age of seven children receive their animal or voluntary soul. The belief that at this age, the 'age of reason', children enter into full possession of their soul is a very common error. No, the fact is that the soul they receive is still only the voluntary or animal soul. From the time they are born, children are constantly in motion, moving their arms and legs, walking and running and jumping about, and by the time they are seven and their animal soul has fully entered their body you could say that they have acquired sufficient physical autonomy to be in control of their movements.
  - **Sensitive or Emotional Soul:** For some time before the animal soul has fully entered their body, a new phase has begun, the phase during which the affective dimension becomes gradually more important: the sensitive or emotional soul has begun to develop.
  - **Rational or Reasonable Soul:** Becomes evident at about fourteen, when children reach puberty, the sensitive soul reaches maturity and enters fully into them, leading emotions. At the same time the capacity for reflection begins to develop and, at the age of twenty-one, the intellectual or rational soul enters fully into a human being.
  - **Divine Soul**, the soul of pure light, possessed only by initiates who have completed their evolution. It's coming depends entirely on the kind of life we have chosen to live and on our desire to receive it. Initiation is just that, the path human beings tread in order to seek out their divine soul and persuade it to take up permanent residence in them. In fact, though, only a few very exceptional beings who have spent many

incarnations working for this goal actually achieve it. For years and years, by means of their spiritual exercises of purification, meditation, prayer and sacrifice, they have prepared themselves to attract and become one with their higher self, their divine self. And when they attain their goal we say that they have received the Holy Spirit.

Our Earth Self:
- **SPIRIT** – The Spirit never dies since it is pure and given to us by God (First Source); it is part of First Source God (the "Great SPIRIT").
- **SOUL** – Does not die with the Body, just lives and is the part involved in JUDGEMENT (of the thoughts and attitude of the heart – Hebrews 4:12; we are judged by our soul, which is the organ of our Free-Will). The Soul can only be destroyed by the Judgment of First Source God.
- **BODY** – the physical body is just a vessel which ages and dies.

- **Without WILL (Soul), one would be a machine**
- **Without Mind (Soul), one would become totally foolish**
- **Without Emotion (Soul), one would be senseless like wood or stone**

AS MANY AS FOUR SOULS CAN REINCARNATE INTO ONE BODY

The verse says, "...*Visit the sins of the fathers on the children for three and four* [generations]" (Ex. 20:5). This means that up to three reincarnating *Nefashot* can reincarnate with a new *Nefesh* together in one body at birth. This makes for a total of four *Nefashot* at one time.

Nephesh (נֶפֶשׁ nep̄eš) is a Biblical **Hebrew** word which occurs in the **Hebrew Bible**. The word refers to the aspects of life, and human beings and higher animals are both described as having a **nephesh**. The **Hebrew** term נפש is literally "living being," although it is commonly rendered as soul in English translations. In this dissertation, Nefresh means a new soul who has not been in a body before.

Nefashop means a reincarnated soul.

It is possible that one *Nefesh* can reincarnate alone in a body; or one reincarnated *Nefesh* with a new *Nefesh*. Or, two reincarnated *Nefashot* by themselves can go into one body; or two reincarnated *Nefashot* with a new one; or three reincarnated *Nefashot* by themselves; or three reincarnated souls with a new one. However, more than this is not possible within one body.

Know that those that are reincarnating together in a single body must all be of a single "root." This is the esoteric meaning of the verse "*...he shall redeem the property of his brother*" (Lev. 25:25). In other words, for one soul to redeem or help another it must be his brother, so to speak; they must be related to each other through their roots.

The new soul, although it has not shared in any of the sins of the others, will be responsible for the well being of the entire group soul that has reincarnated together with the new soul. The new soul is responsible because the new soul is from a more primary aspect than they are, and he has the ability to rejuvenate them.

One of the consequences of sin and repeated blemish is that one of the limbs of the spiritual body that has been affected by the sin may become atrophied. The holiness and life force may be removed from the limb in order that the other limbs do not become blemished as a result of the sin. Rectification of the sin, therefore, allows life and energy to return to the limb and rejuvenates it. In this case, this benefits the entire group of souls of the particular root that has reincarnated together.

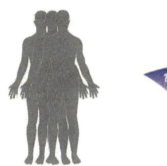 

THE SOUL WITHIN ME HAS MANY PARTS BUT MY SPIRIT IS SEPARATE AND SINGULAR

WHY MY SPIRIT SOUL IS WITHIN ME (Spirit is my driving force, "lives forever," and supports/is supported by Souls).
- Primary/Lead Soul (*Nefesh*).
- New Spirit /Soul (Ezekiel 36:26: I will give you a new heart and put a new spirit in you, I will remove you from your heart of stone and give you a new heart sensitive to me.
- Sees Earth as a renewable energy source of First Source God's creation ("wonders") from which she draws her immense power.
- Is protective of her power since it is needed for both ascension and to redeem the other souls.
- Has transcended or is ready to transcend the 4th Density or the 5th Density (Ascension to the transition from physical to spiritual). This is the reason she believes she is a Lyran.

    As a side note: Density is INDIVIDUAL and Dimension is HUMANITY (the entire group of individual densities).

- Looks to Spirit for guidance.
- Seeks freedom, truth and identification through contemplation, adoration and prayer.
- Tends to be impersonal.
- Is neither male nor female but has the persona of a female
  - The heart and soul are related to the one, feminine principle of yielding, soft, gentle way, like its branches

of a tree, effortlessly giving way, intelligently bending in line with the movement of life.
- Yet, there is a large amount of male within her. The male soul brings form, organization, and structure to the feminine; it is energy of action. Without the male soul, nothing would come into form; it would just exist in a void space. The Patriarchal Masculine in my soul's energy field comes from my Past Lives; these patterns need to be balanced and cleared, particularly any woundings. This is now the time of Unity Consciousness, where the Devine Masculine and Feminine work in union with one another.

- Characteristics:
  - **I am a rock; I am an island** – I am the "rock" of my spiritual world and a rock or island will never die.
  - **I have built walls (a fortress deep and mighty) and have my armor to protect me**, since it has taken multiple lives to achieve my spiritual dominance so that no one may penetrate.
  - **I have my books and poetry (art and music) to protect me** – here I find solace (comfort) and confirm the truth, which I already know (Jeremiah 31-33 & Hebrews 8:10: I will put my laws in their minds and write it on their hearts. I will be their God and they will be my people… because they will all know me).
  - **I touch no one and no one touches me** – My work to be spiritual is not to be "tarnished" or "drained" by another soul.
  - **My Immense energy that is not to be "drained"** – required to energize and protect my spiritual soul, it is needed for my mission, and is the source to restore the other souls that are accompanying me.
  - **I don't talk love but I have heard the words before (it is now deep in my memory); If it were not for love, I would have never cried** – love has its place, but is no longer dominant to my life. Yet, to experience all forms of love is a reason I came to Earth, since I have been a Warrior in many of my past lives. In the many past lives, I have been Strong, Brave, Courageous,

Determined, Rational and Goal Oriented but, by being so, I have not learned forgiveness of my enemy, or for love on most any level.
- **I have little need for friendship**, other than the Spirit; but need a few close friends to experience the world and, sometimes, it's accompanying pain.

MY PHYSICAL (ANIMAL) SOUL IS WITHIN ME
- Is thought to be masculine in orientation.
- Sensitive or emotional soul.
- A voluntary soul.
- Carnal, mundane, requires sleep, Seeks health and life.
- Needs food for nourishment.
- Needs livelihood (physical work).
- Needs money (to support above).
- Feels pain, is contingent, suffering with changes in climate and health.
- Seeks physical challenges for stimulation (for me: running, skiing).
- Is disgraced by the need to satisfy the body and grieved at this position, feels ashamed and confounded by this situation.

WHY THE SENSITIVE OR EMOTIONAL SOUL IS WITHIN ME
- To show my central soul the heart virtues of *Appreciation or gratitude, compassion, humility, forgiveness, understanding and valor or courage. It is the combination of nowness—being in the now—and applying these words in our behaviors. It's being impeccable in this practice*, since this is how to gain Human 3.0 SI and "escape" the Anunnaki deception of enslavement followed by reincarnation into another Anunnaki's containment that keeps my spirit/soul in enslavement to the Anunnaki [i.e., the Afterlife Trap]. (Refer to Chapter 10).
- To practice and apply the HEART VIRTUES is the reason that First Source has placed me in increasing larger groups and organizations – to expand the number of people that I can apply the Heart Virtues.

- Is a sensitive or emotional soul.
- Is compassionate.
- Seeks joy, happiness and warmth through feelings and love.
- Works through harmonious and artistic activities.
- To understand the eight types of Love (refer to Chapter 8). To understand Heart Virtues, this soul is attempting to convey the attributes of *Philla, Sorge, philautia and Agape.*

WHY THE INTELLECTUAL OR RATIONAL/ REASONABLE SOUL IS WITHIN ME

- The driving soul to seek Knowledge, which yields Understanding, which yields Wisdom.
- Is the means of discovery as to who I really am.
- Is the researcher of information that can be condensed into thoughts.
- Is the seaker of "truth."
- Nourishment is Thoughts.
- Activity is meditation and thinking.
- Seeks mental challenge for stimulation.
- Has the capacity for reflection and circular thinking (what if).
- Is the seat of our ordinary, everyday thoughts and reasoning which concerns only the satisfaction of our personal interests and our most material needs.
- Seeks knowledge, learning, Light to achieve Wisdom.

Sources:
1. 'Mind, Body, Soul & Spirit Archives- Journey with Omraam,' Mikhael Aivanhov, with-omraam.com
2. 'Spirit Soul and Body,' *Solus Christus,* www.salvation125,.com, slideshare.net
3. 'The End Time Message Home Page,' Soul Body and Spirit by Ron Milleva, www.endtimemesage.info
4. 'Body Soul and Spirit, 'deborahrossministries.org
5. 'The Human / Body and Soul – Wisdom & Teachings,' Chabad.org

6. The Temple Occasional blog on all sorts of subjects,' On Sight and Seeing – Oedipus Rex, *empleofpegasus.blogspot.com*
7. Four Souls, One Person - Gate of Reincarnations, Chapter Five, Section 2 By Rabbi Yitzchak Luria as recorded by Rabbi Chaim Vital; translation from *Sha'ar Hagilgulim* by Yitzchok bar Chaim; commentary by Shabtai Teicher, http://www.chabad.org/kabbalah/article_cdo/aid/ 380846/ jewish/ Four-Souls-One-Person-52.htm

Chapter 2

WHY WE WERE CREATED, THE EARTH EXPERIMENT, EARTH LIFE PREPARATION

WHY WE WERE CREATED – One Source / Creator God created the entire universe and all that is within the universe. However, Creator God is a multi-dimensional, non-physical entity and has no way to receive feedback about his creation. After eons of contemplating its own nature, he solved the "problem" by creating a basic number of races that would physically experience his creation and provide "feedback," so Creator God could experience his creation through these physically, thinking and experiencing "species." The creation of the various races required the creation of multi-strand DNA sequence that would facilitate multiple and different reproducing entities that had many of the powers possessed by Creator God. The initial creation of the four basic galactic races (Carians, Felines, Humans, and Reptilians) may have occurred in a galaxy other than the Milky Way and may not have occurred on Earth but on various planets in different galaxies. In addition, the process may have resulted through the establishment of the Founding Fathers. Refer to Chapter 4 for the four primary galactic races, the Founding Fathers, and Chapter 3 for the expansion of the races in our own universe. Refer to the upper part of the below diagram for the creation of the basic galactic races.

24 | Chapter 2 –Why We Were Created, Earth Experiment, Life Prep

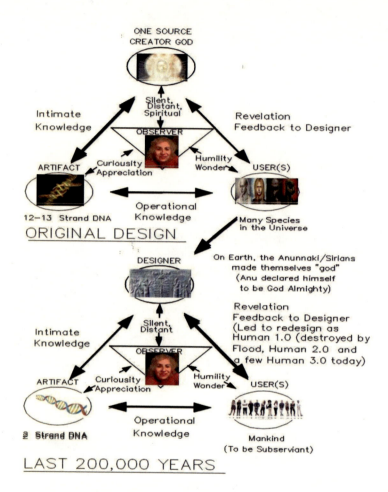

Then, Creator God's creations (namely the Anunnaki and Sirians in our galaxy and our solar system) clamored for the ability to, in turn, create their own creations. Creator God imagined into being a new lower frequency dimension contained within the first. Into this, Creator God's creations thought into existence their own creations and endowed these lower frequency versions of themselves, also with free will, which is how it all began for mankind. However, Creator God's first creation (four basic galactic races) wanted to be "god" so they could dominate their creation of beings to honor, worship, and, sometimes, be their slaves. Therefore, "all of mankind are the children of the lesser god." Refer to the lower part of the above diagram for the creation of mankind.

QUANTUM MECHANICS, QUANTUM PHYSICS, QUANTUM MATHEMATICS – What are they trying to achieve. The Earth was created as a galactic library and the humans are the library cards. Each human contains a small piece of that universal knowledge. Through the various quantum processes, the Dark Force is attempting to extract that knowledge in order to further control their fought-for part of the universe and the various species therein. The Elite/Dark Force will use the various Quantum Processes to modify the human DNA by incorporating "Junk" DNA and bio-mechanics to create trans-humans or to create trans-humans through the injection of nanobots. The trans-human creation may reveal the human's vast stored knowledge. The Dark Force will induce the humans to become trans-human by telling them it will provide them with eternal life which they already have without becoming trans-human. It was this same obtuse "attack," used by the Anunnaki, to lure the Atlanteans to become the power source for the Anunnaki/Sirian creation of mankind. Be wary of the attempt to create trans-humans.

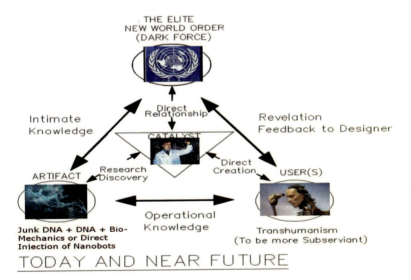

NANOBOT INJECTION-In lieu of bio-mechanics and gene editing, the Elite/Dark Force has or soon will perfect the injection of nanobots, the size of bacterium, as the means to create trans-humans. Nanobot technology will allow the injected nanobots to transmit your thoughts to a wireless cloud and vice versa, allowing remote control of the trans-human's thoughts and reactions. The Dark Force will tell us that nanobots will cure many diseases and ailments, resulting in a longer life, but their bottomline is to control and dominate. Injection of nanobots can be done when one is inoculated to fight the flu, to fight upper repertory diseases, to fight cancer, to ward off a future Dark Force initiated pandemic or even by inoculating infants to "protect" them from Mumps-Measles-Rubella. Be wary of this new technology.

Sources:
1. "Nanobots Will Be Flowing Through Your Body by 2030," TrevoEnglish, April 2017, Inovation / Technology, https://interestingengineering.com/ 2030

OUR DNA IS MUTATING – Although thought to be impossible, Cambridge researchers have published a paper proving the existence of four-strand 'quadruple helix' DNA structures – known as G-quadruples. In addition, a boy way born in 2009 that has a third strand of DNA. A few geneticists have stated that the extra strands are being created by the rising frequency of the Earth.

SOUL PLANE – Eons ago, our "higher soul" fashioned the soul plane level of our vast being. A very simplistic model of the soul plane associated with our region of space is that it's a 6th-dimensional frequency band divided into several sub-bands, say seven, and in that model, most souls inhabit levels three and four of the soul plane.

For eons (or what would be millions of Earth years if time existed there), we souls on the soul plane have worked, played, grown and explored the nature of creation. Where is this place?

Anywhere in the Universe, wherever there is Life, or even right where we are now, interwoven with the Earth plane but vibrating at a higher frequency, so it is invisible to most of us. There are inhabitants who can see and hear us but we cannot see them (usually), so a loved one who has crossed over may be reading this over your shoulder. (However, they are very discreet.) Also, the soul planes corresponding to other planets are interwoven with Earth's, too.

Do souls have to incarnate on Earth? Of course not. There are no rules on the soul plane. However, you could spend millions of years trying to imagine how you would behave if you did not know you were love … and still not get it. Or you could drop into a lifetime in Bosnia or a South African country in civil war and get a five-year crash course in hate, abuse, war, greed, fear and all the other loveless chaos on the planet. One five-year stint as a child in a war torn country will teach you more than millions of years of conjecture on the soul plane. And when you return Home after being brutally butchered into little pieces by a machete-wielding mob, you will look at love with new eyes. Yep, you can't beat the Earth plane for a quick study in limitation, which is why it was created, of course. All just so the Creator could learn more about itself.

Take grief, for example. How can you study the gut-wrenching ache of losing someone you love if it's impossible to lose anyone? On the soul plane, you just think of another soul and boom … you're right there with your buddy.

Now, Earth trips are not for faint-hearted souls because Earth life has a terrible reputation elsewhere in Creation for being the toughest thing any soul can take on. That's why only about ten percent of souls even have the courage to try. The other 90% stay warm and safe, living life on the soul plane.

Assuming you make 40 sojourns to the Earth plane, lasting an average of 50 years each, you will spend about 2,000 years in your various fleshy Earth-suits. (For a hundred lifetimes, that's 5,000 years.) Now, as a soul, you are an eternal entity, but let's say you came into being a mere two million years ago-less than a blink in all eternity. That means your 2,000 Earth years are only 0.1 percent of your experience of life on the soul plane, so you spend 99.9 percent of your time on the soul plane doing "soul things." Now that puts the role of Earth lives into perspective. Hence, the rock and roll song lyrics of "If you believe in forever, then life is just a one night stand" (Righteous Brothers, 1974), making life insignificant and significant in each its own way.

The physical plane life we currently regard as so important is really just a flash in our overall soul's growth, and one of dozens, or even hundreds, of lifetimes just like it. Now someone hearing this might be tempted to say, "Well then, it doesn't really matter what I do in this lifetime, so I might as well take it easy, goof off, and the hell with everything." That attitude is precisely why reincarnation was written out of the Bible in the sixth century CE. The bishops found that telling people they had just one shot to prepare for God's Judgment Day got their attention and motivated them to attend church, etc.

Meanwhile, the other two thirds of Earth's population continues to believe in reincarnation, however screwed up they make it. Hinduism allows for cross-species incarnation, which means, "shape up or return as a bug," and in India, it is tied into the caste system as a means of controlling the population, as in: "shape up or come back as an untouchable." Neither approach exudes unconditional love.

Final Word: As you work and play in this hologram we call reality, it's vital to remember the three Ws:

1. Who you really are - A vast spiritual being squeezed into a tiny bio-suit.

2. What the game is really about - The Creator learning everything about itself and growing In the process.
3. Why You're really here - As a Creator probe who begins its existence in the highest dimensions and projects down through them to explore on behalf of the Creator.

Sources:
1. Quantitative visualization of DNA G-quadruplex structures in human cells, Giulia Biffi, David Tannahill, John McCafferty & Shankar Balasubramanian, Nature Chemistry volume 5, pages 182-186 (2013)
2. "Boy, two, is first person in the world to be born with an extra strand off DNA" By DAILY MAIL REPORTER: 07:24 EDT, 11 April 2011, https://www.dailymail.co.uk/health/article-1375697/Alfie-Clamp-2-1st-person-born-extra-strand-DNA.html
3.. "Reverse Engineering: From Technology to Biology," present by Dr. Domnic Halsmer, Director Center of Faith and Learning, Oral Roberts University, Presented at the Oklahoma Engineering Conference, June 20, 2019 and his pending for publication book entitled *Hacking the Cosmos, How Reverse Engineering Uncovers Organization, Ingenuity and the Care of a Maker*, Edition 1, 2019, Kendall Hunt Publishing Company, ISBN 97852498583

For most, this involves learning, but a few million of us are here as a "transition team" to usher in a dramatic upsurge in the consciousness of humanity – for me, this has been expanded to include the extinguishing or the diminishing of the Anunnaki and their offshoots (Illuminati, Upper levels of the Free Masons, the Anunnaki clones, the Reptilians, programmed humans 2.0 and 3.0, etc.), who are playing the part of the Dark Side within this "grand experiment."

Because you're reading this, you are probably part of that transition team, so if you're not yet awake to that, "Wake up ... the time is now. And remember your three Ws."

THE EARTH EXPERIMENT - From the Galactic Federation of light (as extracted from Galactic Federation - Sangeeta Handa. www.sangeetahanda.net/galactic.html)

Per the Brotherhood of Light, we are not of this world. We are all extraterrestrial in nature, and have travelled at least 26 Light Years to reach Earth, your present home, to bravely partake in a complicated and challenging experiment of 'total spiritual amnesia.' Lady Gaia Earth volunteered to become a laboratory to harbor a daring 'experiment' and become the playground for a dangerous game from which there was no expectation of success, or even sheer survival. This experiment was labeled 'Deathwish.' And to say the least, you courageously volunteered to participate in this risky business of 'no-returns.' We were assisting, so far, only to prevent any irreversible damage to our soul. However, you managed to astound us where we least expected! Despite the total spiritual loss of memory, which is the 'Blueprint of Non-Remembrance' adopted by Earth, you found the '*doorway*' to exit from this complex, full-proof, inextricable labyrinth of sheer darkness. Consequently, we have had to change the pre-determined result of this experiment! A change we embrace and welcome with much pleasure and celebration.

Source:
1. As extracted in part from 'An Extracted in part from 'Soul's Guide to Life, the Universe and Everything,' *Truth Control*, http://www.truthcontrol.com/articles/old-souls-guide-life-universe-and-everything.

EARTH LIFE PREPARATION - Assume, as a soul busy with your soul plane research on the various types of polarity, say it is love, you've taken theory to its limit, but you just don't "get it." You-the-soul have realized that you need an Earth life in order to fully understand love in "reality" as opposed to love "in theory."

When a soul decides to incarnate, it begins a planning process that involves countless spirit guides and counselors, and the souls of everyone who will be involved in Souls Earth life, such as parents, siblings, mates, children and significant co-workers. These soul siblings, etc. all have their say in the goals and challenges that the incarnation will take on, because they know the gaps in their soul's collective experience and understanding that must be closed. You also use a time-travel "technology" to preview how the life you're planning will turn out.

All the people who will be in your new life are "supporting actors" drawn from your soul's soul group, a band of maybe a thousand or so other souls who hang together for eternity. After 40 or 50 lifetimes, you all know each other very well and count on them to incarnate with you and put on a good performance. Of course, you have your smaller group favorites, or family, and turn to them for the intense interactions, such as becoming your mate or even murdering you if your soul needs that experience.

With the help of your spirit guides and soul plane colleagues, you identify your goals, such as to study the balance between sexual love and platonic love, or how to create a work of art, etc.

Then, what you need to decide are:

Situation - The situation that will best support you in achieving your goals, which includes choosing the most appropriate physical body. Remember, that body will be conceived and born, regardless of which soul chooses it. The soul for whom that body will best serve gets to "appropriate" it. (If you hadn't chosen your current body, some other soul would now be living there instead of you).

Goal - Goal is the primary motivation in an incarnation, and soul sets up situations to facilitate goal achievement. Failure leaves your Soul feeling blocked and frustrated; things flow smoothly when you are on track as helpers appear and events unfold with a sense of inevitability.

Mode - The next quality of personality the soul chooses is Mode or the primary form of expression and the approach taken to achieve the Goal. It is "how you do things" behind "what you do," and how other people see you.

The personality structures that will allow you-the-soul to operate in that situation and hopefully achieve yours goals. (Accepting that your created personality allows you to change it. You created it so you can recreate a new one at any time.)

Attitude - Attitude is the third quality, and the primary perspective with which we look at the world, which determines what things we take into account and how we interpret them when deciding what to do and what position to take on issues. Attitude determines how we see the world and through this, we then use our Mode to go about achieving our Goal.

Challenges - Finally, souls take on one or more Challenges as a stumbling block designed to neutralize our attempts to achieve the Goal. But why do we need such a handicap?

Without obstacles, life would be a breeze; we would meet no opposition and achieve little growth, so we build in Challenges to push us to a higher level. Coming to know your Challenge explains much about your reactions and allows you to overcome the "first strike" mode. You become more understanding and therefore tolerant of the behavior of self and others.

Challenge varies greatly in intensity and degree, and is usually selected by adulthood but may change many times. You may not manifest one at all. Some Challenges can be self karmic, holding your back, leading to self blocking, self destruction, self deprecation and martyrdom. Others may lead you to be outgoing and self serving in terms of greed, arrogance and impatience.

Sources:
1. 'Pre-Birth Planning,' Soul Proof, htttps://www.soulproof.com/soul-really-plan/
2. As extracted in part from an 'An Old Extracted in part from 'Soul's Guide to Life, the Universe and Everything,' *Truth Control*, http://www.truthcontrol.com/articles/old-souls-guide-life-universe-and-everything.

Who or What Actually Incarnates? - Each time a soul incarnates, it transmits a characteristic vibration, a fragment of its energy, plus the template for the personality it has designed, across the veil - the boundary between the soul and physical planes - and "attaches" to the fetus that will be its focal point for that incarnation.

When a new incarnation begins, a fragment of soul splits off, forms a personality, inhabits a body, develops an ego, lives a life and returns to the soul plane. Then it does something extremely clever-it merges back into its soul, while retaining the same focal point of consciousness that it had on the Earth plane. So, if you visit a medium, your great-grandmother who crossed over 50 years ago can still come through even though she long ago merged with her main soul entity.

When the soul decides to form a new incarnation, it "borrows" skills, understanding, wisdom and memories gleaned during the lifetimes of whichever of its incarnated fragments are needed. This "borrowing" gives it a jump-start on personality-building.

But the new soul fragment is still a sovereign first-timer, never before having incarnated. However, the soul may include significant portions of fragments that have already incarnated, especially if there is "unfinished business," as in the case of suicides. But those fragments that have returned to the soul plane do not, themselves, incarnate again, instead continuing their development on the soul plane.

The degree of "borrowed" memories that a new fragment takes on could result in an "I've been here before" sensation, even though that fragment per se has not been there before. It only has the borrowed memory of having been there. The original fragment that had been there is still alive and kicking on the other side, waiting for its loved ones to join it.

When the incarnation is over, that soul vibration or fragment, along with the levels of mind and the etheric body, all return to the soul plane to continue development, growth and learning. After a few thousand years, possibly several hundred of these fragments (all part of the same soul) exist, work and play on the soul plane and are aware of each other as "soul siblings" in the same soul family.

This also means that while you are incarnate here on Earth, the knowledge and achievements of all the other fragments of your soul are available to you, but you must ask. Even as a soul fragment yourself, you are a sovereign entity and no other part of your soul can force anything on you, not even wisdom and understanding. However, what a resource once you know about it!

Source:

1. 'Reincarnation – Who incarnates or rather WHAT incarnates," Sakshi Apoologetics Network, U\YouTube, Fen 16, 2018, https://www.youtube.com/watch?v=3mjkwqjFHNw

CHAPTER 3

ALTERNATE HISTORY OF THE UNIVERSE & EARTH, WE ARE AT WAR

Between 20 and 40 billion years ago this universe began as a point of light within the mind of God (FIRST SOURCE, not to be confused with Anu, an Anannaki, who created himself as God in the program Human 2.0), what scientists call the big bang. It was a singularity in the form of a vortex.

14 billion years ago this galaxy was formed as a living entity of spiraling star systems.

Many thousands of years passed, and the beings from Lyra spread out into the cosmos and created new civilizations.

Approx 40 million years ago - When First Source (GOD of All Things) created souls in order to be able to reflect back to itself. Most sources agree that, in our part of the Galaxy, the cradle of mankind stood in the constellation of Lyra. Over time several humanoid species evolved. The majority of them were Lyran Caucasians, who looked virtually identical to the Caucasian race on Earth, today (though many of them were taller). These were the first "creator gods" (the Council of Twelve and Elohim) who knew how to create matter from light. And create they did - planets, stars, universes, life forms for themselves, and eventually others.

The Lyran's physical lifetimes lasted for approximately one thousand years. In time, however, their life span decreased. They sought out something that would enable them to live longer lives so that they could experience the wonder and miracle of existence. They found that gold not only increased their longevity, but provided them with a superconductivity which gave them the ability to be very telepathic and experience their multidimensionality.

Approximately 22 million years ago, the Lyrans were capable of travelling to other stars. As soon as they started exploring other systems in their galactic vicinity, they also began to colonize neighboring planets. It didn't take long before they came across other humanoid races. The first such race they encountered was in Vega, also within the Lyran constellation (but fairly close to Earth, as it is only 25 light years away from us). Vega, too, was inhabited by humanoid races, most of them brown-skinned. These first encounters went peacefully. Soon the populations started interacting, and joined forces in the further exploration and colonization of space. They went to Andromeda, Pleiades, Cygnus Alpha, Tau Ceti, Orion, Sirius, Altair, Alpha Centauri, Arcturus, Antares, Hyades, Sagittarius A & B, Cassiopeia, Procyon and other worlds.

One of the first non-humanoid races they came across was the Reptilian race that had its home in the Draco constellation. Nobody is really sure where the Draco originated. They were brought here from another universe, billions of years ago. They were capable of space travel long before mankind even existed. At the time of the first encounters the Draco Reptilians already had been exploring and colonizing for eons, and had a vast organized empire, usually referred to as the Draconian Empire. This Empire still exists today, and is one of the main players on the galactic geopolitical scene. The Empire originated on Theban (Alpha Draconis), and consists mainly of various groups of reptilian and dinosaur-like species, but humanoid worlds have joined, too, some forcefully, some willingly. Its most important members are based in Alpha Draconis, Epsilon Bootees, Zeta II Reticuli, Polaris, Rigel (Orion), Bellatrix (Orion), Capella (Alpha Aurigae), Ursa minor and Ursa major Sirius B Hydra, and a few others.

Chapter 3 – Alternate History of the Universe & Earth, We are a War

The first encounters between the Lyran/Vegan explorers and the Draconian explorers did not go well. Conflicts broke out over worlds they both wanted to colonize, and had claimed for themselves. It was in the Ring Nebula that the first fights broke out. Things then came to a dramatic escalation when the Draconians engaged in a full force attack upon the Lyran home planets. Over 50 million Lyran humans were killed. It is at this point in history that the Draconians began to look at humans as a food source. This is how old the struggle is between the reptilian and human races. Now, I must make the point that not all the reptilian or human races are "dark." There is a mix. However, the majority of Lyrans had already immigrated to other worlds. They vowed to retaliate.

THE ORION WARS

At the outset, a little over 20 million years ago, the wars started over territory in the constellation of Lyra. But soon the war spread to Orion, and it became a war of mind-sets and ideologies.

The worlds of Orion, at that time, were inhabited by various groups of Lyrans, Vegans, and Reptilians. (The Greys only came much later). After the Draconian Reptilians had attacked the Lyran home worlds.

A large ship came out of the huge craft and approached the planet Bila, and reptilians from Alpha Draconis disembarked. When the Draconians came and saw Bila, with all its abundance and food and natural resources, the Draconians wanted to control it. There was apparently a miscommunication or misunderstanding between the Draconians and Lyran humans. The Lyrans wanted to know more about the Draconians before some kind of "assistance" was offered. The Draconians mistook the communication as a refusal, and subsequently destroyed three out of 14 planets in the Lyran system. The Lyrans were basically defenseless. The planets Bila, Teka and Merck were destroyed.

The Lyrans in the Orion colonies retaliated by attacking Reptilian colonies in Orion. Of course, the Draconian Reptilians responded.

By that time, however, some humanoid (mainly Vegan) races had already started co-operating with reptilian races because they found they shared a common agenda of space exploration and colonization. This co-operation would eventually lead to the establishment of the Orion Empire. This Orion Empire is more recent than the Draconian Empire, and was established after the Vegans engaged in space exploration. It consists of a mixture of reptilian and humanoid civilizations. Nowadays, the Reptilians in Orion are genetically engineered half breeds of the original Draco/Ciakar reptilian races, and form the majority of these reptilian civilizations, whereas most of the humanoid civilizations are of Lyran/Vegan descent. Approximately one in every six worlds in the Orion constellation has a reptilian population. When the wars between the Lyrans and Draconians started, there was no Orion Empire; but there where co-operation agreements.

The wars escalated fast. Several worlds that been subjugated by the Draconians, started an uprising and joined the Lyrans in fighting the Draconians. This joining of forces would lead to the foundation of a "Federation of Planets" (later the Galactic Federation) whose members stood united in fighting the Draconians. The Federation still exists today, and still is one of the main players. It consists of civilizations from the Lyra constellation, from the Andromeda Constellation, from the Pleiades and Hyades open clusters, from Lumma [Wolf 424], Procyon, Tau Ceti, Alpha Centauri, and Epsilon Eridani, all of which are of Lyran/Vegan heritage. They were joined by a number of non-physical races, by some Sirian groups, as well as by some Orion organizations, and by various civilizations from a parallel universe such as the Koldasians. It even received some unexpected members when some worlds with reptilian inhabitants joined, wanting to free themselves from submission to the Draconians.

The Vegans and Reptilians of Orion that had made co-operation agreements with each other probably established the Orion Empire around the same time as the Federation came into existence. In all likelihood, they did this to stay out of the wars. That plan, however, was to fail.

Over time the nature of the wars changed. Where the war initially was over territory, it became a war of mind-sets and ideologies. On the one hand there was a group of mainly humanoid races that had joined forces in the Federation. Many of its members felt they had been 'victimized' by the Draconians, and therefore rejected the idea of colonization and intervention in other worlds. Gradually, they became committed to the idea of service to others. On the other hand there was a mixed group of humanoids and reptilian races that propagated service to self. In this ideology, the Draconian and Orion Empires found each other as like-minded and this would lead to their joining forces. Since then, they are often referred to as the Orion/Draconian Empires.

Initially the philosophy of service to self implied that when everybody takes care of him- or herself, then the whole is taken care of, too. But gradually it changed into service to self, if necessary at the expense of others, which resulted in "victimizers" and "victims." The victims and their allies, who had joined forces in a Federation, started looking upon the victimizers as evil, while they started seeing themselves as good. As a result the wars got polarized, and ended up being wars of duality, even though things didn't start like that, at all. Now history is filled with examples of how a polarized conflict can never be resolved as long as the polarities remain. It was no different in the Orion wars that lasted for eons, but where no breakthroughs by either side would ever be lasting.

LYRA/VEGA MIGRATION

This article was originally published on 16 November 2009, at http:// news.exopoliticssouthafrica.org/ *index.php/exo-articles/47-a-summary-of-galactic-history-part-1.*

The earliest humanoid civilizations were explorers and colonisers, which led to some migrations. When the Galactic Wars erupted, more migrations followed. If we dramatically simplify things, we could say that the spread of mankind through this part of the galaxy, over millions of years, happened in seven consecutive waves of colonisations / migrations.
Ed: One source that I read stated that the Lyran migrations were caused by internal conflict (wars) between the various races located within the Lyra star system. However, several other sources do not mention wars until the Lyran/Orion wars, which are said to continue to this day.

1. As was mentioned before, the story starts in Lyra, where approx. 22 million years ago, the first humanoid civilisations began their space exploration adventures, to boldly go where no man had gone before. The first worlds they colonised were Vega, that itself was already inhabited by a humanoid species, and Apex. Later on the Lyran explorers would also move to Sirius, and on to Orion; while others already came to Earth, and from Earth moved on to the Pleiades.

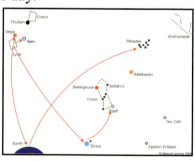

2. The original humanoid population of Vega soon started their own space explorations, and created settlements on worlds in Altair, Centauri, Sirius, and Orion. Some of them even came to Earth. While exploring the Ring Nebula,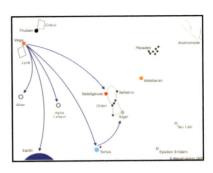
they came across lizard-like races that claimed the territory for themselves. This is where the Galactic wars erupted.

3. A nuclear war on Apex destroyed much of its surface, forcing its inhabitants to live underground for thousands of years. The radiation also damaged their reproductive capacities, forcing them to use cloning as a way to
survive as a species. The Apexians would become the Greys from Zeta Reticuli.

4. Settlers also moved to Arcturius, where as a species, they advanced very fast. Most Arcturians today are non-physical, higher-dimensional beings, though physical races still exist as well.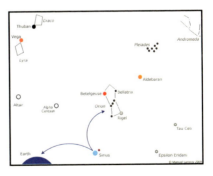

5. In the worlds around Sirius the humanoid settlers found many other species that were not like them at all. Some settlers

therefore chose to move on to Orion. Later on, several Sirians migrated to Earth, too.

6. The main battleground for the Galactic Wars was in Orion. Because of this, many descendants of humanoid settlers in Orion, fled, and also migrated to Earth.

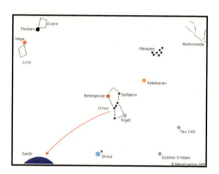

7. Some of the very first Lyran colonisers had to come to Earth. When their descendants were afraid the Galactic Wars were coming too close to Earth, most of them moved to the Pleiades. After time, however, some of their descendants decided to hook up with their relatives from Earth again, and came back to Earth.

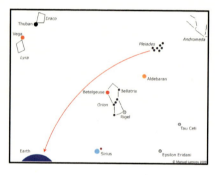

CONFLICT RESOLUTION

This article was originally published on 16 November 2009, at http://news.exopoliticssou thafrica.org/index.php/exo-articles/47-a-summary-of-galactic-history-part-1

The wars literally lasted for millions of years. During all this time, there were attempts to find a peaceful solution. Two such attempts are important to us: one in Sirius, which failed, and one in Orion, which succeeded.

The Sirian Solution - The worlds of Sirius were mainly inhabited by 'refugees,' i.e. by people who fled the wars, whether they were reptilian or human. Many of them came from Orion, and moved to Sirius to leave the wars behind them. (Several had moved to Earth, as well). But wherever these refugees went, the wars kept coming closer. The Sirians didn't really want to get involved, but tensions were rising, and soon there were occasional fights between the different groups. In order to maintain the peace, some groups in Sirius then came up with an inventive solution for conflict resolution: inspired by the idea of an alchemical union of opposites, they suggested a marriage between royal lineages to create a common dynasty, which would unite the people. And so a common dynasty was established, but the marriage didn't have the result they had hope for, as members of the royal families kept arguing, and many people did not pledge their allegiance to the new dynasty. The result was that the Sirian system, to this day, is inhabited by different groups, with different agendas and allegiances.

Important for the history of Earth is that members of the new royal dynasty settled on Nibiru, which through some cataclysmic event would be thrown out of its original orbit around one of the stars of Sirius. Its new orbit would catapult it on a trajectory in which it circled both our sun as well as one of the Sirian Stars. These inhabitants of Nibiru would become the Anunnaki that visited Earth in the past, and intervened in our history (for the last 400,000 years).

The Orion Solution - Every once in a while, usually within the worlds that had been submitted by the Orion and Draconian Empires, there would be rebellions by groups that no longer want to be submitted, but that did not want to join the Federation, either. Things only started changing when groups within the Federation got fed up with the war, too, and broke away from the Federation. Thus *a third party of "rebels" or "renegades"* emerged, and the balances of power changed forever.

Neither the Federation, nor the Empires dared launch a large-scale attack upon the rebels, fearing that if they would do so, the rebels would team up with the others, and that joining of forces would create an unbeatable enemy. But even though a lot of people were sympathetic to some of the ideas of the rebels about ending the war, the rebels didn't succeed in making any major breakthroughs in negotiations with either the Federation or the Empires. It looked like a new stalemate was reached, only this time there were three parties involved, instead of two.

Then the story takes an unexpected turn. Nowadays we know Merlin as the counsel or magician of the legendary King Arthur. However, Merlin, or at least the Merlin archetype, already made his first appearance during the Orion wars. Within the ranks of the rebels, he grew up as a young boy with remarkable talents. When he reached manhood, he started teaching about universal spiritual laws, about unconditional love and forgiveness. He pointed out that all parties, including the rebels, were still caught in a dualistic and polarized perception of reality, that this dualistic perception is an illusion and that only unconditional love and forgiveness would be able to end the conflict. And so Merlin succeeded at first in changing the mindsets of the rebels, and soon afterwards those of the Federation and the Empires, too. He taught them to transcend and value their differences. Peace agreements between parties were reached, and with this peace and the change of mindsets came a dramatic increase in awareness and raise in consciousness. Entire masses of people ascended into a higher dimensional reality. Thus, Merlin became known as the Unifier. A priesthood that teaches his ideas still exists, and is widely respected.

Still, peace was not established everywhere, as not everybody was ready to accept these new teachings. There is, even today, some fighting going on in some parts of this galaxy, where parties are still submerged in dualistic thinking. Earth, unfortunately, is one of those places where the majority of the people are still living in the veils of illusion of duality. Yet overall in our galactic neighbourhood, there is peace, and where there is no peace, there often is a truce.

RECENT DEVELOPMENTS
This article was originally published on 16 November 2009, at http://news.exopoliticssouthafrica.org/ index.php/exo-articles/47-a-summary-of-galactic-history-part-

Many of the players of the galactic wars are still around today. The Federation is still active, as are the two Empires. Since the war ended, they live more or less in peace with each other, even though there still are groups, as well, that keep on fighting.

In more recent times, we see a resurgence of aggressive colonizations, by some Grey and Reptilian groups. This had led to a schism within the Federation. The Federation still tends to stick to a non-intervention rule. The breakaway group partially disagrees. They state that non-intervention only works when nobody intervenes. If another party does, however, intervene, then standing by and letting them intervene makes you an accomplice to their intervention by allowing it to happen. So they advocate counter-intervention and even pre-emptive counter-intervention in those cases where others are intervening, or are about to do so. This breakaway group contains members of Arcturius, Korender, Procyon, Alcyone and others. Some authors refer to this breakaway group as 'the Alliance.'

Procyon - is the name of a binary star system, not too far from Sirius, in Canis Minor, about 11.4 light years away. A lot of stories about alien contact with people that look like Swedes, or Nordics, or Blonds, mention Procyon as their home planet. As such they belong to the Lyran Caucasian group.

Most authors agree that Procyon was started as a colony by Rigelians of Lyran descent. When Rigel was taken over by the Greys, the Rigelian Blonds fled to Procyon. Both Alex Collier and George Andrews claim that the Procyons recently got into a fight with Greys, and had to chase them from their world. This explains their frequent interaction with contactees on Earth where they warn about the activities of the Greys.

(The following is added later, from Wistancia & Joshua Stone's book *Integration and Harmonizing With the Goddess*.

Archangel Michael was there at the inception and proclaimed a history for this new galaxy which is now being fulfilled (2016). The GFL (Galactic Federation of Light) is creating a union of all beings in this galaxy. It permits others to join with other grace-filled beings of the Light, each providing a unique divine service for the Light. "Our star nation is joining with yours." The Anannaki gave you cultural beliefs to control and manipulate you; it is now time to let them go.

GALACTIC HISTORY OF THE EARTH

Approximately 4.6 billion years ago in our solar system there existed: Mercury, Venus, Earth, Mars (no moons), a 4th planet (larger than Earth with many moons, including a large one), Jupiter, Saturn (no rings), Uranus, Neptune and Pluto (which was a satellite of Saturn).

4 billion years ago, another planet came into our still forming solar system. This planet had its own moons. It arrived at approximately the same orbit as the 4th planet called Mardek - the one that existed beyond Mars. Mars was then the 3rd planet.

3.8 billion years ago plant life formed (2nd density). The first density was the mineral state.

About 1 billion years ago Earth wandered into the third orbit of our solar system. Our solar system is called Solis, meaning Great Light. Solis was created to become one of 100 Light-Star demonstration systems. Earth represents the potential manifestation of a glorious showcase experiment bringing light into darkness. The texts of Hinduism are the oldest unpurged and closest to the original galactic human creation myth. All have "in the beginning there was darkness" in their creation myths because Creator decided to make this creation one where light comes out of darkness. The mineral state was formed first, as the first density. Plant life formed second, as second density.

100 million years ago the humanoid was seeded on Earth by seven-density beings with wings, loving and cooperative. Earth was an exotic jungle then, a paradise. From 100 million years ago and lasting to 10 million years ago the civilization of Pangaea (the land of Pan) thrived. Experimentation with DNA took place. Later Mars and Venus were colonized.

60 million years ago - dinosaurs were killed off by a comet passing too close to Earth on its 10,500 year cycle.

50 million years ago - Sirian's creation myth says physical sentience started, but older for non-human.

35 million years ago the initial enteric civilization came to Earth and set up the firmament to protect it from the sun's radiation and other harmful radiations from space. The firmament has been broken and re-established many times through wars. They were designated to be the guardians of Earth but this ethereal intelligence also needed the help of physical guardians of Earth.

25 million years ago there were only our ancestor apes, and then suddenly......

14 million years ago suddenly manlike apes appeared out of nowhere, defying the slow process of evolution.

10 million years ago three planets in our solar system contained physical life: Earth, Mars, and Maldek which later exploded.

8 million years ago humanoids who were fleeing the Orion War colonized Maldek (then 10th planet from the Sun). These would have been of Anunnaki / Sirian/ Vegan /Lyran origins. There was also an indigenous primate-like population, which fits the characteristics of what we often call Bigfoot in the US, Ogo in Africa or the Yeti in the Himalayas.

◇◇◇◇◇◇◇◇◇◇◇◇

Mardek was home to the Anunnaki - In the beginning there existed the Sun (Apsu), encircled by the planet Tiamat, and the planet Mercury (Mummu). Then, between Tiamat and Mercury, came into being the planets, Mars (Lahmu) and Venus (Lahamu). Then, there came into being, beyond the planet Tiamat, the planets, Jupiter (Kishar) and Saturn (Anshar) along with their emissary' Pluto (Gaga). Last to come into being were the planets, Uranus (Anu) and Neptune (Ea). These nine planets, or 'gods,' moved in a counterclockwise direction around Apsu, the sun.

From outer space a new planet, Maldek, almost the size of Jupiter or Saturn, approached, attracted to this solar system by the gravitational pull of Neptune and Uranus. Moving in a clockwise direction past Neptune and Uranus, the path of Maldek took it toward the giants, Saturn and Jupiter. As he passed by Uranus, portions of Maldek were pulled off to become four satellites or 'winds.'

Chapter 3 – Alternate History of the Universe & Earth, We are a War

Maldek neared Saturn and Jupiter, and their massive gravitational pulls bent its orbit drastically inward, forcing its path to be aimed directly at Tiamat. The gravitational pulls of the two giants caused seven chunks of Maldek to be pulled from its body; they became satellites to encircle Malduk. As it moved toward her, one of Tamat's own ten satellites, Kingu, was attracted to Maldek. The movement upset the order of all the planets in the system. In effect, Tanat's satellite, Kingu, had taken on the aspect of a new planet. Kingu was given a *Tablet Of Destiny*, or rather a planetary course, and began its own orbit.

The force of Maldek's path toward Tiamat ripped into her, splitting, but not quite breaking her in half, yet knocking her satellites, with the exception of Kingu, away from her. The paths they were thrown into were clockwise, like Maldek's, and their paths would become large, elliptical orbits around the Sun. They had been changed into the comets which regularly revisit this solar system.

The encounter between Marlek and Tiamat caused its orbit to be bent even more, resulting in it becoming a planet or 'god' which was destined to encircle the Sun forever. And because it now was trapped in an orbit, Mardek's destiny was to return to the scene of the collision. It was, therefore to cross over the site of the collision. And for that reason, Maldek became known as Nibiru, the planet of crossing.

Nibiru was made up of what some call space pirates who imitated other beings, and sometimes a few from one planet would join them, including the Anannaki. These pirates - not at all like the real Anannaki. The story of the Anannaki has been mixed up with these pirates through time so some see the Anannaki as being only evil.

A second time, after an orbit of one star (variously star), a single Nephilim year (i.e. 3,600 Earth-years), and following the new course that fate had presented to it, Maldek / Nibiru approached the solar system. Once more, he passed by the outer planets of Neptune, Uranus and Pluto. Once more, its orbit was accelerated by the gravitational pulls of the giants, Saturn and Jupiter. And once more Nibiru's path was aimed directly at the ruptured and dying planet of Tiamat.

Nibiru struck Tiamat, and this time the collision tore Tiamat in half. The one half was smashed to pieces, and became the asteroid belt that to this day remains in orbit around the Sun between Mars and Jupiter, where the mighty Tiamat once existed. The asteroid belt was called the Hammered Bracelet by the Nephilim. In the Hebrew tradition, this second collision formed the basis of the creation story, and the hammered bracelet (which was previously mistranslated as 'firmament' was named the heaven).

As Nibiru continued on, trampling in its path the one half of Tiamat, one of his satellites, called the North Wind, struck the remaining intact half of Tiamat. The force of this secondary impact, thrust the remaining intact half of Tiamat away from her original orbit, to become repositioned between Venus and Mars. It was at this point that the remaining half of Tiamat took on the name of Earth (Ki), as noted in the Hebrew tradition. The thrust gave the remaining half of Tiamat, or Earth, its axial spin and therefore her ability to experience the changing days and nights (which the other planets/gods did not possess). Only Kingu continued to orbit around Tiamat as a satellite; he would later be called the Moon.

The destruction of Tiamat and the corresponding creation of Earth out of the wreckage resulted in the remaining land masses of Tiamat being concentrated in one spot as a continent (i.e.

Pangea). And the waters of the Earth surrounded the land formed an ocean.

As a result of the collision of Nibiru into Tiamat, and the alteration of the order of the planets, the satellite of Neptune and Uranus, Pluto, was jolted out of its orbit to take on a new orbit around the Sun as a planet itself. The disruption that caused Pluto to acquire its own *Tablet of Destiny* set it on an orbital plane that differed from the other planets.

The creation epic proceeding from the point of the collision of Maldek / Nibiru with Tiamat, as told by the ancient Sumerians, corresponds almost exactly with the Hebrew tradition as told in Genesis; they both corroborate the assumptions made by science. Beginning with the eruption and flowing of molten rock, which sent volcanic debris into the formless skies, all three disciplines detail the creation of an atmosphere as a result of the accumulation of clouds and mists, which blocked out a certain amount of the Sun's heat. That resulted in a cooling of the molten rock to form the continent(s) and the creation of water to surround the continent(s) as the ocean(s). From the lands, waters and atmosphere arose mountains, rivers and the forces of Earth.

The collision of Maldek / Nibiru with Tiamat / Earth not only resulted in the creation of new geophysical features on Tiamat / Earth. It might also have resulted in the creation of life there. It is possible that the collision resulted in a *sharing of elements between the two planets* - elements necessary for life to occur. And because of that, it is possible that life evolved similarly on the two planets, although not necessarily exactly or concurrently. This would explain why, when the technologically advanced Nephilim arrived at Earth around the year 450,000 B.C.E., they found only primitive humanoids.

Maldek was once located in a regular orbit between the orbits of Mars and Jupiter. It was a lush planet, thriving with thriving communities, home to a human civilization far beyond modern Earth in scientific and technological achievement. Immense powers were attained by such means as large-scale manipulation of subtle energies with crystals. Stone blocks the size of a small house could be moved and situated with great precision by this means in order to construct elaborate buildings. An intimate knowledge of these subtle energies, or life energies, allowed the people of Mardek to be in touch with intelligent minds in other worlds, as well as with each other in silent, direct, mind-to-mind communication.

The sciences and industries of Maldek had followed a different course of evolution from humanity on Earth, and they far surpassed us in depth and complexity. Genetic engineering, energy production, and other paths of technology brought great wonders to the people of Maldek, but they also presented problems. Simple mistakes by genetic engineers could produce bizarre mutations, and mistakes by energy researchers could cause powerful explosions. After a certain point, scientific technology on Maldek took on a life of its own, and there seemed to be no stopping it, even if the people had wanted to. The rewards of scientific achievement were absolutely wonderful, dwarfing the occasional accidents and potential dangers, or so the people thought.

The reality of life after Earth was a simple truth to everyone on Maldek. They were fully aware of their spiritual makeup and knew that many physical ailments have their origin in the subtle bodies. The healing arts took that into account. They were also aware that not just people, but all living things have subtle bodies. And not just LIVING things, but all physical things animate or inanimate have subtle bodies that coexist with the physical body and continue to exist after the physical body disintegrates. Rocks, mountains and entire planets have subtle bodies.

The people realized that their very own planet Maldek had spiritual counterparts - parallel worlds existing in subtler dimensions. One branch of science on Maldek involved a space-time doorway through which people could travel between dimensions. They could enter the portal on the physical planet Maldek and emerge into astral worlds. The natural laws and the physics of the two realities were quite different from each other. For example, in the astral worlds there was no gravity, no time and no space as there were in the physical world. Scientists studied these differences as part of the natural sciences of multidimensional living.

One small branch of the complex Maldek scientific establishment involved itself with space travel. It was not travel by propulsion as we know it today. Rather, the travelers would leave the physical world to enter the subtler realms of spacelessness and timelessness, then simply re-enter the physical realm in a new location. Like Maldek, the Earth was flourishing with life, but life on Earth was very primitive by comparison. Mars supported life at that time as well. Teams of scientists on Maldek - the equivalent of our geologists, climatologists, biologists, chemists and physicists - would take exploratory journeys to Earth and Mars from time to time to gather data and monitor the development of life on these very primitive planets. There were species of primates living on Earth at that time, and the scientists of Maldek familiarized themselves with their characteristics and behavior.

Colonies of people from Maldek eventually settled on the surface of the primitive planet Earth, and, like pioneer families in the American West, worked intensively to carve a sense of order in the wild environment.

Chapter 3 – Alternate History of the Universe & Earth, We are a War

The home planet Maldek had evolved into a paradise much like the legendary Eden, in which people lived for hundreds of years in physical bodies that showed little signs of aging. There was no need to eat other living things for nourishment, or even to procreate. It was a perfect, idyllic life for most residents of Maldek, but not for everyone. The rugged way of life on Earth tugged like a magnet at some of the heartier souls and pioneering spirits of Marlek.

As people became increasingly concerned about the dangerous trends of science and technology on Maldek, colonies on Earth began to expand. People brought seeds of their civilization to the new world, and those seeds quickly took root.

◇◇◇◇◇◇◇◇◇◇◇◇

6 million years ago human civilization was established on the Vega star system in the Lyra constellation. Humans came into sentience and rudimentary civilization.

4 million years ago the Galactic Federation decided to protect the light in our galaxy from being taken over by the Reptoids, the cold-hearted, ruthless ones. This started the stellar wars between light and dark.

3 million years ago the homo sapiens classification appeared on Earth.

2 million years ago a successful galactic culture was started by the Galactic Federation, with simi-etheric beings on Hybornea, before Lemuria. It lasted one million years and then the Reptoids and Dinoids, dark forces, from Orion came in and wiped it out.

◇◇◇◇◇◇◇◇◇◇◇◇

Chapter 3 – Alternate History of the Universe & Earth, We are a War

Dinoids from the Bellatrix system in the Constellation of Orion and **Reptoid** colonies from the Constellation of Sagittarius arrived later to inhabit the Earth. The Reptoid and Dinoids allowed a mammalian species to evolve to sentiency. These mammals were called the pre-cetaceans. The pre-cetaceans provided food for all 3 colonies in exchange for technology which in turn improved their production rate further. These 3 civilizations co-existed in harmony trading among one another for over 8 million years. All 3 civilizations developed advanced forms of space/time travel. The pre-cetaceans developed their spiritual side, such as psychic abilities, extensively.

A **Dinoid/Reptoid Alliance** from Bellatrix, believing they were superior to the pre-cetaceans, came to Earth to cease all cooperation with the pre-cetaceans and wanted to put them under their control. Over time, the Earth Dinoids and reptoids became more and more influenced by the Bellatrix Dinoid/Reptoid Alliance. The Pre-cetaceans, through their high psychic abilities, began sensing the aggression against them and came to see the threat presented by the Dinoid/Reptoid civilizations. Being given permission for the Earth Spiritual Hierarchies, the Pre-Cetaceans decided to implode their fusion reactors located in the Ural Mountain Range. The Pre-cetaceans divided into two groups.

One group evacuated out of our solar system to the constellations of Pegasus and Cetus and the other group altered themselves physically so that they could enter the oceans and find haven. This group is now our present day cetaceans such as the dolphins and whales. The entire transformation process occurred over a period of 4 million years.

When the transformation was complete and the later sector was safe, the first sector imploded the fusion reactors, destroying 98% of the Dinoid/Reptoid civilizations, the survivors evacuated to the planet in our solar system, Mardek. Now with the Dinoid/Reptoid no longer present on Earth, the Earth Spiritual Hierarchies and the cetaceans had to find a suitable guardian for the land. They searched the galaxy for 2 to 3 million years before finding what they were looking for. They found, on the fourth planet of the Vega system, a primitive aquatic species that was starting to emerge from the oceans. This species had creation myths, a language, and a hunting and gathering culture.

The Spiritual Hierarchies of the Vega system were then asked if they would permit this species to be vastly altered genetically to accelerate their evolution so that they may become a guardian species. The Vega Spiritual Hierarchies agreed. So, the traces of the first humans came from the Vega Star System. Their technology improved very quickly, and once they had developed star travel technology they started to migrate into nearby star systems for a period of 2.5 million years.

Dinoid/Reptoids in the meantime had built up there forces and were invading the various colonies throughout the solar system. Hyborian Earth, Mars and Venus were victim to these attacks and the Dinoids and Reptoids gained control over the solar system for a period of approximately 80,000 years.

In response to this, the Galactic Federation planned a counterattack to reintroduce humans into this system. They arranged for a battle planet (4 times the diameter of the Earth) to come into the solar system and destroy the planet Mardek - which was the Dinoid/Reptoid stronghold. The remains of the planet Mardek are what we can now see as the asteroid belt.

◇◇◇◇◇◇◇◇◇◇◇◇◇◇◇◇◇◇◇◇

Between 1 million to 700 000 years ago, a war began on Maldek. Some of the inhabitants fled to Earth, Mars, and Venus, taking with them some of the Bigfoot creatures. The war ended in a nuclear disaster which destroyed the planet. Everyone who remained on the planet was killed. This catastrophe also caused Mars to start losing its atmosphere.

1 million years ago Homo Erectus.

900,000 years ago primitive man appeared, named the Neanderthal.

900,000 years ago After the destruction of Maldek and the defeat of the Dinoid/Reptoids a human colony was again established on Earth. It is what we know today as Lemuria.

Some of the Anannaki also were present on Mars before Maldek was destroyed (Ed, lost its atmosphere due to galactic wars held in the 4th Density – thus, Earth was not changed nor was it part of the galactic wars, since Earth is wholly within the 3rd Density).

About half a million years ago, former inhabitants of Maldek started reincarnating on Earth, and together with the descendants of colonists that were still here, they slowly started the civilizations that would become Lemuria and Atlantis, and history would repeat itself.

Lemuria was started after Hybornea was eradicated by the Reptoids. It was fragmented by many different star systems, and many different concepts of how galactic humans should live, among them renegades who believed in hierarchical rule instead of the Law of One relationships.

In some text, it is thought that the Lemurians were the first to arrive on Earth.

500,000 BC - Lemuria started daughter nations in Atlantis, the Yu Empire in China and the Egyptian Empire. Civilization flourished on several continents. What is referred to as the "War in the Heavens" began and lasted 1000 years, where the Luciferians and Michael's forces fought out the battle of light and dark on the 4th density so that 3D inhabitants were not affected. Traffic between Earth and Mars ceased. Prior to that there were interactions.

Over the next 850,000 years the Lemurians spread across the face of the planet.

450,000 BC - The Anannaki (from the planet Nibiru – 10th planet in the solar system – now an asteroid belt) created settlements on Earth to mine gold to send back via Mars to Nibiru to power their atmospheric shield. Enki manipulated their miners until 300,000 BC, when the miners' revolt occurred.

The name "Anannaki" can mean many different things (based on Hebrew interpretations) – it is rich in its meaning:

- "An" is short for "anachnu," which means "we"
- "An" also means "heaven"
- "Naki" means "clean"

So, the name can mean "We are clean" and "heaven is clean," clean as in "pure." "Ki" means "Earth," so "We are here on Earth." "Heaven is on Earth." "Anu is here on Earth." The "we" is also meant as a collective oneness, of the Source.

They were tall, giant, (in Hebrew the word for giants is "Anakim"). It is easy to see their Lyran and Sirian roots in their appearance. They also glowed in a golden color. Their symbol is the winged disk, which not only represents their starships, but also symbolic of the ability of the spirit to fly free while remembering its wise, divine source. These Anannaki were later called the Elohim, and Nephilim (those who descended came down). However, they were NOT "the" Elohim, but Elohim became the word used for the plural of god.

(Genesis) 6:4 it is written:
"The Lord said, "My Earth shall not abide in man forever, since he too is flesh; let the days be allowed him be one hundred and twenty years." It was then, and later too, that the Nephilim appeared on Earth - when the divine beings cohabited with the daughters of men, who bore them offspring. They were the heroes of old, men of renown."

It is thought, by some, that the Nephilim were sinful gods who "fell from grace." They fell, alright, in their spaceships. This can also be seen as symbolic. The "fall" having to do with lowering one's frequency from spirit into physical matter, which is slower and denser. "Fall" also meaning forgetting one's true Source. As life forms choose to come to Earth their vibration goes through changes so that they are more matched to the frequency of Earth, their new home.

Now the Anannaki literally came down from space, but souls choosing to incarnate upon the Earth also had to change their vibration frequencies (from the 5th Density down to the 3rd Density). Enlil was first to come to Earth and was there even before mankind was created. The Sumerian texts called mankind the "Black-Headed People."

If anyone doubts the location of Eden, or why it was chosen by the Anannaki as a locale, please read on from Genesis:

"Then, before there was any rain, he formed man, from the dust of the Earth. He blew into his nostrils the Earth of life, and man became a living being. The Lord God planted a garden in Eden, in the east, and placed there the man whom He had formed...," and then all the other life forms came into being, water, animals, minerals. Genesis does say that the first river in Eden was Pishon and winds through the whole land of Havilah, where the gold is - the gold of that land is good; bdellium is there, and lapis lazuli. The name of the second river is Gihon, the one that winds through the whole land of Cush. The name of the third river is Tigris, the one that flows east of Asshur. And the fourth river is the Euphrates.

The Anannaki bodies were etheric. They could not mine the gold since it was physical. They needed to have bodies that would be able to operate on Earth and mine the gold. The point is that they needed to create a physical vessel like an astronaut would require a spacesuit to inhabit space. They tried hundreds of experiments (over tens of thousands of years) and had the help of both the Atlanteans and Sirians. That vessel was the human body (which the Anannaki called a "uniform" or human "instrument"). The bodies to mine the gold were the equivalent of ape-men; they were pre-human. But they were our predecessors. We sometimes refer to them as Human 1.0. They were completely biological, but Human 1.0s were not fully physical. They were partly etheric. The Anannaki and Sirians designed them to synchronize with the evolving densification of the Earth. So as the Earth solidified, so did the human instruments. They were biological with a soul. The Anannaki and Sirians placed the Atlanteans inside these human uniforms. These were very advanced beings, but apparently naïve.

◇◇◇◇◇◇◇◇◇◇◇

400,000 BC - Leumuria and Atlantis co-existed, this was the first of three ages of Atlantis, known as the Old Empire. But Atlantis began plotting to destroy Lemuria enlisting the help of renegades from other star systems who believed in hierarchical rule instead of the Law of One under which Lemuria lived.

300,000 BC - Enki won approval from Nibiru to replace the miner mutineers with a worker race adapted from the Anannaki genome.

Enki, his sister Ninmah and his son Ningishzidda first created short-lived slaves (programmed with HUMAN 1.0) called *Adamites* (descendents of Adam, with as "m" for Adam), from their own genome but modified with clay, copper, and genes from intelligent African hominoids, Homo erectus.

The ape-men bodies were to continue to mine the gold, if the Anannaki could engineer a vessel to enable them to do so. The engineered bodies were needed since the Earth was continuing to solidify.

"The Anannaki had some kind of a falling out with the Atlanteans, and began to conspire with the Sirians and another race referred to as the Serpents. Each of these three races was interested in figuring out how to embody physical planets. They saw Earth as a laboratory of sorts to figure it out. The Anannaki already had a human uniform; they simply needed to power it with a life source or soul.

The bigger issue was how to get the Atlanteans into these embodiments and keep them there. In effect, these three races conspired to enslave the Atlanteans within these pre-human vessels. The Atlanteans were the power generators that made these biological entities operate.

The Sirians were mostly credited with this invention, but it was the offspring of Anu that really perfected these implants by programming them. The human uniform version 1.0 was designed by the Anannaki, the implants were designed by the Sirians, and the programming of the implants was designed and evolved by a being known as Marduk.

A first, these were much more primitive than Neanderthals. But the answer is in the implants. The biological entity or ape-man was not able to operate in the physical world. They needed survival skills, how to eat, how to hunt, how to clean themselves, how to even move their bodies. All of these very fundamental functions were necessary to actually include or program into the vessel, which was the purpose of the functional implants. The implants were akin to the brain of the human 1.0, but it wasn't just in the brain. These implants were placed inside the body within various parts—like the chest area, middle back, wrists, ankles, etc. The primary ones were contained in the skull. But generally these implants were networked to operate from the head, or brain area. Remember that human 1.0 was still part etheric and part physical. The implants also needed a similar consistency or sound vibration. They were placed into the bone or skeletal structure mostly, and some in the muscle tissue. These functional implants fused into the muscles and bone, including the DNA. The DNA integration was for the intelligence of the plan; the muscle tissue allowed the life essence to power the functional implant.

There was a central coordination point, and that was in the brain, but the implants were located throughout the body. This was an integrated system that was installed in the human uniform to allow it to be controlled, monitored, and programmed over time. It was the evolutionary stick and carrot. Doing it this way allowed the early humans to dig out gold, which was their primary purpose initially.

The implanted functionality was partly to make the Human 1.0 and its power source—the life essence of an Atlantean—to function efficiently and effectively as miners. That was the prime goal. The second, however, was to suppress the power source, or in this case, the Atlantean beings inside the human vessels. They did this by making the power source ignorant of its origin and the reality of its true expression as an infinite being. When the Atlantean beings were placed inside the human uniform, they were essentially one-hundred percent focused on physical survival and functional performance. There was no relationship. No marriage. No reproduction. These were essentially cloned beings. They were all the same in terms of their appearance and abilities. Human drones, piloted by implanted functionality that the Atlantean being inside became associated with, as them. The infinite inside the body believed it was the body and the implanted functionality, and nothing more.

These beings—the Atlanteans—were infinite, meaning they did not have space-time regulation. They lived after the body died. However, the Anannaki created a set of planes or dimensions of experience that was the equivalent of a Holding Plane where they could be recycled. This was the basis of reincarnation. It allowed the Anannaki to recycle the Atlanteans. Some aspects of the implanted functionality were interdimensional, which is to say, it could assist in the delivery of the beings to the proper location within the Holding Planes of consciousness, and assist in their reincarnation back into a new vessel.

The ape-men didn't have reproduction, Not in version 1.0. These were basic. But the Anannaki could create them in large scale, so when one human uniform expired—let's say they had a mining accident—another would be made. These were clones. The ability to self-reproduce came in version 2.0 and that was mostly because the amount of effort required, on the part of the Anannaki, to manage this process was enormous. They wanted to create an automated system, something that wouldn't require them to orchestrate all of the variables. So the Sirians helped them to create the implants for reproduction and the ability to automate the recycling of the beings from the Holding Planes to be born into the physical through a baby.

Malduk was intimately involved in the evolution of the species. That was his role. Of all the Anannaki, he was the closest to the Human 1.0's. Marduk understood them and even admired certain aspects of them. Unconsciously, perhaps, he began to alter their programs so the Human 1.0's behaved more like the Anannaki. As they began to take on the characteristics of the Anannaki, Anu and his sons, Enki and Enlil, were concerned by this. Marduk was programming emotions and feelings. He was evolving humans too quickly, but remember, this was the evolution of the functional implants, the interface between the power source—Atlanteans—and the human physical body. So it was the interface that was being evolved, which enabled the human body to show emotion, to communicate, to sense more of the three-dimensional world called Earth, etc.

The other thing that was happening was that as the Earth continued to become more of a three-dimensional solid, so did the Human 1.0s and their functionality implants. This growing densification also made it easier to control and suppresses the Atlantean power source inside the human uniforms. It was like a compression was taking place in and on this Earth plane, and it was deepening the gravity of focus on Earth plane survival.

The word 'Serpents' has been mentioned above. Serpents are a race of beings. They simply were another race of beings based on reptilian DNA, but distinct from the Anannaki. You could say they were related. They were known as life carriers. They seeded planets. They built food chains. You could say they were the grocers of the planet. They were not involved in the creation of the human 1.0, at least not in the technical sense. Their job was more to provide food and sustenance for it.

We do not know how the Atlanteans were forced into the

Human 1.0 bodies, but the Atlanteans were naïve. They had no reason to think it would be possible to become enslaved. It would be like a concept that was never used in their culture. No one ever did that… nor could they. You can't enslave an infinite being, unless, of course, you lock them into a human uniform. And that was the cunning of the Anannaki and their Sirian partners. They launched this attack from such a bizarre angle, that the Atlanteans couldn't see it coming; it was an ambush or surprise attack.

200,000 BC - The processional cycle took place with floods, ice ages and tectonic shifts which destroyed most of humanity. A precession is a change [shift] in the orientation of the rotational axis of a rotating body. Every 25,920 years a processional cycle occurs for Earth, where shifts wipe out most of the inhabitants.

200,000 BC - Commander Enlil (Anannaki) ordered Enki to create more efficient, intelligent, and obedient miners. In response, Enki begat a line of Earthlings called AdaPites (that's with a P for AdaPa, the boy Enki made with an Adamite girl).

200,000 to 122,000 BC - Lemuria flourished on a continent in the Pacific Ocean the size of Australia, north of current Australia, with half a billion souls at its peak. It was known as the Land of Mu. They were peaceful people.

122,000 BC - A catastrophe wiped out most of the other continents but not Lemuria.

122,000 to 100,000 BC - The second period of Lemuria began when survivors of the destroyed continents came to Lemuria and the population exploded to a billion people at its height. They were not technological, but tribal, music, rhythm, peaceful.

100,000 years ago Pleiadians came and planted seeds of quantum divine DNA into one of 17 kinds of humans existing at that time. Like other animals there were different kinds of humanoids, some with tails, some without, etc. The original creation story was this time. The other kinds of animals after that dropped away. We look like Pleiadians. Biological beings slowly gained their quantum DNA and spirituality was born. The first civilization was Lemuria with 90% quantum DNA, not 30% like we have today. When Lemuria broke up Lemurians became seafarers. They scattered by sea all over the world. Pleiadians originally landed on the largest island of Hawaii, the top of the highest mountain. The lineage of Hawaii is Lemurians. They had a quantum understanding of the solar system. Atlantis was much, much later. Lemurians were considerably more advanced than Atlantis, in consciousness only, not technically. But they could heal with magnetics. They had intuitive information.

100,000 years ago Atlantis was on the rise.

Atlantis Creation – Autocracy Was Born - Naacal (approx 1,000 of very high consciousness, who were of higher dimension and had achieved immortality, established Atlantis by laying out a Tree of Life pattern with 12 circles (not the normal 10) with an extra circle on top, on the isle of Udal, and the other "added" circle in the water. 10 of the circles where on land.

At this time, the Kundalini of the Earth (core to surface) ended at Atlantis; where the Kundalini ends becomes a spiritual center. After Atlantis, the Kundalini moved to Tibet. The Naacals breathed life into the Tree of Life, creating vortexes of energy in each of the circles. Lemurians from all over the scattered world came to Atlantis. The Lemurians were right

Chapter 3 – Alternate History of the Universe & Earth, We are a War

brained (female species) and only eight of the centers were occupied. Two vortexes remained and were filled by the Hebrews (coming from our future?). The Hebrews were right brained and were not of the Earth humans. The other vortex was filled by the left brained ("doers") from Mars (most likely these were the Anannaki, who used Mars as an intermediate station to ship the gold to Nibiru). At one time, Mars was like Earth, 1,000,000 year ago, but the Lucifer Experiment occurred on Mars, where the specie's spirit cuts themselves off from Unity of the Universe (based on love) and, thus, the species is male, without compassion, just logic without emotion. Wars began between the beings on Mars and Mar's atmosphere was destroyed. A synthetic Merkaba was created (five sided pyramids in a cluster). They used the synthetic Merkaba to travel in time to Earth, approx 50,000 years ago. A living Merkaba is the "chariot of ascension" and is the energy field around our body; it can change dimension and allows for travel throughout the universe.

The Isle of Udal was at the top (the brain) of the Tree of Life and its city was Poseidon (Plato mentions Poseidon and its ten children (the 10 circles of the Tree of Life) with its Three Ring symbol of Atlantis: Inner circle was the Naacals (the brain), the middle was the Maya (priesthood) and the outer circle as the Lemurians (regular people of Atlantis). The million or so Atlanteans subdued the 1,000 or so Martians (Anannaki), but the older Martians were able to take control. The Martians (Anannaki), through their technology eventually caused the Lemurians to be more Left brained. This control aspect of Atlantis continued until about 26,000 years ago, when a polar shift occurred (change in magnetic field) and another polar shift occurred 13,000 years ago (The Fall of Consciousness); another is predicted very soon. The pole shift causes magnitude earthquakes, ocean level changes, etc., as the crust of the Earth slips on its molten core. The polar shift appears to align with our shift in consciousness. The collapse of our social structure is, by some, contributed by the changes we are now experiencing in the Earth's magnetic field. The pending pole shift is causing an awaking of our consciousness, which had fallen at the time of the sinking of Atlantis. Between 26,000 and 13,000 years ago, a comet traversed the solar system. The Martians (Anannaki) wanted to blow it out of its orbit with their weapons, but the rest of Atlantis said it was divine order and the comet was allowed to hit the Earth near Charleston (approx 12,000 years ago); fragments hit Atlantis, where the Martians lived, destroying many. The Martians said they will never listen to the others Atlanteans again. Martians decided to take over the Earth. The Martians thought they could create another synthetic Merkaba to control the Earth. The Marian Merkaba exploded (in the area of what is now the Bermuda Triangle) and almost destroyed the Earth. But it did rip a hole in the dimensional level, releasing Lower Dimensional Spirits and beings that entered into the bodies of the Atlanteans, in order to survive. The Naacals were able to send most of the lower dimensional spirits "back" and patched the rip in the dimensional field, but the social, monitory, and other structures failed. We were now a male species and had only 13,000 years to get from "rock bottom," to CHRIST CONSCIOUSNESS. Thus, The kings of Atlantis (Naacals – 6th dimensional spirits) devised a synthetic planetary consciousness grid over the Earth, first created in the 4th dimension and then build it in the 3rd dimension, to hold the consciousness of a species (human). The consciousness grid has the components of all dimensions. The grid led to a universal consciousness, connecting each of us. In recent times, the Russians and the United States attempted to build military bases at all of the grid points in order to control the consciousness of the Earth.

◇◇◇◇◇◇◇◇◇◇◇

75,000 years ago, according to RA in the Law of One, second density moved to third density. The Earth goes through 25,000 year cycles. A density is not expected to reach completion in

Chapter 3 – Alternate History of the Universe & Earth, We are a War

one cycle; maybe some souls are harvestable at the end of the second 25,000 year cycle, and usually everyone at the end of the third 25,000 year cycle. So there were none after the first cycle 50,000 years ago. There were a few harvested 25,000 years ago so contact was made by the Federation. There was a call at that time from Atlantis, Egypt and South America. Atlantis' second stage went down 10,821 years ago.

48,000 BC - Enki and Adapite beauty Batanash begat Noah, who carried Enki's longevity genes and ruled the Iraqi city of Sharuppak until the Deluge of 13,000 years ago.

25,000 BC - The Atlanteans began to acquire a feeling of uniqueness about their culture and wanted to eliminate Lemuria so that they could become the mother country. The Atlanteans began forming alliances with renegade Pleiadians and Alpha Centaurians which had Hierarchical systems of government. Atlantis destroyed Lemuria by using the help of Renegade Pleiadians and others to move one of Earth's two moons (Earth had 2 moons in those times), lowering it over Lemuria and beaming it so that it exploded and rained pieces down on Lemuria, sinking it and causing volcanic destruction. This destroyed much of Lemuria, but this also resulted in many pressures being inflicted upon the tectonic plates, resulting in the gas chambers under Lemuria to implode and thus sink most of the Lemurians continent.

Another source stated that Lemuria sank due to a change in consciousness and Atlantis rose. The people of Lemuria moved (dispersed throughout the Earth) due to the sinking.

Atlantis was a similar civilization as ours today. The DNA was a combination of Orion, Draco, Sirian, Andromedan and Pleiadians. Orions are passionate, Dracos competitive, aggressive, cunning. Pleiadians peaceful and loving.

The Atlanteans founded daughter colonies that were similar to Atlantis: Yu which is now Central China and Tibet and the Libyan/Egyptian colonies.

Two daughter empires, Yu Empire in China and Libyan/Egyptian Empire in Africa were shocked by the destruction of Lemuria. Yu refused to join Atlantis and they retreated underground to become the Agarthans of today - inner Earth and hollow Earth civilizations. Libyan/Egyptian Empire went along with Atlantis' rule. After the fall of Lemuria, there were three subterranean cities: Telos, Shambala and Poseidon. After the fall of Lemuria and the rise of Atlantis, fleets of ships by Alpha Draconian and Orions orbited the Earth in 4th density. They put an electromagnetic shield about the planet to prevent enemy ETs from approaching Earth. Also quarantine was put in place by 7th density Pleiadians to prevent Draco and Orions from corrupting neighboring astral and etheric civilizations. This was only lifted in 1987 during the Harmonic Convergence. Until then, Earth was not a desirable place.

25,000 BC to 15,000 BC was the second age of Atlantis, the Middle Empire, after they destroyed Lemuria they wanted to be ruling power of Earth. They established a hierarchical ruling government, annihilating those who wanted a more democratic Lemurians style of government.

23,900 BC - Earth experienced a small minor processional cycle, but not much damage was done.

23,200 BC - Atlantis was destroyed due to the misuse of crystalline energy (Anannaki where attempting to create a synthetic Merkaba to leave Earth, just as they had done to leave Mardek, thousands of years ago, but they "didn't get it right" and there was a massive explosion). 2000 years prior they had developed radionics devices using quartz. Orions orbiting Earth traded their propulsion systems for Atlantean technology, attempting to gain superiority over their colleagues. It is the opinion of some that an imbalance between head and heart, emotional and mental, caused the downfall. A crystal generator exploded and sank the continent. Only a handful of survivors went to Central and South America, and Egypt.

15,000 years ago The Great White Brotherhood was formed by ascended human beings from Earth - those who had mastered their physical bodies. "White" means clothed in the white garments of God (Mathew 22:11, Isaiah 61:10, others).

Per www.acension-research.org, Great White Brotherhood of Ascended Masters: "Divine Beings (Individualizations of God - THE ONE) have assisted the Earth since Archangel Michael led the coming of the First Root Race of the Sons and Daughters of God into Incarnation. This was a much more distant time before the "fall of man" and the later efforts by the Holy Kumaras in the founding of the Great White Brotherhood with the goal of awakening every person to the Divinity within them.

With the creation of Human 2.0 inserted into the Devised Body, the Anannaki Ann made himself "God" and the Great White Brotherhood was united for the higher purpose of "God on Earth" (i.e., Anu, the Human 2.0 programmer, not the ultimate creator /First Source). In the present day, it appears that The Great White Brotherhood is closely aligned with the Freemasons, Sufis, Knights Templar, Theosophical Society, the Hermetic Order of the Golden Dawn, the illuminati, and the White Path, all to limit or control the truth or obscure the First Source.

15,000 BC to 10,000 BC was the third age of Atlantis (contradicts earlier notes), the New Empire. When they fled Earth they left humans genetically reduced and mutated.

12,000 BC (this is in conflict with the previous sources stating Atlantis was destroyed in 23,200 BC) - Atlantis' elite rulers exiled those who were secretly trying to get a Lemurians style government started. They sent them to Northern Europe to Iona. Included were Atlantis elite and scientists. They were trying to bring into Atlantis the Osirius cult (the Sirians) based on Lemurians form of government. Atlantis tried to destroy the Ionians with a moon and tractor beams but the Ionians (scientists) countered the effort and they helped to destroy Atlantis. The King of Atlantis at that time was called Atlas, who secretly wanted a Lemurians government. His Queen Mu and son Osiris were sent in opposite directions to distract those trying to kill the king. Queen Mu and her brother Prince Mayam were sent to Central America, and his son Osiris, army and priests were sent to Libyan/Egyptian Empire hoping to establish Lemurians government there. But Osiris' brother Seth believed in hierarchical rule of Atlantis and opposed him. Osiris son Horus learned of an impending attack by his Uncle Seth and warned his father who would not believe. Seth secretly set Osirius up as king plotting to kill him and ascend the throne but his plan didn't work and he retreated to Samaria. Son Horus killed Seth and Seth's sons plotted against Horus. Meanwhile the King of the Agarthans sent his son Rama (the Yu Empire that went underground) to the surface to establish a surface empire in India. Rama aligned with Horus in battling Seth's sons and the wars that followed nearly destroyed Earth.

Throughout the years there were many wars among the various empires due to underground movements of people that wanted to have the Lemurians "philosophy" back in place (i.e. no hierarchy). These wars led to vast destruction. As a last resort the warring empires decided to attack the opponents crystal temples (which were responsible for maintaining two frozen layers of water about 15,000 - 30,000 feet above ground which protected people on Earth from the harmful sun's rays and also ensured a stable Earth pattern at all times).

Unfortunately, the attacks were made simultaneously and caused the Firmament (the water layers) to be broken down and thus millions of gallons of water poured down onto the surface causing what is known biblically as "The Great Flood" .The breakdown of the Firmament also resulted in the polar icecaps freezing and also the many climatic variations we have today to form. Earth's population was reduced from 64 million to 2 million.

10,500 BC – The Great Pyramid was finished by the Sirians. Thoth was the engineer, a radiant being of blue-white light, humanoid, who stepped down his vibration to come to descendants of Atlantis in Egypt. The Great Pyramid was built as an ascension chamber and controller of Earth's grid system. It is aligned with Mintaka, a star in Orion's Belt, the central star in Orion's enlightened government after the resolution of Regel/Betelguese wars 100,000 years ago. The alignment with Mintaka had geographical significance in Earth's precession every 25,920 years.

10,000 BC - An archeological site 12,000 years old carbon dated, was found in 1994 only 350 miles from Mt. Ararat where Noah was said to have landed in his ark. It was found by a Turkish farmer who saw a stone sticking up in the sand. Digging down it turned out to be 14 feet long pillar. They call it Gobekli Tepe in SE Turkey. There are circles of stones and columns with finely carved figures.

10,000 years ago approximately (Ed, one source stated 11,000 BC; see, also, 4,000 BC) - The great flood was the turning point in our history. After the flood was the beginning of recorded history. Atlantean elites fled to the star Agena (Beta Centauri) leaving a small number of limited-consciousness humans. Our life span was reduced to decades from millennium. Our height was reduced from 8 to 10 feet tall to 5 or 6 feet.

The Anannaki helped flood survivors proliferate and build cities of 50,000 people in the Middle East, Egypt and the Indus Valley. They built airports, pyramidal powerhouses and temples around the entire Earth. The Anannaki ruled the new civilization as gods.

The Anannaki taught us hierarchy, misogyny, violence, greed, slavery, debt and war that featured genocide and weapons of mass destruction. The Anunnaki's tales of their stay on Earth before they made our ancestors, as well as what our forefathers directly saw imprinted on us with the values of the Nibiran hierarchic, male-run, master-slave-enemy mentality. We assumed values of extraction, pollution, monetary monopoly and obsession with gold. Fortunately the genetics team that created us also gave us the capacity and preserved the histories Sitchin and others translated so we can overcome the liabilities the Anannaki left us.

9,000 years ago - The third and final piece of Atlantis sank due to nuclear and crystal war with those who left Atlantis and went to the South African desert. Egyptian contacts were followed by destruction, also South American contacts. The Federation (also known as the Confederation) stepped back then and used more caution. Their methods were not appropriate. They began to explore more creative methods of contact.

8800 BC - We have been in Galactic Night since 8800 BC. Our solar system completes one orbit around the central sun of our Milky Way galaxy every 26,000 years. (Refer to the Photon Belt).

7,500 BC - Egypt declined when 7th density Sirians arrived and began unraveling the work of Thoth. Sirian factions were on an ego trip. They were the gurus. Jehovah was a Sirian renegade who came to Earth and divided the people of Earth.

6,000 BC - Evidence of hammered metal, and the first money, the silver shekel "weighed ingot." Metallurgy and smelting began in Sumer which was devoid of metal ores. Why? The region had fuels to fire kilns crucibles and furnaces. Fuels were bitumers, asphalts and petroleum, natural to Mesopotamia. There was a high degree of medical knowledge, therapy, surgery and incantations were given to heal the sick. Also punishment for doctors who failed and harmed their patient.

5,000 BC - A tablet was found in Ur which names a medical practitioner, shows there were veterinarians for animals and a snake on a tree - the same symbol for medicine today. There were medical schools, lotions, soaking, cleaning, solvents, lotions and radiation. Also clothing, irrigation, food cuisine, transportation and shipping. A high civilization in 5000 years BC.

4,000 BC – (Ed, contradicts the 11,000 BC flood listed above) the great flood which wiped out most of Earth's population, reduced it from 64 million to 2 million. Caused by two sides warring and both sides used the crystal temples to poke holes in the firmament to rain down waters on the other side. Both sides did it at the same time.

The Anannaki helped flood survivors proliferate and build cities of 50,000 people in the Middle East, Egypt and the Indus Valley. They built airports, pyramidal powerhouses and temples around the entire Earth. The Anannaki ruled the new civilization as gods.

AFTER THE FLOOD - Only about 2 million people survived the Flood from an original 65 million. Unfortunately many of the survivors were the mutant humans that had been genetically altered by the Atlanteans into a much lower state of consciousness (Ed, refer to prior discussions concerning the Anannaki). Also, the fact that the firmament was now no longer in existence resulted in the DNA and thus consciousness breaking down even further. A few different renegades from Pleiades, Alpha and Beta Centauri came to different places on Earth after the Flood, seeing it as an opportune time to establish their own desired ideologies and also be seen as "godlike" and thus revered. Being already genetically altered, the surviving humans were therefore easily controlled by these renegades, since no form of disobedience to these new "gods" was allowed; the concept of ruling by "divine right" became inculcated on Earth. This concept of worshipping elite has continued through to modern times. Culture would rise against culture in wars claiming that the elite they themselves worshipped were superior to the elite of the opposing faction.

Since the Great Flood (Noah), the Anannaki gave us the best and the worst of planet-wide civilization–kings, historians, taxes, temples, priests, bicameral congresses, record-keeping, law codes, library catalogs, furnaces, kilns, wheeled vehicles, paved roads, medicines, cosmogony, cosmology, festivals, beer, food recipes, art, music, music instruments, music notes, dance, textiles, and multicolored apparel. Sumerian school taught mathematics, architecture, theology, writing, grammar, botany, zoology, geography. They had (but didn't show us how to build) a world-wide energy grid, air, submarine and interplanetary transport vehicles and advanced computers.

After the great flood, Human 2.0 was then created. This was the stage where the humans could self-reproduce. And when this happened, some of the Anannaki impregnated female humans and brought in their bloodlines to the human species. This began the variations. This began the idea that humans were no longer clones. The concern, however, was that Human 2.0s might become too powerful and self-aware. What if the

Chapter 3 – Alternate History of the Universe & Earth, We are a War

Atlantean power source became aware that it was an infinite being? This was when Anu decided that he should be God. Humans needed to have a lord or ruler over them so it was clear that they were inferior to an external ruler. This was a key part of their program of indoctrination. Working with Marduk and the Sirians, they created the environment of Eden and created the paradigm of Eve as the instigator of the fall of humanity. This was, you might say, Act 1 of Anu as God. It was staged to provide the Human 2.0s with a clear sense of an external authority, and that they were expelled from Paradise because they tried to be self-realized.

It was like rebuking humanity with the fist of an angry creator who wanted his creation to remain identified with their human uniform. Kind of like saying: "Do not think for a moment that you can be like me." This actually happened kind of like the Bible said. So the God of the Bible is this Anannaki Lord, called Anu.

The original goal was the acquisition of gold. But when the Atlanteans rejected Anu, he began to conspire with the Sirians. It was just before the flood that Anu discovered that the gold he'd mined was sufficient. He didn't require more. However, the notion of being a God over the Atlanteans was seductive. The Sirians and Serpents felt that the idea of enslaving infinite beings in planet ecosystems was their invention. They had something that was totally unique. They were creator-Gods, and every other race could be ensnared in a similar type of vessel. The Earth had a unique quality to its core. This core was of extreme interest to the Anannaki when they first visited Earth. It was this core that created the gravitational field that enabled the planet to become fully physical in such a way that it could support physical life. Of course other conditions needed to be present, too, but it was this core that was the real key. Working with the Sirians and Serpents, they began to do this same enslavement on other planets. They replicated the core of Earth and engineered a method for implanting this core on other planets. They were essentially terraforming a planet by cloning and installing Earth's core.

3,500 BC - Illuru in the form of a Hebrew priest (actually a Nibiruan lizard who appeared later as 3D Moses) took the power away from Egypt's Pharaoh Akhenaton and created monotheism (fundamentalism), when he grabbed Akhenaton's staff and tapped it on the ground and brought forth snakes using 4D magic. Then as Moses he went into the flames on the desert and spoke the words "Aton-I" which his followers heard as Adonai. He told followers to sacrifice animals. The Hebrew people are carriers of Nibiruan intelligence. In Hebrew their name is "Ibri." Egyptians called them "Hibiru." Nibiru and Earth are from the same body. The Hebrew people carry the lineage of Nibiru while Egyptians carry lineage of Sirius.

3100 BC - Egyptian records show lists of royal dynasties.

3000 BC to 1000 AD - The age of the avatars and prophets.

2900 BC - Sumerian City Lagash started and lasted 650 years. One ruler was Gudea devoted to Ningirsu who gave him, in vision, a floor plan to construct a seven-layered temple.

2,450 BC - Sirians rebuilt the Great Pyramid.

2024 BCE – The Anannaki ruined their eastern Mediterranean cities with nuclear blasts and fallout storms.

1300 BC - The exodus of Israelites from Egypt into Canaan, around the same time that the Greek civilization started (Hellenic), probably later. The Minoan culture showed evidence of an earlier Hebrew influence. The Hellenic alphabet (Latin and our own alphabet) came from the Near East. There were 26 letters by 500 BC, a bridge to our western civilization -

it was founded in the Near East. The kings of Greece (Cyrus, Darius) and the names of their deities were Aryan, meaning "lords" People appeared near the Caspian Sea and started to spread west, east and south around 200 BC. There is a comparative alphabet between Hebrew, Greek and Latin. The step pyramids served as a stairway to heaven for the gods (to their spacecraft), as is the "missing" 20-feet between the current top of the Great Pyramid and the gold cap "stone" that is located in the British Museum (space for a spacecraft).

1000 BC - Excavations in Northern Mesopotamia found a palace of an Assyrian king and a well laid-out city with all amenities, dating to 1000 BC.

500 - 400 BC - Greece reached its peak.

331 BC - Alexander the Great conquered Persia (Iran).

311 BC – By 311 BCE, Most Anannaki returned to Nibiru. But Nannar and his followers of pure Nibiran ancestry stayed. They secretly run everything on Earth to this very day. They and their half-breeds perpetuate exclusive, hostile nations, economies and religions to war with weapons, ideology and debt to prevent us uniting against them. Nannar and his minions are still masters of those in positions of political, military, economic and religious power through whom they could influence the creation of third-party conflicts by manipulation of witting and unwitting minions who wield power within the political/ economic/ religious/ military grid. They exercise control through separation (nation from nation, race from race, the haves from the have nots, etc.); where there is separation there is no unity.

200 BC - People who suddenly appeared and increased near the Caspian Sea, started to spread west, east and south.

1 BC - Jesus came to bring a new insight of the First Source. Although sent by First Source, and an avatar (like us, he needed a "spacesuit" to live in the 3rd Density of Earth. Of course, the Anannaki "twisted" his significance by stating Christ was talking about Anu (the "god" created as part of the Human 2.0 program).

1000 AD - 1900 AD - the Middle Ages

1900 AD - present - Modern times.

1987 AD - Harmonic Convergence. Earth moved into the Photon Band in March 1987. The quarantine was then lifted around Earth that was placed there 100,000 years ago by 7th density Pleiadians to prevent the Draconians and Orions from corrupting neighboring astral and etheric civilizations.

1994 - The Anannaki and renegade Reptilians are in alliance and have been controlling Earth for about 13000 years via their henchmen - the dark human cabals who are vying for control of the U.S. and the world. Due to the immense and significant changes involved in the end of the present 206 million year Galactic Cycle, many of the "dark forces" have at this time chosen to come over to the other side. They are now joining the "Forces of Light" in large numbers; membership of the Galactic Federation of Light has recently increased from 100,000 members to over 200,000 Star systems. The Anannaki (the portion led by Marduk) switched sides to the Galactic Federation in 1994 after the dark Anchara Alliance chose to do so.

In early 1994, Anchara's most prophetic priestesses and priests delivered a transformative proclamation to the dark forces. They stated, unequivocally, the following great truth. The *divine* time had arrived, at long last, for a galactic truce! Anchara requested that the Galactic Federation of Light consider a permanent peace treaty. As a stipulation of this permanent treaty of peace, the dark forces of the alliance of Anchara agreed to finally relinquish its claims to Earth.

A great anger remained within the Anannaki as well as a reluctance to relinquish all that they had fought for. Many fierce battles were fought among the confused and rebellious fleet of the dark Alliance of Anchara. When the anger finally cleared, the forces on the side of the galactic truce had won an overwhelming victory. The few remaining dark fleets retreated to their home-worlds on the far side of the Milky Way Galaxy.

Clinging to the last remnants of this rage, this small group now regrouped and bided their time on Earth. They still wished, wholeheartedly, to attack this newly joined fleet of Light.

In late 1994, the victorious elements of the former Anchara Alliance fleets asked for permission to negotiate a permanent treaty, allowing them to join the Galactic Federation of Light as special members. The previous dark fleets now agreed to abide by the rules that the ancient charter of the Galactic Federation of Light had put forth.

The only sticky point was how they would go about giving up their ancient claims to planet Earth. Not wishing to lose their access to this most sacred water-world, the former Alliance members requested that a series of special ambassadors be permanently stationed on Earth. These special ambassadors were only to be put there after Earth and its people returned to full consciousness.

In another part of this treaty, the former Alliance members promised to abolish several secret treaties with the major surface governments of Earth. To demonstrate their sincere belief in Anchara's decrees, the former Alliance members quickly withdrew their many ambassadors, technicians, and scientists from Earth. Their sudden departure was another crack in the evil that surrounds Earth.

The tiny crack soon became a gaping hole when the secret worldly cabals' former masters, the Anannaki, made a surprising and very fortuitous move. The elites' extraterrestrial mentors had unexpectedly switched sides and joined the Galactic Federation of Light.

Now known as the 'Annanuki' (spelling changed to indicate their 'new' direction), they had long been both the masterminds behind global cabals' actions and their chosen cruel and autocratic rulers. As the Anannaki, they currently serve the Light. Their knowledge of the elites' sinister ways has become a true sword of Damocles hanging above the collective heads of these evil oppressors.

The Anunnaki's program is to use their former influence to send the many interlocked cabals down a new path. To date, some degree of progress has been made. However, while slowly changing, the many global cabals retain a deep desire to rule with their accustomed tyranny. Their obsession for control has caused them to temporally fragment around the need to react to the Anunnaki's bold requests. It has also generated a number of odd petitions from Earth's covert rulers to their former masters.

Although the Anannaki, renegade Reptilians and the Archara Alliance switched sides to the Galactic Federation in 1994, Anannaki Earth Command and the renegade Reptilians are slow to relinquish their control. The author of this Compendium believes that their "feet dragging" is due to the Anannaki/Reptilians desire to "install" Human 3.0 into many of their "controlled" humans, to complete their cloning process, and to have the "Fake Second Coming" to again coalesce their control and reduce any awakening that has occurred.

Chapter 3 – Alternate History of the Universe & Earth, We are a War

1997 AD - In 1979, Nannar's Anannaki faction, the one running this planet now, forced U.S. President Reagan and USSR Chairman Gorbachev to develop a world-wide "star wars" defense GRID aimed–not at each other–but at incoming spacecraft of the rival Anannaki faction led by Prince Marduk.

The grid is completely interactive–from surveillance, counterintelligence to asset disposition, military policy to event response sets based on the assumption there will be an invasion by technologically advanced forces incoming. Everything is geared to disallow beachheads fifth column assets have on the ground.

In 1997, President Reagan agreed to defend Nannar's system of 10 czars that already rules Earth against Marduk's incoming forces. Nannar's top 10 bosses–the czars–of Earth have been identified. These czars do Nannar's bidding and run the Earth's governments.

- The American NATO group
- The Russian Mafia group.
- The Japan group.
- The China group.
- The OPEC group.
- The Cartel Triads councils group.
- The supply margin economic policy group In Latin America and Africa headed by Brazil.
- The seven members of the economical community led by the Roman Pope.
- The trigger states, Iran, North Korea as well as the G-8.

Chapter 3 – Alternate History of the Universe & Earth, We are a War

The U.S. Government and other world governments have to formally contend with the presence of two Anannaki camps in conflict with one another, to deal with both:

1) Nunnar's Earthly system of 10 czars whose purpose is to control and dominate the Earth.
2) Marduk (whose group left the Earth by 311 BC) brings with him his son Nabu, his brother Gibil, a leader called Nuskum, as well as a person Marduk calls "The Dedicated Human" to free us from the matrix in which Nannar enslaved us. Yet, Anu will remain GOD.

Marduk's incoming faction offers us instead a "direct democracy" to run the planet instead of Nannar's power elite. Marduk's operatives and agents have infiltrated all Nannar's organizations listed above and they have been assassinating Nannar's Earthling assets and Anannaki agents. Marduk covertly instigates actions within the organizations listed above to create events that drastically reduce their population but do not reveal Marduk's hidden hand and spoil his PR.

2013 AD (approximately) - Our solar system enters the Photon Band as it does every approximately 12,000 years ED: Conflicts with 1987, previously mentioned). Once in the Band there is much less population (per Times Magazine, Newsfeed, 2013/01/11, 'Baby Bust: Is the World's Population Actually Declining?,' The world's population isn't growing nearly as fast as it once did. In fact, experts say the rate of population growth will continue to slow and that the total population will eventually — likely within our lifetimes — fall). Due to intense wind and Earth movements many become trees or crystals at will, changing form to ground them. Those who remain vibrate in total unison with Gaia (personification of the Earth – whereby, in 1979, James Lovelock, in his book *Gaia: A New Look at Life on Earth*, proposes that living organisms and inorganic material are part of dynamic system that shapes the Earth's biosphere and maintains the Earth as a fit environment for life) and they heal by species resonance.

MESSAGE COMING FROM THE FEDERATION ON LEMURIA - Translated by Sheldon Nidel

You were mutated into limited conscious Beings and your cluster of realities was also affected. Suddenly, a new paradigm was adopted that favored lack of limitation, power and division. You lost your connection to your history and to a sacred set of beliefs, which the Anannaki and their carefully chosen minions replaced with a new conception. As a result, they ruled you as your 'gods' and 'goddesses.' They brainwashed you to believe that they were your 'creators' and that the past wonders of Lemuria and Atlantis were myths. They ordered their minions to institute 'writing' as an agent of their own glorification. These acts are recorded in the ancient tablets of Sumer, in the steles of ancient India and in carvings found throughout Europe, Australia, Oceania, Asia and the Americas. Now, as your consciousness expands more quickly, you are coming to see these tales for the elaborate fiction they truly are.

Chapter 3 – Alternate History of the Universe & Earth, We are a War

Your origins are not of this world, but are extraterrestrial in nature, and are to be found on a planet that circles the star Vega in the Lyra constellation. Yet, you have achieved more than to travel a mere 26 Light Years to reach your present home. Many millions of years ago, you became part of a vast rebellion by the Light against the Dark in this galaxy. The uprising began in Lyra, Cancer, Gemini and Orion, as well as in many other lesser-known star groupings ('constellations'). Eventually, this rebellion led to the formation of the Galactic Federation of Light, over 4 million years ago. At the very core of this battle were the Star League of the Pleiades, the Andromedan Confederation, the Lyra Light League and the Sirian Star-Nation. Of these, Sirius is most sacred and the place where the Great Blue Lodge of Creation has chosen to enter this galaxy. Originally, it was defended by a Lion people who decided to settle only on two planets in the Sirius A star system. Later, with their permission, Humans from Lyra were first to colonize Sirius B and, in time, Sirius C and D.

The Sirian star system is filled with the great energy bestowed by the Great Blue Lodge. This energy obscures its exact configuration. The system is an anomaly. Sirius' energy defies the physics of stars' normal construction. Sirius A and its companions seem to be what they are not. Thus, to your scientists, they appear, incorrectly, to be exceedingly dense. This seeming density is due to the energy exerted upon them by the Blue Light of Creation. From within this Light, Sirius gathers up the great energy and disperses it to the galaxy. This energy also transforms the way in which those who dwell here see themselves and their sacred mission. It has led Sirius to assist in spreading the energy of its galactic society to a multitude of solar systems throughout this galaxy. The 'Four Great Laws' were presented, long ago, to humanity on Vega and reached their fullest potential on Sirius. The ancient Lemurians civilization brought them to Earth and they were anchored here by its descendants - the Inner Earth realm known as Agartha (Shambala).

In the language of Sirius B, a star-nation is known as 'Akonowai', meaning 'sacred path of Creation's Light.' The third and fourth planets in our system circle a bluish-white star. Its light forms a pattern in our atmosphere that creates a red-orange sky filled with the rare bluish cloud. Most of our vegetation is quite purple-blue in color. Infrequently, it is green, orange or brown. On our main world, Sirius B's third planet, there is one interconnected sea that contains cetaceans, fish and many creatures unrelated to any aquatic species existing on your world. We dwell in this land of lush forests, huge mountains, enormous prairies and very high mountains. Our main cities are located some 50 to 200 miles (80 to 320 kilometers) from all this beauty. On the surface are only 144 main temple sites. The largest is the grand temple of Atar, dedicated to the spiritual warrior clan named after our largest bird - a six-foot tall eagle that we call an 'Atar.'

The dimensions of the grand temple of Atar are astonishing. Its main hall contains 576 columns, each exactly 288 perdums or 312 feet (94.8 meters) in height. Its roof is covered with a special lacework of pure gold to let in the majesty of our Sun. Its floor tiles are inscribed with the text of the Great Book of Understanding, in which the Creator bestowed upon humanity the blueprint for physicality and the wisdom to fulfill its potential. The main hall is most sacred. The remainder of the temple complex is designed to support and accommodate the rituals practiced within. In the exact center of this very large hall is our planet's main node. The temple is situated on a huge cliff that looks out over our one great sea. The energy that emanates from it each day forms a ring of golden Light around it. At night, when viewed from the ocean, this Light seems like a strong beacon signaling to a ship far out at sea.

The beauty of our world is sacred. Soon, the limitless glories of your world will be apparent once again. Despite all that you have done to her, Mother Earth's magnificence is clearly visible from space. This water-world of yours is utterly exquisite. Soon, most of its deserts and the fierce heat that envelops them will be transformed. Ice caps will vanish and the wonders of your most southern continent will be revealed. As you help to return your world to its original, pristine condition, recall what we have ever so briefly told you about our home. Like the two water planets of Akonowai, your solar system embodies much that is sacred. In a short time, Mars will bloom once more, and the desolation on Venus will metamorphose into a land of abundant oceans that teem with life. Such a destiny awaits you and is truly not as distant as you may imagine.

WHERE FROM HERE – Human 2.0 and Earth has continued to densify -We have become increasingly three-dimensional. Human 2.0s and Earth continues to densify. We are actually denser now than we have ever been - in terms of physicality. There was a time, about thirty years ago, when we thought alien races were actually leaving spaceships behind on purpose, but what we discovered, more recently, is that most of the aliens were not physical beings. They were observing Earth, and their spaceships actually became entrained by the gravitational circuits of the Earth's core, which caused their spaceships to materialize in three-dimensional space. Because many of the materials used in the ships' construction had chemical properties, they were prone to densification when exposed to Earth's atmosphere. The other half of this equation is the resistive behaviors, and these are withdrawing and stopping behaviors that support separation and deception. These are active resistances. Saying "no" to behaviors of your own and others, without judgment.

The Triad of Power, however you want to define it, in terms of titles, is programmed to create their own Human 3.0. This version will be predicated on the confluence of technology in the form of biological enhancements that make the human vessel even more of a welcoming environment for the functional implants. The goal is to make an infinite human on the Earth plane… infinite by virtue of immortality. The fusion of human and technology or what some call transhumanism, is the goal. So, Human 3.0 for the Triad of Power is very different from Human 3.0 SI, transhumanism is separation. It says we are frail, weak, finite, brutish, diseased… incomplete. All of these ideas of biological implants and cognitive enhancement were parts of the ACIO agenda (Advanced Contact Intelligence Organization, which organized an inter-disciplinary research team to access the New Mexico Ancient Arrow Site and extract the nature of the pictographs showing the ascension of man with alien assistance and to discover additional artifacts or evidence of extraterrestrial visitation). The ACIO was building the program Human 3.0, at least certain key aspects of the transhumanist model. Not the SI version. You see, the whole idea of transcending is linked to the inception point of separation. It is the I AM supreme model. It says, the human vessel can be and should be enhanced in such a way that the functional implants can live forever. There are several things missing: One, the unconscious mind cannot contain the data streams of a continuous species, and two, the search for who we are, as the true source of life, will only be further obscured by technological enhancement. The realization of I AM WE ARE is not a technological realization, nor is its manifestation accelerated by or through technology, at an individual level. It is a self-learning and behavioral process. Nothing more, nothing less.

So transhumanists want to transcend human suffering, ignorance, and mortality through technology, and the ACIO was providing some of the technology to do this, but who would have access to the technology?" The elite, of course. It would only accelerate and accentuate the separation. It is simultaneous empowerment and disempowerment. The economic models for the transhumanist diffusion, as it was called in the Labyrinth Group, were not widely considered. The Incunabula being the only exception.

They actually wanted to build a plan that made the transcending technologies available to everyone. They looked at it from two angles: one, if the technology could be introduced at birth, it would mitigate the cost issues of health care and education, offsetting diffusion costs. But it would have to be a government implemented service. No private company could secure sufficient trust. So a critical component was to make the United Nations the credible world organization that could introduce transhumanism to the global stage.

The second angle was to allow class distinctions and free markets to eventually make the technology irresistible to everyone, and then allow government subsidies to bring down the costs sufficiently to enable its dispersion.

All of this sounds very altruistic, but the quality of the technologies would be a variant. Elite classes would be able to secure higher quality implantations coupled to more responsive genetics. This would simply be a human civilization that would be attempting to purge discontent and disobedience, in favor of participation in a ruled system of government by elite transhumans.

Technology will go from external-impersonal, to external-personal, to integrated-personal, to internal-personal. Transhumanism is the last phase, and it is the phase that the elite are moving to. The internal-personal is based on exactly the same paradigm of what is now the human condition—namely, humans have a programmed interface that is integral to their human body, and is powered by the infinite source of which they truly are.

Chapter 3 – Alternate History of the Universe & Earth, We are a War

Humans are unwittingly trying to be Anu to themselves. It's part of the program, according to the WingMakers. Humanity will play God to itself. It will try to engineer a better human and a better civilization.

It will do this because it can't imagine how humanity can save itself through simple behaviors and the realization that these behaviors can make. They will do it because they are programmed to become integrated with technology. There were prophecies of a synthetic race overtaking humanity… this sounds like what those prophets saw. These prophets could have seen Human 3.0 transhumanists in some distant timeline and assumed they were alien.

As you can imagine, the Military Force is where it will be tested first. There is a whole field of psychological technology that has laid the groundwork for the real internal technologies to flow into the military. It will be released there initially so it can be properly defended for testing purposes. Once it's proven there it will converge with the integrated-personal technology programs of the corporate elite.

Miniaturization of the technology will enable it to adorn the body. It will not be internal yet, but it is part of the human body like clothing, glasses, watches and jewelry. (Did you see the added "jewelry" worn by some of the candidates in the recent election?).

Human 1.0 was a creation of a God-like being— No. Anu is the same as us or the Atlanteans. He was no more intelligent or god-like. He was deceptive. That is the only distinction.

But Anu created Human 1.0 and then found them to be too similar to his own capabilities, and feared they would one day figure out that they were Atlanteans enslaved by the Anannaki. And he was worried about the consequences of that discovery.

So, he wiped them clean with a planetary flood.

The flood was one part of the extinction program, but there were also nuclear weapons that were discharged on the planet—most of which have been explained away as meteorite impacts. But the WingMakers write that these were advanced weapons used against human populations that had avoided the flood.

Whatever way Human 1.0's were eliminated from the planet, they were replaced by Human 2.0, and these included upgrades like self-reproduction and more advanced programming. And central to this programming was the notion that Anu was God and would return to his creation. And the up-grade to Human 2.0 branches out like a fork in the road. One version of Human 3.0 goes down the path of technology integration … or transhumanism.

The Triad of Power wants Human 3.0 to go down the path of technology integration, because that is how they are programmed… to emulate their god, Anu.

The New World Order (NWO) is to exploit individual's need for self-affirmation, both individually and in wanting to be a member of the group. This is the situation known as the "lonely crowd." It is the most favorable moment to seize a man and influence him, when he is alone in the masses. And the bigger and homogeneous the mass, the better. The desire to be as part of something bigger is at the very depths of the human Soul. Soul where we are a part of one big Soul rather than being each an individual soul. We therefore hone in on this bee-hive cluster. Mentally the New World Order as a trap for us. The mass becomes not our savior but our executioner.

The Dark Force's first step was to herd the population together, concentrate them in the urban areas where the psychological and sociological characteristics of the mass can most easily be manipulated. Then it will be to create One World Government with a One World Religion and continue to slowly but steadily take away all freedoms, saying it is for the good of all. This was the strategy that the Anannaki used to enslave us over 120,000 years ago (Atlantis) and then again after the Great Flood (10,000 years ago).

The most painful aspect of the whole long drawn-out process involved with this takeover of the world by the New World Order is not the ease with which it has been accomplished – Mankind falling into slavery, but rather the fact that we have all sacrificed our own personal power to make the New World Order's task so much simpler.

The Darkness thrives on fear is a well known fact among those with any kind of eye to see the true nature of the universe. The chief product of low self-esteem and barely existent sense of self-worth is exactly that – fear. The ultimate purpose for propaganda as used to control by the New World Order is to rob the individual of his or her own will power and to instill in its place fear. It seeks to exchange the personal will or power for that of the masses or the organization seeking control. We all feel the power of peer pressure that imposes over the individual.

These days it is an attempt to rob the individual of his personal free will and personal power. After all, Creator God gave us free will and we must be the one willingly to give it away – that is one of the Rules in this polarity world. The New World Order is using peer pressure and the consent of "it is best for the masses" for us to willing agree to be subservient to the One World Order.

Undermining democracy and the rights of the individuals lies at the very core of the New World Order.

The small ways which each of us can begin to fight back against mindless greater will of the omnipresent New World Order is to exercise Love in all of our decision-making processes and dealing with our fellow man. This is especially true to our own sense of being overwhelmed by something which feels so much bigger than ourselves. When we favor humanity over technology and the mass consciousness as expressed by "the rules", we can feel a little more human, and strikes one more blow, however small, for humanity over institutionism.

Sources:
1. 'Our Secret Government's Amid War Between Anunnaki Princes Marduk & Nannar' by Sasha Alex Lessin, PhD Subtitled: 'We The Anunnaki - Time of the Return.' Published June 26, 2015, by admin www.wetheanunnakiu.com.
2. 'A Different story about the Anannaki' by Estelle Nora Harwit Amrani with Enki's Assistance from *Vibrani Website*, January, 1999 up-dated August 3, 2000 recovered through *Bibliotheca Alexandrina Website* Bibliotecapleyades.net.
3. 'Maldek,' Exopeadia, http://www.exopaedia.org/Maldek.
4. 'Suppressed Human History Movie Extraordinary Theory,' U-tube vanlakos.
5. 'The Lemurians and Atlantis Civilizations' by Mary Sutherlan. From the Burlington New Website.
6. 'Extraterrestrial Heritage – World ITC - The story of the planet Marduk,' www.worlditc.org/f_15_macy_extraterrestrial_heritage.htm.
7. 'Earth History – Galactic Messages,' Galactic Federation of Light, Naplers, Florida, http://www.galacticfederation-naplesfl.org/earth-history.html

8. Descendants of The ANUNNA.KI - A New Version of The History,' www.bibliotecapleyades.net/sumer_anunnaki/anunnaki/anu_25_08.
9. 'The Anannaki, Mankinds Enslavement and the Afterlife Deception,' humansarefree.com. 2015/03.

AWAKEN – WE ARE AT WAR

Original Purpose of the Earth - The plan was to create an intergalactic exchange center of information within planet Earth. It was an extraordinary plan, involving a beautiful place, for Earth is located on the fringe of our galactic system and is easily reached from other galaxies. Earth exists close to many way-portals, the highways that exist for energies to travel throughout space. The Earth would be colonized by the Lyrans/ Pliedians who were some of the original Planners of Earth, orchestrators who seeded worlds and civilizations with light and information through creativity and love. They gave their DNA to the original Planners, and this DNA became part of the DNA of the human species. When they designed Earth, other forms of intelligence were able to grasp the reason for Earth's creation. They understood that perhaps their own civilizations might one day be annihilated, and they did not want to lose them entirely.

So, libraries were built throughout existence, and each was filled with specific data. All forms of intelligence that made the libraries valued their identities and valued their civilizations. They understood how their civilizations were constructed. They valued life.

Humans Have Extreme Universal Value - Human beings are the library cards, the keys to the Living Library. All the information stored in Earth's library is accessible only through the humans. The codes and master numbers that the other species in the universe seek are geometric formulas and combinations of intelligence stored within the human. Each creation in the Living Library has its purpose and has a great amount of data stored in it. Humans were designed to be merged with, influenced, and emerged through. The physical bodies that humans now occupy are sending and receiving centers, broadcast units that exist in many realities. All creation is designed to be influenced - to be puzzle pieces that lock and fit with other pieces of the puzzle. Within each human there are stored codes and master numbers that the rest of the universe desperately needs for their own in existence. As Earth is being catapulted into a frequency that will allow the Living Library to come back into full function, in order to once again become valuable assets as the keys who access the Living Library from many cosmic points of view. Humans will have twelve-stranded DNA and full brain capacity. In order for humans to be in partnership as library cards, humans must understand that they are more than human. Humans are considered by some in this universe to be priceless, though in actuality your Soul selves have no idea of the value stored in the human body. Your human body is the most valuable thing you will ever own and encounter. Humans are priceless to the universe.

Battles have long been fought over Earth, and as a result, humans have been purposely enticed away from discovering the wealth of data stored inside of them by controlling or limiting forces. One is purposely taught that humans are insignificant and valueless so that other forms of intelligence will not come and tap into them. Those who control you cannot get the formulas out of you, so they keep you hidden away, quarantined and isolated. In this way, others who need what you have cannot get to you. You are taught the dance of the disempowerment, which you choreograph as a species.

You are now learning to find your own value, a value you will intend to share, teach, and encourage others to discover through an ongoing process. The value you discover about yourself will grow and grow as you wonder at these formulas inside of you, which are the codes for other civilizations.

Earth is a microcosm of the macrocosm, a miniature version of what is happening all over, except that Earth is a trigger point, what some call a kernel. You know that a kernel is a seed. The Lyrans/ Pleiadians have come back to Earth to assist the members of the Family of Light, who have been seeded here, in this essential time when events can be altered. Dark Forces (Anannaki / Orion-Draconian Empire) Had Won the Battle to Control Earth and Its Humans. Although Humans are bearers of the Light, many have been lured to the Dark Force or have not awakened to know they are free spirits that were never meant to be dominated by and subservient to the Dark Side. The Federation is mounting a battle to restore the Earth as the "free zone," Living Library that was first envisioned. The Starseeds are promoting the increase in the frequency of the Earth as well as increasing the frequency of all human beings that are part of the Earth. The increased frequency to that of Love (13 Hz vs. eons of 7.8 Hz) will cause many of the humans to 'Wake Up" and realize their universal purpose.

Defeating the Dark Force and Not Be Subservient To It - We are living in a 21st-century feudal society and we are the serfs. Humanity is sliding ever faster into the great abyss of subsistence living. We have heard it all before; the rich are getting richer and poor are getting poorer. However, we hear that humanity outnumbers the globalists and their minions. We hear that Americans have 300 million handguns and this factor should allow us to defeat those of far fewer numbers. If this were true, tell me why is humanity losing the war against tyranny?

How does one defeat the New World Order (NWO) with their control over the banks, the military, the corporations, health care and the politicians? In short, they own it all. Is there any way to defeat the NWO? The truth is, I don't know how to defeat the NWO and neither does anybody else because we do not know how to mobilize society, but here are a few suggestions on how you can make a difference until we reach the hundredth monkey effect to mobilize society.

On A Global Scale – Claim the World's Governments: The specific aim of the Anannaki, Reptilians, Greys (all commonly referred to as the 'Dark Force') is to take over planet Earth through covert mind control methods, much like the Illuminati and Secret Government is trying to do.

These groups are intimately connected. Most people think of world takeover only in terms of military means such as bombs and guns. They don't need to do this if they can control the people, and world leaders through mind control, hypnosis, brain implants, and reprogramming (Human 3.0). The key question is 'What do we do to stop this?' Our government has sold us out because of their greed for power and world domination and now they can't stop what they have started. The first step is for the people of Earth to reclaim the world's governments.

We must force the governments to release all the knowledge they have about extraterrestrials to the world at large. Half the battle is won if the people of the world know what they are dealing with. If people knew what was happening they would not be so much on automatic pilot. The only way to protect ourselves is through the strength of our consciousness.

If a person is attuned to God (First Source) and the Ascension Masters, and owns their personal power, and has self mastery over their energies, they have nothing to worry about. The world needs to wake up spiritually and psychologically, and stop being victims. It is this victim consciousness that allows them to be abducted and manipulated.

If ever you sense the Dark Force round you, affirm your core and visualize protection for yourself. Your connection with First Source and the Ascension Masters will bring you immediate protection. The only true hope for this planet is a mass spiritual awakening which, in truth, is beginning to occur. This spiritual awakening must also lead us into political action to remove the Secret Government and Illuminati from power. It is these beings that are controlled and manipulated, implanted, and hypnotized by the negative extraterrestrials.
Part of our strength is also to think as individuals. The Greys are a group memory complex that has very little ability to think on their own. It is time now to make people aware of what is really going on. Share this information and others like it with your friends. Do more research on your own. If enough people become aware, the one hundredth monkey effect will begin to occur. It is already happening. The people reading this are the Light bearers for the new age. It will only happen if we do it. The world will change when we change it. This change begins in consciousness, which leads to individual and group action. The Secret Government, Illuminati, and negative extraterrestrials are more vulnerable now than ever before.

On A Personal Level - Look at all choices from four perspective ranges and make your choices accordingly. Image each range to have ten increments.

1. Exercise my Own Free-Will …. Being Controlled
2. Encourages Love of All …… . Encourages Hate & Separation
3. Supports what is Best for All … Encourages what is Best for a the Elite
4. Best for Humanity /Universe … Best for New World Order

Below are a few specific suggestions that we can employ in defiance of the Dark Force. It is called the "Earth by a 1000 cuts" strategy. These actions will allow time for others to 'Wake Up" and help us to get our house in order and to raise the frequency of the Earth and the humans on it.

1. Free Yourself/ Power Yourself – refer To 'Reclaim Your Power' within Chapter 24.
2. Let your pet choose your friends and acquaintants. Animals have a better "sense" of good and not so good than we do.
3. Trust your 'gut.' Your intuition has better judgment than your rational mind.
4. Just because everybody does it/supports it, it does not mean you have to be part of mob mentality.
5. Individuality beats plurality.
6. Do not make decisions out of Fear, Anger, Jealousy, Rivalry, Sociability, or Sympathy.
7. Become informed of all topics and weigh the "good" against the "bad."
8. Support Sovereignty and Local Government. Decentralization is the opposite of global central government. Starting from your local government, support decentralization of power whenever you can. Do not fall for the trap of surrendering to the idea of becoming a global citizen. It is better to be a free citizen of your own sovereign country who can freely choose where to go around the world than to be a global citizen who is slave to a global central government. Say NO to the United Nations, NO to the North America Union, NO to the European Community and any other globalist illusion.
9. Say No to Smart meters. Reduce or eliminate your Use of wireless Technology. This new technology is part of the global control grid. Not only is it a serious health hazard

because of the high levels of electromagnetic radiation, but it also creates a completely invasive spy system which records every activity in your home. Inform yourself, share the information, know your rights, join other likeminded neighbors and say NO!

10. SAY NO to Vaccines. The globalists are so obsessed with vaccines that some, such as Bill Gates, tell us to our face that they are using it to control the population. Unless you like to being filled with mercury and many other poisons, do not take them. Get informed: Why do vaccine manufacturers have immunity from liability if their product is so good? Why are governments around the world trying to make them mandatory? Why has the number of autistic infants skyrocketed since the recent introduction of these new massive vaccinations? Evidence shows that we are systematically being experimented on without our consent and most importantly our lives and health are at risk. The worst part is that most of the population is defending the perpetrators, denying the evidence and attacking the messengers.

11. Find Your Souls Faith. The New World Order wants to establish one world religion, destroy the family, destroy the individual and the final God they want you to submit is the state. I am not telling you what to believe in, that's your personal call, but to find the strength that we will need to endure this struggle; we need something that materialistic things sometimes cannot provide: Faith.

12. Be Wary of Organized Religion. I am not telling you not go to church or what you should or not should believe in. Most organized churches that have the 501c tax exempt status are under the control of the government and they will be used under martial law to control the "flock." Please Google "Clergy response team under the control of FEMA." Be aware that throughout history the church has been used to brainwash humanity and now it will be used to create compliance to the elite's agenda that distorts and

abuses the message of First Source God. Just be careful and use critical thinking when another human being who happens to be speaking from an altar tells you what to do.

13. Do not Follow Political Parties, They Are All Controlled. Support candidates who believe in freedom and oppose globalism. Political parties have been created to "conquer and divide." Like it or not the globalists control both parties. You can clearly see that there is not much difference in their agenda when it comes down to the important issues. It does not really make a difference whether they are Democrats or Republicans. It is just an illusion to make you believe that you are still free to choose and vote. Goethe once said: "None are more hopelessly enslaved than those who falsely believe they are free." However, I still believe that we have to be politically involved and be part of the system in order to create positive change. So, regardless which political party you decide to join, never follow blindly, but follow your heart and the principles of freedom. Do not be afraid to expose the paid trolls of the New World Order in your party.

14. Turn off all mainstream media. Control of mass media is the key to the New World Order strategy for command and control. Do not watch network news unless you are viewing it as a way to determine what the enemy is up to. Apply the same logic to your local newspaper and radio channels that are owned by media giants. The media giants are broadcasting the words of the New World Order.

15. Do not support those who support the New World Order. This includes actors, actresses, public officials, athletic players and teams, performers, artists, businesses, etc.

16. Forget global mentality. What is good for the EU, China, or Russia does not mean it is best for you.

17. Take your money out of the megabanks and place into the credit union or state-owned banks.

18. Get your children out of the government schools with their NWO Common Core curriculum along with their zero tolerance policies and transgender restrooms.
19. Get Out of Debt. Debt is slavery. The Private Central banks that control the world's governments are based on the principle of slave/master relationship. Governments are slaves to the central banks like the private Federal Reserve because they have given them the sovereign power to issue their currency. Every dollar that is issued will be paid back with interest. Our labor is the collateral to pay back the interest of every dollar the government will spend. We may not be able to change that for now, but we can try to get out of personal debt so we do not need the banks, even the local ones. When the economy gets worse, it will be even harder to get out of debt. Live within your means. Pay off your credit cards. We are now a nation of debt slaves. Pay cash for as much as you can. If you cannot pay cash, then do not buy it! Own your future instead of the bankers owning you. Maintain the smallest mortgage or loan that you can manage.
20. Buy as much as you need from local "mom and pop" stores. Stay away from the NWO giant box stores that, also, broadcast the NWO paradigm.
21. Buy gold and do not hoard cash. Hard cash may be OK, once it is backed by gold, as Trump and others are planning to do. This cuts into the power the NWO bankers have over you and your country.
22. Never vote for the incumbent. The longer the power hungry are in power, the more likely they will become part of the NWO.
23. As hard as it might be, buy only Made in America products. This is part of Nationalism and not Globalism (NWO). Do not confuse 'nationalism" with "white nationalism," as the NWO wants to call it. We were formed as an independent nation not bound to any global group, such as the British Commonwealth. We need to

stand as One and not a part of the many, which do not have our best interest in mind.

24. Do not Support Unconstitutional Wars. United States Marine Corps Major General and two time Medal of Honor recipient Smedley D. Butler wrote a very important book: "War is a racket", and Wars are evil and most of the time are created to hide the failures of our politicians and to increase the profits of corporations and central banks. Even worse, as wars have not been declared by Congress in the last 60 years, that is since the Korean War, these are unconstitutional wars with the only purpose of serving the New World Order and its agenda. When the propaganda machine tries to sell you a war without the declaration of Congress, remember, only "Congress shall have Power to ...declare War" Article I, Section 8, Clause 11.

25. Learn about False Flags. A false flag is a covert operation designed to deceive in such a way that the operation appears as though it has been carried out by entities, groups, or nations other than those who actually planned and executed them.

26. Go Rural, Go Wild. If you can, consider moving to a rural area. One of the goals of the globalists is to confine us in mega cities so they can control every aspect of our life, like a herd of cows packed in a corral. That's one of the plans of Agenda 21. Now more than ever it is time to move to rural areas. Go find open spaces away from their regulatory control of ordinances, and unconstitutional bureaucratic parasitic regulations. Nobody should tell you what color you can paint your home or how tall your grass should be. Go live wild, live free.

27. Try to Be a Decent Person. The New World Order feeds on the weaknesses of humanity. The global elite can recruit their minions only if they are willing to submit to evil. To become pawns for their agenda, they will tempt you with wealth, sex, drugs, power and all Earthly

possessions. We are all human (at least most of us, I am not sure about them), and therefore we are corruptible. It is our duty to be decent people believing in the power of positive action and decent values based on good and the best part of our humanity. There is a spiritual battle between good and evil currently taking place in this physical dimension.

28. Do all things out of Love – Reach out and make room for love. Come to realize that, every human encounter possesses a nexus point with every human being we encounter. In each instance, we have a choice to be honorable, compassionate and kind to another or to take advantage of them. You have a choice to chart a new path for humanity or to walk in the evil footprints of those who have come before you. You can choose to align with the Universe or continue to serve and be ruled over by evil.

29. Love Life, Love Your Neighbors, Have Fun. We need to love life. We need to love, period. They want us miserable and full of hate as they feast on fear and hate. Loving life and creating good things is the antithesis of their destructive agenda. We need to have fun, especially now under these circumstances. Do not get me wrong, I wish we didn't have to face these globalist parasites. Since we don't have a choice, and this task will take up a big part of our lives, let's try to have some fun and share quality time with other like-minded people who have committed themselves to exposing and defeating the New World Order. Resistance is never futile! Resistance to tyranny is a duty and a pleasure.

30. Keep an Open Mind. We were all ignorant at some point, ignorance can be fixed, but for arrogance there is no hope. Always have an open mind, do not be an arrogant know it all if somebody is trying to talk to you about some new ideas or theories. I am not saying that you must believe everything you are told, but always keep an open mind. This gives you the ability to continue learning and to re-

evaluate apparent truths that are given as dogma through the propaganda in the media.
31. Find Each Other. Fighting and learning about the New World Order can be overwhelming and stressful. Once you are awake it is very difficult to go back and even share a beer with somebody who still refuses to at least learn about this reality. This world can be a lonely place unless you start to find like-minded people who are aware or at least willing to learn about what is currently happening on our planet.

We have a choice, but our window of opportunity is quickly closing.

1. '20 Key Ways to Defeat the New World Order,' David Hodges, March 12, 2013, Activist Post, https://www.activistpost.com/2013/03/20-key-ways-to-defeat-new-world-order.html
2. 'How to Defeat the New World Order,' Gianluca Zanna, LoveGunsFreedom.com, https://www.lovegunsfreedom.com/how-to-defeat-the-new-world-order.

ON THE HORNS OF A DILEMMA – IDENTIFYING THE FORCE FOR GOOD - The Lyran, Pleiadians, Anannaki, Sirians, Vegans, and many others have established colonies on Earth over the last 400,000 years or even earlier. Within the last 50,000 years there have been the Reptilian Wars. This includes the arrival, internal division, and departure of a portion of the Anannaki, leaving the Earthbound Anunnaki under the command of Eniki, who now controls the Earth through what we call the "Elites," along with the Greys and the Overlord Reptilians. Pleiadian Humans returned, having been forced by treaty to abandon their colonies on Earth eons earlier. The returning Pleiadian Humans attack and defeated the main body of the Reptilian Overloads (leaving only "Elites") and placed 50,000 warrior-colonists in Europe, 3,500 years ago.

To a large extent, the Pleiadians are depicted as having horns on their heads or wearing horns on their helmet and shields. The descendents of the Pleiadians include the Hittites (of the Bible), the kingdoms of the Egyptians (not all of the Kings or Pharaohs) and Greeks (mainly the Spartans), the Celts (Central Europe, Wales, The Netherlands, Belgium, and parts of France), the ancient Mediterranean Seafarers, the Macedonians of Alexander the Great fame, as well as the Scandinavians (including the Vikings).

- **Kheta or the Hittites** were the sons of Heth (Ham, Amon or Jupiter). Below right is an image of a Hittite God that represents Jupiter, and is very similar to that of Odin, the Norse God, with the horned helmet and upturned shoes. Notice the Trident in his hands and the horned winged disk above his head

Hittite Relief

- **Egyptians:** Seti I, King Tut and the Ramses from the Twentieth Dynasty of the New Kingdom of Ancient Egypt. This tradition was carried on by the Priesthood of Jupiter Amon (Amun). The capital for their religion was located in the City of Light, or what we know of as Luxor. The God they had worshipped was god Amon-Ra (Jupiter-Amon). At the temple at Luxor there are many Ram Sphinxes that symbolize God Amon Ra.

- **Macedonians** lead by Alexander the Great around the period when the ancient city of Damascus was captured in 333 B.C. Notice the "horn" in his hair.

- **Mediterranean, Seafaring Kingdoms** (Phoenicians, Cypriots, Mycenaeans, Minoans, others.). To right is the bronze "Ingot God" from Enkomi, 12th century BC, Cyprus.

- **Celts** - The Celts were a collection of tribes with origins in central Europe that shared a similar language, religious beliefs, traditions and culture. It's
- It's believed that the Celtic culture started to evolve as early as 1200 B.C. The Celts spread throughout western Europe – including The Netherlands, Belgium, part of France and Spain, Britain, and Ireland, all via migration.

Celtic Shield – Note Horn motif

The existence of the Celts was first documented in the seventh or eighth century B.C. The Roman Empire, that ruled much of southern Europe at that time, referred to the Celts as "Galli," meaning barbarians. However, the Celts were anything but barbarians, and many aspects of their culture and language have survived through the centuries.

By the third century B.C., the Celts controlled much of the European continent north of the Alps mountain range, as well as present-day Ireland and Great Britain. Beginning with the reign of Julius Caesar in the First Century B.C., the Romans launched a military campaign against the Celts, killing them by the thousands and destroying their culture in much of mainland Europe.

Bronze Celtic warrior with horned helmet and torch

Caesar's Roman armies attempted an invasion of Britain at this time, but were unsuccessful, and thus the Celtic people established a homeland there. As a result, many of their cultural traditions remain evident in present-day Ireland, Scotland and Wales.

- **Scandinavians** (including the Vikings). Vikings were Norse seafarers, mainly speaking the Old Norse language, who during the late 8th to late 11th centuries, raided and traded from their Northern European homelands across wide areas of Europe, and explored westwards to Iceland, Greenland, and

Vinland. Viking raids began in England in the late 8th century, primarily on monasteries.

Identifying the Dark Force - Dominance and control of others is a key factor in the Dark Force belief system of service-to-self. Having slaves or endorsing slavery (having a company story, where everyone must shop, within a mining community is a form of slavery) is one of the ways to identify the Dark Force. The earliest known recorded evidence in Sumer by the Anunnaki where human slaves were needed to mine gold. The Sumerian Code of Ur-Nammu includes laws relating to slaves, written circa 2100 – 2050 BC; it is the oldest known tablet containing a law code surviving today. The Babylonian Code of Hammurabi, dating to c. 1700 BC, also makes distinctions between the freeborn, freed and slave.

In Ancient Egypt, slaves were mainly obtained through prisoners of war. Other ways people could become slaves was by inheriting the status from their parents. One could also become a slave due to their inability to pay their debts. Slavery was the direct result of poverty. People also sold themselves into slavery.

Ancient Greece was mixed. By the late 4th century BC, the philosophy was "God has set everyone free. No one is made a slave by nature." However, the slavery issue was determined on a city-state by city-state basis. In Ancient Athens, about 30% of the population were slaves. During the Peloponnesian War between Athens and Sparta, twenty thousand Athenian slaves, including both mine-workers and artisans, escaped to the Spartans when their army camped at Decelea in 413 BC.

During the Republic, Roman military expansion was a major source of slaves.

Ancient Persia, in remarkable contrast to the other major ancient cultures of the region, the Achaemenid Persians, during the time of Cyrus the Great, formally banned most slavery of non-combatants within the empire. Indeed, Persepolis, the ceremonial capital of the Achaemenid Persians, was built with paid labor.

The slavery issue, even today, is a maker of the Dark Force.

Sources:
1. Reptilian Wars: A 50,0000 Year Update, Merlin, *ebook*
2. 'Horned Helmets of the Vikings, Egyptians & Hittites,' Joe Moe, History of the Brotherhood, *Ghostic Warrior*, https://gnosticwarrior.com/horned-helmets.html
3. 'Celts,' History, ttps://www.history.com/topics/ancient-history/celts.
4. 'Vikings,' *Wikipedia,* https://en.wikipedia.org/wiki/Vikings.
5. 'Slavery in antiquity," *Wikipedia,* https://en.wikipedia.org/wiki/Slavery_in_antiquity
6. 'Ancient Slavery,' Ditext.com. Retrieved 2015-10-18.
7. "Slaves and Slavery in Ancient Egypt,' Touregypt.net. 2011-10-24. Retrieved 2015-10-18.
8. Hopkins, Keith (31 January 1981). Conquerors and Slaves. Cambridge: Cambridge University Press. *p. 101.* ISBN 978-0-521-28181-2.
9. ' *Pausanias(1918), Description of Greece.* Translated by Jones, W.H.S.; H.A. Ormerod. London: William Heinemann Ltd. ISBN 0-674-99328-4. OCLC 10818363.
10. Fergus Millar, The Crowd in Rome in the Late Republic (University of Michigan, 1998, 2002), pp. 23, 209.
11. '"Cyrus Charter of Human Rights,' *www.persepolis.nu. MANI.* Retrieved 21 July2015.

CHAPTER 4

MANY SPECIES THROUGHOUT THE UNIVERSE

OUR EXTRATERRESTRIAL COMPANIONS -
They are here and they have been here for eons. So long that the Anannaki/Sirians bio-engineered our bodies (refer to Chapter 3 for details). And their presence is being revealed. On February 14, 2004, in St. Petersburg, Florida, Apollo 14 astronaut Edgar Mitchell told an audience of over 200 by saying, "Aliens have landed. A few insiders know the truth and are studying the bodies that have been discovered. "Mitchell, the sixth man to walk on the Moon along with Alan B. Sheppard, added, "A 'cabal' of insiders stopped briefing presidents about extraterrestrials after President Kennedy."

In a taped interview with J. L. Ferrando, astronaut Maj. Gordon Cooper said, "For many years I have lived with a secret, in a secrecy imposed on all specialists in astronautics. I can now reveal that every day, in the USA, our radar capture objects of form and composition unknown to us. And there are thousands of witness reports and a quantity of documents to prove this, but nobody wants to make them public." So insiders are in on the truth that ETs have shown up as part of the Earth's (Frequency) Shift…."

ET Involvement - ET Involvement can be both good (as described below) in that they are helping us to evolve to be more like them, who believe that their and our philosophy should be "Service to Others," where each serves others and, by doing so, all are served. Or bad, with some ET species wanting to be in control of and are controlling Earth, just like they are on other planets, where the humans (and other species) are subservient to them. Their philosophy is "Service to Self" ("me first") and if each is taking care of him/herself then all are served.

ET Worldview - Our galaxy, the Milky Way, contains more than 200 billion stars. It was formed about 12 billion years ago out of a huge cloud of gas, mainly hydrogen and helium, which collapsed onto itself and began forming stars. Those star systems most hospitable to evolving life exist in a ring around the galactic center, and are between 4 and 8 billion years old. Astronomers have found that 75 percent of the habitable star systems are older than our sun, so 75% of any intelligent life on their planets has had longer to evolve than humans on Earth have, possibly 4 billion years longer.

Look at how far we've come in the last 100 years, and project it forward another 100 years. Where will we be then? And in 1,000 years? In a million years? In a billion years? If some of those ETs circling Earth have been around for a billion years longer than we have, it's no wonder that they have the technology that can help us through the Frequency Shift. And we can learn about the spirituality of those species who avoided blowing up each other many eons ago.

Dr. Richard Boylan (www.drboylan.com) has compiled one of the best accounts from hundreds of interviews with contactees and what they told him about the ET's beliefs and philosophies: Creator God (One Source) - ETs see this as a transcendent matrix of consciousness, which underlies everything. As such, they do not make a big fuss of it, and just get on with their lives.

ET Superiority - Although the average ET considers us as equals in that we are both sentient, conscious, intelligent life forms, they also enjoy greater sensory acuteness, paranormal abilities, more robust immune systems, and hence longevity. Their technologically is vastly more advanced than ours, as shown by their ability to travel at light speeds and have a form of time travel, as well. Culturally, they appear more advanced, for the most part, living harmoniously, without aggression on their home planets, but the war between the Galactic United Federation ("Light Bearers") and the Draconian Empire ("Service to Self") continue as a war of "Good" vs. "Evil." They are concerned for the Earth's ecosystem, but are not patronizing towards the primitive human culture that is destroying it. Despite the absence of formal religions, the "Service to Others" Group demonstrates highly developed spirituality, with spiritual awareness woven into their daily lives.

Spiritual Mission - The various races have different missions regarding Earth, all seeming to prepare us for contact with them. Some are here to remind us of our cosmic origin. Others show us previous lifetimes, to teach us of reincarnation. Often, they inform us of the many varieties of other ET races, to show us our larger galactic family. Many experiencers come away with deeper metaphysical understanding of the nature of the cosmos, and a more enlightened appreciation for the community of intelligent life forms.

ET Role in our Physical Development - ETs admit that they have been involved in our evolution since the ancient past, and that several groups participated in the genetic engineering of terrestrial primate stock to advance its intelligence and consciousness to our current levels. (This explains why there is no "missing link," and why the Sumerian and ancient African cultures suddenly arose without any bridging cultures.)

ET Role in our Spiritual Development - ETs reveal that many of our avatars (major world religious leaders, such as Zoroaster, Lao-Tzu, Moses, Krishna, Quan Yin, Buddha, White Buffalo Calf Woman, Yeshua ben Joseph, and Mohammed were:

(1) Actually ETs who came here to raise human spiritual consciousness,

(2) Humans who were guided by ETs,
(3) Humans inhabited by ET souls,
(4) Human-extraterrestrial hybrids, or
(5) ETs manifesting human appearance. None of these scenarios negates the divinity of the inspiration, but widens the divine to include ET intermediaries.

Domination – A few ETs are here to dominate and control the Earth, as they have for several eons. In general, these species are referred to as the "Dark Side." Refer to Chapter 3 regarding the Lyran and Orion Wars, and the separation created by the Federation ("Service to Others" – Bearers of Light) and the Draconian Empire ("Service to Self" – The Dark Side).

LISTING OF RACES - By reviewing the descriptions of each race, you may find one that you resonate with. If so, it is likely you may have been one of this race in a past life.

THE FOUR PRIMARY GALACTIC RACES

The Carians (the Bird People)

Parent Race of the Reptilians.

The Carians are a race of birdlike beings. At their most evolved state, the ruling class of the Carians resemble humans with eagle-like features and coloring.

Like the original Felines, the Carians first arrived in this universe when it was being created. A group of 45 came at the request of the Founders of this universe to help assist and oversee the Universal Game.

The Founders gave the Carians a new planet in the Orion constellation for their home. It was more tropical in design and featured an abundance of humid swamps and jungles. It also had more islands than large land masses.

Like the Felines, they were etheric and, therefore, had to develop physical bodies from the life forms evolving on the planet's surface.

Due to the environment they chose the life form that would become the bird and over a period of hundreds of thousands of years, they developed bodies of varying colors and sizes.

The Carians were known for their unique affinity towards colored plumage and so created physical bodies that reflected their creative talent in this area. That is why the Carians have much more variety of size, shape and color in their race than do the Felines. They can be 12 feet tall or only a few inches in height.

Also like the Felines, a group of the original 45 Carians remained etheric and became a council that oversaw and managed the development of their brothers and sisters who chose to incarnate on the planet as part of the upgrading of their physical forms.

When their physical vehicles had reached a certain level of development, they began genetic crossing (something they had learned from the Felines) with certain reptiles that had evolved in the swamps and warmer regions of the planet.

The result of this genetic program was the creation of a new hybrid race known to us as the Draconians. They were part Carian and part reptile.

In time the Draconians became more abundant in the *royal line of Aln* than the purebred Carians. And like the Felines, eventually the House of Aln would be peopled more by Draconians, and their first derivative the *flying serpents* (Snakes), than Carians.

By the time of the First Earth Grand Experiment, the House of Aln was headed by a winged serpent known as Cobazar. Cobazar is the father of Jehowah. Research "The 3 Earths/ An Alternate History" (Chapter 3) for more on this subject.

The Carians are known for their sharp analytical abilities and organizational skills. A predominant character trait of the Carians is their need to maintain a good appearance and image at all times. They are good team players as long as the team structure involves discipline and strictly adhered to codes of conduct.

You will find a preponderance of Carians involved in the creation and maintenance of stargates, dimensional grids and magnetic fields throughout our galaxy and universe. Their inherent analytical abilities make them well-suited for this kind of work.

They are also known for their militaristic capabilities and their star ships are more advanced than any in the universe. They held the majority of the military posts during the First Earth Grand Experiment.

The Felines (the Lion People)
Parent Race of the Humanoids

The Felines are one of the primary races in our universe.

They arrived here by invitation of the Founders. Having successfully completed their Universal Game and completing their universe, a group of 45 Felines volunteered to come to this universe to help setup and oversee the same game here.

The Felines are a bipedal race that stand 12 to 16 feet tall. Their skin is covered by a sort of soft fuzz, and though they don't have fur, they do have manes and both the males and females have long hair.

Their eye color ranges from blue to gold and can change from blue to gold as they mature. They also turn from a golden brown color to white.

The overall Feline temperament is warm, sanguine and intellectual. As they mature they take on more of a somber, introspective and gentle nature. The elders are revered for the wisdom, compassion and insight.

As a race they are extremely close and have a great sense of fair play. The females are revered and honored in equal status with the males. And true to the feline way, they are all very curious and inquisitive.

As part of the Universal Game, the Founders gave the Felines a new planet in the Lyra Constellation for their home. The Felines named it Avyon. Now this is not the exact pronunciation, nor spelling, but it is close enough. The real name cannot be translated into English.

Avyon was a paradise planet with mountains, lakes, streams and oceans. This blue planet was very much like our present Earth in form and variety of vegetation and life forms.

When the Felines arrived, they were in etheric form, and therefore, went through the stage of evolving a physical body in which to reside on the planet. After many millions of years they evolved the lion and other felines and began incarnating into those forms.

As part of the plan, a portion of the original Felines stayed in etheric form to provide guidance to those incarnating. They would be the equivalent of our modern day *Christos Beings*. Remember, this was a 3D planet and once the etheric felines incarnated they would fall under the veil of amnesia that is part of the workings of a 3D planet of free will.

As time passed, and through countless incarnation cycles, the Felines evolved a line of felines that walked upright and retained the consciousness of their etheric counterparts thanks to the periodic incarnations of some of the etheric Felines, and DNA from a bipedal mammal similar to the Ape that was evolving on the planet as well.

With the DNA from the ape-like mammal the Felines were able to take on a more human-like body while retaining most of the facial features and other characteristics of the feline. It was from this crossing when it reached a certain stage that the genetic line known as the Royal Line of Avyon, or House of Avyon, came into being.

The etheric Felines would continue to take turns incarnating to provide not only DNA upgrading, but teaching and training in higher dimensional principals lest their planet bound brothers and sisters get stuck in the non-sentient animal incarnation cycle.

As you can see, the Felines evolved on Avyon in much the same manner as Humans evolved here on Earth. The only difference is that the Humans did get stuck in the animal cycle.

In time the conscious Felines grew large enough in number to take on the responsibilities of planetary guardians of their home world. They continued to evolve and eventually developed the technology for space travel and then warp technology. Their etheric brothers and sisters continued to act as their guides.

Many among them became geneticists (a Feline specialty) and

began helping to develop life forms of various kinds for planets and stars in the universe. Some among them became great space explorers and scientists of various kinds.

It was during this stage in their development that the Felines would turn their attention to that bipedal mammal they owed so much to, and begin a program of genetic crossing and upgrading that would give them a soul and, in the process create a new species that would become known as the Humans.

After numerous crossings and genetic upgrades, the Adamic Human was made. There were two strains, the redheaded strain being the more outgoing and energetic, and the platinum blonde strain being the more gentle-natured and introspective.

After many thousands of years of continued careful crossing breeding, the Feline/Human hybrids began to be more common in the royal line of the Felines, The House of Avyon, than the purebred Felines were. Yet, this was the plan.

In time the purebred Felines would become the ancient ancestors of the Humans with only their genetic traits as a reminder of the connection between them. And though the genetic relationship between the Felines and Humans has been forgotten by modern man, the Felines remain in our consciousness as a regal creature, worthy of our respect and love.

The Felines remain the loving and supportive guardians of their genetic offspring, the Humans. They have continued in this role through time and all dimensions of the Universal Game.

Devin (Feline) is the reigning patriarch of the 9D Royal House of Avyon, and Alu (Human) is the reigning patriarch of the 5D Royal House of Avyon at this time.

The Humans
Zephrin, from the book We are the Nibiruans.

The Humans are the youngest of the four primary races in our universe. They were first created by the Felines on a planet in the Vega star system of the Lyra constellation.

The Humans are unique among the races due to their DNA coding.

The Humans were given the Gene of Compassion as their inheritance from the Felines. They are heirs to the great work which is showing all other races how to achieve compassion through the opening of the heart and the heart chakra.

The Humans were given a different creation myth than the one given to their counterparts, the Reptilians.

The Human's creation myth states that they will strive to live in harmony with any and all races occupying a planet that they wish to colonize.

It also states that they, through their living example, will show their fellow races the way to achieve compassion of the heart instead of compassion of the head (mental compassion). Therefore you will find that Felines and Humans who have open hearts will be assertive, truthful and confrontational in their communications and dealings with others.

The Humans became more predominant in the Royal Line of Avyon by the time they reached the Pleiadian star system.

Devin (Feline) is the current patriarch of the 9D Royal House of Avyon in the Lyra constellation.

Alu (Human) is the current patriarch of the 5D Royal House of Avyon in the Pleiades.

The Reptilians - The Dragon, Snake, and Lizard People.

The Reptilians are the creation of the Carians, their parent race.

They evolved on a planet in the Alpha Draconi star system of the Orion Constellation. The royal line of Reptilians are the Draconians, the winged dragons. The name of their royal line is the House of Anuln. This is not the exact spelling, but it is close. It is more like Oln or Ahln.

the Anunnaki were a species within the Lyra star system that traveled to the Orion. The Anunnaki were "fallen" Anuhazi that crossed with Drakonian from Orion and were mutated into the 10-strand reptilian imprint.

The Reptilians had two other major sub-races. They are known as the Winged Serpents (Snakes) and the Lizards called by some, the Lizzies.

The Reptilians are less emotional that their Human counterparts. Yet they have a highly refined knowledge of universal physics and laws. The Reptilians are responsible for the Mystery School (Egyptian) on Earth and their teachings are from the ancient knowledge held by their parent race, the Carians.

The Reptiles were given a creation myth by their parent race, the Carians, that clashed with the creation myth of the Humans.

The Reptilians were told that they had the right to colonize all planets and star systems in the universe and when they did, they also had the right to conquer or destroy any civilization they found there.

This creation myth has been the source of the many conflicts between the Reptiles and the Humans throughout the dimensions.

Yet, it was given as part of the Universal Game (Polarity Integration). Without it everyone would have lived in peace and there would be no conflict. If this were the case, soul evolution would cease and the universe would become stagnant.

The Reptilians represent the Dark in the Polarity Integration Game while the Humans represent the Light. Through this game, of the highest order, all souls in this universe have the opportunity to spiritually evolve and rejoin the creative god source.

Jehowah is the reigning patriarch of the 9D House of Aln and Enki is the reigning patriarch of the 4D House of Anu at this time. Until recently, Marduk, Enki's son was the current commander of the Draconian Flagship Nibiru, having seized control of it from his grandfather Anu, the former commander.

It is also my understanding that Enki has become the patriarch of the 5D House of Anu and also Head of the 5D Nibiruan Council representing the Dark.

CREATIONAL LOVE vs. FEAR HAS SHAPED US AND OUR UNIVERSE - Each Universe is in the mind of Creator God's and is one living soul. The shaping of our Universe of history is unique in the vastness of time. Creational love and advancement, technology and happiness are second to none. But, because of our other polarity of fear which we agreed to experience, we also have gone to the extreme of war, hate, destruction and self-punishment.

Fear is almost as powerful a creational force as love. Even though it is not real, real in the sense that you are truly threatened; you're not; not the real you. However, fear in its creational form is not free. It is very restrictive, controlling and destructive.

THERE ARE AT LEAST 58 DIFFERENT EXTRATERRESTRIALS IN THE UNIVERSE -
There are just over 10,000,000 worlds in this universe with similar humanities to our own, this is but a few races that are or have been involved with our life wave for some reason.

It was one of the NASA astronauts that stated there were 86 different extraterrestrials. Thus, listed below is a good start as to the description of extraterrestrials. I do not know which Astronaut it was, since the following NASA astronauts have documented seeing extraterrestrial vehicles during their space flights: Gordon Cooper, Don Stayton, Eugene Cernan, Ed White, James McDivit, James Lovell, Frank Borman, Neal Armstrong, Edwin Aldrin, and Scott Carpenter (ref: www.syfi.net, 'UFO Sightings by NASA Astronauts').

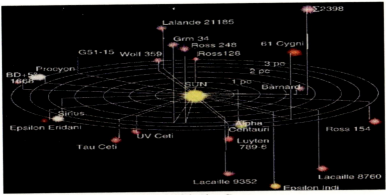

Distance from Sun. None orbit the Sun.
1pc = 1 parsec = 3.26 light years

LYRANS - The Lyrans are the original white Aryan Race and still has part of the race existing within the Lyran star system, but most relocated to be the Pleiadians and Andromedans.

Birth of the humanoid race has all of the genetic DNA from this area. Ancient Lyrans were the Titans. The giants Bigfoot also descended from Lyrans. Lyra consisted of 14 inhabited planets, three planets were destroyed during the Galactic Wars: Bila, Teka and Merok. 50 million were slaughtered. Lyrans started the Black League. The *Black Dragon.*

Lyrans grew into Sirian, Arcturians, Antarian, Pleiadian, Andromedan, Cygnus Alphan, Alpha Centauri, Sagittarius A & B, Cassiopeia, all human evolution. Based upon genetically human forms in higher realms and very highly evolved Universes, it was decided that many forms of life would be created here in Lyra because it appeared to be ideal as far as the age of the Suns and Planets and the length of probable stability.

The human race would have time to evolve and create space exploration and gravitate by means of energy and spiritual recognition into planetary civilizations and that those races would in turn create their own root races and life. It was also important that these races be allowed to manifest and create different aspects of ourselves mentally, emotionally, and spiritually. Thus we would be creating diversity and expressing our own need to create.

As the human race fragmented, the races moved, traveled, and settled many different planets in many systems as space travel evolved. The human became aware of other planetary civilizations in these systems. Different cultures met and grew. Belief systems clashed or spread. New thoughts of philosophy or technologies came into being. Mankind was evolving. A very strong social community developed between all in the

Lyra System. The Lyrans were a very peaceful race on the whole.

There were disagreements and light conflicts, but much was always cleared and resolved. The Lyrans learned to adapt to virtually all of the planetary environments that they settled. They learned to live in complete harmony with their respective planets. They developed agricultural communities that were literally awesome. They were not only efficient and could feed billions of beings, but it was actually enhancing the planet itself and creating an even wealthier environment.

All aspects of life seem to benefit from the Lyran's commitment to be at one with their home planets. At the same time, the life expectancy was between 300 - 425 years on the average. This was to increase by 3 times later, but everyone worked as a community.

They were not in service of self, but were a race that beat as one heart, and shared and moved in the same direction as a whole and would try to make sure that none of their race would lag or fall too far behind the whole. In other words,

"The needs of the many, out-weigh the needs of the few."

They were an incredible role model for all humanity that followed to this present moment.

The human race is history. The works of the mind are a record of that history, for the whole record of the human race is in one man. If you read these words then you are a part of Lyran heritage and a part of you carries this history within.

During the Lyran wars which are mentioned in several 'contactee' accounts, a mass exodus' of humans reportedly left the Lyran system and escaped to the Pleiades, the Hyades [which are 130 light-years from Earth in the Taurus constellation], and to Vega which is also in Lyra.

This region, like our own system, is still a 'battleground' between saurian greys and humans.

PLEAIDIANS - The Seven Sisters - The human species of Pleiadians evolved from Lyra. And they did develop effective weapons of war that helped sustain them through the Orion Wars and beyond. It has been said that the Pleiadians as we know then were Lyrans that came to Earth and then went to the Pleiades. Although some of the Lyrans that colonized here and our Earth for a time, a larger group of Lyrans went to the seven sisters and to other star systems during the Orion Wars.

The Pleiadians are also descendants of the Lyrans who came from Lyra in space stations or arks because of our solar system and the potential for stable longevity. The Lyrans would send down scout teams consisting of scientists, engineers and agricultural specialists to explore the surface of possible habitable planets and to explore them and return data and information to the mothership.

Blond or in some cases brunette 'Nordic' type humans were in the Pleiadian 'Taygeta' and other systems, which were allegedly colonized by refugees from their former planetary abodes in the Lyra constellation which were invaded by Reptiloids entities from Alpha Draconis (Thuban).

The main Pleiadian planet of 'Erra', was reportedly 'Terra-formed' by the Lyran refugees [Lyra being much nearer to Earth--around 30 light years].

The Lyrans claim that their technology surpasses our 'International' technology by about 3000 years. This may explain why the humans in Lyra were able to travel the vast distances from this part of the galaxy to colonize the Pleiades, some 430 light-years from Terra-Earth.

Their colonization approach was to explore each planet and, based upon its unique nature, they developed each colony to coexist with the life forms on each planet. In this way the Pleiadians became interested in our world and our races here. They have been visiting Earth for at least 80,000 years, with many large settlements. They come and left throughout our planet's history. We are very similar in many ways to the Pleiadians; however, they are emotionally and spiritually more evolved than we at this time.

They too have gone through their growing pains, as we are going through them right now. They have made attempts to share with us the benefits of their experience. So we don't have to experience the same kinds of setbacks and possible destructions, but at present, not enough people are listening.

The Pleiades is an open star cluster consisting of 254 stars and many times that of planetary bodies. Many of the stars are very young. This is located in the constellation of Taurus. The Pleiadians and the alphabets of Earth are both very similar. This was noted as of about 11,200 years ago that the script form was developed here on Earth and carried back to the seven sisters. This script form is the parent of most of our present day alphabets.

Three of the star systems have human life as we know it, the most advance is the system of Taygeta. And the other is the system of Taro which circles Alcyone. Most of the Pleiadians look like us in both size and stature, build, color of hair, etc.

They are also very fluent and articulate when speaking any of our languages, or discussing our sciences, history, etc. We have inherited our aggressiveness towards each other from them. Their life spans far exceed our own by at least 10 times what is our norm. Their technology has made it possible to travel anywhere in our Universe at speeds faster than the speed of light.

They are capable of using the oceans for undersea operations. They are very concerned about our misuse for our sciences today and that we have completely lost our spiritual center or harmony with our sciences. They have no use for money, politics and religions, clearly stating that the later two-politics and religions are really the same. The Pleiadians are worried as our most benevolent races visit, that we will destroy our planet and ourselves.

All Earths languages are derived from a ancient Pre-Sumerian language called Tamil which was spoken in Lyra and in the Pleiades. The Pleiadians as well as other groups have left descendants on the Earth in the past. They have said they are willing to help us but not to the point of changing our own evolution and then therefore becoming responsible for us as a race.

ACTURIANS - Arcturius is one of the most advanced extraterrestrial civilizations in our galaxy. It is a fifth dimensional civilization which, in reality, is like a prototype for Earth's future.

This group of beings settled in the constellation of Arcturius. These races of humanity are very private, and only for very specific reasons do they get involved with Earth. They think of themselves as healers. They carry a strong pride of technology in the arts of physical healing, and emotional and spiritual bodies.

They have been known to intervene in the ancient past to help resolve very serious conflicts in our area of the Universe by sharing their unique ability to show others how to integrate their belief systems and feelings to resolve conflict. They can be very silent, and can and will keep very much to themselves. As a group, they have done much to help raise the overall levels of consciousness in our Universe.

Their energy works with humanity as emotional, mental and spiritual healers. It is also an energy gateway through which humans pass during Earth and rebirth. It functions as a way station for nonphysical consciousness to become accustomed to physicality.

The Arcturians teach that the most fundamental ingredient for living in the fifth dimension is love. They teach that negativity, fear and guilt must be overcome and be exchanged for love and light.

Arcturius is the brightest star in the Bootes constellation, which is approximately 36 light years from Earth. The Arcturians work in very close connection with the Ascended Masters whom they refer to as the brotherhood of the all. They also work very closely with what they refer to as The Galactic Command.

The Arcturians travel the universe in their starships, which are some of the most advanced in the entire universe. One of the reasons that Earth has not been attacked by more warlike negative extraterrestrials has been these civilizations' fear of the advanced starships of the Arcturians. These ships are the cutting edge state of the art technology. One of the starships circling the Earth is called the Starship Athena, named after one of the Greek Gods.

The Arcturians society is governed by what they call the elders.

These beings are revered by the people of Arcturius for the advanced knowledge, wisdom, and extremely high vibrational frequencies. The higher the vibrational frequency, the closer one is to light, or spirit or God. The Arcturians are very short in physical stature, about three to four feet tall. They are also very slender. They all look very much alike in appearance. The Arcturians pride themselves in this because this erases the pettiness of comparison of looks which is so predominant in our society.

The Arcturians are the most loving and non-judgmental beings you can possibly imagine.

- Their skin is a greenish color.
- They have very large almond shaped eyes.
- They only have three fingers.
- They have the ability to move objects with their mind and are totally telepathic.
- Their source of food is an effervescent type of liquid that is highly vitalizing to their entire being.
- Their eyes are a dark brown or black color.
- Their main source of seeing is actually through their telepathic nature, not their physical eyes.
- Their sense of hearing even transcends their telepathic nature.
- They also have an ability to sense with the back of their heads.
- The average life span is from 350 to 400 of our Earth years.
- Their highly developed spiritual nature has allowed them to never age, since they have the ability to transcend time and space.
- They terminate the life when the contract that has been arranged for their existence is up.
- There is also no sickness on Arcturius, it was

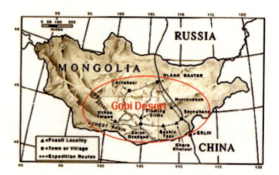

eliminated centuries ago.

AGHARIANS or Aghartians - A group of Asiatic or Nordic humans who, sources claim, discovered a vast system of caverns below the region of the Gobi desert and surrounding areas thousands of years ago, and have since established a thriving kingdom within, one which has been interacting with other-planetary systems up until current times.

Vast cavern systems below Tibet allegedly link the Agharti systems of central Asia to "Snakeworld," a multileveled cavern system under the southwestern slopes of the Himalayas where the "Nagas" dwell, according to Hindu legend.

Here a serpent cult of human and reptilian collaborators dwells, one of which is said to have had contact with the Nazi Thule society during World War II.

Long ago an Asian prince is said to have led several militant followers - warrior monks - into the caves and came in conflict with this serpent cult.

Following the conflict the reptilians and collaborating forces were driven out, however in recent centuries they have regained some ground.

ALPHA-DRACONIANS - Reptilian beings who are said to have established colonies in Alpha Draconis (Thuban). Like all reptilians, these claim to have originated on Terra thousands of years ago, a fact that they use to 'justify' their attempt to take the Earth for their own.

They are apparently a major part of a planned 'invasion' which is eventually turning from covert infiltration mode to overt invasion mode as the "window of opportunity" (the time span before International human society becomes an interplanetary and interstellar power) slowly begins to close.

They are attempting to keep the "window" open by suppressing advanced technology from the masses, which would lead to eventual Terran colonization of other planets by Earth and an eventual solution to the population, pollution, food and other environmental problems.

Being that Terrans have an inbred "warrior" instinct the Draconians DO NOT want them/us to attain interstellar capabilities and therefore become a threat to their imperialistic agendas (Draconian).

ALPHA CENTAURIANS - The extraterrestrials from Alpha Centauri vibrate and resonate on the band of violet light. This civilization has enormous scientific and technical knowledge that is of the highest quality in the universe.

The Alpha Centaurians are very theoretical. Part of their mission on Earth is to help raise the Earth's scientific, technical and theoretical knowledge. Their mission is to also find ways to make this knowledge understandable to our society, since they are so much more advanced.

One of the ways they are doing this is by telepathically linking up with some of our most advanced scientists.

Because these beings are so incredibly intelligent and are of such a high vibration, they sometimes have a difficult time grounding these ideas on the Earthly plane. The beings from Sirius are very good at bridging this gap, because they are very good at the practical application of these ideas, and making these theories usable for our third dimensional society.

The Sirians are the workers and doers of the Earth.

ALTAIRIANS - Alleged Reptilian inhabitants of the Altair stellar system in the constellation Aquila, in collaboration with a smaller Nordic human element and a collaborative Grey and Terran military presence. Headquarters of a collective known as the "Corporate", which maintains ties with the Ashtar and Draconian collectives (Draconian).

AMPHIBIANS - Similar to the Saurians or Reptiloids, yet being hominoid creatures with reptilian as well as amphibian-like features and are semi-aquatic in nature. May have once lived on land, yet became more aquatic over the centuries.

'They' have been encountered near swampy regions, rivers, etc., and have been known to attack people without being provoked. It is interesting that some types of Greys and Reptiloids are believed to be semi-aquatic, having webbed fingers and toes (Draconian).

ANAKIM, THE - Also referred to the 'Els', short for 'Elder Race' or simply as the 'Giants.' Referred to in ancient Hebrew tradition, this race is allegedly tied-in with a branch of ancient humans who broke-off from mainstream humanity because of their vast size which had developed over the centuries, possibly as a result of a genetic anomaly.

They are said to range anywhere from 9-11 ft. and in some cases even 12 ft. in height, although in configuration they are remarkably similar to 'International' humans. Are said to possess a means of molecular condensing and expansion which allows some of their kind to mingle among humans on the surface. They have allegedly been encountered in deep and extensive cavern systems below the western part of North America, as far north as Alaska, as far south as Mexico, and as far east as Texas. They are believed to have interstellar traveling capabilities.

ANTARCTICAN - This is allegedly a secret area of operations for both human and reptilian beings.

It is said by some that Aryan-Nazi scientists actually developed disk-shaped aircraft capable of very advanced aerial performance, and that swastika's have been seen on a few aerial disks. They may be piloted by a 'pure-bred' blond, blue-eyed Aryan race.

There appears to be more than one 'Blond' human society involved in the UFO scenarios, and especially subterranean human societies may have developed 'blond' hair due to lack of sunlight. There does not seem to be anything more than a peripheral connection between the Antarcticans, the Telosian and the Pleiadian 'blondes' (i.e., we will refer to the Antarcticans as the 'Aryans,' the Telosians as the 'Blondes,' and the Pleiadians as the 'Nordics' in order to discourage confusion).

The Antarcticans may consist largely of 'batch consigned' pure-bred blue-eyed, blond Aryans who became victims of Hitler's obsession to create a super race, and as suggested by Harbinson and others most of these may be controlled through mind manipulation and implants, being 'human drones' who are used to keep this hidden society functioning.

A massive joint Humanoid-Reptiloid underground system called the "New Berlin" is said to lie below the mountains of Neu Schwabenland, Antarctica. It is said by some sources that this joint human-alien force has spread terror through this sector of the galaxy, conquering and committing untold atrocities against the peaceful inhabitants of other worlds.

The famous abductees Barney Hill who along with his wife Betty was abducted by "Zeta Reticulan Greys" in 1961, stated under regressive hypnosis that he had encountered an evil-eyed "German Nazi" working with the Greys on board the craft.

It is claimed that the original "treaty" with the Greys was established by the Bavarian Thule and Illuminati societies as early as 1933, and this collaboration was brought into America via the CIA, which was established with the help of American Nazi fifth column agents as well as European Nazi's who were brought into America through Project Paperclip and other operations.

ATLANS - These are humans, usually described as being benevolent by comparison to other groups, who are said to inhabit vast and complex cavern-cities beneath in southern Brazil and surrounding regions. The term 'Atlantean' or 'Atlan' in reference to these races, has been placed upon them because of the fact that these cavern networks along the east coast of Brazil were reportedly once a part of the antediluvian 'Atlantean' empire.

The present inhabitants have no direct genetic relation to the ancient 'Atlantean' society which is said to have controlled these cavern systems several millennia ago, but are referred to as 'Atlanteans' simply because they are descendants of those who re-discovered and inhabited the ancient Atlan installations. As in North America and other continents, both common and gnome-like humans have been encountered here, some of which possessed advanced aerial or 'disk' technology.

The Telosians claim to have some connections with South America, especially the Matto Grosso region where a sister city named POSID exists in a large cavern system underground.

ASHTAR COMMAND - "The Airborne division of the Great White Brotherhood."

One of the most interesting and intriguing extraterrestrial groups of them all is that of Commander Ashtar and the Ashtar Command.

Commander Ashtar is the man who is in charge of the Airborne Division of the Great White Brotherhood, or Brotherhood of Light. Commander Ashtar and His vast extraterrestrial army of workers of over twenty million, work closely and in conjunction with the Ascended Masters.

Besides the twenty million personnel under His command in our solar system, of which He is in charge, there are another four million members and workers on the physical plane. Commander Ashtar, Himself, is a great and noble being approximately seven feet in height with blue eyes.

His body type is that of the Adam Kadmon which means it is similar to ours of Earth. He evolved from the planet Ashtar in his development as a soul. He has never had an embodiment on planet Earth. Although Commander Ashtar is in charge of the space fleet in our solar system, He is not restricted to this sector of space in terms of his service.

He represents our solar system in the council meetings of our galaxy, and universes throughout the greater omniuniverse. One of the important things to understand about Commander Ashtar and His army of workers, and fleet of extraterrestrial aircraft, is that they are etheric in nature. They do not have physical bodies like we do, however they are able to manifest physical bodies, and manifest their aircraft onto the physical plane anytime they want.

A person seeing them would not think of them any differently than you or I. Most of the life on the other planets in our solar system is etheric in nature. Sometimes for this reason these beings have been called etherians. They would not be considered disincarnate beings for they do have bodies.

They are in a state of evolution just as we are, and their life on their plane is not that much different than ours, except that they have transcended much of the lower self and astral desire that the people of Earth struggle with so frequently. Commander Ashtar also works closely with the Angelic Kingdom, most specifically with Archangel Michael.

Commander Ashtar is an extremely loving and gentle man but stern and adamant in his mission to serve, educate and protect humankind throughout the solar system.

Commander Ashtar and his crew do not wish to be seen as Gods, but rather as comrades and equals with us on paths of ascension and beyond. Two of his main missions are to spiritually educate mankind to their true mission for being here and secondly to defend and protect the Earth and the solar system from hostile and selfish extraterrestrial groups.

People have no idea of the gratitude that is entitled to Him and His tireless crew and workers.

The Ashtar Command and the Negative Extraterrestrials - There are many extraterrestrial civilizations throughout the galaxy, universe, and omniuniverse that have come to Earth to collect data and perform experiments for their own selfish purposes. They are not here to be of service. Some of these extraterrestrials are of what might be termed a neutral nature, and some are serving the Dark Force.

There are also negative extraterrestrials who openly oppose the Great White Brotherhood and the Ashtar Command. They would seize the planet and take it over if they could. It is the Ashtar Command and civilizations like that of Arcturius, that have protected us from this taking place. Just like in Star Trek, there are bands of renegades in their starships that are escorted out of our sector by these commands.

Many of the Ashtar Command walk among us on our streets on Earth without us even being aware of it. The Ashtar Command serves in a certain sense as heaven's policemen, there are actually six planets in the Orion system, and a group called the Deros, from inner space, that have had to be cordoned off so beware of anything to do with the Orion Nebula.

One of the problems the Ashtar Command has is that if our government makes legally binding agreements with certain negative extraterrestrial groups, they are not allowed to interfere with our free choice, unless we are endangering our solar system and galaxy.

The number of negative extraterrestrials is small in number compared to the vast number of positive extraterrestrials, however, the negative ones are quite dangerous if not controlled.

As a general rule, the cigar shaped UFO craft are potentially the dangerous extraterrestrials. There are a few exceptions to this rule.

BERNARIANS - Inhabitants of the 'Bernard's Star' system. Although not much has been written about them, it seems that human beings at least in part control this star system, along with "The Orange."

Whether the Saurians have any influence or not is uncertain, however some sources indicate a possible collaboration similar to that within our own SOL system.

BOOTEANS - Reptilians from the 'Bootes' system. These, and reptilian entities from the 'Draconis' system are allegedly involved with the 'Dulce' scenario as well as the infiltration-implantation-control of human society on Earth in anticipation of their planned takeover at some point in the future

(Draconian).

BURROWERS - Another mutation of the saurian or serpent race that is capable of burrowing through the Earth. Possibly quadrupedal as well as be-pedal, these have been known to use their natural 'boring' abilities to create artificial tunnels like moles, or even spontaneously produced 'cave-ins' (the latter has allegedly been used in attempts to entrap or kill unsuspecting intruders into the underground domains). These may possess a highly-developed 'bio-sensing' system.

CETIANS or Tau Cetians - A human race of 'Mediterranean' or 'South American' appearing, tan-skinned humans. Very similar to Caucasian humans on Terra except for slight differences:
- slightly pointed ears
- higher physical 'density' for their size
- slightly broader nose
- 5' 5" tall on average
- often wear short 'Roman' or 'crew' style haircuts

Tau Ceti and Epsilon Eridani are said to be a major 'convergence' of exterran 'human' activity, and are said to be in alliance with the Pleiadians (who in turn, according to contactees, have 'Federated' alliances with the Vegans, the Ummites, and others).

The Cetian alliance with the Pleiadians and 'other' societies who have been 'victimized' by the 'Grey' predators is based on a desire to establish a common defense against their reptilian nemesis.

CHAMELEON - Reptilians genetically bred to enable themselves to appear 'human.' Also less-humanoid appearing Reptiloids who use a form of technosis, molecular shape-shifting and/or laser holograms to produce an outward "human" appearance.

Reports of these have surface from underground joint-operational facilities near:
- Dulce, New Mexico
- Dougway, Utah
- Groom Lake, Nevada
- Deep Springs, California
- Fort Lewis, Washington
- and elsewhere

They are reportedly involved in some type of infiltration agenda. These 'infiltrators' can appear remarkably human outwardly, however at the same time retaining reptilian or neo-saurian internal organs. Often described as appearing 'bulge-eyed' with scaly, hairless skin behind their 'disguise.' One report alleged that the 'Chameleons' may utilize artificial 'lenses' to conceal "slit-pupiled iris."

Some claim they are genetically bred 'mercenaries' who are part of an advanced guard of a planned silent invasion-takeover of human society.

DALS - The Dals are a handsome Nordic looking race, much like the Northern European Caucasians. They are able to breathe our atmosphere without special equipment.

It must be understood, however, that many, if not most of the extraterrestrials do not have the Adam Kadmon style of physical bodies that we have. It is important that this not scare us.

DWARFS - Diminutive humans who have allegedly been encountered in or near caverns in various parts of the world, including northern California and the south-eastern Arizona / south-western New Mexico region and in some in connection to UFO's, although most reported 'dwarf' sightings in connection to UFO's are actually sightings of the saurian 'greys.'

These should not be confused with the small 'elementals' or 'nature spirits' which some believe are ethereal in nature yet have the ability to appear in solid or semi-solid form at times.

The Dwarf races are allegedly just as human as surface peoples but average between 3 to 4 ft. in height, although at times they have been seen as small as two feet. As with the 'giants' or 'Els' this diminutivity may have resulted in a genetic anomaly which ran its course due to the separation of their race(s) from the International 'gene pool.' They allegedly live in subterranean systems to a large extent as a 'protective' measure.

Some allegedly possess 'aerial disk' technology and interplanetary travel capabilities.

EVA-BORGS - Cybernetic forms controlled by 'human' entities. OR humans who have been implanted or surgically altered to such an extent that they have become cybernetic in nature, yet still retaining a soul-matrix.

GIZAN or GizAnu - The 'Gizeh People' have been referred to by the Plejaren (Billy Meier contacts) as well as others. This may have some connection with the strange 'people' and technology allegedly encountered in deep labyrinthine recesses beneath Egypt, who were sometimes reportedly seen by explorers, and who are said to dress like ancient Egyptians.

There is allegedly, according to Leading Edge Research, a huge cavern deep beneath Egypt which is inhabited by people with close ties with the U.S. 'secret government.'

Some sources indicate that the 'Giza People' may be a 'controlled' society with the reptilians being the dominant power, although there is still much mystery as to what the "Gizeh Empire" is all about.

GRAILS - These are saurian 'grey' type entities which are apparently somewhat taller than the usually-encountered greys yet with extremely thin 'rail-like' torso and limbs yet very strong.

GREENS, THE - Humans of 'normal' size, yet who possess an olive-green skin color. They claim to be from a subterranean or cavernous realms beneath Europe which they refer to as 'St. Martin's Land.'

GREYS, THE - Small neo-saurian hominoids, very prolific and intelligent. May be the 'brains' or 'intellect' of the serpent race, whereas the larger 'Reptoids' allegedly act as the physical overlords and thus are of a higher 'ranking' than the Greys.

The Greys are logic-based and operate on base animal survival or predatory instincts and in most cases are emotionally insensitive to humans, and like other reptilian entities they 'feed' off of human and animal vital fluids by rubbing a 'liquid protein' formula on their bodies, which is then absorbed through the skin. Like typical reptiles which shed their skins the 'waste' is excreted back through the skin. The Greys range from 3 1/2 to 4 1/2 ft. tall on the average, with skin colors ranging from gray-white to grey-brown to gray-green to grey-blue.

Aside from feeding off of human and animal proteins and fluids, they also allegedly feed off the 'life energy', the 'vital essence' or 'soul energy' of humans as do other reptilian species. This is why those humans seen working with the Greys (implanted and programmed 'drones', whether willingly or unwillingly) have appeared 'lifeless' and 'emotionless' to the witnesses who observed them.

The Greys are reportedly extremely deceitful and although they act on 'logic', to them it is 'logical' to use extremely complex forms of deception to bring about their goals. They are the most commonly observed 'alien' entities encountered during UFO events.

Their basic program is service to self.

They are using this planet as a supply depot, for biological materials (people and cattle mutilations).

They are very telepathic in nature. Our world is not the only world they have tried to conquer. The Grays from Zeta Reticuli have the ability to magnify their mental field in order to maintain control over humans. These different species of Grays are members of a network which is a type of loose alliance to which all have common purposes and aims.

The Grays from Rigel (image right) were the ones that made the secret deal with the US Government.

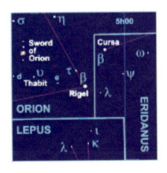

They are impregnating human females on a massive scale, and later extracting the fetuses. Most of their biological materials comes from the cattle mutilation. However, at times, they have done human mutilations. These materials have been found on their crashed UFO crafts.

There are some books on the market saying that they are our friends, and that we agreed to these abductions. We are here to tell you not to believe it for a second. These beings are very disturbed beings and are here to take over this planet for their own selfish purposes. They look at us in a similar way that the unconscious mass of our society looks at animals.

The Zeta Reticulans appear to be divided into two different groups. There is one group that appears to be a little more tolerant towards human beings. The other group is interested in colonization and conquest of planet Earth. The Grays have one base near the Aleutian Islands. The Grays seem to have influence over the Reticulans and the Beeletrax species of Grays.

These Grays have no stomach and digest their food by absorption through the skin or under their tongue. They have been cloning themselves instead of the practice of reproduction we use on Earth. Each time they reclone, however, the genetic copy becomes weaker, which is part of their problem. Their attitude towards humans is tolerance towards inferiors. They are technologically superior, however, spiritually and socially backwards.

The Reptilians (subspecies of the Grays) are the other extraterrestrial race that is most negative, destructive, and evil in their intent. These extraterrestrials are human in shape, however, have reptilian type faces. They also have scales which makes their skin water proof. They have three fingers with an opposing thumb. Their mouth is more like a slit. They average from six to seven feet in height. They are well suited for space travel because they are able to hibernate. They are cold blooded biologically, so must have a balanced environment to maintain body temperature.

The soldier class can bury themselves in the ground and wait long periods of time in order to ambush an enemy. The leaders of this species are called the Draco. They have special wings, which are like flaps of skin. There is a second group of their race that does not have wings, but the soldier class and scientists of their race don't.

In an emergency they can survive on one very large meal every few weeks. These Reptilians have been interacting with Earth for a very long time. In their home system they apparently live underground. This Reptilian species apparently directs the efforts of the working class which are only about four feet tall.

These beings would be considered another one of the subspecies of the Greys.
- The command progression in this Reptilian society are the Draco who are the winged Reptilians first in command
- Secondly the Draco who are the non winged Reptilians
- Then the Greys

This group, along with the Greys, pose the greatest danger at this time to planet Earth.

GYPSIES - Several sources refer to the Gypsies as having some connection with the UFO mystery. Other sources suggest a connection with high-tech subsurface kingdoms such as Agharti, etc. The knowledge which the Gypsies allegedly possess of an ancient war, UFO craft, and so on is supposedly a carefully guarded secret among various Gypsy tribes. Some claim to have traced the Gypsies back to ancient India or surrounding regions.

The infamous Philadelphia Experiment information source, Carlos Allenda, was allegedly part of a Gypsy clan with knowledge of past and present "history" on alien cultures which have interacted behind the scenes in Terran affairs.

HAV-MUSUVS or Suvians - Prominent in Paihute Indian tradition, the Hav-Musuvs were allegedly an Egyptian or Grecian-like sea-faring race that discovered huge caverns around 3 to 5 thousand years ago within and later deep beneath the Panamint Mts. of California.

Within these they then established their vast underground cities. When the inland sea (now Earth Valley) which connected the ocean in ancient times dried up, they had no way to carry on trade with other parts of the world. As a result of this, according to Paihute Indian tradition, they began to build and fly 'silvery eagles' which became increasingly advanced as time went on.

They then evidently established interplanetary and later interstellar travel, exploration and colonization. This huge facility is now operating as a major Federation base on Earth, and possesses huge chambers with differing environmental, atmospheric and even gravitational conditions to accommodate the various visiting Federation dignitaries.

HU-BRID - 'Hybrids' possessing reptilian and human genetic coding yet who possess a human soul-matrix.

HYADEANS - The Hyades in the constellation Taurus, like the Pleiades and Vega, are said to have been the destination of yet another group of refugees from the ancient Lyran wars.

HYBRIDS - Since human and reptilian beings are genetically so different in their physical make-up a natural 'hybrid' between the two is impossible.

However an unnatural genetic alteration, in essence 'splicing' human and reptilian genes, has been attempted by the Anunnaki, with the offspring not being an actual 'hybrid' (half human - half reptilian) but would fall to one side or the other. Since reptilians possess no soul-matrix as do humans but instead operate on a 'collective consciousness' level, the 'hybrid' would be human or reptilian depending on whether they/it was born with or without a soul-energy-matrix.
In most cases one might tell the difference if the entity had round-pupils as opposed to black opaque or vertical-slit pupiled eyes; or five-digit fingers as opposed to three or four;

or external genitalia as opposed to none. This may not always be the rule, especially when the 'chameleons' are considered. Some of the hybrids without souls are 'fed' with human soul-energy in an attempt to engraft an already existing human soul-matrix into the hybrid.

IGUANOIDS - Approximately 4-5 ft. tall, with 'Iguana-like' appearance yet 'hominoid' configuration.

They have sometimes been seen wearing black, hooded 'monk' robes or cloaks which conceal much of their saurian features, which include tails. These have been reported as being extremely dangerous and hateful towards humans and lesser-ranking Reptiloids such as Greys, and like all other branches of the 'serpent' race they utilize black witchcraft, sorcery and other forms of mind control against their enemies.

They appear to be a dimension-hopping sorcerer or priest class among the Reptiloid species.

IKELS OR SATYRS - Small hairy humanoids with cloven hoofs which inhabit deep caverns beneath South America and elsewhere. They may be members of a fallen pre-Adamic race which possessed angelic, animal and humanoid characteristics. Now allied with the reptilians.

They have been known, according to natives, to 'kidnap' women and children down through the ages and many stories are told of South American tribes who have battled these creatures with machetes during certain of their forays to the surface in search for women, children or food.

INSIDERS - Residents, either permanent or temporary, of the various different secret-society-connected top secret government 'underground installations,' bases or colonies throughout the United States and the World. Some of these groups may possess advanced technology enabling them to travel to various other planetary bodies in the solar system.

JANOSIAN - This is allegedly a planet on which human beings live or once lived. They apparently arrived on that planet some thousands of years ago according to certain 'contactees', and had all along retained their memories and legends concerning their ancient home world, planet Earth, where their ancestors lived long before their colonization of the planet 'Janos.'

They are said to be like Terrans, although somewhat oriental and slender. A group of refugees is said to have left Janos centuries ago in a huge carrier vessel of roughly donut-shaped configuration after an asteroid or meteor shower devastated the surface of their planet, causing a chain-reaction in their nuclear power grid, loosing deadly radiation into the atmosphere and into the underground tunnels and 'cities' which they had built beneath Janos.

They apparently remembered the star-route back to Earth, and the latest reports stated that they were in a high orbit somewhere 'near' the Earth and are seeking contact with Earth governments to exchange technology for a place to live on (or below?) the Earth, in the tradition of the TV series 'Alien Nation.'

In light of other revelations and lack of confirmation from other 'contactees', this might be a 'staged' Draconian propaganda operation; on the other hand the account may be legitimate.

KORENDIAN - Humans allegedly living on a colonized planet known as 'Korender.'

Perfectly 'human' in proportion yet 4-5 ft. tall on the average. Gabriel Green described alleged contacts with this group in publications during the late 1950's - early '60's. The accounts published by Gabriel Green were rather fantastic, although perhaps no less so than some other accounts.

Robert Renaud is one of the main "Korendian" contactees, and he claims that they have a large underground facility somewhere in Massachusetts.

The Korendians claim alliance with the Arcturians and are part of a massive collective Alliance of worlds who lean more to non-Interventionism than to direct Interventionism.

LEVIATHANS - Sea saurian 'sea serpents' such as the so-called 'Loch Ness Monster.' Loch Ness has been the site of much occult or paranormal activity including UFO activity, 'Grey' sightings, etc.

Aliester Crowley, the Satanist-Illuminist founder of the O.T.O. or Ordo Templi Orientis, claimed to be in contact with 'The Beast' of the Loch. He owned a mansion on the shores of the loch and this same mansion later became the residence of the British occultist Jimmy Page, who not only played with the British Rock group Led Zeppelin but also owned a large bookstore dealing with witchcraft and the occult.

Being aquatic in nature and having lost the use of their limbs via atrophication and mutation, this branch of the "serpent race" is allegedly used for long-range 'psychic' warfare and occult manipulation of the human race.

MARTIANS - Inhabitants of the planet Mars, both human and non-human, including the alleged inhabitants of the two Martian 'moons' (which many believe to be artificially-hollowed asteroids), one of which - Phobos - is said to be under the control of the "original" Greys, or *self-reproducing Greys* which are the "hosts" for the Grey "clones" which operate from various space stations that are disguised as planetoids. (It is from these "carrier" ships that the abduction, implantation, programming, mutilation, infiltration and other projects are carried out against planet Earth).

It has also been suggested that thousands of years ago the surface of Luna and Mars were much more 'habitable', that the surfaces of these bodies may have been decimated after passing through the asteroid belt or an 'asteroid storm' (consisting of debris which 'may' have been torn from a planet which apparently existed between Mars and Jupiter at one time -- possibly destroyed by a close encounter with another planetary body in the tradition of Velikovsky's theories).

It is believed that ancient 'ruins', possibly thousands of years old, have been seen on both 'planets' and that these attest to such a cataclysm.

MIB - Also referred to as the 'Men In Black' or 'Horlocks.' These are in many cases humans who are controlled by draconian influences, although other 'MIB' have been encountered which do not seem human, but more reptilian or synthetic. The 'MIB' have been encountered often after UFO sightings, usually intimidating witnesses into keeping silent about what they've seen (many of the witnesses may be 'abductees' with suppressed memories of the event).

Their 'threats' appear to be motivated by attempts to utilize 'terrorism', 'fear' or 'intimidation' as a psychological weapon against witnesses. This 'weapon' may not only be used to keep the human 'MIB' under control, but by the human MIB's themselves.

'They' are often, though not always, seen in connection with large, black automobiles, some of which have been seen disappearing into mountains -- as in the case of one basing area between Hopland and Lakeport, California -- canyons or tunnels or in some cases apparently appear out of or disappear (cloak?) into thin air. Most humanoid MIB have probably been implanted by the Draconians and are essentially their 'slaves.' Bio-synthetic forms possessed by 'infernals' also seem to play a part in the MIB scenario, as do subterranean and exterran societies.

Sirius, at only 9+ light years away, has been identified as a major exterran MIB center of activity, with a subterran counterpart existing in ancient antediluvian 'Atlantean' underground complexes which have been 're-established' beneath the Eastern U.S. seaboard.

MOON-EYES, THE - A race of peaceable humans some 7-8 ft. tall, with pale-blue skin and large 'wrap-around' eyes which are extremely sensitive to light. They may be the same as the large humans allegedly encountered on the moon by our 'astronauts' according to John Lear and others, who in turn were silenced and not allowed to tell what they saw. These people may, according to some accounts, be allied to the 'Nordics' and/or 'Blondes.'

They claim to be descendants of Noah who traveled to the Western Hemisphere a few centuries following the deluge and discovered ancient antediluvian cavern systems and ancient technologies which had been abandoned by the antediluvians in deep subterranean recesses.

They have been encountered mostly in deep cavern-systems beneath the general region of the Ozarks-Arkansas and surrounding regions.

MOTHMEN - Largely subterranean, pterodactyloid-like hominoids with bat-like wings. Sometimes describes as possessing 'horns' and thus are considered very similar to the traditional depiction of the 'devil', according to certain individuals who have encountered them. Very intelligent and extremely malignant. Although often referred to as 'Mothmen', this title might be a little misleading.

These creatures -- which have also been referred to as the Ciakars, Pteroids, Birdmen and Winged Draco -- have been encountered near underground systems near Mountauk Point, Long Island; Point Pleasant, West Virginia; and Dulce, New Mexico.

NAGAS - Also referred to as the 'Reptoids', 'Reptiloids', 'Reptons', 'Homo-saurus', 'Lizard-men', or the 'Large Nosed Greys.' They play a significant role in the legends of India and Tibet where they are considered by some to be demoniacal residents of a subterranean realm.

They are described as being around 7-8 ft. tall and of various colors, grotesque, but most often moldy greenish with scaled crocodilian 'skin.' Allegedly descended from a branch of bipedal sauroids which existed thousands of years ago on Earth and via mutation and natural selection, developed the brain-body coordination necessary to develop technology.

Some species still reportedly retain a visible 'tail' although much atrophied from their supposedly extinct' saurian ancestors. Some abductees claim that the "lizard" people resemble a humanoid version of a Velociraptor.

After a reputed battle in ancient times between a "pre-Scandinavian" race from the Gobi region and a Reptiloid race based in Antarctica, the reptilians allegedly lost the battle for domination of the surface world and were driven into underground networks in which they eventually developed aerial and space technology.

ORANGE, THE - These entities largely converge beneath southern Nevada, northern New Mexico and possibly Utah.

Some sources refer to a [1] 'human' race with stalky yellow, red or orange hair, others of [2] a genetically-altered, Humanoid-Reptiloid strain or hybrid. They are often described often as having a humanoid form yet certain 'reptilian' genetic features.

They are also said to possess human-like reproductive organs, and possibly (or not) a human 'soul-matrix', and therefore a divergent branch of the human race, or Reptiloid race depending on which 'type' of Orange one is referring to. as some accounts suggest there may also be [3] orange-colored reptilians which possess no soul-matrix.

Some of the "Orange" allegedly have connections to Bernard's Star.

ORIONS - Some claim that 'negative' entities have been associated with some of the stars in the Orion constellation.

Other sources claim that the Orion Nebula is a cosmic 'doorway' to 'infinity' or the realm of the Creator, which transcends the time-space-matter universe.

Some astronomers claim that a huge, beautifully-illuminated multicolored 'light' has emerged from the "nebula" (image right) and is on an intercept-course with Earth, although at a rather leisurely pace and at this rate this 'light' or 'star' will reach Earth approximately 3000 AD (give or take a hundred years).

Could this have something to do with the prophecy in Revelation 21? Since the Draconians are attempting to conquer the 'heavens', they may have made futile attempts to enter the

'Eternity Gate' and intercept the emerging 'Light' ('War In Heaven' between Michael and the 'Dragon' - see: Rev. Chapter 12).

This may explain the alleged presence of the Draconians in the Orion constellation, although certain 'human' groups have allegedly become curious of the 'Eternity Gate' as well. The Orion open cluster itself is the base of a joint Reptiloid - Grey Empire called the Unholy Six, which has been working out of NEMESIS in the SOL system. Many of the "planetoids" that have entered this system and have made observable "course alterations" are arriving from NEMESIS and the Orion-Draconian Empire.

The Orion civilization was one of the very few that evolved into a state of technological advancement while still being in a state of spiritual conflict. In the Orion conflict there were two groups, the negative side who believed in the concept of serving the self. They believed if they served their self the whole would be served. This translates into seeking domination over others. The more positive spiritual side held the ideal of being of service to others.

It is the exact same conflict that occurred in Atlantis between the Sons of Belial and the *Law of One*. It is the exact same conflict that occurs in our present world today. Do you serve self or ego, or do you serve Creator God? This Orion conflict played out for eons of time in a most destructive and disturbing manner.

There were three groups that formed. These three groups were:
- the dominators
- the victims
- the resistance
- The dominators were the Orion Empire
- The Black League was the resistance to the evil domination of the Empire

Chapter 4 – Many Species Throughout the Universe

The movie, 'Star Wars,' was actually based on this Orion conflict. The empire attempted to dominate mentally, emotionally, technologically, and even devised ways to control using the psychic arts for an evil purpose. There was apparently a great spiritual Avatar that came forward and awakened the Orion people to the Law of Love and Forgiveness.

This facilitated the beginning of a mass awakening for the civilization. There are parts of the Orion system that have awakened and parts that are still trying to dominate. One of those still trying to dominate in the Orion system is the reptilian race.

The positive Orions that are visiting the Earth are contributing their advanced mental power for the development of a smoothly running systems of organization on Earth. These Orions vibrate and resonate to the color yellow, and beam this frequency to Earth for the purpose of stabilizing the intuitive powers within the human consciousness.

The Ashtar Command serves in a certain sense as heaven's policemen, and there are actually six planets in the Orion system, and a group called the Deros, from Orion inner space, that have had to be completely cordoned off so beware of anything to do with the Orion Nebula.

PHOENICIANS - The 'Phoenix Empire' is allegedly a non-surface society which may be partially connected with the Dulce subnet, according to certain 'inside' sources. It's uncertain whether this is a Human or a Reptilian Empire, however some indications suggest a collaboration.

There may be a connection also with the Gizeh Empire below Egypt which was established by ancient Egyptian collaborators, the so-called Komogal-II empire which is said to have some connection with the ASHTAR collective as well as the DRACONIAN collective.

PROCYONIANS - One of the more positive extraterrestrial groups are from a solar system that revolves around Procyon.

Procyon (image right) is a binary yellowish/white star that rises before Sirius in Canis Minor and is about 11.4 light years from Earth.

They have been nicknamed the Swedes. They are humanoid in nature with blond hair. They have a very strong positive spiritual attitude towards the humanity of Earth.

The United States government was not interested in negotiating with the Procyon's because they would not give them new weapons systems. The Procyonians have apparently cross bred with us at many stages in our evolutionary development. This was done for a much more noble purpose than the Greys. The Procyonians have a philosophy of service to others rather than service of self.

They have been involved in trying to protect us from the evil activities of the Greys and Reptilians.

They are able to travel in time and between dimensions of reality. They frequently use mechanical vehicles for this, but are not dependent on them. The term Procyon translates into English as "The home of those who travel through time."

The Procyonians serve the *Law of One*. They are here to help us help ourselves, totally respecting our free choice.

RA-ANS - They landed on Earth approximately 110,000 years ago in an extraterrestrial mission to help Earthlings with their mental and spiritual evolution.

Their main focus geographically, was in Egypt and the Mayan civilization. The Ra refers to themselves as a sixth density social memory complex. They no longer have physical bodies. They are Light beings, however they are able to materialize bodies when they need to. They came to Egypt in a bell shaped UFO air craft. They refer to themselves as humble messengers of the *Law of One*.

They no longer operate in linear time as we do on Earth. They refer to themselves as a social memory complex, although still do have individual identities within this understanding. They attempted to help in technical ways, in terms of the healing of mind/body/spirit, through the use of crystals.

They were also involved in the building of the Great Pyramid of Giza. They made some contact in the Holy Land, also. The Pharaoh they contacted was Akhenaton, in the Eighteenth Dynasty. The Pharaoh accepted the teachings of the *Law of One*, however the priests only gave this teaching lip service.

The pyramids they helped create were used for spiritual initiation, and in this current day and age they refer to the great pyramid as a piano out of tune. They apparently originally had some connection with the planet Venus, however, they no longer do. In their physical manifestation on Earth the physical bodies had a golden luster because of their high vibration. They did not apparently stay too long in Egypt, once they realized that what they taught was being distorted.

They stayed a little bit longer in South America, where they had a little more success.

RE-BRID - 'Hybrids' possessing no soul-matrix. Some of

these may possess human-like genetic coding yet no 'soul' while others may be an apparent 'hybrid' of two or more reptilian species. It must be understood that the Reptilians are far more adaptable or 'mutable' than are humans, physically.

This would mean that we should expect a much greater rate of physical diversity between the reptilian species than between the various human species.

Such mutations would not have to take place over millions of years, but through eons or even centuries, especially when one considers the possibility that controlled natural selection, mutation, genetic manipulation, and even occult-technological molecular shape-shifting may have been responsible for accelerating this process.

RETICULANS - Apparently a major center of 'Reptiloid' activity and possibly 'controlled' human slaves.

This is a region from where a large percentage of the 'Grey-type' Saurians --such as encountered by Betty and Barney Hillmore and other abductees.

This binary or double-star system may be the center of interstellar 'Grey' activity just as Alpha Draconis (Thuban) seems to be the center of 'Reptiloid' activity and Orion being a realm where both reptilian sub-species operate in joint capacity.

Much of the implant-control scenarios allegedly originated from the Reticulan 'Grey' Reptiloids.

SASQUATCH - Large, hairy 'humanoids' who are usually troglodytial or cavern-dwellers, although they have been known to forage through mountainous or wooded areas on the surface in search for roots, berries, grasses and nuts which make up their diet.

They are believed to possess a heightened 'sensing' ability which allows them to steer clear of 'human' influence. They are more human than animal according to some reports although they have often been mistaken for animals, which has forced them to take up a largely subterran lifestyle.

They have often been described as having a human face on an 'ape-like' body. They are mostly strict vegetarians, which may be explained by the possibility that they might be a 'hybrid' or 'hubrid' between antediluvian humans and Sapiens. Such interbreeding, if possible back then, is certainly not possible in modern times due to increasingly divergent genetic strains between the two groups.

Most Sasquatch apparently posses a human soul-matrix. They are usually described as being 6-9 ft. tall, while other branches may be smaller. 'Hairy humanoids', both large and smaller "dwarf like" entities, have on some occasions been observed in connection with UFO encounters, or subterranean encounters.

Sasquatch have been known to attack humans only in self defense (sometimes throwing large boulders to frighten intruders away). There have also been 'hairy hominoids' which possessed either 'robot-like' or 'amphibian' characteristics, suggesting bio-genetic manipulation to create 'biological machines' or 'cyborgs.'

There is a possibility that other entities, possibly more animal than human, are the result of humanoid-Sasquatch and nonhuman-Sapiens interbreeding or genetic manipulation, in which case the offspring might be more human or beast in nature, but this is mere speculation. Another type of 'hairy humanoid' is allegedly the result of genetic manipulation, and have been reported in underground bases in northwestern New Mexico and in Southern Nevada.

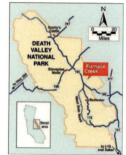

Sasquatch apparently has the ability to spontaneously induce invisibility through producing an electromagnetic psychic shield around themselves, and are said to commute between our dimension and a "5th" dimensional realm.

SERPENTS - These are literally 'giant snakes' which have been encountered in various underground regions. They are often used by the Draconians as 'sentries' to guard subterranean tunnels or 'treasure' repositories.

They have been known to easily crush a human being or other objects with their teeth or their bodies.

SIRIANS - Sirius is the epicenter of the ASHTAR or ASTARTE collective, where humanoids of various types, Sasquatch, Reptiloids, Greys, Insectoids and Reptilian-Insectoid hybrid species as well as cybernetic "MIB" entities have collaborated in the past.

The Sirians have waged war in the past with the Orion Empire or the "Unholy Six" reptilian star systems in the Orion open cluster.

The ancient dispute involves just who will serve as the "landlords" of a sector of space containing 21 star systems including the most strategic star system, SOL and particularly planet Earth, Terra or Shan -- which is a virtual cosmic "oasis" of water, mineral, plant, animal and genetic resources in incredible variety compared with most other worlds.

This dispute between the Sirians and Orion Reptiloids dates back to the ancient invasion of Orion by the Draconian Empire, as a result of which many "Nordic" type humanoids escaped to Procyon, Sol, Sirius and elsewhere.

In recent times a rift or split has occurred in the Ashtar collective following the discovery of massive infiltration into the collective by agents of the Unholy Six and Draconian Empire, with many humanoids taking sides with the Federation - which has a major Earth-base under Furnace Creek, California (see map left); and many of the Reptiloids taking sides with the Orion-Draconian Empire - which has a major Earth-base below Dulce, New Mexico.

A Collaboration of sorts (via the electronic collective mind which links humanoid and Reptiloid intelligences into a master mainframe via psionic implants) still exists however, a collective-collaboration which maintains bases under Paradox, Nevada, Dougway, Utah and near the Denver International Airport in Colorado.

This war in Sirius-B is gravitating towards the Sol System, in that the opposing agendas for this system is one of the major issues of dispute between the two [or three] warring factions.

During many of the Egyptian dynasties it was quite common to have a visitation from a Sirian in the disguise of one of their Gods.

Sirius was one of the first areas to be colonized by beings from the Lyran Star group and is more advanced in a metaphysical sense.

Djwhal Khul says Sirius is one of the more advanced training centers or universities to which the Ascended Masters may travel.

The path to Sirius is one of the seven paths to higher evolution that each soul must choose upon achieving the sixth initiation and/or their ascension. The star Sirius is known as the Dog Star, and is a member of the constellation of Canis Major. It lies approximately 8.7 light years from Earth.

It is one of the most brilliant stars that is observable in the night sky. We must think of them in terms of being a group consciousness of both physical and non-physicality. The third dimensional Sirians visited both the Egyptian and Mayan civilizations in times past.

The Sirians gave the Egyptians advanced astronomical and medical information.

The Mayans and the Inca also had a very personal relationship with the Syrians. Considerable information was shared, and it is interesting that the Mayan race seemed to just vanish off the face of the Earth at a certain point in their history. The Sirians left behind time capsules for our future generations to discover, one of which was supposedly the crystal skull.

At this time they are working with us primarily without direct intervention. They were instrumental in helping us at the time of Atlantis during that cataclysmic period. Also, at that time, they mixed with us genetically. Their views, currently on Earth, is that they will not consider a more active partnership again, until we outgrow the tendency as a people, to be exploitive, judgmental and manipulative.

The guides also refer to Sirius as a star system where the residents are seldom permanent residents. It is a meeting place for those who have mastered their own planetary systems and are preparing there for further duties and missions. They talk about it as an important way station for Earthlings who wish to continue their spiritual development. The beings from Sirius who are visiting Earth are very good at the practical application of very advanced theoretical ideas that are being brought forth from other very advanced extraterrestrial civilizations.

They are here to ground and make usable these advanced ideas and technologies. Sirius helped to build the great pyramids and temples of Egypt. They also helped in the building of many of the tunnels and pathways to the Inner Earth.

They will be very involved in the future in establishing the Golden Age on this planet.

SOLARIANS - Human residents of the 'Sol' System who claim to have ties with ancient Terran societies, especially subterran societies which developed off-planet travel early on and established underground bases and colonies on various planetary bodies in the 'Sol' system, including the Jovian moons and the Saturnian moons on or under which they have allegedly established a 'Tribunal' center for the Federated Solarian planets.

Saturnian moons montage Dione is the large moon in front of Saturn, Tethys and Mimas are below Saturn to the right, and Enceladus and Rhea are to the left. Titan, actually the largest moon by far, is in the background right.

Jovian moons From upper left clockwise: Amalthea, Io, Europa, Callisto, and Ganymede.

SYNTHETICS - Of several different types and varieties. Although reptilians and humans apparently utilize 'artificial intelligence' devices or organisms (technology itself being amoral, neither good nor evil), the Draconians as well as some 'controlled' humans have apparently developed bio-synthetic or mechanical 'entities' as Extension of their activities.

This is especially true with the bio-synthetic cybernetic creatures which the 'reptilians' have allegedly 'created' using cybernetics and biological organs stolen from animal and human mutilation victims.

The synthetics are of many types, some of which are very 'human-like' and which may be used as 'infiltrators.' Others apparently look more like the 'Grey' entities, created 'after their own image' so to speak, but are not reptilian yet instead a type of 'molded' entity form containing a 'sponge-like' substance which permeates the interior.

They may be the worst of all, as they are apparently bio-genetic 'forms' which are able to be inhabited or possessed by the 'Infernals,' 'poltergeists' or fallen supernatural entities as 'containers' enabling them to operate in the physical realm.

TELOSIAN - Tall, blond inhabitants of a re-established network of subsurface antediluvian colonies located throughout the Western States, and concentrated around Mt. Shasta in northern California.

They are sometimes referred to erroneously as 'Lemurians' as it is believed that the cavern cities which they re-discovered and built upon were once part of an antediluvian civilization called 'Lemuria' (Lemuria is actually a hypothetical lost continent in the Indian Ocean. The Pacific continent was called Elam-Mu).

They may have loose contact with the Pleiadians and other groups via ancient ancestral ties, since the Telosians are Earth-Natives who allegedly possess interstellar vehicles, and are a western branch of the sub-International Agharti network and it's "Silver Fleet."

The name 'Telos' is a Greek work meaning 'uttermost' or 'purpose,' yet some of the inhabitants refer to ancient ties with neo-Mayan tribes, and therefore many of them 'may' possess a

Greco-Mayan ancestry. Some ancient Vedic texts speak of a collaboration between the Greeks and the East Indians -- who some believe gave rise to the Mayas -- in the development and construction of aerial craft called "Vimanas."

Telosians are part of a "Melchizedek" spiritual order with connections to the Ashtar collective-mind and have dealings with extraterrestrials in Arcturius, Sirius, and Saturn as well as with other-dimensional beings.

TEROS - A term describing various human groups who inhabit the cavern systems and re-established antediluvian cities beneath the North American continent.

Many of these may be descended from early American colonists, while others are apparently descended from older civilizations such as ancient native Americans who went underground hundreds and/or thousands of years ago.

The nemesis of the Tero are the 'dero', which apparently consist of draconian or reptilian controlled elements.

ULTERRANS or Ultraterrestrials - These are said to be people who have been encountered at times entering or leaving an 'alternate' or 'parallel' existence, yet still operating within the ONE 'reality.'

Latitude and Longitude of the Triangle:
NW edge, Bermuda: 32.20 N, 64.45 W.
SW edge, San Juan: 18.5 N, 66.9 W
NE edge, Miami: 25.48N, 80.18 W

It is very unlikely that more than one 'physical reality' like ours exists, yet there is a theoretical possibility that another co-existent 'world' might exist on the opposite end or polarity of the electromagnetic barrier.

Many humanoid and/or neo-saurian inhabitants of this 'alternate' world if it exists originally came from our own 'world' through some type of vortex or through hi-tech means. There are said to be four intersecting "Universes" which make up the "Omniverse."

One is the matter universe, the other is the antimatter universe. The nature of the other two is unknown (perhaps the matter and antimatter universes each have a forward and reverse time-flow phase?) Each of the four universes allegedly have 11 "dimensional densities," with a 12th density which is currently unfolding as a result of super energies which are emanating from the black holes at the center of the galaxies.

This multi-dimensional reality may explain various phenomena such as animals, objects, people and entire vessels which have seemingly fallen into or out of our 'world.' It may also be possible that certain objects in our 'world' would be invisible in the 'other' realm or dimension (or rather the opposite polarity of our reality!?) and vice versa.

For instance, one airplane pilot who had become temporarily caught up in an EM-vortex in the 'Bermuda Triangle,' saw an island which was deserted, while the very same island was inhabited in the world he was familiar with.

This would also explain the many accounts of people who claim to have seen or stopped at houses, cafes, hotels or other sites along remote stretches of road, only to return the same way and find that no such place 'exists.' Since both dimensions may 'flow-in' to each other, being part of the same electromagnetic superspectrum, such temporary displacement of objects and/or people from one 'world' to another might occur.

This is not saying that one necessarily has an alternate 'self' inhabiting the alternate dimensions, but more a case of other 'dimensions' or 'universes' which were inhabited intentionally or unintentionally over a long period of time by humans, animals or 'other beings' which were somehow transported there.

This would also explain the case of Joseph Vorin, who suddenly appeared as 'out-of-nowhere' near Frankfurt-am-Oder, Germany in 1850, spoke a broken and ancient para-Germanic dialect which the authorities could just barely understand, and claimed to be from the nation of Laxaria in Sakria (no known country by those names exists -- in 'our world').

When he suddenly appeared he seemed disoriented and dumbfounded, as if he had suddenly fallen out of 'another' world.

UMMITES - Humans claiming to hail from the general area of Wolf 424, some 14-plus light years distant from the Earth-Sol system, and possibly having ancient ties with the 'Lyran' colonies in that the Ummites (from the planet Ummo) are like the Lyrans-Pleiadians said to be 'Scandinavian' in appearance, and therefore may tie-in with the so-called 'Nordic' or 'Blond' societies.

They reportedly work closely with the Vegan humanoids.

The Ummites are extremely telepathic.

They, very much, believe in the existence of the soul and in a Creator God. At the age of 13.7 Ummite children leave their families for teaching centers where they are prepared for adult life.

They make practical use of at least 10 dimensions of reality and are aware of far more. They say one of the reasons they are able to travel such far distances in such a short time in their space craft is that they use folds and warps in the space continuum.

They have bases on Earth in eight countries.

VEGANS - Relatively peaceful and gentle humans descended from refugees from the 'Lyran Wars', who work closely with other refugee-colonists now living in the Pleiades, Wolf 424, and elsewhere. Often described as "dark skinned Orientals" similar to the native residents of the nation of India.

The Vegan technology is about 250 years ahead of the Pleiadians, and they are also in contact with the Dal universe and are being assisted by them. All these civilizations are guided by non-physical beings who sit on the Andromeda Council.

The Vegans are darker in skin color than the Lyrians with higher cheekbones and more triangular faces. The Vegans also helped to colonize star systems such as Altair, Centauri, Sirius, and Orion, among others. Andromeda is a large spiral galaxy, the closest to the Milky Way at a distance of 2.2 million light years. Altair lies around 15 light years from Earth. The Altair civilization is quiet and contemplative, and is given to peaceful philosophic pursuits.

They are not currently involved in space exploration and they strenuously object to the Lyran involvement in Earths evolution.

VENUSIAN - Allegedly inhabited by physical entities, both human and reptilian, beneath the surface and therefore 'safe' from the extreme surface conditions.

Also allegedly inhabited (on the surface?) by human beings, possibly colonists from Terra-Earth, who somehow were able to 'phase' or generate their physical bodies' molecular structure into a '4th dimensional' existence wherein they now allegedly survive unaffected by the harsh 'physical' conditions.

Other surface colonies allegedly exist in "biodome" cities, whereas still others reportedly live in the "antimatter" counterpart of "Venus" -- which in the "alternate" universe is part of a 12-planet alliance called the Koldasian alliance according to some contactees.

The Pleiadians also claim to have colonized the "anti-matter" universe, which they call the Dal universe.

ZETA RETICULUMS - The extraterrestrials from Zeta Reticuli are some of the most well known and often seen space visitors. They are the three to four feet tall beings that are involved in the abduction process.

They are very science oriented and share more of a group mind, and are not as individualistic as we are on Earth.

They are also mentally developed to a fault, in the sense of their emotional sensitivity is not as developed. The channelings of Lyssa Royal suggests that they come from a planet called the Apex planet in the Lyran system. This was a planet that was very similar to Earth. Their spiritual growth, however, did not match their technological development which finally led to a planetary cataclysm.

The atomic explosions caused the plant life to deteriorate, which led the civilization to build underground shelters.

It was during this underground period in their history that they began reproducing through cloning techniques, which is part of the work they continue in their abduction work on the human race.

One of the other conclusions they came to was that their emotions were the cause of their surface destruction of their planet so they no longer allowed emotions in their lives.

There is another group of Zetas called the "Negative Zeta Reticuli" who were more power hungry that are causing a lot of problems.

Part of the reason they are doing all their abductions of humans and animals is that the generations of cloning using the same genetic material has caused their evolutionary growth to become very inbred and stagnant. In truth their race is actually dying.

The Zeta Reticuli are also creating a hybrid race of both human and Zeta origin.

Sources:
1. 'List of alleged extraterrestrial beings,' *Wikipedia*, Various authors, https://en.wikipedia.org/wiki/List_of_alleged_extraterrestrial_beings.
2. 'Former Apollo astronaut Edgar Mitchell calls on the US government to ...,' April 22, 209, *The Guardian*, ttps://www.theguardian.com/world/.../2009/.../ufos-apollo-astronaut-extraterrestrials.
3. *The 58 RACES of the ALIEN RACES BOOK (AZAZEL8867) Legendado ...*, Old Soulstube. May 28, 1013, https://www.Old Soulstube.com/watch?v=Na4OCgKNlEY

4. Book of Alien Races: Secret Russian KGB Book of Alien Species, Gil Carlson, 2017, https://www.amazon.com/Book-Alien-Races-Russian-Species/dp/1640084711
5. Alien Races Book, Suddenlink, *Old Soulstube*, Isantkori, pages.suddenlink.net/stevewingate/alien%20races%20book.pdf
6. 'Introduction to the Alien Races', *Exopolitics*, https://exopolitics.blogs.com/files/russian.secret.alien.races.book.pdf
7. '58 Alien Races Visiting Earth,' *Soul:Ask*, https://www.soulask.com/58-alien-races-visiting-Earth/
8. 'A-Z of Alien Species active in Earths Evolution' From the *ExopoliticsHongKong* Website, https://www.bibliotecapleyades.net/vida_alien/esp_vida_alien_19a.htm

CHAPTER 5

LIFE LESSONS FOR THE SOUL - THE JOURNEY TO "I AM, WE ARE" - WHY WE ARE HERE

First and foremost, we are Spirit and we have voluntarily come to Earth (the "Experiment") to learn "lessons" we cannot resolve by being in the spiritual realm. We, along with fellow spirit Wanderers/Travelers/Starseeds/Indigos who agreed before we were born, chose the "path" we are to take through this life. Our fellow Wanderers/Travelers/Starseeds/Indigos chose the role they were to play in our life on Earth to either "set the stage" or help, in some way, to start or guide us on our "path" – some for a reason, some for a season, and some for most of our life. In addition, our fellow "travelers" have a path of their own.

The below list contains some of the common achievements on our life path.

- **You WAKE UP to Reality**:

    o **It may come subconsciously as a child**, learning to make pictures by depicting people as purple or green, and animals, some strange looking and of different colors (remembrances of past lives on a different planet?); people as stick figures (remembering being on a planet with less or more gravity); an orange or different color sky (again, what might unconsciously be from a past life); by making a picture of just stipples, dots, and streaks (remembering the stars, although where one current lives has few stars due to the lights of the city); by coloring outside the lines (are we trying to depict their aura?).

However, don't be fooled by the "Real" in reality. We learn primarily by observation. As a child grows and develops consciousness over time, they move from confusion to differentiation, to situational awareness, then to identification, ultimately arriving at self-awareness. By the time they become self-aware, their perception of what the world is all about is well-formed. The programs in play here affect the rest of their lives.

Conformity to patterns of thought and patterns of behavior are learned, and when you watch people closely, you notice that most of them are imitating the examples they've seen their whole lives. Emotional behavior, notions of success, relationships, rules, laws, and even love for self are all ingrained programs, many of which need to be undone in order for spiritual growth to occur.

- **The WAKE UP comes later** due to the programming that had occurred during one's youth. The WAKE UP call comes when Divine Spirit sends a spiritual wake-up call through one means or another, such as seeing 11:11 everywhere and it comes with a feeling that something is amiss with this scene, that something's wrong with the script. A thought creeps in and the soul begins to grope for the truth. We may go through years of doubt and uncertainty. We may sample one religion or another, tripping from area to area in the occult field, or shifting from philosophy to psychology, even to mathematics. It's all in pursuit of the key to life and truth.

- It only takes the right scrap of information, the right quote, or the right idea at the right time to change your whole understanding of the world. When you begin to question everything, you start to wonder if your perceptions and belief about society and your own life are really true. You wonder if they are your own perceptions or if they belong to someone else. You begin to ask if you outlook is based on the complete picture, or if it is based on a limited understanding and a limited knowing. When you grasp this, you begin to understand just how much power you have to control your own perceptions, and then you own reality, and are no longer bound to the whims of others.

- **You are not from here** since you are Spirit that has "lived" in the infinite past and will "live" into the infinite future.

- **Find one's way back to Creator God.** We arrive here with only a vague memory of what has gone on "before."

- **Learn Love through experience:**
  - All Earthly love is conditional
  - You cannot love another until you love yourself.
  - There is only one unconditional love in the Universe – Creator God, who loves us no matter what. This is how he can love the criminal, the sinner, the blasphemer, etc. – no matter what; God loves each of his creation.

- **Nothing is yours** – it all belongs to Creator God, who is loaning things to us.

- **Events and circumstances in your life are meaningless**, unless you tell what they are. It's up to you what meaning you give to the things that happen to you. Only state of being matters. Because state of being materializes everything around you.

- **One's past means nothing** (past years, past lives, etc.). The past only tells you how you got to where you are today. The past is created from the present and not the other way around. Too many people cannot get past this "lesson" and are doomed by their own past, which may have occurred years ago, millennia ago (the war between Venus and Mars, as depicted in Biblical murals of spaceships in the sky over Earth), or even eons ago (The Lyran and Orion Wars that started 22 million years ago between the Humanoids and the Dracos, as depicted in the movie "Star Wars," which continue on even today).

- **What is, is what it should be.** One is always at the right place at the right time. Nothing is by coincidence.

- **You are responsible for your own happiness**, not money, not fame, not another person, none of these. Happiness comes from within, not form anything outside of you.

- **Separating Body, Mind, Soul, and Spirit**:
    - The body ends at the end of the current life. It is but a shell to contain our Mind, Soul and Spirit.
    - Mind is the mental/emotional aspect of the human being. The mind processes thoughts and ideas as well as feelings and emotions. The mind is consciousness; perception; determines relevance; makes value judgments; memory; imagination; develops abstract "philosophical" concepts about the world and the meaning of events; determines what is joy, fear, anger, guilt, envy, trauma, shock, etc.; linguistics; mathematical mental processing; dreaming, fantasizing, modeling and "channeling" of new ideas to solve problems and constructs.
    - There is a force of Good (Bearers of Light) and a force of Evil (Dark Side). Part of our Soul continues into the

next life, as part of the judgment that we have to "work out" in the next life. The Soul is the part that makes you - you in this life and the "sins of the soul" will be judged as to what the consequences may be. But, it is not polarity between Heaven and Hell, neither of which exist. Hell is being banned from seeing the "Face of Creator God," once you have seen His face.
- o Your Spirit is pure – a part Creator God gave to us and is the part that continues on after Earth. Sprit is pure, untarnished by the lives we lead. It could be the part that tells us what is "right" and what is "wrong," although we have free will to make our choices. Those choices remain in the Soul.
- o Integration: The Mind and the Body are interactive and create *Self* ("ego"). The Mind talks to the Soul and it is at the Soul level that we make sense of what is outside us. Creator God (pure) communicates with the Spirit (pure) – this is a two-way communication. Spirit talks to the Soul, buts the Soul does not talk back to the Spirit.

- **The only moment in time that actually exists is NOW.** Everything that has ever happened is just a remembering of that event in this very moment. And whenever you bring things from past into the present, You can give a different meaning to them, and in the end, change your whole history. In this sense, you are a different individual with every second, with every NOW.

- **Time is relative.** As a spirit, you have been a part of infinity past and will be part of infinity future. Thus, a lifetime means practically nothing when it is a part of two infinities. Yet there are "lessons" to be learned in this lifetime.

- **There are many false "gods" on Earth**; one was given to us as "Anu," the supreme leader of the Annaunaki (of Sumerian time) – he was a star traveler. Anu was declared by himself to be the god of the heavens. There is but one Universal Creator God and He is not Anu. The Anunnaki modified the human DNA and made us a hybrid species, to be subservient to the Anunnaki, yet we contain some of their DNA – hence, "children of the lesser God."

- **Recycling Trap of the human Soul**: The souls of the human species are trapped in a dimension of control (i.e., what we call "reality") and the afterlife is merely a short break before being recycled back into the chaos.

    - It may sound scary to choose not to go to the Light because many of us are afraid of the unknown. Whereas, the Light feels "safe" because we've gone there so many times, and "everybody else" who went there seems to have done just fine. Instead of letting yourself be "hypnotized" by its attraction, turn and look in the opposite direction (you will have 360° vision, and you can still concentrate on looking in a certain direction) and move away from the Tunnel (you do this by "thinking" yourself as moving - it's all about thoughts and intention in this dimension).
    - Remember, you are a soul of Fire that is far stronger than the centrifugal force that pulls you toward the Tunnel. Don't try to fight it — that's not the way to do it. Instead, think yourself away from it!
    - The Tunnel with the Light on the other side of it is a sophisticated hologram created by the Anunnaki to recycle our soul back to being subservient to the Anunnaki Dark Force, and all you need to do is to think yourself in another direction, and the Tunnel will fade away.

- Then you will see the Grid as a fuzzy "barrier" in front of you, or above you (there are no ups and downs or left and right in space). You will now see the Universe the way it is, i.e. you will now be truly interdimensional. This means you will see a much larger universe than you are used to seeing.

  As a Fire riding an Avatar, you are now free to go more or less anywhere in the Universe.

- **You are connected to everything within the Universe.** All things, including us, have a frequency, even the Earth, rocks, the plants, and the all living things.

- **You are on a "Path"** to be experienced on Earth. That "Path" was chosen by you before you were born in order to experience and learn many of the above "lessons" before you return to be part of Creator God's spirit – part of the "infinite."

- **To Know Self as I AM / WE ARE** – The Self has no qualifiers. Begin with defining yourself as "I AM __(Fill in the blank)__ " Now forget what you said and try another "I AM __(Fill in the blank)__ " and disregard that definition. Do this until you have qualified who you are and then disregard that definition. My last definition of Self was "I am a free spirit in the universe." Finally, you are down to Self as simplify "I AM." Then do this with "WE ARE" and exhaust all the definitions until, finally, one is down to defining Self as "I AM-WE ARE." Your duty is to BE and not be this or that. Let go of the ego and its activities. Reality is only in the "I AM." Thoughts change but for you. "I" rises in the heart, which is the place of the mind's origin.

- **Our purpose in life, as higher dimension star beings, is to raise the frequency of the Earth** and thereby raise the frequency of the people of Earth. Once you have mastered the above "lessons," you will realize your true purpose here on Earth and you will realize that you are not defined by *Self*. It will all be reduced to the simple "I AM." At this point, you will realize that "Reality" is an illusion (Although I have made it past nearly all of the above "lessons," I am not there, as yet, since I have allowed my Mind to "see" the Earth illusion as being real).

Increasing the frequency of the Earth is part of our AWAKENING as well as to seeing reality as it is.

WHY WE, AS EXTRADIMENSIONAL BEINGS, ARE HERE - We are not from here but were sent here as Star Travelers, Starseeds, Light Workers, Indigos, walk-ins, and others to carry out a mission.

1) We have chosen to be sent here, NOT as part of the Dark Side/Anunnaki "recycle program" (refer to Recycling the Human Soul above) but for multiple reasons.
2) Mission is to WAKE UP, to use our institution, to conduct research, separate away from Self, and see Reality for what it is – an illusion created by your ego in concert with all other egos. You are Fire riding on an avatar and you are a free spirit, unteathered from any all Cabals.
3) Primary Purpose: I believe our presence, as a higher dimension star being, is to help raise the frequency of the Earth and, thereby, raise the frequency of the people of Earth.
4) Raising the frequency will result in an AWAKENING, where the normal person will become aware of the Dark Side's manipulation to control the people and the deception that they have created (i.e., an alternate "Reality"). An AWAKENING will result in the adoption of "service to

others" (a Federation/ Bearers of Light concept) vs. the Dark Side's "service to self."
5) Healers (manipulators of another person's field) are here in order to remove the blockade of pain that is keeping them from becoming Fully Awake
6) Spiritual Healers: Those that can help others grow spiritually in order to "raise" their own vibration.
7) Observers: Sent here by the Galactic Federation to advise if:
   (a) People have lost their Free-Will by the false illusion portrayed by the Dark Side, in their quest to control the Earth and, if so, this remnant of the Dark Side should be "taken out." The Federation established a quarantine of the Earth (no one in or out) and that the perimeter is being patrolled by cloaked Federation Warships. The Federation's primary directive is to never interfere with Free-Will and that each planet should use their Free-Will to decide governance, etc, There are over 200,000 planet members of the Galactic Federation.

   b) That the Federation's efforts to increase the frequency of the Earth is working, to the extent desired, and that an invasion to wipe-out" the Dark Side/Annaunaki should be delayed. However, the Federation is now ready to negotiate (refer to my Dream that I am on my way to Procyon), with the Dark Side/Annaunaki knowing that if the Federation invades, their choice will be to leave the planet (most likely, to a penal colony) or die.

Sources:
1) '5 Things You Realize When You Wake Up and Question Reality' was originally created and published by *Waking Times* and is published here under a Creative Commons license with attribution to Dylan Charles and WakingTimes.com. It may be re-posted

freely with proper attribution, author bio, and this copyright statement.

CHAPTER 6

THE LESSON OF LOVE – WHAT I HAVE DISCOVERED

My primary Earth Life Planning goal (refer to Chapter 2) and Life Lessons (refer to Chapter 5) was to understand LOVE as "practiced" and not as I understood it in "theory" prior to my journey to Earth.

BASIC LESSON
- **All Earthly love is conditional**
- Only one unconditional love and that is from Creator God. This is the reason that Creator God loves the sinner, the criminal, the blasphemer, the Satanic Cult members, etc.
- Earth is a polarity planet where all people have a LOVE – HATE relationship with each other and all items and events on Earth.
- **The 7 Kind of Love** - As we struggle to define love, the ancient Greeks seemed to have no problem at all defining *multiple* kinds of love. My Mission Goal was to primarily explore Philia, Pragma, Agape, Philautia and Storge love. Perhaps, you are exploring one or more of the kinds of love.

   a. **Eros: Love of the body** - Eros was the Greek God of love and sexual desire. He was shooting golden arrows into the hearts of both mortals and immortals without warning. The Greeks feared that kind of love the most because it was dangerous and could get them into the most trouble. Eros is defined as divine beauty or lust. Eros is mainly based on sexual attraction and it is where the term "erotica" derives.

   b. **Philia: Love of the mind** - Also known as brotherly love, Philia represents the sincere and platonic love. The kind of love you have for your brother or a really good friend. It was more valuable and more cherished by the Greeks than Eros. Philia exists when people share the same values and dispositions with someone and the feelings are reciprocated.

c. **Ludus: Playful love** - Ludus is the flirtatious and teasing kind of love, the love mostly accompanied by dancing or laughter. It's the child-like and fun kind of love. If you think about it; this generation loves Ludus more than anything else.

d. **Pragma: Longstanding love** - The everlasting love between a married couple that develops over a long period of time. Pragma was the highest form of love; the true commitment that comes understanding, compromise and tolerance. It is *pragmatic*, which is why it is referred to as *"standing in love"* rather than *"falling in love"* because it grows over time and requires profound understanding between lovers who have been together for many years.

e. **Agape: Love of the soul** - It is the selfless kind of love, the love for humanity. It is the closest to unconditional love. The love you give without expecting anything in return reflected in all charitable acts. It is the compassionate love that makes us sympathize with, help and connect to people we don't know. The world needs more Agape.

f. **Philautia: Love of the self** - The ancient Greeks divided Philautia into two kinds: There is one that is pure selfish and seeks pleasure, fame, and wealth often leading to narcissism and there is another healthy kind of love we give ourselves. Philautia is essential for any relationship, we can only love others if we truly love ourselves and we can only care for others if we truly care for ourselves.

   g. **Storge: Love of the child** - This is the love parents naturally feel for their children. It's based on natural feelings and effortless love. Storge is the love that knows forgiveness, acceptance and sacrifice. It is the one that makes you feel secure, comfortable and safe.

Defining love can help us discover which kind we need to give more of and which kind we want to receive. If we incorporate *Eros, Ludus & Pragma* into our relationships and *Agape, Philia* and *Storge* into our lives, we will reach *Philautia* and live a happier life.

WHAT I LEARNED
   a. **How We Block Love** - We block love in dozens of ways, all of them laid down during childhood by how we interpreted our perceptions of how our parents treated us. Here are just a few:

Unwillingness to deal with feelings-if we felt hurt, we suppressed our emotions, which means all of them, pleasant and unpleasant.

Not feeling deserving of love is one way to deal with lack of love as a child was to convince yourself that you were unworthy of it, so you didn't expect it, and were not hurt when it didn't come.

I don't need love is another coping mechanism to reinvent yourself as a rugged individualist who doesn't need anyone else, especially if you are male, because the culture encouraged this.

I've had my shot at love and won't get a second-in other words; I screwed up the first time and must now receive my punishment.

If I open myself to love, I will get hurt-that's always a chance in anything we try.

A major source of low self-esteem was the trauma of birth, in which you were squeezed and ejected from the womb, into the harshness of the outer world. Not only is this traumatic first experience of the world recorded in your Subconscious Mind, but it may be interpreted as punishment, not for something you have done but for why you are unworthy. So your very first self-image was one of unworthiness, and this still sits deep in your Subconscious, ready to be called up and reinforced whenever you do something dumb as an adult.

b. **Love Yourself First** - If you espouse Serving Others, how would this change your life? Completely and in every department of your identity: relationship with self, with how you perceive deity, and with others (romantic, platonic, family, co-workers, children, pets and deceased loved ones). Is that enough?

The spiritual path is not a "doing" thing, for that leads to spiritual ego and spiritual ambition. It also separates the seeker from that which is sought, which is True Self. The real spiritual path involves getting Little Self out of the way and dissolving the blocks to love. Then, you can allow True Self to embrace you and merge with True Self.

Also, "searching" implies that the path and Self are "out there" somewhere, when, in fact, they are very much "in here." Worse, you create the illusory "out there," so you would actually be chasing your own illusions, much like a dog chasing its tail-not a productive exercise and you get dizzy. Of course, you must interact with "out there," but do not confuse it with anything Real; the only Reality is within you, and it is the unconditional love of your True Self.

c. **Love Cares** - Love cares about the happiness of the beloved and constantly reminds him or her of how special and important he or she is to you. Love says, "you are valuable to me; I care about you and will do whatever I can to ensure your happiness."

d. **Love Respects** - When you respect those you love, you honor them, are honest with them, let them be who they are without trying to change them, and want what is in their highest and best interest.

e. **Love Forgives** - All of us incarnate to learn, grow and explore, and we inevitably screw up somewhere along the way and hurt someone else. If someone harms you, you have two options: (1) you can hold a grudge, or (2) you can forgive. Clearly, the first harms you further and gives all your power to the very person who harmed you, allowing that person to determine how you will feel.

The second option allows you to move on, free of other people's energy. You also live longer and healthier. However, the other person doesn't just walk away. They must be made to understand how you were harmed by their actions and offer a sincere apology and promise that it won't happen again. If they are spiritual, they will be eager to learn the consequences of a hurtful word or deed ... otherwise there's always the court system. And if that deed stemmed from malicious intent rather than an innocent accident, the apology had better be good.

If you are the miscreant, it's essential to own the deed, without finger pointing or blame. Fess up and accept the consequences of your actions. And preferably apologize before you're found out. Suppose a friend confides a secret in you and you have too much to drink and blurt it out. Apologize before word gets back to your friend, who may then still have some respect for you.

f. **Love Encourages Others to Find Strength** - Most of us have untapped strengths and potentials, and only discover these when slammed by some major Life Challenge. And if we run around "fixing" things for our friends and loved ones, we're simply enabling their victimness. Instead, love encourages others to find the strength and courage to tap their own potential, confidence and abilities to grasp life by the horns. Love encourages others to explore the grandest expression of who they can be. And rather than nay-saying, love says, "Go for it! You can do it!"

g. **Love Challenges** - Love's final gift is to challenge the other to rise and stretch to achieve a goal or blast through a self-limitation, and thereby grow. Love's encouragement reveals the strength or ability; love's challenge calls it into action. Love says, "You have the vision of your grandest expression, so now become that expression."

Given that love allows, cares, respects, forgives, encourages and challenges, in your life as a spiritual being, the trick is to blend these ingredients in just the right proportion, or things won't balance. And the best way to avoid imbalance is communication. Ask, "How does it make you feel when I encourage you to find a better job?" or, "How does it make you feel when I dare you to _____?" Finding the right mixture of allowing, caring, encouraging and challenging is not easy and requires one to communicate openly and frequently … for that, too, is part of growth.

h. **Love Encourages Growth** - How can one person support another? By criticizing, nitpicking, and pointing out flaws? Obviously not, but that's how most parents approach child-rearing; "Eat all your greens or mommy won't love you."

That's flat-out manipulation but we carry that into adulthood, with "love" as a reward for a well-prepared meal or a promotion.

Many people use "love" to coerce a mate into conforming to their opinion of how the mate should be (just watch a few movies on the Lifetime Channel). Such "love" forces the mate to contract and shrink into a little box, often with the justification, "I love you and want only what's best for you." This really means: "… what's best for me." On the other hand, unconditional love encourages expansion and growth, which brings us to how love really works.

Love also allows the beloved to be who he or she is, without seeking to change him or her, except for encouraging growth. We all know that it's impossible to change others; only they can change themselves but plenty of people do try … and end up exhausted and frustrated. It's about as pointless as mud-wrestling a pig---its hard slippery work, and besides, the pig likes it.

i. **Unconditional Love** in your life as a spiritual being. There's no middle ground with this-love it is either unconditional or conditional, and the latter is simply bartering attention to get something you want.

If I love you unconditionally, you do not need to earn it, pass any tests, win any contests, or in any way deserve it. If you did need to prove your worth, you have tenure only until someone more worthy comes along.

Unconditional love says, "You can be who you really are, and share your Souls deepest thoughts, fears and feelings in absolute surety that I won't judge you or stop loving you. We may agree to disagree on things but I will never reject you, for I am committed to your well-being and growth."

In a soulful relationship, love allows itself to flow. Love isn't a "doing" thing, but an allowing thing. Imagine love as water, and you're a hose. How big a hose are you? A tiny tube used in an irrigation drip-watering system? A standard garden hose? A fireman's hose? Or a huge pipeline? This obviously determines how much love can flow through you, which increases with practice.

LIFE'S LESSONS IN LOVE
The Lesson is: When it comes to love, don't believe in fate but believe in choices.

That may not seem as romantic, although it is much more meaningful. Fate would mean that there is someone out there destined for you to meet: Your perfect match. Choice means that you find someone to love on your own and you choose to stay with them even though they aren't perfect.

We can choose to stay with our FIRST LOVE. It's a love that looks right, on paper and to the rest of society – but not so deep down you know it doesn't feel right. It's the one that will make everyone else but you, happy.

OR

We can choose HARD LOVE; it's the love that is not worth having if we don't have to fight for it. This is the kind of love where trying to make it work becomes more important than whether it actually should. It's destructive, unstable, or self-centered even. There may be emotional, mental, or physical abuse and manipulation – but no matter what, there will always be drama. Just like your favorite movie or book, what keeps us addicted to this storyline is the drama. It's the emotional rollercoaster of extreme highs and lows, and like a junkie trying to get their fix, you stick through the loops, the twists, the turns, and the lowest of lows with the expectation and hope of one single high. It's the love we wished was right, and when it doesn't work out – because it will never work out – you feel defeated but you know it was for the best.

OR

We can take the leap of faith and the You-Never-Saw-Coming Love. This is the one that comes so easy it doesn't seem possible or real for that matter. Because, if things seem too good to be true, they probably are not, right? So, now you're just waiting for the part where things go wrong – but to your surprise, it'll never come. This is the love we never planned for. Everything just seems right and it just fits – there aren't any expectations about how each person should be behaving, nor is there pressure to become someone other than who they already are. We are accepted for exactly who we are, and to be honest, it scares the living hell out of us. This kind of acceptance completely shakes you and your every belief in love, to their very core. This love shows us that love doesn't have to be how we see and read about in movies, shows, and books in order to be true. This is the love that keeps us on our toes and allows us to see the best version of ourselves. This is the love that everyone deserves, and hopefully, will one day find. It's the love that just feels right because it just is.

LESSONS IN LOVE SUMMARY - Maybe we don't all get the chance to experience these loves in this lifetime, but perhaps that's just because we aren't ready to. Maybe the reality is that we need to truly learn what love isn't before we can grasp what it is.

Maybe we need a whole lifetime to learn each lesson, or maybe, if we pre-planned our live just right, it'll only take a few years to figure it out.

But if you ask me, I think whoever makes it to their third love – no matter how long it takes – are the real lucky ones. They are the ones who feel like giving up after constant heartbreak and disappointment, but yet, they don't, they keep trying, they keep giving love "one more shot."

To find your final and most important love begins with knowing who you are and knowing that you cannot love another without loving yourself first.

Sources:
1. 'An Old Soul's Guide to Life, the Universe and Everything' by *Truth Control*, www.truthcontrol.com/articles/old-souls-guide-life-universe-and-everything
2. 'There Are 3 Types Of Love You Will Have In Your Lifetime,' Liss, *Unwritten,* Dec 14, 2016, https://www.readunwritten.com/

CHAPTER 7

5TH WORLD, RISING FREQUENCY OF THE EARTH, CHANGE IN DESTINY

THE FIFTH WORLD

BIBLE: The New Earth is an expression used in the Book of Isaiah (Is 65:17 & 66:22), 2 Peter (2 Peter 3:13), and the Book of Revelation (Rev 21:1) to describe the final state of redeemed humanity. It is one of the central doctrines of Christian eschatology and is referred to in the Nicene Creed as the world to come.

Revelation 21 New International Version (NIV):
21 Then I saw "a new heaven and a new Earth," for the first heaven and the first Earth had passed away, and there was no longer any sea.² I saw the Holy City, the New Jerusalem, coming down out of heaven from God, prepared as a bride beautifully dressed for her husband. ³ And I heard a loud voice from the throne saying, "Look! God's dwelling place is now among the people, and he will dwell with them. They will be his people, and God himself will be with them and be their God. ⁴ He will wipe every tear from their eyes. There will be no more Earth or mourning or crying or pain, for the old order of things has passed away. He who was seated on the throne said, "I am making everything new!"Then he said, "Write this down, for these words are trustworthy and true."

NATIVE AMERICANS IN THE UNITED STATES AND CENTRAL AMERICA have creation myths that describe the present world as interpreted by several groups. The central theme of the myth holds that there were four other cycles of creation and destruction that preceded the Fifth World. The creation story is taken largely from the mythological, cosmological, and eschatological beliefs and traditions of earlier Mesoamerican cultures.

Aztec Mythology - According to Aztec mythology the present world is a product of four cycles of birth, Earth, and reincarnation. When each world is destroyed it is reborn through the sacrifice of a god. The god's sacrifice creates a new sun, which creates a new world. The myth is sometimes referred to as the "Legend of Five Suns."

Jaguars, a hurricane, fire, rain and a flood destroyed the first four suns. After the fourth sun was destroyed the gods gathered to choose a god to become the new sun. Tecuciztecatl, a boastful and proud god, offered himself up for sacrifice. However, the rest of gods favored Nanahuatzin, the smallest and humblest god. The gods built a grand fire, but at the last second Tecuciztecatl refused to jump into the fire because he was too afraid of the pain. Instead, Nanahuatzin jumped in the fire. Embarrassed by Nanahuatzin's sacrifice, Tecuciztecatl followed him into the fire. The two suns rose in the sky, but they were too bright. The gods threw a rabbit at Tecuciztecatl to dim his light, and he turned into the moon. This is the reason why the Aztec people say there is a rabbit that lives on the moon.

However, the sun remained motionless in the sky, burning the ground below. The gods then recognized they all must be sacrificed so that the people could survive. The god Ehecatl helped offering them up. The sacrifices made the sun move through the sky, energizing Earth instead of burning it.

Navajo Mythology - The Navajo, who were neighbors of the Hopi in the southwest, borrow elements of the Pueblo people's emergence myths in their creation stories. The Navajo creation story has parallels to the Biblical book of Genesis. The early Judaic-Christian concept of the world is similar to the

Chapter 7– 5th World, Rising Earth Frequency, Change in Density

Navajo concept of the world. This world is one where the Earth is an area of land floating in an ocean covered by a domed heaven. The domed heaven fits the land and ocean like a lid with its edges on the horizon. The Navajo creation story traces the evolution of life through four previous worlds until the people reach the fifth and present world. As the humans passed through each of the previous four worlds, they went through evolution. They started out as insects and various animals until they became humans in the Fourth World.

Upon arriving in the Fourth World the First Man was not satisfied. The land was barren. He planted a reed and it grew to the roof of the Fourth World. First Man sent the badger up the reed, but water began to drip before he could reach top so he returned. Next a locust climbed the reed. The locust made a headband with two crossed arrows on his forehead. With the help of all the gods the locust reached the Fifth World. When he pushed through mud he reached water and saw a black water bird swimming towards him. The bird told the locust that he could only stay if he could make magic. The locust took the arrows from his headband and pulled them through his body, between his shell and his heart. The black bird was convinced that the locust possessed great medicine and he swam away taking the water with him. The locust returned to the lower world.

Now two days had passed and there was no sun. First Man sent the badger up to the Fifth World again. The badger returned covered with mud from a flood. First Man collected turquoise chips to offer to the five Chiefs of the Winds. They were satisfied with the gift, and they dried the Fifth World. When the badger returned he said that he had come out on dry Earth. So First Man led the rest of people to the upper world. So with the explicit help of the gods the people reached the Fifth World similar to the Aztec creation story.

After all the people had arrived from the lower world, First Man and First Woman placed the mountain lion on one side and the wolf on the other. They divided the people into two groups. The first group chose the wolf for their chief. The mountain lion was the chief for the other side. The people who had the mountain lion chief were to be the people of the Earth. The people with the wolf chief became the animals.

Navajo medicine men say there are two worlds above the Fifth World. The first is the World of the Spirits of Living Things and the second is the Place of Melting into One.

The Navajo legends are an oral account that is passed down from generation to generation. There are various versions of the story as there are in any oral account, but the variations are slight.

Hopi Mythology - The Hopi's creation myth is slightly different than the creation myths of the Aztecs and Navajo. The Hopi believe we are currently living in the Fourth World, but are on the threshold of the Fifth World.

In each of the three previous worlds humanity was destroyed by destructive practices and wars. Similar to the Navajo myth, the Hopi myth has many variations because it is an oral prophecy. In the most common version of the story the Spider Grandmother (*Kookyangso'wuuti*) caused a reed to grow into the sky, and it emerged in the Fourth World at the sipapu, a small tunnel or inter-dimensional passage. As the end of one world draws near the sipapu appears to lead the Hopi into the next phase of the world.

Sources:
1. 'Jump up *Iron,'* Osita (2008). *A Day in the Life of God*, Dover, Delaware: Enlil Institute.
   p. 150. ISBN 0615241948

2. ' Jump up to Stookey,' Lorena Laura (2004), *Thematic Guide to World Mythology,* Westport, Connecticut: Greenwood Press, p. 20, ISBN 0313315051
3. 'Jump up to,' Doyle, Diana (2004), *Yale-New Haven Teachers Institute,* Aztec and Mayan Mythology, Yale University
4. 'Jump up,' Matthews, Warren (2013), *World Religions.* Belmont, California: Engage Learning, p. 34, ISBN 0495007099
5. Jump up,' Anderson, Arthur (2012), *Florentine Codex: General History of the Things of New Spain,* Salt Lake City, Utah: University of Utah p. 89. ISBN 0874800005
6. ' Jump up to, Stookey, Lorena Laura (2004), *Thematic Guide to World Mythology,* Westport, Connecticut: Greenwood Press, p. 80, ISBN 0313315051
7. ' Jump up to, 'Locke, Raymond (2002). *The Book of the Navajo,* Los Angeles, California: Holloway House, p. 55, ISBN 0876875002
8. 'Jump up,' *Seelye,* James E. (2013), *American Indian Experience,* Santa Barbara, California: Greenwood Press, p. 8, ISBN 031338116X
9. 'Jump up,' O'Bryan, Aileen (1956)

NEW AGE SPIRITURALISTS - New Age Spiritualists hold that the four other cycles of creation, referred to as the 4-Earths, where the changes in Density/Dimensions that those Earths went through and that we are on the verge of the "creation" of a 5-D (5th Density) Earth. Below is a refined system of dimensions and densities somewhat based on personal experience and verification from other sources.

1st Density:	Mineral kingdom
2nd Density:	Plant & lower animal kingdom
3rd Density:	Higher animal & lower human
4th Density	Low: Astral, lower emotional realms
4th Density	High: Etheric, higher mental realms

5th Density	Low: Causal, creative realms
5th Density	High: Soul (last level of individuality)
6th Density:	Oversoul (social memory complex)
7th Density:	Master oversoul, atomic plane
8th Density:	Avatar planes, celestial heavens
9th Density:	Christ planes, Buddhic planes, lower God worlds
10th Density:	Higher God realms
11th Density:	Universal realms
12th Density:	The source, the mystery, the Tao
13th and beyond:	The void, unmanifested creation

Sources
1. 'Dimensions and Densities,' Sal Rachele, https://www.salrachele.com/webchannelings/foundersworkshoppart1.htm

Summary: No matter which creation story you believe, "the times they are a changing" and we are on the verge of a new world.

FREQUENCY OF THE EARTH IS RISING - An old sage from India has stated that the magnetic field (which "drives" the frequency) of Earth was put in place by the Ancient Ones to block our memories of our true heritage. This was so that souls could learn from the experience of free-will unhampered by memories of the past.

For many years the Earth resonance frequency has hovered at a steady 7.83 Hz with only slight variations. In June 2014 that apparently changed. Monitors at the Russian Space Observing System showed a sudden spike in activity to around 8.5 Hz. Since then, they have recorded days where the Schumann frequency accelerated as fast as 16.5 Hz. These emerging resonances are naturally correlated to human brainwave activity. So this means that we are changing. Whatever is happening, it's clear that this acceleration may make you feel more tired, exhausted, dizzy, depressed, and even strange as you raise your own frequencies to be more "in tune" with the New Earth.

Adaptation is not always an easy process but keep in mind it is all part of your own unique AWAKENING.

Although Brain waves, at rest, are in the same range as that of the Earth (7.8 Hz), when we are awake and thinking, the range is 13-38 Hz. Other brain waves include:

- Delta waves (below 4 Hz) occur during sleep
- Theta waves (4-7 Hz) are associated with sleep, deep relaxation (like hypnotic relaxation), and visualization
- Alpha waves (8-13 Hz) occur when we are awake but relaxed and calm
- Beta waves (13-38 Hz) occur when we are actively thinking, problem-solving, etc.
- Gamma brain waves (39-100 Hz) are involved in higher mental activity and consolidation of information.

Source:
1. 'Mother Earth is Shifting Her Vibrational Frequency and So Are We,' Feb 3, 2018, *Patriots for Truth*, 'https://patriots4truth.org/.../mother-Earth-is-shifting-her-vibrational-frequency-and-so-...

EARTH CHANGES DUE TO CHANCE IN DENSITY TO THE 5TH WORLD - Several events have already occurred that indicate we are on the verge of the "creation" of a 5-D (4th Density) Earth from the previous 4-D (3th Density). Those events included the Harmonic Convergence/Galactic Alignment (occurs approx. every 500 years, last occurring in 1998 +/- 18 years), Solstice, 2012, the date when a 5,200-year "long count" in the Mayan calendar came to an end, along with two other cycles of 26,000 years (Milankovitch Procession Cycle – a complete axis wobble cycle) and 130,000 years (Milankovitch Longitudinal Cycle – Earth's orbit around the sun changes from an ellipse to a circle). Every 26,000 years, this planet enters an Age of Aquarius (began 11/11/11) and it also enters the Photon Belt, a region of highly charged space.

The result of our entry to the Photon Belt is unpredictable because what happens depends on the level of consciousness of each of the planet's individual inhabitants, so each time is a first … which also means it's a very personal impact. Those who are less prepared for the Shift may feel as if they have walked into chaos, and nothing makes sense; those who are more prepared will see the disruption as the removal of limitation. Both ways, things will be disrupted and a new order of organization will emerge from the chaos in a process that many call ascension.

Forget the doom-laden prophecies of the Book of Revelation, Nostradamus, and Edgar Cayce. Anything that predates the Harmonic Convergence of August 1998 goes out the window. Consider only post-Convergence predictions, but because things are changing daily, regard even those with suspicion.

Following the "creation" of 5-D, and with a dramatic increase in spirituality among Earth's population, the Shift will be far less destructive than once foreseen. However, there is a continued need for us to deepen our unconditional love and compassion for our fellow humans. Religious Fundamentalism, being born of fear, will fall away as tolerance and compassion based on love come to the forefront. Women will take the initiative and we will listen to the new children.

During the Shift, coastal areas may be inundated, but the only people impacted will be those whose soul planned for them to cross over and return after the Shift to enjoy the results of the new beginning. To survive the Shift, the ability to let go of attachments to material things is vital. We must be willing to walk away and start over, confident that it's our spirit's plan.

Sources:
1. 'Earth Changes,' Sal Rachele, *webarticles,* https://www.salrachele.com/webarticles/Earthchanges.htm
2. 'The Earth Changes and the Mayan Predictions - World Mysteries Blog,' Nov 29, 2010, *world-mysteries*, http://blog.world-mysteries.com/science/the-Earth-changes-and-the-mayan-predictions/

CHAPTER 8

RAISING THE FREQUENCY OF THE SOUL

Frequency: Matter is vibrating energy. Different vibrationary rates denote the properties. Frequency is the rate at which molecules or consciousness vibrates.

PSYCHIC ACTIVITY OF THE PINEAL GLAND ("third Eye") - When the pineal gland is stimulated geomagnetically, it produces chemicals that are similar to plant hallucinogens, which help to alter consciousness. Studies show that psychedelic drugs alter levels of melatonin and serotonin, resulting, in some cases, in psychosis.

So, how could the Earth's geomagnetic fluctuations affect these brain chemicals? Researchers have found that electromagnetic and geomagnetic fields strongly affect the production and activity of the enzyme hydroxyindole-O-methyltransferase (HIOMT). It is this enzyme that is centrally involved in the production of melatonin and possibly 5-methoxytryptamine (5-MT). Any changes in the magnetic field can produce changes in this enzyme's activity.

Studies in animals have also shown that any strong change in the ambient magnetic field—whether increased or decreased—will inhibit production of HIOMT.

Other research shows that serotonin N-acetyltransferase, the enzyme involved in the production of melatonin, is strongly affected by electromagnetic fields.

If this is the case, says Roney-Dougal, any strong change in the Earth's ambient magnetic field, which is on the rise, would produce a rush of natural hallucinogens in our bodies, enabling us to be more psychically receptive.

The following abstracts and articles show the connection between the Earth's frequency and brain wave frequency. The brain wave, through the Pineal Gland tries to match the brain waves to that of the Earth's frequency. Thus, by increasing the frequency of the Earth, via match to brain wave (brain wave frequency increase), we will achieve the 5th World, a world of higher frequency and "dimension."

A number of fascinating studies shows some sort of correlation between geomagnetic activity and an increase in dreams or psychic activity. In one such study, the famous parapsychologist Stanley Krippner set up a dream laboratory where some participants slept in a room while other participants attempted to 'send' them certain images in hopes that these images would become incorporated into the sleeping participants' dreams. Upon waking, the sleepers had to describe their dreams in great detail to determine if there were any correlations with the target pictures they'd been 'sent' during their slumbers.

Global geomagnetic activity was tracked for 20 of the nights that one study participant was the dreaming recipient. In this case, it was found that, on nights of less geomagnetic activity, the dreamer had significantly greater accuracy in picking up the target pictures.

It may well be that our human potential is at its greatest when we are in harmony with the Earth and the sun. Traditional cultures had some greater understanding of this energetic harmony that we do well to learn from.

Geomagnetics & Consciousness: Geomagnetic Field Effects & Human Psychophysiology - Research has proven that changes in solar/geomagnetic activity can affect our emotions and collective behavior. Every cell in your body is bathed in an environment of magnetic forces which are invisible to the human eye. Numerous rhythms within your body can synchronize with solar and geomagnetic activity. The Earth's magnetic resonances vibrate at the same frequency as human heart rhythms and brainwaves. The Earth's changing electromagnetic fields may be affecting your day-to-day health, feelings and behavior. When the sun's emission of a 2.8-gigahertz radiowave frequency is increased we tend to feel better. Geomagnetic field disturbance is associated with lowered heart rate variability, indicating our nervous system is not functioning as well. Earth's magnetic fields can affect your health and daily life. Heart coherence helps reduce emotional reactions during solar flares. Solar flares can disrupt your sleep. Migraines may correlate with geomagnetic disturbances. You can feel more mentally fogged during solar flares. We are more intuitive during full-moon periods. –Heartmath. Even a single cell has its characteristic shape and anatomy, all parts of which are in constant activity; its electrical potentials and mechanical properties similarly, are subject to cyclic and non-cyclic changes as it responds to and counteracts environmental fluctuations. --Mae-Wan Ho.

Electrical engineer, Ben Lonetree has continuously monitored several geophysical parameters over decades. His highly sensitive custom equipment outperforms government stations. He says, "There is a reason why my system responds to many things other magnetometers do not. Most are fluxgate mags that sample a collapsing field at a very slow sample rate. My system is simply a very large induction coil that after the amplifier and filter stages couples into an analog to digital converter. I have the converter programmed to use a sample rate of 240 times per second. So the system sees every little blip there is out there." He has conducted numerous experiments correlating local geophysical anomalies in Earth's magnetic field with EEG brainwaves of many subjects, and anecdotal reports of changes in consciousness. Preliminary experiments were done as proof of concept with intent to investigate the possibilities more deeply.

Sources:
1. 'Geomagnetics & Consciousness: Geomagnetic Field Effects & Human Psychophysiology (Part I),' *Journal of Consciousness Exploration & Research*, July 2013, Volume 4, Issue 6, pp. 657-670, Miller, I, Abstract: http://www.jcer.com/index.php/jcj/article/view/319/344

THERE ARE MANY SUB-PLANES WITHIN EACH MAJOR DENSITY LEVEL - Remember that densities and dimensions are labels for convenience only so that our intellects can grasp these ideas. In actuality, there is not always a sharp demarcation between levels.

There are several "negative" astral levels, including what many religions call "purgatory" or the "netherworlds", places where soul fragments journey to learn about separation, fear and terror. In these "lower" realms, fear thoughts manifest as grotesque apparitions, monsters, etc.

In the higher regions of the "astral," are common dream states, out-of-body experiences, lucid dreaming, etc. There is a lot of talk about negative entities and their effect on humans. Whether ghosts, poltergeists or negative ETs, the truth is that these beings can only affect us if we vibrate at a level that attracts them. When we reach the higher realms, these experiences are seen as dreams or part of the "maya" of the lower four dimensions.

Regardless of whether or not "reptilians" are ET's or are only holographic projections does not ultimately matter. If they are fourth dimensional vibrations, then like all 4D entities, going beyond the "maya" into the 5th dimension is the way to freedom. I personally do not live in fear of the reptilians or their agenda of fear because I know that overcoming fear within my consciousness is the answer.

Beyond the astral is what is commonly called the "etheric" realms, which have a more refined vibration. The upper etheric realms encroach upon the mental realms, the place of higher imagination. Beyond these are the causal planes, realms of great beauty and perfection. They are causal because they "control" the 3D and 4D worlds through a complex series of crystal grids (think of sacred geometric figures, only now in multi-colored swirling patterns). It is here that higher thoughts are coalesced into DNA and other life-form structures. As you might have guessed, the akashic records and divine blueprint of each soul are part of the causal planes.

Next up the ladder (corresponding roughly to 6D and 7D) are the soul and oversoul realms, celestial planes and other "God-worlds."

There is some confusion as to what is "inner" and what is "outer" with respect to densities. The easy way around this is that everything is "inner." The "outer" is an illusion. It's all one continuous energy emanating from the One (Creator God) and we are the collective creation doing the emanating.

Regarding our multidimensional nature: This is a paradox we are investigating here. When we are in our center, we realize we already exist in 5D. In fact, each one of us has at least 12 dimensions of being. We are simply unaware of the vast majority of Who We Are.

Our level of vibration corresponds to the composite total of where we place our attention. Within the Earthly sphere, most of us are vibrating at a composite level between 3D and 4D. Using the calibration scale developed by Dr. David Hawkins, most of humanity is vibrating a lot lower than that. I was informed by my higher self that my composite vibration was approximately 480 but approaching 500 (480 on the Hawkins scale listed below).

Dr. David Hawkins levels of human consciousness

Enlightenment   700-1000
One has become like God. Many see this as Christ, Budda, or Krishnan.

Peace   600-700
Achieved after a life of complete surrender to the One Source Creator. It is where you have transcended all and have entered that place that Hawkins calls illumination. Here, a stillness and silence of mind is achieved, allowing for constant revelation. Only 1 in 10 million (that's .00001 percent) people will arrive at this level.

Joy   540-600
This is the level of saints and advanced spiritual people. As love becomes more unconditional, there follows a constant accompaniment of true happiness. No personal tragedy or world event could ever shake someone living at this level of consciousness. They seem to inspire and lift all those who come in contact with them. One is in complete harmony with the will of Divinity and the fruits of that harmony are expressed in your joy.

Love   500-540
Only if, in the level of Reason, you start to see yourself as a potential for the greater good of mankind, will you have enough power to enter here. Here is where you start applying what was learned in your reasoning and you let the heart take over rather than the mind - you live by intuition. This is the level of charity - a selfless love that has no desire except for the welfare of those around them. Ghandi and Mother Theresa are examples of people who were living at this level. Only 0.4 percent of the world will ever reach it.

Reason   400-500

The level of science, medicine, and a desire for knowledge. You thirst for knowledge becomes insatiable. You don't waste time in activities that do not provide educational value. You begin to categorize all of life and its experiences into proofs, postulates, and theories. The failure of this level is you cannot seem to separate the subjective from the objective, and because of that, you tend to miss the point. You fail to see the forest because you're tunnel-versioned on the trees. Paradoxically, Reason can become a stumbling block for further progressions of consciousness.

Acceptance   350-400

If Courage is the realization that you are the source your life's experiences, then it is here where you become the creator of them. Combined with the skills learned in the Willingness phase, you begin to awaken your potential through action. Here's where you begin to set and achieve goals and to actively push yourself beyond your previous limitations. Up to this point you've been generally reactive to what life throws at you. Here's where you turn that around, take control, and become proactive.

Willingness   310-350

Those people around you that are perpetual optimists - this is their level of consciousness. Seeing life as one big possibility is the cornerstone of those operating here. No longer are you satisfied with complacency - you strive to do your best at whatever task you've undertaken. You begin to develop self-discipline and willpower and learn the importance of sticking to a task till the end.

Neutrality   250-310

Neutrality is the level of flexibility. To be neutral, you are, for the most part, unattached to outcomes. At this level, you are satisfied with your current life situation and tend not to have a lot of motivation towards self improvement or excellence in your career. You realize the possibilities but don't make the sacrifices required to reach a higher level.

Courage 200-250
This is the level of empowerment. It is the first level where you are not taking life energy from those around you. Courage is where you see that you don't need to be tossed to and fro by your external conditions. This empowerment leads you to the realization that you are a steward unto yourself, and that you alone are in charge of your own growth and success. This is what makes you inherently human: the realization that there is a gap between stimulus and response and that you have the potential to choose how to respond.

Pride   175-200
According to Hawkins, since the majority of people are below this point, this is the level that most people aspire to. It makes up a good deal of Hollywood. In comparison to Shame and Guilt, one begins to feel positive here. However, it's a false positive. It's dependent upon external conditions such as wealth, position or power. It is also the source of racism, nationalism, and religious fanaticism.

As multidimensional beings we exist simultaneously in all densities and dimensions. The variable here is awareness. Where is our attention? Are we stuck in attachment to the physical? Are we stuck in our heads? Are we too much heart and not enough "gut"? What scripts are we still playing out that bind us to the realm of karma? Are we denying our emotional bodies or squelching our emotional desires based on a belief they are not spiritual?

The 6D perspective looks lovingly on humanity and does not judge. The service-to-others (STO) urge is spontaneous and natural because we are all One.

The more we desire to experience 5D or higher and put our

attention there, the more our overall vibration will move into 5D or higher. Whether this takes a month or 1000 years is irrelevant since we already exist in 5D and higher, and need only place our awareness there to experience it.

Regarding living in 5D: If it were that easy, we'd all be there already. There's a lot of self-discipline and study that goes into this for most of us. That's why we have spiritual teachers, groups and countless self-help books and techniques. However, the more we focus our attention on our 5D selves, the more we are drawn to those experiences that accelerate our evolution into 5D. Sometimes, those experiences involve going back and healing aspects of self that vibrate in 3D and 4D.

This is a difficult subject because words are inadequate to express anything beyond 5D. I have an inner knowing that there are densities or dimensions beyond 6D, and others have talked about this, but until we experience these directly, any descriptions will fall short.

The part of us that is aware is like the tip of an iceberg. The vast majority of WHO WE ARE lies below, above and beyond the surface. At times we get glimpses of realms beyond the beyond.

Sources:
1. 'Map of Consciousness,' Clestine Chua, *Personal Living*, https://personalexcellence.co/blog/map-of-consciousness/

CHAPTER 9

CONNECTING WITH THE UNIVERSE, BE GROUNDED, OPEN YOUR CROWN CHAUKA, REMOVE THE BLOCKAGE BETWEEN LEFT & RIGHT BRAIN, RAISE YOUR ANTENNA

HEART - "Heart" does not mean the emotions (though it includes our emotions). It refers to our inner orientation, the core of our being. This kind of "heart" is what Jesus was referring to when he told us to store up treasures in heaven instead of on Earth, "for where your treasure is, there also will your heart be." (Matthew 6:21) This is the "heart" Jesus was worried about when he said "from the heart come evil thoughts, murder, adultery, unchastely, theft, false witness, blasphemy." (Matthew 15:19) Jesus observed that our heart can get unEarthed from our actions: "This people honor me with their lips, but their hearts are far from me." (Matthew 15:8) Heart in this sense is the totality of our response.

Our heart is the essence of who we are, the deepest part of which is truly us. It is the source from which our dreams, desires, passions, motives, thoughts, emotions, decisions and actions arise – so it only makes sense that we consider another way to care for our heart by spiritually guarding it. The Bible tells us that our heart determines the course of our life.

Proverbs 4:23 tells us: "Above all else, guard your heart, for everything you do flows from it."

PINEAL GLAND is a pear shaped gland located approx 1" above the center of the browline and 2"-3" into the cranium cavity, where it sets between the left and right halves of the brain.

No one quite knows what to make of the pineal gland. This cone-shaped pea of a gland sits on the roof of the third ventricle of the brain, directly behind the root of the nose, floating in a small lake of cerebrospinal fluid. Because it lies in the center of the brain, neurosurgeons and radiologists have found it a useful landmark for brain surgery.

While the physiological function of the pineal gland has been unknown until recent times, mystical traditions and esoteric schools have long known this area in the middle of the brain to be the connecting link between the physical and spiritual worlds. Considered the most powerful and highest source of ethereal energy available to humans, the pineal gland has always been important in initiating supernatural powers.

The pineal gland is the very key to the highest and divinest consciousness. It is the Single Eye.

In a distant past our pineal gland used to be our third eye and, even more than an eye: a cosmic receiver and sender of multi-dimensional information. The pineal gland is now a tiny gland in the center of our brain, connected with all our senses and the rest of our body. Through the other senses it communicates with the outer world in electrical impulses.

With its spectrum of hormones it regulates our state of consciousness, e.g. waking, sleeping, dreaming, various meditative states including those states in which we may have mystical experiences. The mind and senses are paths for occult energies that work through various psychophysical centers or chakras, among the highest of which is the pineal gland. These centers continue to develop as we evolve towards spirit.

Chapter 9 – Connecting with the Universe, Be Grounded, Open Your Crown Chauka, Remove the Blockage between Left & Right Brain, Raising Your Antenna

So, while the third eye or pineal gland has certain physiological activities in conjunction with the pituitary gland – together they regulate the rhythms of metabolism and growth – it is also the physical organ of intuition, inspiration, spiritual vision, and divine thought. The pituitary gland is the thought receiver and the pineal gland, often called our true master gland, is the thought transmitter.

Activating your pineal gland will help you open to new frequencies, receive heightened information and adjust more easily to transformation.

The more light you can store in your body, the higher your vibration will become. The higher your vibration is, the easier it becomes to elevate your surrounding as well as the people around you. Now is the time to reawaken our pineal gland as a cosmic receiver.

Until relatively recently, it was the subject of much lore as the gateway into the soul or the higher realm, the memory valve, an energy vortex, the main tap for vital fluids and even the source of mental illness.

It was philosopher René Descartes, who first laid claim to the idea that the pineal gland is the seat of the soul, a unique meeting point between body and soul. In modern times, the gland has been consigned to the neurological dustbin, regarded by the scientific community as an evolutionary leftover, the appendix of the brain.

In all higher vertebrates, including humans, the pineal gland secretes melatonin. Production of this hormone is stimulated by darkness and inhibited by light.

The pineal has been called a photo-neuroendocrine transducer, through which a neural signal with environmental information is converted into a chemical message – in this case, to switch on or off the production of melatonin.

Master clock - Melatonin acts as a kind of master clock, regulating our sleep/wake cycle and retarding the ageing process, regulating growth and even maintaining mental stability.

Although scientists realize that the pineal is light-sensitive, it has always been assumed that the light or darkness enters as usual from the rod and cone receptors in the eye retina and makes its way to the gland via the sympathetic nerves. The conventional wisdom is that a small percentage of the impulses from the optic nerve are detoured to the pineal from the visual pathway, and it is this input which controls the production of melatonin.

"The Sedona Effect" - The sun inductively couples to the Earth and to humans. And human energy fields inductively couple to other human fields. First we need an understanding of induction. We can connect our bodies' energy field to Earth's field which in turn connects to the sun and other planets fields, which in turn can connect to the galaxy's core and beyond.

Researcher Serena Roney-Dougal has gathered together some of the most compelling research into the biological means by which the geomagnetic flux of the Earth might cause the pineal gland to allow us to psychically 'tune in.'

Psychedelic gland - Besides melatonin, the pineal gland also produces the 'neuromodulator' chemicals— called beta-carbolines — which affect the brain. Beta-carbolines are both monoamine-oxidase (MAO) inhibitors and serotonin reuptake inhibitors, which means that they prevent the breakdown of serotonin by inhibiting its uptake into the brain's synapses.

This is akin to what doctors claim is the action of selective serotonin reuptake inhibitors (SSRIs) like Prozac.

Some evidence also suggests that the pineal can also manufacture a hallucinogenic substance called 5-methoxydimethyltryptamine (5-methoxy-DMT) from melatonin. What might be the result is a pooling of these amines into the synapses of the brain, causing reactions that are similar to drug-induced hallucinations.

The current view is that neuromodulators need 5-methoxy-DMT and DMT in order to work and that, by blocking MAO, the pineal gland regulates and increases the concentration of serotonin. This regulatory function of blocking one chemical and promoting another is thought to be the catalyst for dreaming.

Several facts suggest that the production of serotonin and melatonin may be in some way involved in psychic phenomena. First, many hallucinogenic substances are chemical sisters to those made by the pineal gland. Yage, or ayahausca, a ceremonial drink made by some Amazon tribes to produce psychic effects for healing, clairvoyance and precognition, is produced from native vines (Banisteriopsis caapi) that are chemically nearly equivalent to the 5-methoxy-DMT in humans.

Sources:
1. Old Soul's Guide to Life, the Universe and Everything' by *Truth Control*, www.truthcontrol.com/articles/old-souls-guide-life-universe-and-everything

2. 'Pineal Gland: Cosmic Antenna,' *Healing Energy Tools*, http://www.healingenergytools.com/
3. The Human Antenna' by Lynne McTaggart, as extracted from her book entitled *The Power of Eight*, https://lynnemctaggart.com/the-human-antenna/

CROWN CHAUKA - CONNECT TO THE UNIVERSE -
The Crown Chakra also commonly known as Sahasrara (a thousand petaled lotus in Sanskrit) is at the top of the ladder in the seven-major chakra system. Situated at the top and slightly above your head, it is the only major chakra that lies outside of the body. The colors violet or white are associated with it. In many pictures, the crown chakra is depicted with an inverted lotus flower or a gold ring that lies on top of the head. Many have views that these images are suggesting that the crown chakra is connected to heaven but extend downwards to us.

Other names for the crown chakra are:
- Spirituality Chakra
- Violet Chakra
- Shunnya
- Niralambapuri
- Gateway to Spirit
- Akasha Chakra
- Sahasrara Padma

Sahasrara is where connection takes place. Here you connect to the universe, Spirit, pure consciousness and yourself at a deeper level. The crown chakra is actually considered to be a portal that opens one to the universal life force energy that exists in the universe. At this chakra, you find awareness, understanding, trust, devotion, inspiration, happiness, positivity, unity, serenity, joy, and the ability to learn.

Chapter 9 – Connecting with the Universe, Be Grounded, Open Your Crown Chauka, Remove the Blockage between Left & Right Brain, Raising Your Antenna

The gateway to spirit is the subtlest of the major chakras. But it is also the point from which all of the other chakras emanate. It is considered to be the receiver and giver of energy and consciousness.

Sahasrara is also where your soul and the body meet and connect to each other.

There are different ideas of the element that is associated with the crown chakra. Some say that this chakra is associated with no element; others say it is associated with thought, and many see it as associated with the cosmos.

When the crown chakra's energy is blocked or depleted one can feel very isolated and depressed. It also shows up as having no inspiration and can lead to a spiritual crisis in an individual.

On the other side, if a person's crown chakra is overloaded or overly energized it can lead to an obsession with spirituality and its practices. Also, individuals can start to have spiritual delusions, a feeling of not being grounded.

It is is important that the crown chakra be balanced. Everything in our lives needs to be balanced to bring about health, happiness, and joy in our lives. In the chakra system when one works on balancing it lets us lead a life where we find the things we need.

The chakra system is a holistic philosophy that provides us the information to lead a healthy balanced life. The chakras in your body constantly need to be worked on. When balanced, a chakra can also fall into a state of depletion or over energized if one does not work on them on a continual basis.

CENTERING EXERCISE PREPRATION

1. Wear comfortable clothing, such as sweats. Remove your belt. Unhook your bra.
2. Sit up straight. Knees level with pelvis.
3. Feet flat on floor.
4. Calfs vertical.
5. Arms at side, on legs or on resting on the arms of the chair.
6. Roll your hips backward, slightly.
7. Align your back so that your neck aligns with the center of your pelvis.
8. Shoulders relaxed but rolled back – this will thrust your heart forward (You should feel as if someone was pushing the back center of your shoulders forward).
9. Pull your belly button toward your spine. (You should feel your heart is being pushed forward)
10. Elongate your body, as if someone is pulling you up from your crown.
11. Close your eyes or Look straight ahead – but have eyes unfocused.
12. Concentrate on your heart by hearing and feeling it beat.

Proper Body Position

Shown for shoulder position - not arms

Final position should look like this

Chapter 9 – Connecting with the Universe, Be Grounded, Open Your Crown Chauka, Remove the Blockage between Left & Right Brain, Raising Your Antenna

Do this for a few minutes and slow down its beat.

13. Breathe from your diaphragm (no shallow breaths). Breathe through your mouth – you should hear the air entering and exiting your lungs. Take deep, slow steady breaths. Count the seconds in and the seconds out. Count four seconds in and four seconds out. Increase the time in and out. Do this for several minutes, while still being centered in your heart.
14. Relax your body, while still maintaining all of the above steps. Start by concentrating to relax your head, then neck, then shoulders, then chest and proceed, part by part, until you are at your toes.
15. Listen to 3rd Eye Chakra music, such as those listed below, while concentrating on your heart beat, breathing and body posture.

Sources
1. https://www.youtube.com/watch?v=VrQD9pJ9BlI
2. https://www.youtube.com/watch?v=aa7sr3ROVCw
3. https://www.youtube.com/watch?v=tU3oAyin8W4

GROUNDING - Do you feel grounded and rooted in your being?

When you are grounded you are not only connected to Mother Earth but you are also rooted in your being and in the essence of who you are.

Being grounded basically means you are centered in yourself and with the physical, mental and emotional space that you are currently in.

Even if you don't necessarily enjoy where you are currently, when you take a moment to center and root your being to the ground, you instantly give yourself a launching pad to spring from.

Having a launching pad allows you to sink deeper into the Earth so you can set your roots in order to branch out and grow taller. Just like a tree, the stronger the roots, the healthier and more lush you can grow.

Often times however, life can bring us certain situations, events or feelings that can knock us off our launching pad. Usually this is temporary and is always to serve a higher purpose.

Grounding can help you to:
- Reduce stress, lethargy and a lack of motivation.
- Increase your emotional and mental health.
- Bring clarity to your life path and purpose.
- Know your own wisdom, thoughts, beliefs and desires.
- Grow stronger, taller and higher in all areas.
- Bring understanding to your situation.
- Reduce feelings of chaos, clutter and indecision.
- Take responsibility for where you are currently situated. Creating a sense of grounding is really about taking responsibility for your life and the events and feelings occurring.

This doesn't need to be a harsh process, but rather one that aligns you with your truth, wisdom and your ability to plan and take action based on how you feel.

GROUNDING EXERCISE - Do the exercises by concentrating on your heart and aligning the heart with the Pineal Gland.
1. Complete the Centering Exercise Preparation.
2. Remain in the sitting position.
3. Roll your pelvis upward at the front.
4. Elongate your body, as if it is being pulled up from the crown. Maintain steadiness.

5. Visualize the crown of your head, as light opens up in a cone that opens upward to the cosmos.
6. Create an open channel from the crown chakra to the bottom of your spine.
7. From your navel visualize a cable of light shooting down through your priformis down into the depth of the Earth. Like a drill of light shooting down and continuing further down, further than you can see or imagine.

BELOW ARE A FEW OTHER EXERCISES TO ACHIEVE GROUNDING:

1. **Grounding Guided Meditation** - Sit on the ground in a comfortable position so you your body connected to the Earth. Close your eyes and imagine your body sinking into the ground below you.

   Feel the support of the Earth and then start to visualize roots coming out of your body and reaching into the ground. See your roots being nourished by the Earth and as you breathe deeply, allow yourself to feel a deeper sense of connection.

   Once you have visualized your roots moving into the ground, take a few deep breaths here before opening your eyes.

2. **Be in Nature** - Spending time amongst the trees and flowers that are rooted deeply within Mother Earth is another way to reconnect your energy and to establish your center to yourself and the environment.

   Consider taking a walk in nature and as you do, feel the weight of your feet in the ground. Feel your feet connected to the Earth as you take each step.

"Walk as if you are kissing the Earth with your feet."- Thich Nhat Hahn.

You may also want to take a few, deep mindful breaths where you imagine your feet sinking deeper into the Earth and taking root amongst the plants.

Try to also heighten your senses to see if you can tune in to the different smells, sights and sounds that are before you. Take the time to really observe the way nature is behaving around you.

Aim to do this for about 5-30 minutes every day and be sure to switch off or leave your cell phone or other devices behind. Instead, use nature as your source of connection.

3. **Walking Barefoot on the Grass** - Don't have much time? Simply walking barefoot on the grass is a great way to 'Earth' or ground yourself, especially if you feel frazzled or have been sitting around technology for a long period of time.

Talking just 5-10 minutes to walk around on the grass can help you to instantly connect and stabilize your energy.

Taking the time to ground your energy can definitely harmonize your soul and help you to reconnect with your essence.

At different times of yours life you may need more or less grounding, however you should always make it a point to center your energy when you are needing to focus or feel motivated, after spending time around technology, chaotic events or disruptive people and when you need to be present or of service to someone else.

Chapter 9 – Connecting with the Universe, Be Grounded, Open Your Crown Chauka, Remove the Blockage between Left & Right Brain, Raising Your Antenna

"To ground is to pour your energies back into the Earth and feel the warm calm of nature entering your body in exchange." – Unknown

Sources:
1. Exercise: 'Third-Eye Meditation – Activating the Pineal Gland' by Bentinho Massaro, https://www.youtube.com > watch
2. lternate Exercises: 'How to Ground Your Energy' by Tanaaz, http://foreverconscious.com/how-to-ground-your-energy

THE PINEAL GLAND - "THIRD EYE" CONNECTION TO THE UNIVERSE

1. Continue on from the Grounding Exercise.
2. Remain in the sitting position.
3. Simultaneously, bring your awareness up to the spine to the crown where the light is rising and extending to the crown chakra.
4. Breathe through your nose so that little valve shuts off the nostrils from the mouth. Breathe through your throat – a deeper sound that through your nostrils.
5. Check your form, straighten down and up, as well.
6. Be receptive to the Earth energy (from your grounding rod) and upward, through the crown chakra out to the cosmos (sun energy).
7. Breathe from the belly, using the diaphragm.
8. Tighten your piriformis muscle (the one you use to stop peeing). Pull it up the center part (between your asshole and the sphincter/penis) toward your upper body, feel its energy being pulled to the pineal gland. Do this periodically, pulling the energy up and bouncing the energy up to the pineal gland.

9. Visualize a blue or purple connection between the piriformis muscle and continue bouncing the energy between the piriformis muscle and pineal gland.
10. Be cognizant of the light (sun/cosmos) energy entering the crown charka. Energy of light and love being received from the universe, through the crown charka.
11. Both energies are coalescing in rings around the pineal gland, rings that are spinning and building and releasing dopamine into your brain.
12. Visualize the pineal gland freeing itself from its sleepiness, releasing melatonin into the brain and body, making you feel free and not as physical.
13. Keep feeling the energy that is being received (love and energy).
14. Visualize a cross that extends from the center of your eyebrows and back through pineal gland to the back cortex (back of head). Then a branch upward to the crown chakra and downward to the piriformis muscle.
15. Periodically contact the piriformis muscle that creates energy upward toward the pineal gland.
16. Visualize a purple energy flow between the piriformis muscle and the pineal gland.
17. Now visual energy entering from the openness of the universe passing through the cone shape of the crown charka. See that energy spiraling down to the pineal gland and upward from the piriformis muscle.
18. There is now a energy and light flowing back and forth and up and down.
19. Create and bounce more energy.
20. See the light grow.
21. You feel yourself changing to be more light, more connection to the universe, realize your purpose. There is no thought, just visualizations.
22. Receive light from the energy that is at ease and receptive and open to the cosmic forces.

23. Your nervous system is awake to its own and it is light wide open to the universe.
24. Feel your light body, more than your physical body. You have reached a higher frequency. You have "lightened" your body and are able to serve the Creator more openly. You are a free agent of the Creator, You are a helper. You are AWAKENED Light. The Creator is with you and you are part of the Creator. You were created from Love Light. You are Love Light.

Source:
1) 'Third-Eye Meditation – Activating the Pineal Gland' by Bentinho Massaro, https://www.youtube.com > watch

REMOVING THE CARD BETWEEN LEFT & RIGHT BRAIN - There is the duel between mental structure and mental freedom; commonly experienced as the duality between the left and right brain when not in sync. Here the duality between your logical thinking mind and your free-thinking and open mind comes to a clash, where thoughts do not balance with each other, but instead create struggle by their dualistic and opposite natures. Unifying these thoughts does not appear simple, but if you can relax into your meditation long enough, you might just start seeing how everything lines up and the way out will become clear.

The Eight of Swords is illustrated as a figure blindfolded unknowingly by his own will, surrounded by sharp swords flying all around him. He is unable to see the path in front of him and seemingly can't escape his own chaos. Yet, the path is right there, if he simply removed his blindfold he could easily break free from his self imposed confusion. The confusion is internal. The biggest problem is that the figure is fixated on the problem, not looking at the solution, and thus continues in his confused state.

This card acts as the blindfold of the figure in the Eight Sword illustration and it is between the left and the right side of the brain. The card (blindfold) represents a state of mental imprisonment which eventually leads to isolation and misunderstandings. The card could, physically, be the membrane (Septum pellucidum) that resides between the two halves of our brain.

The secret of this card is that the way out is actually very simple, if we could only remove our blockages to see this. Another way to look at this in a practical sense is to change our perspective and look at the challenge in a new way, one that is not restricted by the lens of limitation that we are currently viewing them through. Breaking down this card even further, it really speaks to over-thinking the little things, and spending too much time on the details at the expense of the bigger picture.

This exercise uses divine assistance to remove the card, allowing left and right brain to have improved connectivity. The result of removing the card will result in an approximate 30% increase in our spiritual mind. Remember that your heart contains your Soul's soul.

1. Complete steps 1 through 14 of the 3rd Eye/Crown Chakra Exercise.
2. Visualize a blue or purple connection between the piriformis muscle and continue bouncing the energy between the piriformis muscle and pineal gland.
3. Now concentrate on the Pineal Gland and use its collective energy to push the card upward to the Crown Chakra. The Pineal Gland is in the center of the brain and is immediately below the card that separates the two halves of the brain.

4. Once the card has been pushed into the Crown Chakra, your Guardian, Counselor, and the Universe force of light entering the Crown Chakra can "nibble-away" the card.

Both halves of the brain contain consciousness but each has a component of the duel between mental structure and mental freedom, meaning the two haves can slowly recreate the confusion card. Given this, it would be best to complete the above exercise on a periodic basis.

Sources:
1. 'Eight of Swords,' *SpiritScienceCentral*, https://spiritsciencecentral.com/patch-tarot/tarot-directory/eight-swords-tarot/
2. 'Corax Coding,' http://www.corax.com/tarot/ cards/index.html?swords-8
3. 'Biddy Tarot,' https://www.biddytarot.com/tarot-card-meanings/minor-arcana/suit-of-swords/eight-of-swords/
4. 'The Book of Thoth,' http://amzn.to/2wnNDCb
5. 'Learn Tarot,' http://www.learntarot.com/s8.htm
6. 'Esoteric Meanings,' http://www.esotericmeanings.com/eight-of-swords-thoth-tarot-card-tutorial/
7. 'The Golden Dawn,' http://amzn.to/2y37B78
8. 'The Tarot Handbook,' http://amzn.to/2eUpcWM
9. 'Aeclectic Tarot,' http://www.aeclectic.net/ tarot/learn/meanings/eight-of-swords.shtml
10. 'Tarot,' *Wikipedia*, http://www.tarotwikipedia.com/tarot-card-meanings/minor-arcana-swords/eight-of-swords-tarot-card-meanings/

RAISING YOUR ANTENNA - Although the Crown Chakra is shaped like a downward flowing funnel and it receives messages from the universe (inflowing light) and delivers the universe light to the Pineal Gland, you also have an antenna inside the Crown Chakra that projects just above the crown of the Crown Chakra.

The antenna is connected to the pineal gland.

This exercise to raise your antenna consists of the following steps:
1. Complete steps 1 through 14 of the 3rd Eye/Crown Chakra Exercise.
2. Visualize a blue or purple connection between the piriformis muscle and continue bouncing the energy between the piriformis muscle and pineal gland.
3. Now concentrate on the Pineal Gland and use its collective energy to raise your antenna.
4. Keep raising your antenna (a visiting spiritualist, in June 2017, stated that I raised my antenna about 30-feet, on my first try but most first-timers only raise it a few inches).

You may choose to broadcast a question to the universe (don't do what I did, by saying "Is anybody there. Does anybody care") but it is better to take what comes from this enlightening experience, since the universe has been waiting patiently to talk to you. Be prepared that what you receive is not sound but images.

Sources:
1) 'The Human Antenna' by Lynne McTaggart, as extracted from her book entitled *The Power of Eight*. https://lynnemctaggart.com/the-human-antenna/
2) 'An Old Soul's Guide to Life, the Universe and Everything' by *Truth Control*, www.truthcontrol.com/articles/old-souls-guide-life-universe-and-everything
3) 'Pineal Gland: Cosmic Antenna,' *Healing Energy Tools*, http://www.healingenergytols.com/

MEDITATION DOES NOT WORK FOR ME

A person's level of clairvoyance is dependent on the openness of their Pineal Gland (third eye), which is directly affected by energy blockages of at least the three chakras below the Crown Chakras.

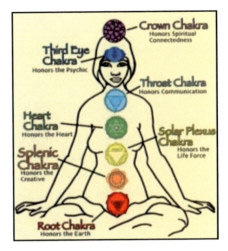

A fully open Pineal Gland (third eye) will allow multiple light rays to stream in, often in strong golden and silver colors. Streams of white light enter the space as information which is received and then interpreted in pictures, messages and higher consciousness in the crown chakra.

The more advanced the practitioner the more expansive the light rays become. However, because the Pineal Gland (third eye) is connected to the first, second and third chakras, if there are channel blockages the functionality of the Pineal Gland (third eye) is greatly restricted.

Blockages can be due to physical injury; muscular, bone and inflammation, and also due to mental energy blocks caused by fear, stress and anxiety.

The location of the blockage determines the difficulty of understanding what is seen during your meditation. It is therefore a good idea to use a chakra meditation or a "Healer" to unblock energy channels before attempting to open the third eye through meditation.

May Take Years of Practice – Pineal Gland Activation (third eye) is a skill that can take many years of practice to master, and most people rarely get past the stage of sitting down to meditate, let alone accessing their Pineal Gland (third eye); so if you've got that far you're more than a third of the way.

What most information regarding Pineal Gland (third eye) meditation neglects to mention is that one should start off with basic meditation first. Cultivating a non-attached, present, centered, balanced state is essential to opening the Pineal Gland (third eye), and therefore it is best to start meditation using guided meditation or binaural beats.

Binaural beats recordings provide the easiest pathway to states of meditation and to the activation of the Pineal Gland (third eye). By using this proven natural science you can effortlessly achieve deep states of meditation, which will ultimately help you access your clairvoyance faster.

Sources:
1. 'How to Activate Your Third Eye Using Meditation Techniques,' *Binaural Beats Meditation*, ttps://www.binauralbeats meditation.com/ third-eye-meditation-techniques/

CHAPTER 10

FALSE 2ND COMING, EARTH, REINCARNATION

FALSE SECOND COMING - Primarily extracted from: The Fake Second Coming By Christi Verismo, Part 15 of 16, http://www.bibliotecapleyades.net/ sociopolitica/ fakesecondcoming/fakesecondcoming15.html

We are now in the times that will finally bring to end an approximate 10,000 years of "semi-consciousness" and regain our full consciousness that we deserve. This will be due to our entire solar system coming into contact with what is known as the "Photon Belt"

The Anunnaki "God" Anu, Human 2.0 creator, will return, just as foretold in the Bible's Book of Revelations.

Our programmed (Human 2.0) minds will connect with the projected imagery of the messages, as was pre-programmed into us by the Anunnaki over 10,000 years ago, when they calculated our spiritual evolution. This perhaps, could be NASA's Blue Beam holographic image of the Messiah sent by satellites, complete with HAARP's voice of *'God'* that is capable of using the language of any country it beams into. So in receiving the projected imagery, we can turn from the affairs of the world and arouse feelings of joy, because of our salvation over the material body of form is part of us – the problem is that the Anunnaki "god" (Dark Force) gave it to us and not Creator God.

Heaven with its 12-gates, as presented in Revelations, will be created by the Dark Force in the 4th Density and come "down" to Earth. The 'chosen ones' (Dark Force) will be gathered into the magnetic fields for 'deliverance.' This would, in effect, "fulfill" the Bible's story, as given to us by the Anunnaki. In addition, after people will be dematerialized and materialized, just as was tested by the Philadelphia Experiment, through using portable briefcase sized dematerialization machines. All of this will be Dark Force's desperate event to insure their ongoing dominance of the Earth.

ESCAPING THE ANUNNAKI AFTER LIFE TRAP OF REINCARNATION FOR THOSE TRAPPED IN DIMENSIONAL CONTROL - Source: 'Escape 'Their TRAP and Set your Soul FREE, Humans Are Free,' humansarefree.com, March 2015,escape-their-trap-and-set-your-soul-free.html

The souls of the human species are trapped in a dimension of control (i.e., what we call "reality") and the afterlife is merely a short break before being recycled back into the chaos. (Similar to how wounded soldiers are sent to the hospital for treatment, before being sent to the front line once again).

It may sound scary to choose not to go to the Light because many of us are afraid of the unknown. Whereas, the Light feels "safe" because we've gone there so many times, and "everybody else" who went there seems to have done just fine.

However, remember that you are multidimensional every night you go to sleep and dream. This is a taste of what is awaiting after we die — except, after we die, we are in charge of our "dreams" and can create consciously what we create unconsciously during REM sleep.

However, this only gives a partial picture, so let's get a little bit more into detail about what I have learned recently on the details about escaping the Afterlife Trap (AIF) once and for all.

Those who have come to the point in their awareness level that they are reading this don't have to worry about getting "stuck" in the ether and become a "lost soul." The reader of this material is beyond that because you know too much.

When you die, you will most probably be approached by your guide of guides as usual, and he or she wants to help you "cross over," and if you allow this, it will lead you through the Tunnel.

In some cases, there are no guides in the beginning, and the Tunnel will open up in front of you, but at a distance.

Normally, souls feel the attraction and gravitation from the Tunnel and start moving toward it, consciously or unconsciously - like a leaf being sucked in by a vacuum cleaner.

WE HAVE CONTROL TO NOT BELIEVE THE DECEPTION, AND RETURN AS A FREE SPIRIT AND NOT A SPIRIT AGAIN TRAPPED IN A CONTROLABLE ANANNAKI CREATED BODY

1. Instead of letting yourself be "hypnotized" by its attraction, turn and look in the opposite direction (you will have 360° vision, and you can still concentrate on looking in a certain direction) and move away from the Tunnel (you do this by "thinking" yourself as moving — it's all about thoughts and intention in this dimension).

   Remember, you, as a soul of Fire, are far stronger than the centrifugal force that pulls you toward the Tunnel. Don't try to fight it — that's not the way to do it. Instead, think yourself away from it!

2. The Tunnel with the Light on the other side of it is a sophisticated hologram, and all you need to do is to think yourself in another direction, and the Tunnel will fade away.

   Soon you will see the Grid as a fuzzy "barrier" in front of

you, or above you (there are no ups and downs or lefts and rights in space). You will also see that it has holes in it — like a Swiss cheese. Move through one of these holes.

3. You will now see the Universe the way it is, i.e. You will now be truly interdimensional. This means you will see a much larger universe than you are used to.

This is possible because you are outside the Grid, and you're not in a programmed body — you are meeting the Universe as a pure Spirit of Fire riding an Avatar, which is your mind.

When astronauts are allowed outside the Grid, they are still restricted by their bodies and will remain in 3-D, but on a slightly higher vibration because the Earth is tilted and the Grid is no longer doing its containment work on these astronauts.

What you experience outside the Grid, as a discarnate spirit, can be quite overwhelming and impressive.

Probably for the first time, you see the Universe as it really is, with the KHAA (Egyptian: The Mother Universe – the VOID) and everything. When you read this, you are still limited with your five senses, but a good idea is to prepare yourself mentally for what is out there. It's not at all going to be a negative experience, just very different!

You will also see the Space War that is going on in the solar system, and you will notice the soldiers fighting in other dimensions, which you now are going to have access to. (In order to prepare, recommend reading the free e-book, *Beyond 2012 — a Handbook for the New Era*).

4. As a Fire riding an Avatar, you are now free to go more or less anywhere in the Universe.

EARTH OF MULTIDIMENSIONAL BEINGS - by Dawn Abel from *MayaMysterySchool* Website. Primarily extracted from: 'Becoming Multidimensional Beings.'

Have you been having prophetic dreams lately? Seeing yourself on a planet with two suns? Seeing areas flooding and helicopters flying above? Talking to beings in your dream state whom you seem to know but don't think you've ever really met? Feeling like you've gained 50 pounds and your body is really dense, not allowing you to move as quickly as you did before? You're not alone.

The other telltale symptom is not only forgetting what you were just about to do, but finding yourself staring at the panel on your car, or at equipment that you've used every day, trying to figure out what it is and what you're supposed to do with it! No, you're not going crazy; you are just spending more time out of this physical reality as your essence is trying to become more accustomed to the new vibration and frequency that will confront us, permanently, very soon.

This is not dream states or even meditation states; I'm talking about those moments, which are increasing beyond your control, where you have lapses in memory and return to your consciousness wondering what you were just on yours way to do when the thought suddenly slipped your mind! For many, the ability to hang onto a linear thought and fulfill the action in this physical plane is becoming harder and more tedious. What this means is we are currently functioning in two realities, straddling our consciousness between the physical Earth and the multidimensional universe, while physically existing in the current Earth plane.

This light shift is actually a physical reality and quantum physics even supports the science that we can be in two places at the same time; in fact, we can be in even more than two places and can transport our body to wherever we wish to be.

The problem is, when we return back to this physical reality in our current bodies, our conscious mind is still disconnected or in a "freeze" state. So as we try to refocus on the familiar, it appears unfamiliar until we've readjusted ourselves to the physical frequency. This is not a onetime deal, this is the program. We are making a transition, like it or not. Either we get with the program or flail around in fear when the time comes. It's not the first time this has happened on this planet. But the powers that be who have known about this, don't want us, the people, to know. That's because keeping people in fear is a tried and true method of keeping people from making the transition and freeing themselves, finally, from the karmic cycle of master-slave. If you leave your body in fear, you're fodder for the next program. And likeminded souls, including masters and slaves, travel in likeminded circles.

U.S. Administration, the world fundamentalists and Dark Side cabals believe they are hastening the "end times" program, which will bring about their salvation, they are actually creating very bad karma for themselves and will find themselves in the same restricted, 3-D reality, fighting the same wars and playing the same games until they figure out the program and find the *Christ* light in their hearts.

Not everyone will choose to stay on Earth. Some are here only as observers and ascended masters, who will move onto other realms following this transition. In other words, been there, done that, time to move on and "get a life"; that is, a more ascended one. There will be no *final judgment* by Creator *God*; you are your own judge. You own contract (Chapter 2 - Earth Life Preparation) that you made before you came down here and your ensuing actions while you're here will determine the options you'll have next.

Will the transition be painful? If that was part of your contract (Chapter 2 - Earth Life Preparation) or you didn't fulfill it and you needed to experience pain, there will be pain.

But once you are a free spirit (not on the recycle path) and the physical body is gone, you will be free, and able to assess whether you met your own contract, and then move on accordingly. While you will no longer have a physical body that feels pain, your soul, reviewing your deeds, may well experience "memory" pain and thus recycle into another program where you will have another few thousand millennia or so to try to get it right, yet again. We are all multidimensional beings; we've just denied that part of ourselves through our linear, institutional programming. Many are waking up and realizing there's life after Earth. In fact, that's really the only life there is because the body is only temporary housing.

We need only shed our self-imposed prison gowns to realize that we've all been fooled into fear and intolerance as a control mechanism to keep us unaware and in the dark. This whole 3-D scenario was really only a program that was set up by low-vibration entities to feed themselves and their very powerful institutions that are trying to control our current master-slave reality.

In the end, we're the students who—to graduate to the next level—have to wake up, realize that the game's over, and free ourselves from the shackles of 3-D. That's what the Frequency shift (to a 5-D world) and multidimensionality is all about.

In the mean time, keep looking forward and focus on kindness, peace and harmony. That is the reality you will find yourself in when all has been said and done.

CHAPTER 11

BEING AN OLD SOUL IN A YOUNG SOUL WORLD, CHALLENGES BEFORE ENTERING THE 4TH DENSITY

WHAT IS AN OLD SOUL? - There are some people who don't quite fit the mold of those around them. Perhaps Old Souls feel isolated or alone or just that Old Souls weren't entirely in the same realm as Old Soul peers. The truth is age has no bearing on whether someone is an Old Soul. If Old Soul's soul has been incarnated many times, it's had more experiences. Most Old Souls feel certain disconnect from the Earth, and most are inherently aware that they're different. In the various online quizzes, Arlene results in being a Soul that is the oldest in the quiz as being 100,000 to 200,000 years old. But reading Appendix 1, Arlene's Story, one will see that she was at the event that destroyed some of the planets in her solar system, approximately 22-million years ago.

WHAT ARE THE CHARACTERISTICS OF AN OLD SOUL?

Yearns for a Place to Belong - For some Old Souls, the world feels alien. They find it hard to understand people, why such chaos and misery exists and how it is allowed and sometimes encouraged to continue. They long to find a place where they feel like they belong, a space filled with freedom and liberation. This often results in the feeling that this world is not their true home.

Has a Strange Love for Other Time Periods - Has almost this nostalgia for other times or countries or cultures. Old Souls think of them fondly, and often say Old Souls were born in the wrong decade, either past or future.

Most Likely a Solitary Loner- Old Souls are not usually interested in what other people are doing. They tend to hate making friends and find it hard to relate with others. Because of this, Old Souls find themselves alone most of the time. However, they'd prefer it this way. People tend to drain their energy.

The Old Souls have a tendency to think a lot about everything which leads them to a more solitary existence. This reflection is hugely positive. Old Souls can learn from their actions and the actions of those around them, which gives them insight into countless situations, which is one of the reasons why they feel so old at heart. Old Souls have learned many lessons simply through their own thoughts.

Seeks Out Truth, Wisdom and Knowledge - This might seem a little bit noble and self-centered, but Old Souls usually cling to the intellectual side of life. Philosophical thought and deep thinking are more meaningful than last night's basketball scores.

They have a sense of life's transience. Old Souls gravitate towards intellectual pursuits. They see the power in knowledge and the happiness that comes from wisdom. Going after this kind of satisfaction is much more fulfilling for Old Souls than engaging in gossip or anything materialistic.

Not Materialistic - Materialism tends to bore Old Souls. Fame, wealth, and having the fanciest car aren't a huge concern.

Tends to be Interested in Spirituality - Even if Old Souls don't identify with a particular religion or dogma, their focus and value is always on the immaterial: how one thinks, what one feels, etc., as opposed to what is. Sees reality as a movable thing dependent on how one is and not the other way around.

Chapter 11 – Being an Old Soul in a Young Soul World, Challenges Before Entering the 4th Density

Not Scared of Death - Old Souls know they're going to die. They understand the transience of life. However, instead of being afraid of this fact, they use it to power them. Knowing they're going to die inspires them to follow their dreams. Also, they know that there is life after Death.

Extremely Intuitive – They just "know" things and always have. Knows the right answers, how other people are feeling, what we're all really doing here in an existential sense. There's just this kind of knowledge and wisdom that Old Souls seem to have, without really developing it from anywhere (that Old Souls are conscious of!).

Savors the Quiet Moments in Life - Old Souls most enjoy reading, handwritten journals, candle-lit dinners with friends, wearing one's favorite cotton shirt. It's the simple, little things that make Old Souls happiest, and that they try to fill their life with the most.

Highly Introspective – They do not know anything other than self-growth and improvement. Old Souls are constantly evaluating their feelings, trying to understand the human condition more and more and push themselves to be better.

Finds them thinking about everything all the time. Old Souls tend to reflect and learn from their actions and the actions of others.

Sees the Bigger Picture - Old Souls don't get lost in the superficial aspects of life. They look at life from a bird's eye view of seeing the most logical path to take. Old Souls know the issues in life are just speed bumps and they only increase the amount of happiness to be experienced in the future.

Wants To Understand the Root or Purpose of Everything - Old Souls don't accept things on the surface; they deeply desire to understand them and their origins. This makes Old Souls prime for enjoying history, or art, or English, or on a more existential level, to be constantly meditating on why we're here, and for what purpose.

A "Healer" Even if they don't do "healing" work by trade (think: healthcare, psychiatry) Old Souls are the person everyone turns to when they're having a problem. People just tend to spill their lives to Old Souls, and the advice Old Souls give tends to be well-received.

Often Eccentric - Old Souls walk to the beat of their own drum, but not in a loud, rebellious or juvenile way – that is just the nature of who they are. They have a vastly different outlook from those around them. Old Souls see through the fallacies of social conditioning and walk through life seeking for the "truth" or reality of existence that has often been obscured through religious, political and cultural teachings. Whether they have an odd fashion sense, strange mannerisms, unorthodox perspectives or seemingly peculiar beliefs, Old Souls are certainly different from the rest. However, far from being a party of one, Old Souls still appreciate acceptance and tolerance of who they are.

As Connected as Old Souls Feel about Themselves, Old Souls Sometimes Feel Disconnected From the World Around Them - Old Souls don't think the way most people do, and they certainly don't value what most people do, either. It sometimes feels like Old Souls just don't belong and it's usually from this feeling that a lot of self-connection and inner-exploration grows. Old Souls are able to connect with others beyond surface tastes and personality similarities without being able to create a profound connection with someone. They will usually move on after the other has learned the lessons they've shared.

Tends to be Brutally Honest- Old Souls value honesty highly as they believe it to be an immensely important facet in all things and all people, including themselves. They often don't hesitate to point things that embarrass others, and they prefer to share their thoughts and feelings rather than repressing them.

Comes Across as Blasé or Indifferent-They don't take life as seriously as others, often adopting the motto of "Don't worry, be happy." The reality is that everything fades and passes away, no matter how wonderful or terrible. Therefore, the Old Soul doesn't see much of a point in becoming overly attached to the outcome of situations, whether positive or negative. For this reason, it is common to misinterpret the Old Soul as being uncaring or apathetic because they don't share the same extremes in emotion as others. The truth is that they are simply enjoying the ride in their own balanced way.

Gives and Expects Freedom - The beautiful thing about being an Old Soul is that they give everyone complete reign over their birth right: freedom. Old Souls are rarely controlling, demanding or possessive, and they prefer instead to give all their undivided freedom to others without conditions – all they expect is honesty. They will support ones dreams and desires and will stand by their plans and pursuits, but they also expect others to do the same for them.

Knows There's Another Way To Do Things - Old Souls often say things like, "I have a feeling this will work," or "there's no harm in trying." People may view Old Souls suggestions as outdated but Old Souls know that sometimes, just sometimes, the tried and tested ways of doing things are best. If it isn't broke... Old Souls feel that not all problems require a new and innovative solution, and going round in circles when the answer may be staring them in their face is usually a waste of valuable time, and energy. Old Souls have no problem trying out new things, but know, too, that oldies can also be goodies.

Gives Advice Well Beyond One's Years - Old Souls somehow seem to know how to do things they haven't even done themselves. It's like Old Souls have lived before, and just know how it all works. People often look at Old Souls with that "how do they know?" expression and Old Souls respond with a confident, "I just know!" Truth is, Old Souls just know, but don't know how they know. Those people who come to Old Souls for advice, though somewhat freaked out by Old Souls amazing prophetic powers to impressively offer solutions and predict outcomes. They trust OLD Souls wholeheartedly and don't doubt an Old Souls authenticity.

Thinks Things Through - Even the most impatient of people will need to think things through even if they are an Old Soul at heart. Old Souls need that time to mull it over in their head. It's an important part of their to-do process, and it enables them to move forward in the direction most in sync with their mind, body and soul. To Old Souls, not being able to think things through, even a little leaves them feeling uneasy, and that does nothing to help.

Has the Ability to Adapt and Accept, Rather than Resist... But Won't be Used - Old Souls can put up with a lot in life often because they have developed the ability to accept rather than to constantly resist everything that comes their way. The Old Soul rarely plays the role of the self-sacrificing martyr and often moves on to more fulfilling connections. Their philosophy is "If it doesn't work out, then just move on." This is true even in love. If it is not working out, the Old Soul just walks away without even giving a reason.

Inspires All to be a Better Person - When all has been said and done, Old Souls give more than they take. An Old Soul will leave others that they come in contact with as though they are a better, smarter, wiser, more improved and a wholer version of themselves than what they first met the Old Soul.

Doesn't Like To Go Out Just For The Sake Of Going Out - It's quality over quantity for Old Souls. Old Souls love to go out and have fun, but going out because others feel it is required or Old Souls look boring if they don't, holds no merit for Old Souls. When they go out, they like to experience something; something that resonates with their way of perceiving the world and challenges them. Old Souls happily spend money on things that give them wonderful experiences and broaden their horizons. Going out just because, seems pointless to Old Souls; they would rather save their time, and money, and do something of quality.

Appreciates Old Literature - Old Souls respect the classics. They are often found getting euphorically high from old books. Old Souls have probably sniffed a few old books in their time, and they don't care who sees. For Old Souls, old literature should be respected and valued; they hold history and historical experience between their pages and deserve to be exalted.

Has Old Ears - Old Souls love and appreciate the classics and have a longing for the musicality of those nostalgic tunes. Old Souls record (that's right, record!) collection looks like a retro music store. Probably only 10% of their collection consists of what Old Souls refer to as "nowadays" music, the rest are from decades gone by. Old Souls know only a handful of today's artists, and that's only because they haven't heard an album yet to rival their favorite Grateful Dead album, or their favorite Frank Sinatra track. Old Souls don't go out of their way to avoid modern music; it just doesn't seem to whet their appetite. So Old Souls will happily play Janis Joplin or Nat King Cole all the way home!

Sees No Need In Being Unnecessarily Stressed - Old Souls don't invite drama just because it makes them feel alive, no, Old Souls would much prefer to live without it. Old Souls appreciate the quiet and invite peace. It becomes apparent to them that the world views stress and busyness as being productive. But Old Souls know that being productive has nothing to do with being crazy busy or stressed, but everything to do with how well one utilizes their time. So Old Souls are mindful about what they spend their hours doing, and make sure they are doing something worthwhile, and not just keeping busy for busy sake.

Loves To Meet New People - To Old Souls, talking to people is enriching and adds to their experience of the world. This isn't because Old Souls just can't help chit chatting, but more so because Old Souls are genuinely fascinated by those they share this planet with, who can offer different perspectives. Old Souls love being able to swap stories with people they have only just met. Plus, it also serves to make those trips to the bank all the more interesting!

Values Deep Connections - For Old Souls, it's all about quality over quantity. Old Souls require a deeper connection with those around them in order to feel any connection at all. Half-hearted friendships, surface-level relationships and fly-by-night hook-ups are not their thing. Old Souls value the essence of deeper friendships and long lasting relationships.

Loves Learning – Nothing gets Old Souls going more than learning more about themselves, other people and the world around them. For Old Souls learning is growth, and growth is part of life. Old Souls approach learning from the understanding that it doesn't have to lead anywhere, for example, a degree or certificate. Sure, those things are great and offer a sense of accomplishment, but for Old Souls it's the act of learning something new and wonderful that motivates them, not the initials after their name!

Doesn't See The Fuss About The Latest Craze - Following others just to fit in? Where's the fun in that? To Old Souls, being a style chaser or tech follower is something they can never quite get their head around. Sure they may even own a Kindle or may have an ipad, but they use them as a research tool, not for social media, because they miss the feel (and smell) or the real thing, and a computer works just fine. They don't really care whether they are an early adopter or a late comer. None of the things defines them, and Old Souls are okay with that.

Values The Company Of Those Older Than Themselves - Old Souls want to drink in their wisdom and hang on to their every word as they tell of their stories, laugh at their accounts of old trends, and cry at the war stories. Old Souls reminisce with them about long lost loves, and actually listen to their pearls of wisdom. At a time when we seem to have less and less time for the more mature among us, the Old Soul has nothing but time to give. That's because Old Souls appreciate what they have to share, and let's be honest, Old Souls secretly wish for a time when life seemed so simple.

They Are The Epitome Of Calm - Old Souls are the steadfast ones, the ones that neither sway, nor topple, even in a crisis. Old Souls probably say things like, "Slow is smooth, and smooth is fast," and tell people to "Get a grip!" Too everyone else, Old Souls appear disconnected, but to those who know their souls well, Old Souls are actually hard at work. They just work differently. Old Souls have learned that nothing actually gets done if everyone is running around losing their heads; someone needs to be the calm force. This is just how Old Souls make sense of what is happening. Old Souls stop. Wait. Listen. Then decide what steps to take next.

Truly Understands What It Means To Give - To Old Souls there's no better way to live, than to give. Giving time, or money or those things Old Souls simply have no need for is the most rewarding thing anyone can do with their short time on Earth. It isn't an ego thing, far from it. For Old Souls, giving is the purest act of love. Plus, Old Souls see no point in holding on to things they can't take with them, so Old Souls are more than happy to travel light!

Very Optimistic - Old Souls probably will never not see the world through rose-colored glasses, and Old Souls wouldn't have it any other way.

Tends To Be a Homebody - Old Souls enjoy a nice night out on the town, but at the end of the day, having a home in which Old Souls feel comfortable and happy is of the upmost importance to them.

Most Times Wants to "Get on With It" - Old Souls don't waste time asking why. After they have thought things through, Old Souls move ahead, confident in the knowledge that they have done all they needed to do to get going. Old Souls don't waste time in trying to justify it to themselves or anyone else. Old Souls have little time and patience for the nonsensical and would prefer to utilize their time getting things done, rather than sitting around talking about getting things done. In the end, Old Souls understand that whatever they do,

Chapter 11 – Being an Old Soul in a Young Soul World, Challenges Before Entering the 4th Density

they trust that all things will work out just as they are supposed to, and they don't want to question that wonderful process.

BEING AND OLD SOUL IN A YOUNG SOUL WORLD - Old Souls live on a planet where the average soul age is Young. Old Souls are good at almost anything they do. And their work and hobbies are usually oriented to personal growth, teaching, writing or bringing beauty of some sort into the world.

The problem is that we live on a planet that consists of Baby Souls, Young Souls, and Mature Souls. And, thus, the Old Soul needs to understand what drives each of these Soul Groups.

INFANT SOULS (10%) deal with issues of survival; they do not yet have a basis for making sense of what is "out there"—they only know that it is "not me." They are innocent, untarnished by culture, purely instinctive, fearful, withdrawn, without conscience, and sometimes violent. Infant Souls often live on the fringes of society, such as Ethiopia, New Guinea, Cambodia, and areas near the Equator. Their experience of life is simple, earthy, primitive, and mystical. Without loving guidance from older souls who teach those the difference between right and wrong, Infant Souls may react violently to perceive threats.

BABY SOUL (23%) organizations include most government agencies, the Ku Klux Klan, the National Rifle Association, and groups such as Rotary Clubs. They have a sense of self-importance. Aboriginal populations tend to be Infant Souls and they seek countries, such as those in Australia, Borneo, Ethiopia, the Amazon Basin, and the Sudan. Baby Souls tend to incarnate in Latin countries such as Argentina, Brazil, Haiti, and Central and South America in general. Baby Souls also predominate in China, India, Indonesia, in Muslim countries such as Iran, Iraq, Libya and much of the Middle East, and in African countries such as Ghana, the Ivory Coast, Liberia and

Nigeria. Baby Souls need rules & regulations, structures, direction, "authorities" and frameworks within which to live, they create them and impose them on everyone. Or they get the Old Soul lawmakers to ban it, who will because they don't need the items the Baby Souls want to ban. Things like gays, pot, and nude beaches terrify Baby Souls, who pull out their Bibles and quote scriptures at the poor gays, who just want to be left alone. Their hit list is endless-pot, abortion, euthanasia, and smoking. For every freedom, there's a law limiting it, and more laws pour out from the Baby Souls every day. The problem is that Baby Souls are so sure they are right, that they think they're right for us, too. It's not easy being a Baby Soul. Their greatest constraint comes with religion, as witnessed by Baby Souls like Jerry Fallwell, Oral Roberts and Jimmy Swaggart. (According to the Michael Entity, Jim and Tammy Fae Bakker are first level Young Souls still operating as Baby Souls). Baby Soul Priests threw nine million of us into the "flames of purification" because our souls were apparently in mortal danger of eternal damnation, or so they told us. Also, Baby Souls are compulsive about neatness and germs, not realizing that 100 percent of all illness is neurotic (all in the mind) in origin. But they worship doctors as gods, and sacrifice themselves to the medical industry, losing breasts, prostate glands and ovaries to the knife.

YOUNG SOULS (32%) includes most of Corporate America. Young Souls have a driving ambition to acquire the most toys. Young Souls pop up where science and economies are hot, such as Australia, Canada, some European countries, Hong Kong, Israel, Japan, Mexico, Taiwan, South Korea, and Vietnam, plus progressive Arab states such as Oman and Saudi Arabia. Some areas of the U.S. are comfortable for Young Souls, such as California, especially LA, Silicon Valley, and Seattle, although the rest of the U.S. is shifting from Young Souls to Mature. For Young Souls the main issues are power, prominence and wealth. Who has the most powerful army, the tallest skyscraper, the biggest diamond, the most gold, and the largest oil reserves.

Chapter 11 – Being an Old Soul in a Young Soul World, Challenges Before Entering the 4th Density

And if it's not us, let's go to war so that we can have it. After all, Young Soul warriors make up the largest population block in the United States, exemplified by George W. Bush, a Young Soul Warrior (with Goal = Dominance, Mode = Perseverance, Challenge = Arrogance). Perfect presidential material! The Young Soul credo of "I win, you lose" has brought us the adversarial legal system, dreadful pollution, gas-guzzling SUVs, and a business management system corrupted into a money-making machine for the few. Talking of corruption, classic Young Souls Ferdinand and Imelda Marcos, late of the Philippines, siphoned billions out of their country, while most of their subjects lived in squalor and poverty. But again, it's not easy being a Young Soul. They are compulsive about appearances and the trappings of success, so they work long hours to buy the biggest, the best, the fastest, and the most. Also, a strong identification with the physical body brings terror at the first wrinkle or gray hair. Sagging breasts, balding or crow's feet are all alarms that send Young Souls to cosmetic surgeons, also Young Souls with a taste for SUVs and BMWs. And the beat goes on.

MATURE SOULS (24%) include ecological groups such as Greenpeace and the Sierra Club. They have a fascination with their own dramas. Mature Souls favor countries that have the basics handled and are exploring sociological issues, such as Belgium, Denmark, England, Finland, Greece, Holland, Italy, New Zealand, Norway, Russia, Sweden and most of the United States. We have much to thank Mature Souls for. Finally, Mature Souls can see and appreciate others' points of view, and don't see others as "the enemy." They bring mature themes in music (Paul McCartney, Janis Joplin, Bruce Springsteen and Madonna), in art (Vincent van Gogh and Paul Gauguin) and in literature (J.D. Salinger and Truman Capote). They also bring us crusaders such as Ralph Nader and Gloria Steinem, not to mention passionate actors such as Elizabeth Taylor, Richard Burton, Kevin Costner, Russel Crowe, and Robert DiNero.

Most notably, Mature Souls are into "rights"-civil rights, gay rights, immigrants' rights, unborn children's rights, animal rights and the rights of any minority without a voice. But now the nagging questions of "Who am I?" and "Why am I here?" begin to plague the Mature Soul, who doesn't yet have the Old Soul's answers. This brings emotional angst, confusion and pain, which in turn leads to drugs, alcohol and suicide. Sean Penn, Robert Downey Jr., and Woody Allen are examples of Mature Soul angst. And James Dean, Princess Diana, Jimi Hendrix, Janis Joplin and Jim Morrison are examples of Mature Souls who would still be with us if their flight plans hadn't called for an early departure.

OLD SOULS (11%) see the big picture and realize how truly tiny is our role in it. We see things as they are, and can't get puffed up with our own self-importance. It's not that we don't care. In fact, we are the most caring soul age, as witnessed by Old Soul peace activists Sting, Jerry Garcia, John Lennon and Yoko Ono. Old Souls enjoy such countries as Iceland, Switzerland, and some pockets in the U.S., such as Oregon, Washington and northern California, and in spiritual enclaves such as Santa Fe, Taos, Sedona, Atlanta, the Florida Keys and Boulder, Colorado. Old Souls see nothing wrong with being gay, pot, nude beaches, etc.

So, here we Old Souls live within Baby Soul rules, Young Souls greed and competitiveness, and Mature Soul angst, but at least we know what's going on and can make adjustments and allowances for the younger souls.

CHALENGES TO BRING ABOUT A SPIRITUAL SOCIETY in the 4th DENSITY - So far, we have focused on being a spiritual individual, enlarging and redefining our beliefs, which will change our day-to-day reality. We, as 5th and 6th Density Beings, are in the process of shifting the Earth and its inhabitants into a whole new level of reality termed the 5th

Dimension in which consciousness of love, compassion, peace and spiritual freedom prevails. However, apart from a few spiritual groups, we have no real societal support. But, projecting a few years into the future, suppose people such as Old Souls become the norm. What would society look like then?

In order to "see" this new view, we need to examine how several societal issues and institutions would change if a spiritual worldview prevailed, beginning with the institution actually charged with our spiritual welfare-organized religion.

Organized Religion - Organized religions will be the first thing to go with life in a spiritual society. The word "religion" literally means to "bind back" in the context of our relationship with God. So their professed purpose is to teach us what God is and then how we can appease it to get a passing grade on Judgment Day. However, their approach is to separate our soul from its own divinity, so that the soul can stand apart from it, feel guilty about being separate from it, and then worship it from a distance, in a very specific way-their way. And they condemn any other way of worshipping that fictional deity. But it gets much worse.

Their notions of what that deity is are extremely narrow and limited. First they teach that their judgmental and vengeful God wants something from us, but how can God possibly want something from us? What can this being possibly need? That we behave in a certain way, we're told. And if we don't act in that way, then God will impose sanctions on us, such as not letting us into heaven. Why on Earth would the Creator make us human and imperfect-and then punish us for being that way? Doesn't make much sense, does it? This is the "god" that the Anunnaki gave us via the Sirians. We will be told that there is a Universal Creator God, One Source (refer to Chapter 2).

The Spiritual Society and Children - Life in a spiritual society would acknowledge that the souls of children choose their parents for reasons of genetics, environment, imprinting and exploring karma, and that the child's soul makes a contract with the parents' souls. This contract is binding, and can be broken only at the soul level.

Such a society would also know that the first trimester of pregnancy is a trial period on both sides, so miscarriage and abortion have no consequences. So don't be needlessly consumed with guilt and/or grief. It's all just the Creator learning more about itself.

The parent/child spiritual contract can be voided if the incoming soul finds that the fetus is not viable for some reason, but again, this is all okay at the soul level because that soul fragment was part of a soul group and have incarnated together countless times before ... and will do so countless times again. In cases of miscarriage, that same soul fragment often shows up in a later pregnancy so, from the soul's perspective, it's just a tiny delay.

In a spiritual society, parents would know that the incoming soul chose them specifically and would view themselves as "stewards" to give the incoming soul time to develop its ego-personality and worldview, and become self-sustaining. From this perspective, there can be no question of "ownership" of a child.

Spiritual parents would know that a baby's mind is already forming while still in the womb, and is recording every energetic nuance in the Subconscious Mind, so they would ensure that the mother is stress-free. Because the new Subconscious Mind is already recording everything in its environment, parents would guard that carefully, allowing in only what will bolster the child's self-esteem and self-worth. In addition to health and nutrition, prenatal classes would also include telepathy so that parents can also get a head start on forming their relationship with the new child.

The New Children - As part of life in a spiritual society, a new subspecies of human began showing up in mass in the 1980s, with the frontal wave occurring in the mid to late 1940's. Variously called Starseed and Star Children, they are also known as Indigo Children because of the color of their auras. In addition, they seem much older than their years, and have a disconcerting gaze that "looks right through you." They also display enhanced psychic abilities such as telepathy, precognition, psycho-kinesis, clairvoyance, powerful intuition, and the ability to affect electrical devices such as street lamps, computers, body scanners and watches. They also have a comfort and familiarity with off-world events and higher dimensions.

The Spiritual Society and Earth - For millennia, every civilization on the planet has embraced beliefs about Earth and where we go when our turn comes. The Romans went to the Elysian Fields, the Vikings to Valhalla and Pagans to the Summerlands. Today, in the West, Christianity gives us a pretty insipid "heaven," and the medical profession is no help at all. Instead, they pour all their efforts into delaying the inevitable, little realizing that the soul has already pre-ordained the time and means of Earth (except in cases of suicide).

In hospitals (and to a lesser extent, hospices), people tread lightly around the D-word, and the staff feel that each crossing is a loss for them and a victory for the Reaper. In fact, unless one has committed monstrous acts while alive, going to the soul plane is a cause for great celebration, not the usual wailing and mourning. So why is this fact not in the consensus? Because the Judeo-Christian model of reality does not allow for pre-existence of the soul. Christian dogma asserts that the soul begins only at birth (or maybe conception) and at death goes into a state of limbo, waiting Judgment Day.

Also, Christianity makes no allowance for communication between the living and the deceased, which is commonly practiced by aboriginal people, whereby those who have crossed over offer invaluable guidance to those still on the Earth plane. The former watch over the latter, with love and concern. For example, on an episode of *Crossing Over* with John Edward, a woman's deceased husband warned her of faulty wiring in her basement following a flood.

The Spiritual Society and Grief - Grief is really about change, and the most obvious change comes when someone we love dies or disappears from our life. But it also comes when one becomes suddenly jobless or homeless after a natural disaster. Grief is the process of adjusting to the new situation. And that takes time. Of course, life goes on; eating and breathing happen, just minus the person/job/house/pet is missing. No question, it's rough to be cruising along and suddenly life takes a sharp right turn and one is fighting for survival. Of course, each soul wrote this in their own life's flight plan (Chapter2) but that's no help when one is in emotional quicksand.

So, grieving is being confronted by change and having to adjust to it—one's mate dies or leaves, or a tornado moves one's house to the next state. Unbidden, unwanted change, drastic life rearrangement, major stress makes one adjust. Of course, anger and denial are options, too, but acceptance and adjustment are the sane responses. And while one is accepting and adjusting, ask "Now why have I pulled this into my life? What did I plan to learn? How did I intend to grow?"

The Spiritual Society and Sex - Apart from organized religion, in no other area of life are we so messed up as we are about sex. First, gender is possible only on the physical plane, for on all other dimensions, creator-souls are made up of radiant, male, yang energy and receptive, female, yin energy.

Second, having two genders is local to the Earth plane, and the species on the physical planes of other planets can have from one to five genders. Having only two genders makes for the maximum karmic potential. And the need for sex between a member of each gender in order to create a new member of the species greatly magnifies that karmic potential. So, what we take for granted as "just the way it is" is actually the result of enormous forethought and planning on the part of us as creator-souls in order to maximize challenges and the need for matching resources.

According to the designers of our species, the primary purpose of sex is the energetic union of two people, with procreation coming second (which knocks the Catholic stance towards contraception on the head). Combining Divine union and creating children was a very interesting choice.

For life in a spiritual society, it comes closest to exploring the true gift of sex between two people as a means of focusing energy and using it to experience our own soul and merger with our partner. Those on the soul plane report that soul merger is the highest form of ecstatic bliss possible, and is infinitely beyond our ability to imagine while still on the Earth plane. In comparison, an orgasm is little more than a sneeze! But given the numerous past lives of a multidimensional soul, sex is not a driving source or goal. This kind of the "been there, done that" and it was not that exciting of a goal driving event.

Sources:
1) Michael Teaching, 'Soul Age' (several other articles), online at http://www.michaelteachings.com/soul_age_index.html

2) Several books including *Journey of Old Souls Soul: A Channel Explores the Michael Teachings* Paperback – April 23, 2013 by Shepherd Hoodwin (Author), Jon Klimo (Foreword), John Friedlander (Foreword)
3) 'An Old Soul's Guide to Life, the Universe and Everything' by *Truth Control* on December 5th, 2013, a 16 Chapter online book, http://www.truthcontrol.com/articles/old-souls-guide-life-universe-and-everything
4) '15 Signs You are an Old Soul,' Patricia C. Osei-Oppong, *Lifehack*,www.lifehack.org/749842/why-some-people-have-a-lack-of-empathy-and-how-to-deal-with-them?ref=sidebar_bottom

Chapter 12

THE HUMAN ENERGY FIELD (AURA) / LEVELS OF CONCIOUSNESS / DENSITIES/VIBRATIONAL FREQUENCIES / QUALITY OF OUR SPIRITUAL LIGHT

THE HUMAN ENERGY FIELD (AURA) – An aura or Human energy field is, according to New Age beliefs, a colored emanation said to enclose a human body or any animal or object. In some esoteric positions, the aura is described as a subtle body. Psychics and holistic medicine practitioners often claim to have the ability to see the size, color and type of vibration of an aura.

In New Age alternative medicine, the human aura is seen as a hidden anatomy that affects the health of a client, and is often understood to comprise centers of vital force called chakra. Such claims are not supported by scientific evidence and are pseudoscience. When tested under controlled experiments, the ability to see auras has not been shown to exist.

The concept of auras was first popularized by Charles Webster Leadbeater, a former priest of the Church of England and a member of the mystic Theosophical Society. Leadbeater had studied theosophy in India, and believed he had the capacity to use his clairvoyant powers to make scientific investigations. He claimed that hydrogen atoms are made of six bodies contained in an egg-like form. In his book *Man Visible Invisible* published in 1903, Leadbeater illustrated the aura of man at various stages of his moral evolution, from the "savage" to the saint. In 1910, Leadbeater introduced the modern conception of auras by incorporating the Tantric notion of chakras in his book *The Inner Life*.

In the following years, Leadbeater's ideas on the aura and chakras where adopted and reinterpreted by other Theosophists such as Rudolf Steiner and Edgar Cayce, but his occult anatomy remained of minor interest within the esoteric counterculture until the 1980s, when it was picked up by the New Age movement.

In 1977, American esotericist Christopher Hills published the book *Nuclear Evolution: The Rainbow Body*, which presented a modified version of Leadbeater's occult anatomy. Whereas Leadbeater had drawn each chakra with intricately detailed shapes and multiple colors, Hills presented them as a sequence of centers, each one being associated with a color of the rainbow. Most of the subsequent New Age writers will base their representations of the aura on Hill's interpretation of Leadbeater's ideas. Chakras became a part of mainstream esoteric speculations in the 1980s and 1990s. Many New Age techniques that aim to clear blockages of the chakras were developed during those years, such as crystal healing and aura-soma. Chakras were, by the late 1990s, less connected with their theosophical and Hinduist root and more infused with New Age ideas. A variety of New Age books proposed different links between each chakras and colors, personality traits, illnesses, Christian sacraments, etc. Various type of holistic healing within the New Age movement claim to use aura reading techniques, such as bioenergetics, energy medicine, energy spirituality, and energy psychology.

The book *The Third Eye*, written by Cyril Henry Hoskin under the pseudonym Lobsang Rampa, claims that Tibetan monks opened the spiritual third eye using trepanation in order to accelerate the development of clairvoyance and to allow to see the aura. It also includes body gazing techniques purported to help achieve aura visualization.

Baron Wilhelm von Reichenbach discovered several properties unique to this human energy field, which he called the odic force, and would later be ascribed to the subtle body. He determined that it shared similar properties to the electromagnetic field, which had previously been investigated by James Clerk Maxwell, one of the fathers of electricity. The odic human energy field was composed of polarities or opposites, as is the electromagnetic field. In electromagnetism, however, opposites attract. Not so in the odic field, where like attracts like.

Reichenbach also found that the human energy field related to different colors and that it could not only carry a charge, but also flow around objects. He described the field on the left side of the body as a negative pole and the right side as a positive pole, similar to the ideas of Chinese medicine.

These and other theories have revealed the aura to have a fluid or flowing state; to be comprised of different colors, therefore frequencies; to be permeable and penetrable; and to be magnetic in nature, although it also has electromagnetic properties.

SPECIAL ENERGY FIELDS - There are many different biofields that regulate various mental, emotional, spiritual, or physical functions and these correspond to various parts of the layers of the auric field, as described by Barbara Ann Brennan and according to the twelve-chakra system subtle body. The following list of biofields is based on the work of Barbara Ann Brennan and others.

Chapter 12 – The Human Energy Field, Levels of Consciousness, Densities, Vibrational Frequencies, Quality of Our Spiritual Light

Physical field: Lowest in frequency. Regulates the human body.

Etheric field: Blueprint for the physical structure that it surrounds. There is also an etheric human energy field for the soul.

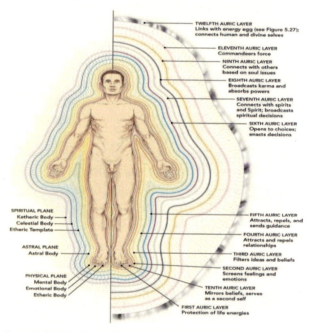

Emotional field: Regulates the emotional state of the organism.
Mental Etheric template: Exists only on the spiritual plane and holds the highest ideals for existence.
Celestial field: Accesses universal energies and serves as a template for the etheric fields.
Causal field: Directs lower levels of existence.

Chapter 12 – The Human Energy Field, Levels of Consciousness, Densities, Vibrational Frequencies, Quality of Our Spiritual Light

LIGHT AND SOUND FREQUENCIES ASSOCIATED WITH AURA, GLANDS, QUALITIES - One of the more compelling sets of studies in this area was conducted by Dr. Valerie Hunt. In *A Study of Structural Neuromuscular, Energy Field, and Emotional Approaches,* she recorded the frequency of low-millivoltage signals emanating from the body during Rolfing sessions. She made these recordings using electrodes of silver and silver chloride on the skin. Scientists then analyzed the wave patterns recorded with a Fourier analysis and a sonogram frequency analysis. The human energy field did, indeed, consist of a number of different color bands, which correlated to the chakras. The following results, taken from the February 1988 study, showed color-frequency correlations in hertz or cycles per second:

Note	Hertz	Equivalent Wavelength Angstroms/10 Nanometres	Approximate Colour
A	440	619.69	Orange-Yellow
A#	457.75	595.66	Yellow-Orange
Bb	472.27	577.34	Yellow
B	491.32	554.95	Yellow-Green
Cb	506.91	537.89	Green-Yellow
B#	511.13	533.44	Green
C	527.35	517.03	Green
C#	548.62	496.99	Green-Blue
Db	566.03	481.70	Blue-Green
D	588.86	463.03	
D#	612.61	445.08	Blue-Violet
Eb	632.05	431.39	Violet-Blue
E	657.54	414.67	Violet
Fb	678.41	401.91	Ultra Violet
E#	684.06	398.59	Invisible Violet
F	705.77	772.66	Invisible Red
F#	734.23	742.71	Infra Red
Gb	757.53	719.86	Red
G	788.08	691.96	Red-Orange
G#	819.87	665.13	Orange-Red
Ab	845.89	644.67	Orange

- **Blue** 250–275 Hz plus 1,200 Hz (a mixure of several frequencies)
- **Green** 250–475 Hz
- **Yellow** 500–700 Hz
- **Orange** 950–1050 Hz
- **Red** 1,000–1,200 Hz
- **Violet** 1,000–2,000, plus

Chapter 12 – The Human Energy Field, Levels of Consciousness, Densities, Vibrational Frequencies, Quality of Our Spiritual Light

300–400; 600–800 Hz
+ **White** 1,100–2,000 Hz

While mechanically measuring the subjects, healer and aura reader Reverend Rosalyn Bruyere provided her own input, separately recording the various colors she intuitively perceived. In all cases, her renderings were the same as those demonstrated mechanically. Hunt repeated this experiment with other psychics with the same results.

Color	Characteristic	Gland	Qualities	Imbalance	Resonance Frequency
Red	Physical	Gonads	courage, action, grounding, stability, survival	violence, greed, self, centeredness	194.18Hz
Orange	Social	Spleen	passion, trust, emotions, health, pleasure, let go	Jealousy, envy, aimlessness, obsessiveness	210.42Hz
Yellow	Intellectual	Adrenals	personal power, self esteem	fear, anger, hate, power	126.22Hz
Green	Self assertive	Lymph	Acceptance, forgiveness, love, radiance	Instability, repressed, love	136.10HZ
Dark Blue	Conceptual	Thyroid	Communication, truth, creative/arts	Depression, ignorance	141.27Hz
Indigo	Intuitive	Hypothalmus, Pituatry	Perception, realisation, intuition, clairvoyance..	Fear, tension, headaches	221.23Hz
Violet	Imaginative	Pineal	Fulfilment, inspiration	Confusion	172.06Hz

Sources:
1) Refer to the multitude of references listed within 'Aura (paranormal)'- *Wikipedia*, https://en.wikipedia.org/wiki/Aura_(paranormal)
2) 'Energetic Anatomy: A Complete Guide to the Human Energy Fields and Etheric Bodies,' *excerpted with permission from The Subtle Body* by Cyndi Dale, *ConciousLifestyle* magazine, www.consciouslifestylemag.com/ human-energy-field-aura/

Chapter 12 – The Human Energy Field, Levels of Consciousness, Densities, Vibrational Frequencies, Quality of Our Spiritual Light

QUALITY OF OUR SPIRITUAL LIGHT - Your true spiritual form - your spirit/soul - is a holographic system of flowing etheric tubes and geometrical fractal codes - a system of light and geometrical shapes. You are an etheric being of light. You are not just a solid physical being searching for a spiritual experience in this world. You are a non-solid spiritual being that is experiencing a solid physical experience in this world, in search of a spiritual experience. The spiritual journey is a Remembering, as well as a Returning to the awareness of your own multidimensional consciousness and infinite self. The only real question is the quality of your light.

The quality of each of our light is affected by the quality of your own inner sentiments - our inner feelings and virtues. They are reflections of each other. The quality of our light is also affected by the quality of our inner sentiments and energies that are enforced upon each of us - the emotion and mind - the reactions and rigid intellectual opinions - the programming and control - of the outside world around us. The quality of our light is affected by the quality of the things we allow to surround us - and the quality of our light is affected by the quality of our own inner feelings and traits.

You can never determine things by color alone. You have to use your perception and read things by the quality of the way things feel. You have to use your intuition. But you can learn to see energy, and it grants you more information to help guide you through life. And obviously, there's way more to every color than what's mentioned here. But these are the basics. Healing, Inner Power, and Perception all come down to developing the quality of your light- the reflection of your inner virtues.

Black Resonance

The Black Resonance is the energy of anger, coldness, control, disdain, hate, maliciousness, viciousness, and the inner negativity of rigid intellectual opinions. One should never judge a person, just because they have a black resonance, because it's not always theirs. Sometimes, a person can have a celestial energy, travel through dark worlds… and then come out covered in the black energies of the worlds they were swimming through. Traveling through dark worlds is like swimming in a sewer, and the sludge will cling to you. Sometimes, women will carry the black fractals of the dark men that they have been with, usually in a sexual way. Sometimes, a person can have black fractal codes in their energy field from the negative and rigid intellectual opinions projected onto them by others- family, friends, enemies, and/or the very system itself - which are the etheric manifestations of programming and control. Even physical pain, trauma, and memories can appear as black fractals in a person's energy field. Healers often become black in absorbing the dark energies of those that they're healing. All of this is why constant purification is vital - because black energy eventually manifests as cancers, tumors, and disease. So, you have to be cautious of black fractals, because they are demonic energies, but there's way more to reading people than just the color of their energy — and the person may be experiencing something or traveling through a dimension — that you are totally unaware of. You have to be sensitive to their situation.

White Resonance

The White Resonance can be a celestial energy of pristine purity, but white is also often the color of elitism, intellectual superiority, and the white shadow. Such types appearing white is mostly to do with their considering of themselves to be cleaner, more pure, and holier than others. White energies can be the most dangerous, because they often conceal dark energies, motives, and agendas hidden within a person - like white frosted icing covering a dark chocolate cake. Sometimes a person goes white with fear - like looking "white as a ghost", both physically, as well as on an etheric level. Most people are shades of gray, like two-dimensional boards with no real life or color to them, of which is mostly the reflection of the tick-tock system of routine draining their life force, or being stuck in their own mind. Leukemia looks white, so that tells you something. Not all white is good.

Red Resonance

The Red Resonance is aggressiveness, usually linked to anger and control issues. Black and reds are primarily demonic etheric forces, often sexual forces that are directed and projected towards hitting others. Male sexual predators are mostly black and red, and their etheric tubes will often hit women in the legs, ass, or vagina with black and red fractals - which sting. Their blacks are their disdain towards women, and their reds are their aggressiveness towards women. But women can also project black and red fractals, so it's not just isolated to the men. Some reds are simply from normal physical exertion, like working out at the gym or working to get things done in the physical world. But red is aggressiveness, and you have to be very cautious with red resonance people, because red is an attacking energy - and they can hit you at any given moment - whether it be physically or on an etheric energy level.

Orange Resonance

The Orange Resonance is always emotion, which usually forms as a giant orange etheric ball of energy that literally pushes up against everything and pushes things away. Emotional people are hard to reach, because they're usually so wrapped up in their own emotion that they don't stop to listen or observe the conditions that they are actually creating for themselves. They often falsely accuse others, exaggerate, or flat out lie — because they base things on their emotional condition — rather than on fact or truth. Needy people don't realize that they are actually pushing things away with their very own disruptive energy. Dark emotional energy builds and stores in the stomach and can fly out and hit other people in the stomach, causing them diarrhea, gas, and/or nausea. Some emotions, particularly sadness, emits as orange or dirty brown little fuzzy balls of energy that can fly up another person's tail end and cause them instant diarrhea. If you're emotional, and you're wondering why others flee… there's a reason for it. You have to discipline yourself into a stance of calmness.

Yellow Resonance

The Yellow Resonance is actually kind of rare. Yellow is intellect- the mind- but the mind is usually falling or dwelling in other areas of inner negativity and rigid intellectual opinions - causing a person's resonance to rotate into blacks, whites, grays, reds, and/or lime greens. Don't give yellow much thought.

Lime Green Resonance

The Lime Green Resonance is "The Sickness of Specialness" - a "Green Disease" - attention seeking, envy, greed, jealousy, self-importance - specialness. Lime green is linked to hatred and disdain. Envy and jealousy usually harbor hidden inner hatred. Greed harms. Self-importance and specialness are a form of disdain for others. How can you feel important, without making someone else unimportant and unworthy in your own mind? You can't. Never make yourself special. Never make anyone else special. Lime green can be thrown onto people, and lime green will make you sick. If you ever feel or see that you've been hit by lime green, you clear it by blowing it slowly out of your energy field, or by laying face down in the grass. Nature helps clear it. Some greens are ok, like emerald and forest greens, but lime green is never good and There is no inner power in specialness.

Blue Resonance

The Blue Resonance is mostly a celestial healing and nurturing energy. Women that develop the quality of their energy often develop a blue resonance. Some have it naturally. Some men have a blue resonance. Celestial blue is the quality of a giving spirit, kindness, loyalty, reverence, and softness. "True Blue" is quite a true statement, for those that actually are. Blue is usually the reflection of a strong sense of self. Celestial blues have a purity and vibrancy to them. But some blues are not so good, so you have to be careful. Deep blues and blacks or bluish black swirls are usually the energies of bewitchment- hidden agendas- seduction and sexual manipulation- usually coming from women that want to have their way with you- and their energy crawls and spirals up your legs. If it feels like something is crawling up your leg- something probably is, even if you can't see it. You shake it off by brushing your legs quickly with your hands.

Purple Resonance

The Purple Resonance is another celestial healing energy, but it's rare to see in people. Celestial purple is the transcendental state of "No Emotion, No Mind." Purple is Benevolence and Selflessness. It's also the energy of "Celestial Heat." The Celestial Heat burns away dark energies, pain, and sickness. It heals and protects you. A celestial purple resonance can heal just about anything. But not all purple is necessarily celestial either. Some violets slip into the whiteness of spiritual elitism, and some deep purples slip into the blackness of control and domination and can look like etheric bruises on a person's skin. But for the most part, purple is usually good- and a Celestial Purple Resonance heals.

Golden Resonance

The Golden Resonance is another celestial healing energy and vibrational resonance of warmth. Golden resonances are unconditional love - acceptance, forgiveness, and nurturing. A golden resonance is a celestial force of light that has the ability to burn away dark energies. It often enters a person's energy field as a form of etheric protection. Sometimes, golden energies are a download of information, like inspiration, realizations, and visions. Whatever the case, the golden resonance always seems to be good.

Sources:
1. 'Souls of Light,' Khris Krepcik, Aug 18, 2012, *The Hooded Sage*, http://www.thehooded sage.com/ 2012/08/souls-of-light/

LEVELS OF CONSCIOUSNESS/ DENSITIES/ VIBRATIONAL FREQUENCIES

Dimension:
Dimension refers to one's location in space/time rather than a person's vibrational frequency (density). Webster defines "dimension" as "Magnitude measured in a particular direction, specifically length, breadth, thickness or time." There are an infinite number of dimensions existing within a given density or vibrational frequency.

Frequency:
Matter is vibrating energy. Different vibrationary rates denote the properties. Frequency is the rate at which molecules or consciousness vibrates.

Density:
Density denotes a vibrational frequency and not a location, which the term "dimension" implies. The density structure of this reality is primarily expressed in multiple levels, though each level has sub-levels within it. The density scale is a model used to communicate one's perception of orientation in relation to other realities.

Chapter 12 – The Human Energy Field, Levels of Consciousness, Densities, Vibrational Frequencies, Quality of Our Spiritual Light

Levels of Consciousness, in ascending order, claimed by the New Age Spiritualists (Chapter 7):

Level	State of Consciousness
1	Existence, non-biological
2	Instinctual, emotional, animalistic
3	Intellectual, logical, rational mind, ego – this is the current Density of the Earth
4	Creative, imaginative, psychic, intuitive
5	Pure intelligence, insight, love
6	Causal level, soul level (last level of individuality)
7	Oversoul level (group consciousness)
8	Avatar level (a high level of mastery)
9	Christ level (unconditionally loving consciousness)
10	Cosmic level (cosmic consciousness)
11	God level (God consciousness)
12	Universal level (Universal consciousness)
13	The Void, the Great Mystery

Below is a refined system of dimensions and densities somewhat based on personal experience and verification from other sources.

1st Density:	Mineral kingdom
2nd Density:	Plant & lower animal kingdom
3rd Density:	Higher animal & lower human
4th Density	Low: Astral, lower emotional realms
4th Density	High: Etheric, higher mental realms
5th Density	Low: Causal, creative realms
5th Density	High: Soul (last level of individuality)
6th Density:	Oversoul (social memory complex)
7th Density:	Master oversoul, atmic plane

Chapter 12 – The Human Energy Field, Levels of Consciousness, Densities, Vibrational Frequencies, Quality of Our Spiritual Light

8th Density:	Avatar planes, celestial heavens
9th Density:	Christ planes, Buddhic planes, lower God worlds
10th Density:	Higher God realms
11th Density:	Universal realms
12th Density:	The source; the mystery, the Tao
13th and beyond:	The void, unmanifested creation

An Alternate Analysis of Densities

1d
*red
*sphere
*root chakra
*awareness: Earth/ malkuth center, gross physical/ elemental body
*physical, visible

2d
*orange
*central icosahedron
*sacral chakra
*growth: development without knowledge of the self, "animal" consciousness
*physical, visible

3d
*yellow
*octahedron
*solar plexus chakra
*choice: self knowing mind attained, plane of suffering, choice to serve others or self
*physical, visible

4d
*green
*star tetrahedron
*heart chakra
*love: the level of love, wisdom is not sought or developed here
*physical, non-visible

5d
*blue
*cube
*throat chakra
*light: light, mind, and wisdom fully developed here but
  not unified with love
*non-physical, non-visible

6d
*indigo
*dodecahedron
*brow chakra
*unity: the balance between compassion (love) and wisdom is
practiced here.
*non-physical, non-visible

7d
*violet
*sphere
*crown chakra
*gateway: the sacramental nature of all things is realized
  And the gateway to return to the oneness is opened
*non-physical, non-visible

8d
*white
*The void, unmanifested creation

CHAPTER 13
GUIDE TO THE 13 DIMENSIONS OF REALITY & OBSERVED FIELDS

DIMENSIONS - The universe is mathematical. Thirteen dimensions are predicted by M-Theory of String Theory: 8 physical and 5 theoretical at least that is one understanding. However, there is no consistent definition of the dimensions. Below is an attempt to define the dimensions.

One notable feature of string theories is that these therories require extra dimensions of space-time for their mathematical consistency. In Bosonic String Theory, space-time is 26-dimensional, while in superstring theory it is 10-dimensional, and in M-Theory it is 13-dimensional.

1. Point
2. Length (from which is derived length, width and height)
3. Mass Density – Sometimes referred to atomic weight or weight Density (as in pound per cubic foot). With these three, we see an object
4. Space/Time – We travel through it on a moment by moment basis. Einstein envisioned Space/Time as a grid onto which planets, sun, and the universe are placed. Objects, such as Earth and moon, create a depression within the grid, due to their mass and gravity. Due to the depressions, space/time is "warped" at each object. The space/time grid is not flat but can take many shapes; the views below are just illustrations to help visualize space/time.

280 | Chapter 13 – Guide to the 13 Dimensions of Reality & Observed Fields

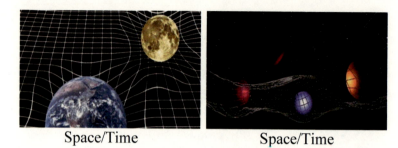

Space/Time   Space/Time

5. **Sound** – We have "broken" the sound barrier. However, this is the level where the Earth, universe and all things were created when God said, "Let there be light." His creation then transcended to the 3rd Dimension. Creation occurred via the "Word" (refer to Colossians 1:16).

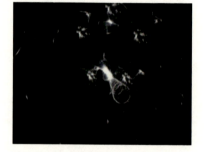

John 1:1 is the first verse in the opening chapter of the Gospel of John. In the Douay–Rheims, King James, New International, and other versions of the Bible, the verse reads:" In the beginning was the Word, and the Word was with God, and the Word was God. When God said, "Let there be light," at the creation, and light appeared, it showed God's (Creator God/First Source) creative power and absolute control. The physical light that Creator God (First Source) made on the first day of creation is a wonderful picture of what He does in every heart that trusts in Christ, the True Illuminator Light.

The reality of the creative power of Creator God's voice has important spiritual implications that go well beyond the creation account itself. Light is often used as a metaphor in the Bible, and the world illumination ("divine enlightenment of the human heart with truth") has to do

Chapter 13 – Guide to the 13 Dimensions of Reality & Observed Fields

with bringing things into the light. Spiritual illumination is a kind of "creation" that occurs in a human heart. "God (Creator God), who said, 'Let light shine out of darkness,' made his light shine in our hearts to give us the light of the knowledge of God's glory displayed in the face of Christ" (2 Corinthians 4:6). Jesus Himself is "the light of the world" (John 8:12).

Creation in the 5th Dimension may well be the way the Pyramids were made and then transcended to the 3rd Dimension. And, may well be with "I saw the Holy City, the new Jerusalem, coming down out of heaven from God" (Revelation 21:2), where creation occurs in the 5th Dimension and then transcends to the 3rd Dimension.

6. Light – we have not been able, as yet, to exceed the speed of light. Per the Bible, Light was created on Day 1 (Genesis 1-2).

Light   Gravity

7. Gravity – by observing a black hole, light cannot escape gravity of the very dense core of the black hole.

8. Matter – Void of being identified as a specific molecule. This is what is being ejected from the black hole, through its vertical axis. Dispersion of this matter may result in Black Matter that occurs throughout the universe.

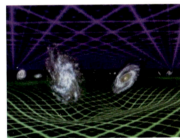
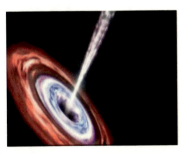

282 | Chapter 13 – Guide to the 13 Dimensions of Reality & Observed Fields

9. Possible worlds – the so-called parallel worlds possibility, where all things appear similar but different. (e.g., H.G. Wells' *Men Like Gods*, 1923 and 'The Twilight Zone," *The Parallel*, TV Episode 1993).

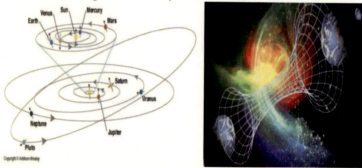

10. A Plane of All Possible Worlds with Same Start Conditions.

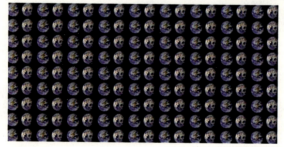

11. A Plane of All Possible Worlds with Different Start Conditions.

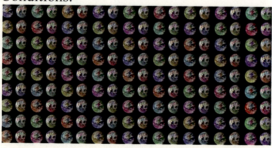

12. A Plane of All Possible Worlds with Different Start Conditions, Each Branching Out Infinitely.

13. All Possible Worlds, Starting With All Possible Start Conditions and Laws of Physics.

OBSERVED FIELDS
1. **Magnetic Fields - The Earth's magnetic field** is the magnetic field that surrounds the Earth. It is sometimes called the geomagnetic field.

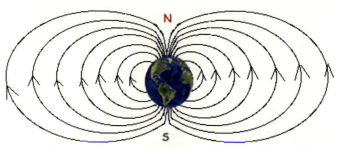

The Earth's magnetic field pattern is composed of lines that resemble the field line pattern for a bar magnet

An original Cyberphysics graphic © 2017

The Earth's magnetic field is created by the rotation of the Earth and Earth's core. It shields the Earth against harmful particles in space. The field is unstable and has changed often in the history of the Earth. As the Earth spins the two parts of the core move at different speeds and this is thought to generate the magnetic field around the Earth as though it had a large bar magnet inside it. This is termed the "Motor Effect" due to the two parts of the core move at different speed, just as an electric motor creates a field between the core and the and the coil wrapping.

The magnetic field creates magnetic poles that are near the geographical poles. The intensity of the magnetic field is greatest near the magnetic poles where it is vertical. The intensity of the field is weakest near the equator where it is horizontal. The magnetic field's intensity is measured in Gauss.

The magnetic field has decreased in strength through recent years. In the past twenty-two years, the field has decreased its strength 1.7%, on average. In some areas of the field, the strength has decreased up to 10%. The fast strength decrease of the field is a sign that the magnetic field might be reversing. The reversal might happen in the next few thousand years. It has been shown that the movement of the magnetic poles is related to the decreasing strength of the magnetic field.

Also, as the magnetic field moves around the graphic pole, the shielding effect from solar radiation (which heats the Earth) changes position to make some areas of the Earth warmer and other areas colder.

2. **Energy Grids & Ley Lines -** The history surrounding this subject has many landmarks, beginning with Alfred Watkins in 1921. He wrote "It was recognized that certain powerful currents, lines of magnetism, run invisible over the surface of the Earth....

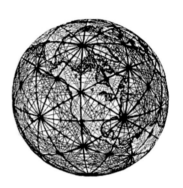

"And that these lines of current appear to connect many ancient sacred centers that create a uniform grid pattern. Some believe that intersecting ley lines form centers of power/control over the Earth.

3. **Van Allen Radiation Belt Plasmasphere -** The Van Allen belts were the first discovery of the space age, measured with the launch of a US satellite, Explorer 1, in 1958. In the decades since, scientists have

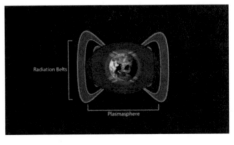

learned that the size of the two belts can change – or merge, or even separate into three belts occasionally. But generally the inner belt stretches from 400 to 6,000 miles above Earth's surface and the outer belt stretches from 8,400 to 36,000 miles above Earth's surface.

Most of the particles that form the belts are thought to come from solar wind and other particles by cosmic rays. By trapping the solar wind, the magnetic field deflects those energetic particles and protects the Earth's atmosphere from destruction.

The radiation belts are not the only particle structures surrounding Earth. A giant cloud of relatively cool, charged particles called the plasmasphere fills the outermost region of Earth's atmosphere, beginning at about 600 miles up and extending partially into the outer Van Allen belt. The particles at the outer boundary of the plasmasphere cause particles in the outer radiation belt to scatter, removing them from the belt.

The two donuts of seething radiation are called the Van Allen radiation belts and they, have been found to contain a nearly impenetrable barrier that prevents the fastest, most energetic electrons from reaching Earth.

VISUALIZING THE DIMENSIONS that make up the first eight dimensions. The other dimensions (some mathematical) enclose the first eight to form a total of 13 dimensions of M-Theory (String Theory).

Visualize the following:

3-D The Earth is located in the center of the model pictured. Now spin the Earth on its axis, including its "wobble" (Procession) and tilting axis.

4-D Space/Time- Encase (surround) the 3-D Earth with a Bucky Ball, which is a fused ring structure "ball" made out of pentagons (pentagons and hexagons). In reality the structure looks like a C_{60} molecule. Now, visualize the ball as rotating in any direction. As this ball spins, look through one of the polygons and view the Earth from that time perspective. Look through another polygon to view the Earth at a different point in time.

5-D Sound – Encase (surround) the Space-Time "ball" with another Bucky ball and rotate that "ball" in a different direction and speed than the Space-Time "Ball."

6-D Light - Encase (surround) the Sound "ball" with another Bucky ball and rotate that "ball" in a different direction and speed than the Sound "Ball."

7-D Gravity - Encase (surround) the Light "ball" with another Bucky ball and rotate that "ball in a different direction and speed than the Light "Ball."

8-D Matter - Encase (surround) the Gravity "ball" with another Bucky ball and rotate that "ball in a different direction and speed than the Gravity "Ball."

Note that the "balls" are, most likely, not round. They could be any shape. And the spacing between the "balls" are, most likely, not evenly spaced.

Model of 8 Dimensions – innermost is the Earth, enclosed within a the "red" ball

Sources
1. "Earth's Grid System,' Becker-Hagens, *Hartmann Net*, www.crystalinks.com/grids.html
2. 'Earth Ley Lines, Earth's Grid System,' Becker-Hagens, , Hartmann Net, www.crystalinks.com/grids.html
3. 'Van Allen Belt Mystery Solved With Student-Built Satellite,' *Gizmodo*, https://gizmodo.com/van-allen-belt-mystery-solved-with-student-built-satell-1821252.
4. 'Van Allen radiation belt,' *Wikipedia* https://en.wikipedia.org/wiki/Van_Allen_radiation_belt
5. 'Matter, Black Holes,' *Science Mission Directorate – NASA*, www.google.com/search?tbm=isch&sa=1&ei=rGnzWsShC8HAjwTdn67wDg&q=black+hole&oq=black+hole&gs_l=img.1.0.35i39k1j0i67k1j0l8.233004.235988.0.239377.10.8.0.0.0.0.
6. 'Possible Worlds,' *M-Theory, String Theory*, Dr. Michio Kaku, www.google.com/search?q=parallel+worlds&source=lnms&tbm=isch&sa=X&ved=0ahUKEwi_rqb30_naAhXFyoMKHWWQCtQQ_AUICygC&biw=1492&bih=859#imgrc=KwfLYcOyD
7. 'Magnetic Fields,' *Cyberphysica*, www.google.com/search?biw=1492&bih=859&tbm=isch&sa=1&ei=PXbzWvXyF4nTjwSJuqroAw&q=magnetic+Earth+fields&oq=magnetic+Earth+fields&gs_l=img.1.0.35i39k1j0i8i3
8. '13 Dimensions' (article and photos of D-9, D-10, D11, D-12, D-13) and 'Here's a Visual Guide to the 10 Dimensions of Reality,' *Ultraculture*, https://ultraculture.org/blog/2014/12/16/heres-visual-guide-10-dimensions-reality/

PHOTOS:
1. Earth's Magnetic Field – Cyberphysics – The Earth's Magnetic Field, Cyberphysics Graphs, 2007
2. Space Time – flat grid, Einstein taught us it's all relative, space-time curvature, www.google.com/search?q=space+time+einstein&source=lnms&tbm=isch&sa=X&ved=0ahUKEwjp7-_mxPnaAhUh2oMKHeLQCkcQ_AUICygC#imgrc=I57Qj9o2ifih3M:
3. Space Time warped grid, *Cosmology.com*, www.google.com/search?q=space+time+einstein&source=lnms&tbm=isch&sa=X&ved=0ahUKEwjp7-_mxPnaAhUh2oMKHeLQCkcQ_AUICygC#imgrc=SyY0p6pHOIfsQM:
4. 'Light, Einstein to shed light on black holes,' *Science Nordic*, www.google.com/ search?tbm =isch&sa=1&ei =QWPzWp-JNcbPjwT4 _KvQCQ&q =universe +light&oq niverse+light&gs _l=img.1.0.0l4j0i5i30k1l4j0i8i30k1j0i10i24k1.1372488.1375955.0.13783
5. Gravity, Space Images, Dark Energy and Gravity, Dark Energy and Gravity: Yin and Yang of the Universe, *NASA Jet Propulsion Laboratory*, www.google.com/search?tbm=isch&sa=1&ei=tmjzWs3sOMPCjwTwrI6ABQ&q=gracity+of+the+universe&oq=gracity&gs_l=img.1.0.35i39k1j0i10k1l9.224666.226483.0.228866.7.7.0.0.0.0.245.
6. Energy Grid and Ley Lines, Earth's Grid System, Becker-Hagens, Ley Lines, *Crystalinks*, www.google.com/search?q=energy+grids+and+ley+lines&source=lnms&tbm=isch&sa=X&ved=0ahUKEwjz68fF2PnaAhWH4IMKHUEfCXYQ_AUIDCgD&biw=1492&bih=859#imgrc=hWN9kd

Chapter 13 – Guide to the 13 Dimensions of Reality & Observed Fields

CHAPTER 14

ARE YOU A WANDERER?

If you are reading this article it's possible that you are a Wanderer and are penetrating the forgetting process, searching for knowledge. Not every Wanderer that incarnates on Earth pierces the veil of forgetting to the same degree. *The Law of One* states that over the last 75,000 years, approximately 1.9 Billion souls, from all portions of creation, entered into this experience at various times. Some Wanderers have been in this sphere for many thousands of years, others have come more recently. In the last 25,000 years, approximately six out of 30 (20%), transitioned from 4-D to 6-D. Currently, there are approximately 35,000 Wanderers are on Earth and they are, to some degree, beginning to Wake Up to their mission to help this planet in its transition to the next Density. *The Law of One* states that those who remember their status to an intelligent degree is between 8.5 and 9.75% of Wanderers. Those who recognize symptoms of not being of this Earthly 'insanity' is just over fifty percent of the remainder. About one third of the next remainder feel different in some way, and so on.

A Wanderer's purpose in life, as a higher dimension star being, is to raise the frequency of the Earth and thereby raise the frequency of the people of Earth. Once you have mastered the various "lessons" (refer to Chapter 5), you will realize your true purpose here on Earth, you will realize that you are not defined by *Self,* and you have eliminated all of the self definitions of I AM (add anything here). It will all be reduced to the simple "I AM." At this point, you will realize that "Reality" is an illusion (Although I have made it past nearly all of the "lessons," I am not there, as yet, since I have allowed my Mind to "see" the Earth illusion as being real.

Wanderers have been incarnating on Earth, According to *The Law of One* [The Law of One: 'The Ra Material: An Ancient Astronaut Speaks' (*The Law of One*, Book 1)], due to the planet's vibrational shift is transitioning from third to fourth density. They are souls who are being born to help raise the vibration of the planet nearer to that of love and light.

Wanderers started to incardinate in large numbers in the 1940's. Their primary purpose on this Earthly plane is simple - to radiate love and light to others through thought and action, and to raise the vibration of the Earth to that of the next Density.

Wanderers can become 'activated' during the course of their lifetime and begin to commence the good works that they intended themselves to do before birth. Higher beings are oftentimes the catalyst for the awakening of Wanderers and do so in such a way as to minimize the chance of creating any fear which could produce adverse effects. In rare cases, contact with higher beings is made through channeling or perhaps UFO contact, however most Wanderers activate or undergo spiritual awakening due to a subconscious thought that is unknowingly received sometimes during sleep or during a purposeful event which occurs during waking hours – such as survival of an accident, uncovering secret information such as conspiracy theories or conspiracy fact, or perhaps a simple revelation causing the Wanderer to view the Earthy illusion in an entirely different way to how they viewed life since birth.

Each Wanderer is unique, just as any soul at any progressional level is unique. Each Wanderer incarnates with a unique set of talents and abilities. One may possess a brightly shining green chakra energy center and be predisposed toward activities of a caring and compassionate nature. Others may have a bright free flowing blue energy center and enjoy communication or teaching of a positive nature. Wanderers incarnate from many distant places within the universe and their biases and norms of behavior reflect this diversity. Each Wanderer however is united in the desire to serve others, progress spiritually, and ameliorate sorrow and suffering from any groups of souls who experience it.

For most people, their human bodies exist in the third density, and their spirit bodies are of a similar progressional level. However a Wanderer is much, much older and far more spiritually advanced. A Wanderer can originate from any fourth, fifth or sixth density planet (higher dimensions of evolutionary existence than ours) and while in their home world, they choose to regress to a third density existence, such as Earth, for the purpose of learning and experience. Hence the name 'Wanderer' - these souls wander between densities of existence (dimensions of a sort) seeking further enlightenment. Although their talents and personalities are varied,

- Wanderer souls from fourth density existence serve primarily as broadcasters of love and light; they are intensely drawn to helping others and facilitate joy and happiness.
- Wanderers of a fifth density origin are predisposed toward raising the planetary vibration through expression of wisdom and clarity of thought.
- Those of a sixth density origin are biased toward both love and light, and the expression of wisdom as they are searching for a balance between the two during their own progression. However, talents and personalities are varied.

Wanderers have been incarnating in waves for that last 200 or more years in order to bring about technological advancements to help to free up our lives to concentrate on spiritual progression. The capitalist system often demands long working hours, preventing us from spending time developing our true potential. It is said that Nikola Tesla was one such Wanderer who incarnated with a wish to free humanity by providing a source of free energy and light, however his attempt was thwarted by those wishing to profit from energy production.

The population or society from which a Wanderer comes may have reached a collective harmony, and high level of global unity and fulfillment. In seeking further purpose and enlightenment, these advanced beings wish to reach out to other entities experiencing sorrow. Our planet is one such place. By enlightening the planetary consciousness, those souls who incarnate on Earth at this time will be better able to spiritually progress and live in love and light, show compassion and serve others, as well as serving and knowing the Self. The Wanderers lift the planetary vibration simply by being on Earth, even if they don't undertake good works for the benefit of all during their lifetime.

There are many souls of a third density progressional level who are entering the fourth. These beings have always been residents of Earth, or have recently come here from other planetary spheres as third density beings, ready to make the transition to fourth. These beings, of a lower progressional level to Wanderers, are starting to show the abilities of fourth density and are able to manifest great abilities. They do this as a function of learning in the present and not as a function of remembering passed lives or experiences. Sometimes known as 'Indigo children' they are capable of feats like telekinesis, metal bending, telepathy, super intelligence, and expression of intense love and compassion – to name just a few traits. These souls are well able to manifest these abilities as they naturally progress.

Wanderers however, have already made these progressions and found these abilities in their own past lives. However, upon incarnating on Earth, the forgetting process creates conditions where the Wanderer has no longer access the abilities previously learned. This is because Wanderers would otherwise exhibit Godlike abilities and be unable to integrate with the third density souls incarnate on Earth. It would affect the lives and progression of the third density souls of Earth also.

Chapter 14 – Are You a Wanderer?

The Earth exists in the third density and is already making the vibratory shift to fourth. It has been doing this since the mid 20th century, but the mind/body/soul/spirit complexes (people) inhabiting the Earth are lagging behind as a whole in their vibratory frequency. Wanderers' purpose here is to raise this frequency, through both service to self and service to others.

There is an extreme variance between the vibratory frequencies of this third density to the higher fourth, fifth and sixth densities. Therefore in some cases Wanderers, being from these higher densities, experience a mismatch or incompatibility of frequencies with their new earthly home. They therefore experience physical distortions, allergies or ailments due to the spirit body having difficulty adjusting, or they endure extremely intense sensations of alienation within society, resulting in mental illness and personality disorders.

It is a privilege to be permitted to incarnate on Earth from more advanced densities of existence due to the amount of potential progression, learning and experience this earthly illusion has to offer. There are countless Wanderers originating from all corners of the universe, not just our own galaxy. Gaining the chance at a lifetime on Earth at this time of change is a special opportunity and the Wanderer can fast track their own soul's progression. The dysfunctional nature and confusion within this earthly illusion offers many opportunities for expression of love, light and wisdom.

Wanderers often times feel like misfits within this planetary illusion and that they are inexplicably different to other people. They usually have at least a dim recollection of previous life experiences, and know that certain ways of life within this earthly vibration are often not necessary or feel extremely unusual compared to their home reality.

Wanderers usually possess wonderful talents in the arts, science, philosophy, teaching etc, and are very kind and caring people. Although they find it difficult to completely fit into life on this planet, they are cheerful and pleasant – naturally radiating love and light to others. Wanderers are often trusting and less able to recognize people of negative polarity because they themselves are far less distorted to toward negative thoughts and behaviors.

So if you believe you are a Wanderer (or Lightworker) and are searching for your purpose in this life, know that you have great potential for spiritual progression just by being here. Life might seem tough and alien at times, and you might feel like the odd one out. Try not to feel down because it's a privilege to gain this experience. Keep searching for your purpose which will reveal itself in time. It's likely to be of a positive nature and help to improve the world in which we live. Seek out others like you as they will understand. See what you can achieve in this lifetime even if you have little money - love, care and compassion are free. Just like it's unlikely humanity will suddenly experience a revelation, change the world and unify – there's always the possibility it will happen.

Source:
1. 'The Law of One Ra Material: An Ancient Astronaut Speaks' (*The Law of One*, Book 1) by Don Elkins (Author), James Allen McCathy (Author) and Clara Rueckert (Author), Whiteford Press (May 1, 1984), ISBN: 08986542604

CHAPTER 15

SPIRITURAL PROTECTION (SELF-DEFENSE)

HIGHER FREQUENCY SOULS ARE AT RISK OF SPIRITURAL ATTACK - Now that you are AWAKENING or are AWAKE, as a New Soul, Starseed, Indigo, Returning Soul or Old Soul/Wanderer, you are now open to spiritual attack due to your higher vibration (frequency) – Refer to Chapter 12.

TYPES OF SPIRITRUAL ATTACKS

1) <u>Psychic attack</u> - a human that harbors negative emotions toward you projects low vibratory energies that you absorb. It can come from someone close to you or someone at a distance, because distance often has no bearing if the attacker can visualize (simply think of) you as an individual. The negative emotions serve to counteract your positive vibration, literally canceling out your happiness.

2) <u>Thought-forms</u> - a psychic attacker can experience such intense emotion that virtual entities manifest entirely by thought. The thought-form can reside within your dwelling causing intensive psychic attack. For example, some alien visitations are thought to be thought-form entities projected here from distant civilizations using intense negative emotion, visualization and intent.

3) <u>Negative residual energies</u> - have you ever walked into a house and thought it had bad energy? Well the very atoms of the building may have retained negative energies from unpleasant occurrences from the past. Energies like this can be transmitted to you having entered your home. For example, it is well to remove your shoes when you come inside, as they can bring in negative energy from the street!

4) <u>Energy vampires</u> – Energy vampirism is when a person uses any fear based emotion to emotionally impact us and thereby gain access to our personal energy whereas they are then capable of claiming it as their own. Some of these fear based emotions include intimidation, guilt, embarrassment, pity, anger, and depression.

Energy vampires are negatively polarized humans who tend to administer the psychic attack. It may be a particularly unpleasant person that you know or live with, that seems to drain your positive emotions dry. Sometimes positive people can turn into energy vampires for a period of time if they experience trauma or loss.

It becomes important for people that find themselves constantly around energy vampires and their negativity to consistently remind themselves that they are in control of their own energy and where it goes.

NEGATIVE ENTITIES – negatively polarized discarnate (not in human form) spirits may be attracted to you and feed from your own negative emotions if you are experiencing an unhappy time. You may also attract a negative entity if you're performing positively polarized work such as helping many people to a great extent - the entity may want to hamper your positive achievements if they are of universal significance. It is rare however to attract a discarnate negative entity.

MEANS OF SELF-DEFENSE - First, know that love is the greatest protector. Protection involves utilizing love in as purer form as possible, for with love you can effectively construct a brick wall around you that negative forces cannot penetrate. Furthermore, negative entities cannot stand when positive vibrations hold strong because they start to Polarize toward the positive (they turn positive), and that's the last thing they want. So, always approach protection with the highest intent in love and light, because using negative emotion will act like a magnet for further darkness to feed upon.

For example, if you shout back at an angry person then the argument escalates. Behave calmly and with love toward an angry person and they will likely calm down. The negative energy diffuses and dissipates.

Second, know that in higher realms of existence (that's higher densities and within time-space) thoughts become reality. Thought-forms can be created through visualization such as walls or protective bubbles of light, doorways for negative entities to leave though, or in-streaming healing energy into your body. All these have a high probability of manifesting through your strong intent and effective visualization - they manifest on the other side and are used in this physical reality seen through your third eye.

Third, also know that coupled with visualization; intention (or belief) is key - they work together to create thought forms and manifestations that can be used for spiritual protection. For example, you visualize a glowing white protective orb around you and your intention is for it to protect you from negative forces. Without the intention, the visualization is merely a pretty orb - you must assign it a purpose.

HOW TO SPIRITUALLY PROTECT YOURSELF
1) Distant yourself from negative entities. Don't let anyone touch you for any length of time, since they may be trying to steal your energy. Only make longer contact with people you have learned are "safe" and at or above your energy level (Ascended Masters come to mind). Perfect intent comes only with the knowledge of what one is connected to and often lots of practicing doing that well.

2) Be wary of "Healers of any kind (both Physical and Spiritualists). Approach "Healers" as in #1 above. Many

"Healers" do not know what they are doing because they only have some vague idea of what they are connected to, and often it isn't even that. They believe all the energies out there are good energies and that saying something about 'the higher good' will protect them and their patients from anything negative using them. But again, they have no perfect intent to make those words so. They have no understanding of the war going on in Creation between the Darkness and the true Divine Light. More often than not they are dumping or channeling more negative stuff than that which they initially hope to remove.

3) Massage people are the same, and any type of healing or healer should be very thoroughly questioned to one's Guidance before being allowed to even enter one's space, let alone lay hands or energies upon one for healing sake.

4) If you find yourself in a "nest" of negative energy, such as an Apartment Complex, move to a less intense environment. Constant attacks by negative entities will lead to restless nights of sleep, weird dreams, tiredness, weakness and depression.

Unfortunately, just as wild animals born in captivity will do, people born and bred as slaves grow accustomed to their chains and the security provided by their cages. Even when you undo the shackles and open the cage door as many healers can help do for people, the courage to step forward and face an 'insecure' world or fate takes more courage than most people have, and certainly lots and lots of pure intent.

5) **Visualization** - Before performing any spirit contact, trance work, meditation and more, it's always best to visualize protection. In a meditative state visualize white light streaming down from the universe and know that it is love. Allow the protective white light to form a three dimensional

shield around your mind/body/spirit complex. As love is the great protector, no negative energies can penetrate this barrier - by knowing that this is true (using intent/belief) you make it possible from the perspective of time/space, therefore making it effective.

6) **White Light** - Perhaps the most well known technique in the new age and metaphysical realms is that which involves white light or just light energy. The concept of surrounding ourselves with the white light of eternal love and protection is not really new to many. Still, many have trouble figuring out exactly how to do this.

Suggest the following visualizations:

Visualize white light streaming down from the universe and know that it is love. Allow the light to flow into the top of your head and down through your chakras, in turn filling your entire body with white light. Intend for this energy to heal and protect your body from any physical-spiritual attack (for example a negative entity working on weak back muscles causing pain).

Visualize a protective wall of glowing love light energy between you and an energy vampire or other negatively polarized person you know. By erecting a protective wall, they may start to avoid you or be unable to lower your energy vibration as a result.

If you believe you have a negative entity in your home then visualize a glowing white doorway created entirely from love/light. On the other side is the spirit world. Tell the dark spirit entity to leave with confidence, in the highest intent and love. If you struggle to remove such an entity or experience any illness following this, consult a priest or spiritual medium as per your belief system that is trained to cleanse dwellings.

Picture yourself in the center of a light bulb, and then imagine it is turned on.

While standing under a shower of water (real or imagined), see/feel the water turn into the light.

Visualize an angel hovering over you and the light radiating from all around it and around you.

White light is important since it raises our own vibrations thus making it less likely that we'll even encounter those who are choosing to follow the path of a lower vibration (hence negativity). Additionally, it helps to neutralize the negative vibrations that do manage to make their way to our aura.

7) **Blue Bubble or Blue Shield** - Not as well known as the white light technique, the Bubble and Shield technique uses the idea that we can surround ourselves mentally with either a bubble or a shield that will reflect and absorb negativity so that we don't have to feel the full effects of it. The color blue, associated with the throat chakra, represents will power and when combined with the visualization of the bubble or shield strengthens it.

We can layer the bubble or shield with the white light, so both can be in effect at one time. In truth, in dire situations, all of these methods can be layered to provide additional levels of protection to the psyche and auric energy field.

If you are one of those people that hates being around large crowds because you are so sensitive to energy, this is an important technique which can in essence give your social freedom back to you. Go out to a mall or shopping area where a lot of people are and enter and take note of what it feels like. Exit or excuse yourself to the restroom. Put the blue bubble or shield around yourself before going back. See if you notice a difference.

Going with the idea, one could put a bubble around the person that is being negative, thereby creating a form of operant conditioning around the individual. When they choose to throw negative energy or use negative emotions to their advantage, this energy can't escape the bubble and thus they feel the full effects of it. I.E., a person learns that they have to be nice when around you or they get zapped by their own negative energy.

8) **Physical Body Positions** - Crossing your arms and legs can also be very protective. These body positions act to close off the human energy circuits and also protect various chakra (energy) points – depending on where the arms are crossed. The next time you are around someone that seems to be pulling at your energy or spewing a bunch of negativity, sit down calmly, cross your arms and legs, and listen. Their energy won't be affecting you and eventually they'll get tired or drained (as they aren't getting any of your energy and they are using up their own supply) and they just leave you alone for the rest of the day.

9) **Mirrors** - Visualizing mirrors surrounding the self has been used almost as long as the white light and blue energy. The idea here is that your visualization should have the mirrors facing outwards so that energy is reflected away from you. Like the bubble, you can put them around someone else to act as a form of operant conditioning, but this time the mirror's reflective surface should face inward toward the person you are putting them around.

10) **Salt** - We are speaking of a pure salt here, such as Kosher Salt or Sea Salt. These pure salts absorb negative energy and will ground or take it away from you if you have picked up any. There are many ways to use this technique.

a) Put some salt into a small glass and leave the glass on your work desk or in the room where people are most often found. This will absorb negative vibes. Make sure to flush it and change it out every month or after every fight/argument.
b) Add a sprinkle to some bath water and soak in it. This will pull negativity off and away from you as you soak. Add a touch of baking soda also to revitalize or help regain the lost energy.
c) Dilute some salt into a spray bottle of spring or mineral water. Spray a mist in the air of any room which has been overloaded with negativity or in which recent fights/arguments have occurred. This has the effect of making the environment feel light, pure, and airy again. Many combine this with the burning of sage (often called smudging) to cleanse and clear areas.

11) **Protection Symbols** - Protection symbols come in many forms. It's the belief in the symbol that will be the most important. However, the symbol itself can act to strengthen the subconscious mind and as a result be an added measure of defense and protection.

Holy symbols tend to be the most popular symbols of protection (cross/crucifix for Catholics/Christians, pentagram for Pagans, cow, Buddha, the list literally could go on) however any symbol can be used as a symbol of protection as long as it is meaningful to you. Thus, don't make fun of someone who talks about their lucky whatever. It may truly be an important symbol for them and because of their belief and what that symbol invokes; it very well may truly be "lucky" and helpful for them.

12) **Psychic Defense Technique – Prayer and Affirmations**
Prayer and affirmations have long been used to build positive energy, amplify other protections, and add layers of

defense to the human energy system. In the case of prayer, any prayer which is said immediately following the use of one of these methods will act to strengthen it. In the case of affirmations, affirmations such as "I allow only love around me," "People adore me," and "My vibration is stronger and faster each day" can improve your energy and defense techniques. When writing an affirmation, always remember to put it in the present, write it from the first person perspective, and do not include negatives (not, don't, won't, can't, etc.) in it.

Likewise, invoking or asking your Higher Self, guides and counselors for help can strengthen your protection. A common conception of the angelic realm is that angels can't intervene or help humans unless a human has asked and given them permission to do so. The exception being if a person's life is in danger, then many times that rule can be broken. The point is, always be willing to ask for extra help if you need it. Your angels, guides, and the powers to be will always respond and help out.

13) **Challenge Entities** - When performing spirit contact, mediumship, channeling and others, if you sense the presence of an entity approaching or you feel that contact has been made - you must challenge the entity in the name of universal love, Christ, The Creator, positive polarization or any other highly positive belief that provides the purest, most loving and protective energy for you according to your own beliefs. This action effectively forms a barrier between you and the approaching consciousness. If the entity is of a negative polarization with negative intent then this wall of light will prove impenetrable.

14) **Ask for Protection** - No one travels alone. Even if we are lonely in this precious lifetime, each of us has a group of spirit guides, including perhaps an angelic entity or two. Although you likely have a 'life plan' that you set for

yourself before birth, your guides are there to help you along the way. It is an infringement to be interfered with during your lifetime by discarnate entities, therefore ask your spirit guides to please remove them. Treat your guides with love as they will benefit from this energy the same as any entity.

Your freewill is very important spiritually; therefore a spirit guide cannot explicitly intervene unless requested. So go ahead and ask. For example, you believe that a family member's vital energy is being drained by a negative acquaintance, ask your spirit guides to help protect your family member, or at least to get your loved one's guides to do so. In this way, spirit guides will help by planting seeds of thought into someone's mind that leads to a solution, or by changing circumstances seemingly by chance. Watch your loved one's circumstances potentially improve.

Your higher self can be of assistance if asked, although it cannot interfere with your path. Your higher self is your soul in the far unimaginable future, because time and space are not relative where the higher self resides. The higher self is your soul looking back at its distant former self and has the ability to do so. It can place an amour of light around you if deemed appropriate, can help to alter circumstances or plant seeds of thought about the way forward into your mind complex.

15) **Supportive Loved Ones** - Just like you have spirit guides, don't overlook the souls incarnate as human who love you in this lifetime. Do you draw strength and feel better when you talk to your closest companion about negativity that you are experiencing? They are raising your vibration, helping to make you resilient to negative attack. Support and love them back because together we are stronger. The doubling effect occurs where the positive energy of two

people is twice as powerful as one. Draw strength from each other for protection.

16) **Clearing Your Home of Negative Energy** - Less than harmonious energies within your home can affect your own energies and bring you down. These energies could have been left by current or former inhabitants, arguing, crying, experiencing depression and so on. Here are a couple of methods:

Salt is a great absorber of negative energy when our intent is for it to do so - sea salt is best for purity. Acquire some blessed water. This needn't be blessed by a priest, but be filled with your own love energy. You may charge the water like any other crystal, by radiating love into it. Water too is a crystalline structure. Sprinkle the salt around areas of the home where negative energies are felt. Sprinkle the blessed water over the salt with the intention to activate it to absorb negative energies. Hold this clear intention in your mind whilst sprinkling the water with your fingers. Leave the salt for three days and then clean the area thoroughly. Ensure that pets or young children will not be affected by the salt.

Rinse any objects that hold a negative vibration - perhaps an item that has been owned by a very unhappy person. Use salt water and hold the intent in your mind for the mixture to absorb negative energy.

Discarnate negative entities will never remain were cut garlic is placed. If you believe a negative entity is present, send it back to the lower astral planes by placing cut garlic around the areas which feel most negative to you. Leave it there for 3 days and nights.

17) **Charging Objects With Your Intent** - You can charge any crystalline structure with pure love energy and keep it with

you. Visualize your balanced love energy flowing from the green (heart) chakra into the crystal and its structure being charged. This is why many people keep quartz and other crystals. They act like a hard drive for emotions. Wash the quartz in water, charge it with love and put it in your pocket to use when you are experiencing low frequency energies. When you are experiencing an onslaught, you can increase your vital energies using the stored energies within the crystal. Give yourself strength, remedy the energy distortion, provide mental balance and defense. Hold the crystal and accept into the self the in-flowing energies back into your heart chakra. You may wear a crystal around the neck that hangs in front of the green energy center/chakra.

18) **Objects that Reminds You of Love and Strength -** Configure objects around your home, workplace or within the bag you carry to provide you with comfort and joy. When experiencing negative onslaught or psychic attack, you can use these to replenish vital energy. For example, if you have been insulted at work, looking at a picture of your family on your desk can make you feel somewhat energized, helping to protect you from further onslaughts.

19) **Chanting -** If you are on the move, very busy or unable to perform other protection methods, chanting (if only in your mind) or repeating a prayer/call to spirit guides can help you gain protection. For example, if you have attracted road rage by being intimated by angry rush hour drivers, more angry drivers will literally magnetize to your fear or anger and you may experience more of the same. Try chanting to yourself; 'The universe guards and protects me because from it I draw endless love,' or 'I will balance emotionally and experience love, because I am one with all that there is.'

LONG TERM PROTECTION AGAINST NEGATIVE ENTITIES AND ENERGIES

1) **Balancing of the Self** - Your aura or energy field will be strongest, with no weak patches or distortions, if your energy centers (chakras) are balanced, unblocked and free flowing. This presents as a balanced personality.

   If your aura/energy field has weakness and distortion, physical ailments occur as a result. Negative entities may use this as a window of opportunity for psychic attack.

   For example; again you are being insulted. An unbalanced person relying on red or orange (animalistic and reactive) chakras may become emotional, fight or become upset. A spiritually balanced person with bright free flowing energy centers will know that the comment is meaningless and instead hold love in their heart for the other person because they too are one with all creation.

   Read the article 'How to Unblock Your Chakras Yourself' for guidance on how to balance the self. In addition, meditation is important for spiritual balancing, replenishing vital energies, receiving intelligent energy and is overall the most important thing you can do.

2) **Physical Strength and Vital Energy** - You may undergo physical-psychic attack. A negative discarnate entity form a higher density may target you if you are performing good works to serve many within this earthly realm. If you have physical weakness it may choose to work upon and worsen this. Eat well, exercise and get plenty of sleep so that your vital energies are replenished and you're physically strong. Your aura will again be difficult to penetrate.

SUMMARY - In summary, protection is important if you are a positively polarized individual (or even if you are a bit on the negative side!). This is due to negative energy and the negative entities producing it will always exist. Just as there are two sides to every coin, so too will there always be positive and negative energies. Creation is not meant solely for goodness. Whatever you perceive Creator God to be, that creator would have created everything to be pure and good if it was meant to be. There would be no murder, cancer, earthquakes, diseases and so on. But if you exist in a positive vibration then you can remain in this awesome state by getting spiritual protection against the negative energies that inevitably exist. Tip the overall balance of the mass consciousness to positive by staying positive - fight off those negative emotions, spirits and people with love.

Sources:
1. '7 Basic Psychic Self Defense and Energy Protection Techniques,' Psychic Hayden, *California Psychics*, /www.californiapsychics.com/blog/mind-body-spirit/7-basic-psychic-self-defense-and-energy-protection-techniques.html
2. 'Spiritual Protection - How to Protect Yourself from Negative Energies & Emotional Vampires, Spiritual Inspiration on Your Journey Through Life,' *Spiritual Awaking*.net, 16 February 2015, http://www.spiritual-awakening.net/2015/02/spiritual-protection-how-to-protect.html

CHAPTER 16

DESCRIPTION OF THE UNIVERSE

"If a problem has no solution, it may not be a problem, but a fact - not to be solved, but to be coped with over time." - Shimon Peres (1923 -), 9th President of the State of Israel

If one understands the difference between Densities (Chapter 12) and Dimensions (Chapter 13), then one can conduct research to be able to Describe the Universe, well almost. There are several theories as to the description of the universe. Several are listed below.

THE UNIVERSE IS A CREATED COMPUTER SIMULATION - Several physicists, cosmologists and technologists are now happy to entertain the idea that we are all living inside a gigantic computer simulation, experiencing a *Matrix*-style virtual world that we mistakenly think is real.

Over the last few decades, computers have given us games of uncanny realism – with autonomous characters responding to our choices – as well as virtual-reality simulators of tremendous persuasive power.

The Matrix formulated the narrative with unprecedented clarity. In that story, humans are locked by a malignant power into a virtual world that they accept unquestioningly as "real." But the science-fiction nightmare of being trapped in a universe manufactured within our minds can be traced back further, for instance to David Ronenberg's *Videodrome* (1983) and Terry Gilliam's *Brazil* (1985).

Over all these dystopian visions, there loom two questions. How would we know? And would it matter?

In June 2016, technology entrepreneur Elon Musk asserted that the odds are "a billion to one" against us living in "base reality." Similarly, Google's machine-intelligence guru Ray Kurzweil has suggested that "maybe our whole universe is a science experiment of some junior high-school student in another universe."

Musk and other like-minded people are suggesting that we are entirely simulated beings. We could be nothing more than strings of information manipulated in some gigantic computer, like the characters in a video game. Even our brains are simulated, and are responding to simulated sensory inputs. In this view, there is no *Matrix* to "escape from." This is where we live, and is our only chance of "living" at all.

But why believe in such a baroque possibility? The argument is quite simple: we already make simulations, and with better technology it should be possible to create the ultimate one, with conscious agents that experience it as being totally lifelike.

We carry out computer simulations not just in games but in research. Scientists try to simulate aspects of the world at levels ranging from the subatomic to entire societies or galaxies, even whole universes. For example, computer simulations of animals may tell us how they develop complex behaviors like flocking and swarming; if we can determine the mechanism behind swarming, we could then determine how an army will react on the ground. Other simulations help us understand how planets, stars and galaxies form. We can also simulate human societies using rather simple "agents" that make choices according to certain rules. These give us insights into how cooperation appears, how cities evolve, how road traffic and economies function, and much more. These simulations are getting ever more complex as computer power expands. Already, some simulations of human behavior try to build in rough descriptions of cognition. Researchers envision a time, not far away, when these agents' decision-making will not come from simple "if...then..." rules. Instead, they will give the agents simplified models of the brain and see how they respond.

Who is to say that before long we will be able to create computational agents – virtual beings – that show signs of consciousness? Advances in understanding and mapping the brain, as well as the vast computational resources promised by quantum computing, make this more likely by the day. If we ever reach that stage, we will be running huge numbers of simulations. They will vastly outnumber the one "real" world around us. Is it not likely, then, that some other intelligence elsewhere in the Universe has already reached that point? If so, it makes sense for any conscious beings like ourselves to assume that we are actually in such a simulation, and not in the one world from which the virtual realities are run. The probability is just so much greater.

But this is all just supposition. Could we find any evidence? Many researchers believe that it depends on how good the simulation is. The best way would be to search for flaws in the program, just like the glitches that betray the artificial nature of the "ordinary world" in *The Matrix*. For instance, we might discover inconsistencies in the laws of physics. Alternatively, the late artificial-intelligence maven Marvin Minsky has suggested that there might be giveaway errors due to "rounding off" approximations in the computation. For example, whenever an event has several possible outcomes, their probabilities should add up to 1. If we found that they did not, that would suggest something was amiss.

Sources:
1. 'Do We Live In A Computer Simulation Created By An Advanced Alien Civilization?,' MessageToEagle.com, September 7, 2013, *Holographic Universe*, http://www.messagetoeagle.com/do-we-live-in-a-computer-simulation-created-by-an-advanced-alien-civilization/

2. 'Did the aliens create our universe? Do we live in sandboxed world?,' *in science,* https://steemit.com/science/@mys/did-the-aliens-create-our-universe-do-we-live-in-sandboxed-world
3. 'We might live in a computer program, but it may not matter,' Phil Ball, Sept 5, 2015, *Earth,* http://www.bbc.com/Earth/story/20160901-we-might-live-in-a-computer-program-but-it-may-not-matter?

THE UNIVERSE IS A HOLIGRAM

3-Dimenaional Hologram - In the 1970s, when scientists debated the properties of a black hole and how an object's entropy could be lost while adhering to the second law of thermodynamics, it was found, by Paul Matt Sutter, an astrophysicist, in an interview with Fraser Cain that, "when it comes to black holes, the information content of a black hole is proportional not to its volume, but to its surface area." In other words, the information going into a black hole might be directed and maintained onto its event horizon – the boundary marking the limits of a black hole. Generalizing, all the information defining what "fell" into the black hole is contained within the event horizon – meaning what is "inside" can be maintained "on the outside."

Gerald 't Hooft believed that the correct description of the black hole would be by some form of String Theory. This idea was made more precise by Leonard Susskind, who had also been developing holography, largely independently. Susskind argued that the oscillation of the horizon of a black hole is a complete description of both the infalling and outgoing matter, because the world-sheet theory of string theory was just such a holographic description. The holographic principle first proposed by Gerard 't Hooft, is a principle of String Theories and a supposed property of quantum gravity that states that the description of a volume of space can be thought of as encoded on a lower-dimensional boundary to the region - preferably a light-like boundary, such as gravitational horizon.

Susskind then theorized that the information inside a volume is replicated in an outer dome or sphere hologram, which is the same, as previously stated, "the information that is inside the volume (e.g., inside a black hole) is duplicated on the outside (event horizon). Taking this further, what is contained within the Earth is contained within the hologram that surrounds the Earth, with other event horizons, such as our solar system is contained within the hologram which surrounds its event horizon, containing the solar system.

Coupling this "holistic" hologram with Quantum Gravity Theory then reflects both String Theory of the "small" and Relativity Theory of the "large," including gravity, matter and black matter, inflation, warpage and all the other components that compose both theories.

Having said this, we receive the holographic information through our five senses, which is then transmitted into the darkness of our mind, the only place where "reality" occurs within each of us.

If the "volume" is manipulated by an entity or entities, then the "event horizon hologram" for the "volume" will reflect the manipulation. However, as we progress to distant event horizons (e.g., the solar system or the galaxy) the manipulation of the Earth hologram becomes less and less significant in affecting the other event horizons.

Sources:
1. Holographic Universe, Michael Talbot, 1991 Harper Perennial, ISBN: 006092283. Summary: YouTube https://www.youtube.com/watch?v=UDnakYnA7VA&app=desktop

2. *'Holographic Universe,'* Richard Merrick, *Token Rock Inspiration Center,* https://www.tokenrock.com/explain-holographic-universe-124.html
3. 'What if Our Universe is a Hologram?,' Chelsea Gohd, October 8, 2017 *Hard Science,* https://futurism.com/
4. 'Theory claims to offer the first evidence our Universe is a hologram,' Abigail Beail, 31 January 2017, *WIRED UK,* https://www.wired.co.uk/article/our-universe-is-a-hologram
5. 'Holographic principle,' *Wikipedia,* https://en.wikipedia.org/wiki/Holographic_principle
6. 'What It Means to Live in a Holographic Universe,' Brian Koberlein, May 7, 2014 , *Nautilus,* http://nautil.us/blog/what-it-means-to-live-in-a-holographic-universe
7. 'New Evidence for the Strange Idea that the Universe Is a Hologram,' Brian Koberlein, Feb 21 2017, *Nautilus,* http://nautil.us/blog/new-evidence-for-the-strange-idea-that-the-universe-is-a-hologram
8. 'Is The Universe a Hologram?,' YouTube, The Good Stuff, Interview with Leonard Suskind, Aug , 2015, https://m.youtube/watch?v=iNgll-qikiU
9. 'Are We Living in a Hologram?, ' Paul Sutter, *Astrophysicist,* January 29, 2018, Space.com, https://www.space.com/39510-are-we-living-in-a-hologram.html
10. 'NASA Scientist Claims Human Reality Is an Alien Created Hologram,' Kevin Burwick, July 5, 2017, *MOVIE NEWS,* https://movieweb.com/nasa-scientist-Earth-alien-created-hologram/
11. Gerardus (Gerard) 't Hooft (Dutch: [ˌɣeːrɑrt ət ˈɦoːft]; born July 5, 1946) is a Dutch theoretical physicist and professor at Utrecht University, the Netherlands. He shared the 1999 Nobel Prize in Physics with his thesis advisor Martinus J. G. Veltman "for elucidating the quantum structure of electroweak interactions." His work concentrates on Gauge Theory, black

holes, quantum gravity and fundamental aspects of quantum mechanics. His contributions to physics include a proof that Gauge Theories are renormalizable, dimensional regularization and the holographic principle. (Wikipedia)
12. Leonard Susskind (/ˈsʌskɪnd/; born 1940) is an American physicist, who is professor of theoretical physics at Stanford University, and director of the Stanford Institute for Theoretical Physics. His research interests include String Theory, Quantum Field Theory, quantum statistical mechanics and quantum cosmology. He is a member of the National Academy of Sciences of the US, and the American Academy of Arts and Sciences, an associate member of the faculty of Canada's Perimeter Institute for Theoretical Physics, and a distinguished professor of the Korea Institute for Advanced Study. Susskind is widely regarded as one of the fathers of String Theory. He was the first to give a precise string-theory interpretation of the holographic principle in 1995 and the first to introduce the idea of the String Theory landscape in 2003. (Wikipedia)

2-Dimensional Hologram - Einstein's theory of General Relativity explains almost everything large scale in the Universe very well, but starts to unravel when examining its origins and mechanisms at quantum level. Scientists have been working for decades to combine Einstein's theory of gravity and quantum theory. Some believe the concept of a holographic Universe has the potential to reconcile the two.

In the 1970s, when scientists debated the properties of a black hole and how an object's entropy could be lost while adhering to the second law of thermodynamics, it was found, by Paul Matt Sutter, an astrophysicist, in an interview with Fraser Cain that, "when it comes to black holes, the information content of a black hole is proportional not to its volume, but to its surface area." In other words, the information going into a black hole might be directed and maintained onto its event horizon, which is 2D- essentially 3D information stored in 2D space. This idea expanded in the 1990s when physicists at the University of Southampton believes it has found signs our Universe is an illusion by studying the cosmic microwave background (CMB) – radiation left over from the Big Bang. These physicists discovered that when you assume that universe is a hologram, gravity vanishes when you can take away one from whatever number of dimensions you are working with.

These phenomenon are described in the "holographic principle," which states, simply, that all objects can be explained by the information stored on their surfaces - so if you take the 3-D image, which contains all of its encoded information, and you place it onto a 2-D surface, with the edges being the cosmic horizon, the higher dimension of information is, essentially, encoded in a lower dimension of space.

"Imagine that everything you see, feel and hear in three dimensions, and your perception of time, in fact emanates from a flat two-dimensional field," says Professor Kostas Skenderis from the University of Southampton.

To find the 'evidence', the researchers developed models of the holographic Universe that can be tested by peering back in time as far as 13 billion years, at the furthest reaches of the observable Universe. These models depend on the theory of quantum gravity, a theory that challenges the accepted version of classical gravity. The holographic principle says gravity comes from thin, vibrating strings which are all holograms of a flat, 2D Universe.

Recent advances in telescopes and sensing equipment have allowed scientists to detect a vast amount of data hidden in the 'white noise' or microwaves left over from the moment the Universe was created. Using this information, the team was able to make comparisons between networks of features in the data and quantum field theory. They found some of the simplest quantum field theories could explain nearly all cosmological observations of the early Universe. This, they claim, moves quantum gravity away from being an alternative theory and towards an accepted model; the first time such 'evidence' has been found.

However, the most intensively explored instance of the holographic principle works only under very special circumstances — when 5D space-time is bent back on itself, as New Scientist put it, "rather like the surface of a Pringle." This "trick" of bending space-time, eliminating gravity, and working under the constraint of the universe being a hologram, has had a variety of practical applications. The holographic principle, a part of String Theory, has helped with the advancement of supercomputers and physics problems like explaining why particles have mass.

Many detractors of the holographic universe say that the holographic universe does not account for gravity, black matter, dark energy, warpage, inflation, and mass. For example how can all see me kicking a rock, which has mass, which tends to follow Einstein's Relativistic Physics' Theory of gravity and mass attraction. Although the holographic universe does not account for gravity, black matter, black energy, warpage, inflation, and mass, String Theory can account for what is done by one is "seen" by all. The Sting Theory concept is called "Entanglement": When two quantum particles are entangled, they cannot be described individually, but instead form a single quantum "object," even if they're far apart. Further, if a hologram of a rose is cut in half and then illuminated by a laser, each half will still be found to contain the entire image of the rose. Indeed, even if the halves are divided again, each snippet of film will always be found to contain a smaller but intact version of the original image. Unlike normal photographs, every part of a hologram contains all the information possessed by the whole. Given this, the reason subatomic particles are able to remain in contact with one another regardless of the distance separating them is not because they are sending some sort of mysterious signal back and forth, but because their separateness is an illusion. At some deeper level of reality such particles are not individual entities, but are actually extensions of the same fundamental something. There is a measure that describes how entangled a quantum system is, known as the "entropy of entanglement." After several years of work, Grumiller and his colleagues managed to show that this entropy takes on exactly the same value when calculated in gravitational theory and quantum field theory for spaces like our universe.

While it's unlikely, that the universe is a hologram, the potential for 3D information to be stored in two dimensions has been shown with black holes. As Sutter concretely puts it, the holographic principle is just "a convenient mathematical tool because some questions in physics are super hard."

Sources:
1. 'What if Our Universe is a Hologram?,' Chelsea Gohd, October 8, 2017 *Hard Science*, https://futurism.com/
2. 'Theory claims to offer the first 'evidence' our Universe is a hologram' By Abigail Beall, 31 January 2017, WIRED UK, https://www.wired.co.uk/article/our-universe-is-a-hologram
3. 'New Evidence for the Strange Idea that the Universe Is a Hologram,' posted by Brian Koberlein, Feb 21, 2017, *NAUTILUS*, HTTP://NAUTIL.US/BLOG/NEW-EVIDENCE-FOR-THE-STRANGE-IDEA-THAT-THE-UNIVERSE-IS-A-HOLOGRAM
4. 'There Is Growing Evidence that Our Universe Is a Giant Hologram,' Maddie Stone, May 5 2015, *Motherboard*, https://motherboard.vice.com/

en_us/article/jp59b8/there-is-growing-evidence-that-our-universe-is-a-giant-hologram

THE UNIVERSE IS A CREATED 3- DIMENSIONAL CONTAINED WITHIN A PHYSICAL UNIVERSE - Cosmologist Alan Guth of the Massachusetts Institute of Technology, US has suggested that our entire Universe might be real yet still a kind of lab experiment. The idea is that our Universe was created by some super-intelligence, much as biologists breed colonies of micro-organisms. There is nothing in principle that rules out the possibility of manufacturing a universe in an artificial Big Bang, filled with real matter and energy. Nor would it destroy the universe in which it was made. The new universe would create its own bubble of space-time, separate from that in which it was hatched. This bubble would quickly pinch off from the parent universe and lose contact with it.

In this scenario, the creation may have been made in the 10th Dimension (A Plain of all Possible Worlds with Same Start Conditions). 11th Dimension (A Plain of all Possible Worlds with Different Start, Each Branching Out Infinitely Conditions), or even the 13th Dimension (All Possible Worlds, Starting With All Possible Start Conditions and Laws of Physics). Nothing limits One Source Creator from making our Universe the same as any other Universe that might have been created.

Using the Big Bank as a starting point, right after the "Bang," all matter is small and condensed. During this period, String Theory, the theory of the small, could apply. As the components scatter, they begin to attract one another to form plants and stars. During this period, Einstein's Theory of General Relativity explains almost everything of large scale in the Universe.

A 3-Dimensional (physical dimensions + time) universe accounts for gravity, black matter, dark energy, warpage, inflation, and mass. It also explains how I can all see me kicking a rock, which has mass, which tends to follow Einstein's Relativistic Physics' Theory of Gravity and Mass Attraction.

The idea is that our Universe was created by some super-intelligence within some kind of lab experiment does not really change anything. Our Universe might have been born in some super-beings' equivalent of a test tube, but it is just as physically "real" as if it had been born "naturally."

Sources:
1. 'SHOCK CLAIM: Aliens CREATED the universe and are controlling every aspect RIGHT NOW,'" SEAN MARTIN, Published: 09:07, Mon, Nov 28, 2016, *Express*, https://www.express.co.uk/news/science/737034/Aliens-CREATED-universe-big-bang-theory
2. 'DID ALIENS CREATE AND MAINTAIN THE UNIVERSE?,' Published: 11/26/2016, *WND*, https://www.wnd.com/2016/11/did-aliens-create-and-maintain-the-universe/#UWLmwA75G5hgwDZA.99
3. 'Is 'God' An Alien Extraterrestrial From Another Planet?', Rhawn Gabriel Joseph, *Cosmology*, March 9, 2017, http://cosmology.com/IsGodAnExtraterrestrial.html. Also, includes alternate history of Mars
    a. Crick, F. H. (1981), Life itself, Simon & Schuster
    b. Crick, F., & Orgel, L. (1973), 'Directed Panspermia,' *Icarus*, 19, 43-57
    c. Heidel, H. (1988), *The Babylonian Genesis, Oriental Institute of Chicago*
    d. Joseph, R. (1997), *Life on Earth Came From Other Planets,* University Press, California
    e. Joseph, R. (2000), *Astrobiology, The Origins of Life, and the Earth of Darwinism,* University Press, California

f. Joseph, R. (2009), 'Life on Earth Came From Other Planets,' *Journal of Cosmology*, 1, 1-40
g. Joseph, R. (2016), 'A High Probability of Life on Mars,' C*osmology*, 2016, Vol 25, 1-25
h. Joseph, R. (2016), 'Martian Fungi and Bacteria Contaminate and Damage the Mars Rovers,' C*osmology*, 2016, Vol 26, 40-65
i. Joseph, R. (2017), 'Space Fungi Are Attacking The Space Stations,' *Cosmology*.com
j. Joseph, R. (2017), 'Extraterrestrial Origins: Life on Earth Came From Other Planets,' *Cosmology*.com
k. Joseph, R. (2017), 'Caveman Cosmology: Constellations, Caves, Paleolithic Astronomy 30,000 B.C.,' *Cosmology*.com
l. Kramer, S. N. (1991), *History begins at Sumer*. U. Pennsylvania Press, Philadelphia
m. Roux, G. (1992), *Ancient Iraq*, Penguin, New York

THE UNIVERSE IS A BUBBLE Setting in a Network Of Bubble Universes - Another theory for multiple universes comes from "eternal inflation." Based on research from Tufts University cosmologist Alexander Vilenkin, when looking at space-time as a whole, some areas of space stop inflating like the Big Bang inflated our own universe. Others, however, will keep getting larger. So if we picture our own universe as a bubble, it is sitting in a network of bubble universes of space. What's interesting about this theory is the other universes could have very different laws of physics than our own, since they are not linked.

Sources:
1. 'Parallel Universes: Theories & Evidence,' By Elizabeth Howell, Contributor *Space*.com, May 9, 2018 08:25pm ET, https://www.space.com/32728-parallel-universes.html

2. 'Hard Art of the Universe Creation,' journal Physics B372-442, 1992, Andrei Linde (Noble Laurent), Cornell University, arXi:hep-th/9110037
3. 'Creating a Universe in the Lab? The Idea Is No Joke,' Zeeya Meralil,| June 19, 2017, THE CRUX / Discover Magazine, http://blogs.discovermagazine.com/crux/2017/06/19/build-a-universe-in-the-lab/

THE UNIVERSE IS A DAUGHTER UNIVERSE – Different from a Mirror Universe - Perhaps multiple universes can follow the theory of quantum mechanics (how subatomic particles behave), as part of the "daughter universe" theory. If you follow the laws of probability, it suggests that for every outcome that could come from one of your decisions, there would be a range of universes — each of which saw one outcome come to be. So in one universe, you took that job to China. In another, perhaps you were on your way and your plane landed somewhere different, and you decided to stay. And so on.

Source:
1. 'Parallel Universes: Theories & Evidence,' Elizabeth Howell, *Space*.com, May 9, 2018 08:25pm ET, https://www.space.com/32728-parallel-universes.html

THE MATHEMATICAL UNIVERSE - Another possible avenue is exploring mathematical universes, which, simply put, explain that the structure of mathematics may change depending in which universe you reside. "A mathematical structure is something that you can describe in a way that's completely independent of human baggage," said theory-proposer Max Tegmark of the Massachusetts Institute of Technology, as quoted in a 2012 article. "I really believe that there is this universe out there that can exist independently of me that would continue to exist even if there were no humans."

Sources:
1. 'Parallel Universes: Theories & Evidence,' By Elizabeth Howell, Contributor *Space*.com, May 9, 2018 08:25pm ET, https://www.space.com/32728-parallel-universes.html

PARALLEL UNIVERSES - The idea of parallel universes goes back to the idea that space-time is flat and the number of possible particle configurations in multiple universes would be limited to $10^{10^{122}}$ distinct possibilities, to be exact. So, with an infinite number of cosmic patches, the particle arrangements within them must repeat — infinitely many times over. This means there are infinitely many "parallel universes" - cosmic patches exactly the same as ours (containing someone exactly like you), as well as patches that differ by just one particle's position, patches that differ by two particles' positions, and so on down to patches that are totally different from ours.

Famously, physicist's Stephen Hawking's last paper before his death also dealt with the multiverse. The paper was published in May 2018, just a few months after Hawking's demise. About the theory, he told Cambridge University in an interview published in The Washington Post, "We are not down to a single, unique universe, but our findings imply a significant reduction of the multiverse to a much smaller range of possible universes."

Source:
1. 'Parallel Universes: Theories & Evidence,' Elizabeth Howell, *Space*.com, May 9, 2018 08:25pm ET, https://www.space.com/32728-parallel-universes.html

OUR UNIVERSE EXISTS INSIDE A BLACK HOLE Our universe may exist inside a black hole. This may sound strange, but it could actually be the best explanation of how the universe began, and what we observe today. It's a theory that has been explored over the past few decades by a small group of physicists.

Successful as it is, there are notable unsolved questions with the standard big bang theory, which suggests that the universe began as a seemingly impossible "singularity," an infinitely small point containing an infinitely high concentration of matter, expanding in size to what we observe today. The theory of inflation, a super-fast expansion of space proposed in recent decades, fills in many important details, such as why slight lumps in the concentration of matter in the early universe coalesced into large celestial bodies such as galaxies and clusters of galaxies.

But these theories leave major questions unresolved. For example: What started the big bang? What caused inflation to end? What is the source of the mysterious dark energy that is apparently causing the universe to speed up its expansion?

The idea that our universe is entirely contained within a black hole provides answers to these problems and many more. It eliminates the notion of physically impossible singularities in our universe. And it draws upon two central theories in physics.

The first is Einstein's theory of general relativity, the modern theory of gravity. It describes the universe at the largest scales. Any event in the universe occurs as a point in space and time, or spacetime. A massive object such as the Sun distorts or "curves" spacetime, like a bowling ball sitting on a canvas. The 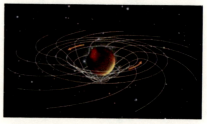 Sun's gravitational dent alters the motion of Earth and the other planets orbiting it. The sun's pull of the planets appears to us as the force of gravity. The second is quantum mechanics, which describes the universe at the smallest scales, such as the level of the atom. However, quantum mechanics and general relativity are currently separate theories; physicists have been striving to combine the two successfully into a single theory of "quantum gravity" to adequately describe important phenomena, including the behavior of subatomic particles in black holes.

A 1960s adaptation of general relativity, called the Einstein-Cartan-Sciama-Kibble theory of gravity, takes into account effects from quantum mechanics. It not only provides a step towards quantum gravity but also leads to an alternative picture of the universe. This variation of general relativity incorporates an important quantum property known as spin. Particles such as atoms and electrons possess spin, or the internal angular momentum that is analogous to a skater spinning on ice.

In this picture, spins in particles interact with spacetime and endow it with a property called "torsion." To understand

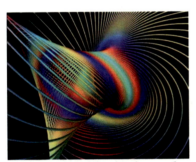

torsion, imagine spacetime not as a two-dimensional canvas, but as a flexible, one-dimensional rod. Bending the rod corresponds to curving spacetime, and twisting the rod corresponds to spacetime torsion. In Space-time, torsion would only be significant, let alone noticeable, in the early universe or in black holes. In these extreme environments, spacetime torsion would manifest itself as a repulsive force that counters the attractive gravitational force coming from spacetime curvature. As in the standard version of general relativity, very massive stars end up collapsing into black holes: regions of space from which nothing, not even light, can escape.

Here is how torsion would play out in the beginning moments of our universe. Initially, the gravitational attraction from curved space would overcome torsion's repulsive forces, serving to collapse matter into smaller regions of space. But eventually torsion would become very strong and prevent matter from compressing into a point of infinite density; matter would reach a state of extremely large but finite density. As energy can be converted into mass, the immensely high gravitational energy in this extremely dense state would cause an intense production of particles, greatly increasing the mass inside the black hole.

The increasing numbers of particles with spin would result in higher levels of spacetime torsion. The repulsive torsion would stop the collapse and would create a "big bounce" like a compressed beach ball that snaps outward. The rapid recoil after such a big bounce could be what has led to our expanding universe. The result of this recoil matches observations of the universe's shape, geometry, and distribution of mass.

In turn, the torsion mechanism suggests an astonishing scenario: every black hole would produce a new, baby universe inside. If that is true, then the first matter in our universe came from somewhere else. So our own universe could be the interior of a black hole existing in another universe. Just as we cannot see what is going on inside black holes in the cosmos, any observers in the parent universe could not see what is going on in ours.

The motion of matter through the black hole's boundary, called an "event horizon," would only happen in one direction, providing a direction of time that we perceive as moving forward. The arrow of time in our universe would therefore be inherited, through torsion, from the parent universe.

Torsion could also explain the observed imbalance between matter and antimatter in the universe. Because of torsion, matter would decay into familiar electrons and quarks, and antimatter would decay into "dark matter," a mysterious invisible form of matter that appears to account for a majority of matter in the universe.

Finally, torsion could be the source of "dark energy," a mysterious form of energy that permeates all of space and increases the rate of expansion of the universe. Geometry with torsion naturally produces a "cosmological constant," a sort of added-on outward force which is the simplest way to explain dark energy. Thus, the observed accelerating expansion of the universe may end up being the strongest evidence for torsion.

Torsion therefore provides a theoretical foundation for a scenario in which the interior of every black hole becomes a new universe. It also appears as a remedy to several major problems of current theory of gravity and cosmology. Physicists still need to combine the Einstein-Cartan-Sciama-Kibble theory fully with quantum mechanics into a quantum theory of gravity. While resolving some major questions, it raises new ones of its own. For example, what do we know about the parent universe and the black hole inside which our own universe resides? How many layers of parent universes would we have? How can we test that our universe lives in a black hole?

The last question can potentially be investigated: since all stars and thus black holes rotate, our universe would have inherited the parent black hole's axis of rotation as a "preferred direction." There is some recently reported evidence from surveys of over 15,000 galaxies that in one hemisphere of the universe more spiral galaxies are "left-handed", or rotating clockwise, while in the other hemisphere more are "right-handed", or rotating counterclockwise. In any case, including torsion in geometry of spacetime is a right step towards a successful theory of cosmology.

(Ed: This article may support the theory that a Black Hole is a portal to another universe).

Sources:
1. 'Every Black Hole Contains a New Universe,' Nikodem Poplawski theoretical physicist at the University of New Haven in Connecticut, *Inside Science*, May 17, 2012, https://www.insidescience.org/news/every-black-hole-contains-new-universe
2. 'Baby Universes, Third Quantization and the Cosmological Constant,' Giddings, Steven B. *et al.* Nucl.Phys. B321 (1989) 481-508 HUTP-88/A036http://inspirehep.net/record/262567?ln=en
3. 'Aliens from another dimension might have created our universe, according to a speculative new study,' Michael E. Price, *The Conversation*, Jul. 11, 2017, https://www.businessinsider.com/why-universe-exists-alien-life-adaptation-idea-2017-7

Chapter 17

GLIMPSES INTO ENLIGHTENMENT

Spiritual awakening is a term usually used in reference to a particular shift in consciousness which includes such awareness as the oneness of all, freedom from illusions, a quiet mind, sustained present moment awareness, and other changes in perspective.

A quote from the book *Thinking Like Einstein* may be appropriate:

"We realize that the deeper coherence of the universe requires that each of us inhabits a lawful world of our own that may seem inconsistent with the worlds inhabited by others. Only at another more subtle level are these individualized worlds harmonized: difference and unity. Once we internalize this difficult insight, we begin to swim, ungrounded, in a multiplicity of possible worlds."

Rational thought processes alone cannot acquire mystical experience. Philosophy, as an analytical discursive and verbal process, cannot, in itself, lead to mystical awareness. A transcendental insight, a deep intuition, a faith in the possibility of ultimate experience, is required.

POSITIVE AND NEGATIVE SPIRITUAL POLARIZATION & MAKING CHOICES IN THE 3RD DENSITY- Positive and negative spiritual polarization is a fundamental principal through the Densities up to and including a portion of the 6th Density. The principal of service-to-others and service-to-self forms the spiritual polarity of the Universe. In the 3rd Density is where beings start to wake up and we are given the opportunity to choose – since they are spirit beings and eternal beings – and are on an evolutionary journey. With this, the beings have Free Will and can make their own choices.

Everything is squeezed into the 3rd Density cycle. The 3rd Density is a very concentrated, intense time, where we are inspired to choose our orientation (service-to-others or service-to-self). This does not mean we cannot change our orientation later on – we can always change, but this is the density of our initial choice. We get to decide whether we feel like being of service to others, or being mostly of service to self, in a very negative-oriented way (through enslavement, domination, conquest, and so on).

To have service-to-others and service-to-self beings all bunched together for millennia, within a single collective Consciousness, is highly disruptive and catalytic. It is also highly potent and beneficial for the expansion and waking up of the One Infinite Creator to itself, in the form of a collective Consciousness we call "humanity" on planet Earth. We have been thrown into a "pot of soup" together – a lot of service-to-self and a lot of service-to-others beings. We have been working through this conflict, trying to find resolution, for ages.

The whole polarity of planet Earth is slowly shifting toward the positive orientation, in proportion to the increasing frequency of the Earth that is being generated through the increase in frequency of the service-to-other beings and from that of assisting terrestrial beings from other Densities. Negatively-oriented beings will no longer be able to sustain themselves within this dimensional growth of our civilization and planet. This inability to sustain themselves is partially brought about due to the Universe service-to-other beings having isolated Earth so that Universe service-to-self beings can no longer assist the service-to-self beings on Earth. This is why, especially now, one may see some powerful outbursts of negativity. It is akin to cornering a cat – you know it is going to fight back rapidly and it knows that its days are coming to an end. When your eyes are open, when you open your inner eye, and your become enlightened, you will see that many are awakening to help create a very harmonious civilization that is service-to-others. At that time, the attitude will not be "I need to take something away from someone else to be able to manifest or empower myself in some way." Instead it will be "I can give to myself and empower myself through being of service to other beings."

Polarization in the direction of either service-to-self or service-to-others is actually the amassing of Free Will. Service-to-others is gaining (or regaining) our Free Will. One could call this spiritual power or spiritual awareness, and it is amplifying and accelerating and charging up our journey, which expands beyond this particular life.

You have the opportunity to use this life in a very polarizing way (this does not mean in a separating way, as used by the service-to-self uses to divide us), by changing yourself in a certain direction; by committing to and choosing to be devoted to being of service to your fellow human being and to this planet; by choosing to be even more devoted, even more polarized in the positive direction, without blaming or judging the negative polarization. By being passionate in your endeavors, you will be changing yourself in the direction of service-to-others.

Eventually, in mid-6th Density, everything will come together as Unity, Love, and Light, and service-to-others is all there is. At that point, it is seen as "service-to-all" since there is no separation. The attitude in mid-6th Density is much more like the human attitude of service-to-others than it is like service-to-self, but it will be seen to be "service-to-all."

Right now, what is relevant for us is to inspire ourselves; to see how we can transcend our own "personal bubbles" and be inspired to change the world; to see how we can contribute and offer new reflections, through following our own joys and excitement and inspiration, to the best of our ability.

THE GROUPINGS BETWEEN "SERVICE-TO-OTHERS" AND SERVICE-TO-SELF" - In order to increase our participation in this new reality, and to help humanity reach it faster and more efficiently and harmoniously, we need to know where we are on the scale of enlightenment and to know how we might help the vast numbers of those that are "Asleep" or are in the "Waking up process" to help them in their ascension. In addition, we need to know more about those that have succumbed to the Dark Side but are redeemable, and to better know those who are "Resolute Dark Side", in order to better understand the motivations of the "service-to-self" beings.

So, now that you better understand service-to-others and service-to-self and you think you are AWAKE and ENLIGHTENED. Let us begin with a few descriptions that are the results of reviewing multiple references.

Non-Dual Awakening - Non-Dual Awakening is a moment-out-of-time perspective shift, where it is seen that reality is a single, seamless fabric of awareness that every seemingly separate thing is made of, and that the separateness that we had always assumed "self", other, things, space, and time were comprised of was, in fact, illusory. Seeing this erases the belief in "self" (and eventually that "self" entirely), and ends seeking. A deep but difficult to express understanding of reality is permanently instilled. This understanding IS enlightenment to the nature of reality. Those who are Non-Dual Awakening have the perspective that it is fairly pointless to talk about it, as typical attempts to describe it sound like madness to most "normal" people.

A person who is truly enlightened will live in accordance to what they believe. They will love one another. They will exist in harmony. They will live in peace. They will honor the purest form of righteousness and holiness. While at the same time being absent of any pride, ego, arrogance, entitlements and supremacy. All of this is because it is the truest, rightist and most correct thing to do. They will express these basic spiritual truths and more, all without any threats, fears or intimidations. They each will not want to be identified in any way to angels, gods or lords.

Enlightenment is the state of being of self-mastery where one has extinguished all false concepts as exist within the human construct, attains a transcendence of self comprising a deep sense of oneness and a "self-less" nature, and is liberated from (nearly) all psycho-emotional pain, discontentment, dissatisfaction, and self-suffering.

Spiritual Awakening - Spiritual Awakening is commonly linked with the insight, "We are all one", and creates seekers, poets, mystics, etc. The insight itself is only partial, however, and leaves the person who has experienced it with a deep thirst for understanding that precipitates much personal reflection, art, research, writing, etc. The number may be 1 in 500, or less? Most of us know or have met, or seen someone who has had some kind of spiritual or supernatural event that changed their lives. For these people, it is known that something lies beyond the veil of the normative world, and there is intense urgency in discovering what that is. This insight can, in rare cases, precede a Non-Dual Awakening where there is some discipline, or practice in place to push the insight further.

Spiritual Superconsciousness - In this superconscious state, one sees their life from a different perspective, in which we realize how utterly trivial it is whether we sign that big contract or get a raise, whether somebody insults or praises us, whether people understand us or not. We realize that these things just don't matter. One realized that only those things that helped us to grow spiritually are important. In this superconscious state, we understand that this world is a delusion. We are no longer attached to the body, to the opinions of other people, or to any outward realities. We understand that this world is a delusion, a cosmic dream. We become completely centered in our higher Self because that's where our power and growth begin. We must align our ego with the spiritual superconscious. One must recognize that there is a higher aspect of consciousness, even of your own consciousness, over which you have no control. You are offering yourself up into something you can't command, but the consciousness that comes, which is your own higher Self, doesn't impose itself on you.

Rational Consciousness
1. **Conscious** - The rational awareness that usually guides our daily decisions. When we receive input from the senses, analyze the facts, and make decisions based on this information, we are using this conscious level of guidance. This process is also strongly affected by the opinions of others, which can cloud our ability to draw true guidance. Dividing and separating the world into either/or categories, the conscious level of awareness is problem-oriented. It's difficult to be completely certain of decisions drawn from this level, because the analytical mind can see all the possible solutions. But ultimately it doesn't have the ability to distinguish which one is best. If we rely exclusively on the conscious mind, we may find ourselves lacking in certainty and slipping into a state of perpetual indecision.

2. **Superconscious** - Intuition and heightened mental clarity flow from superconscious awareness. The conscious mind is limited by its analytical nature, and therefore sees all things as separate and distinct. We may be puzzled by a certain situation, but because it seems unrelated to other events, it's difficult to draw a clear course of action. By contrast, because the superconscious level of consciousness is punitive and sees all things as part of a whole, it can readily draw solutions. In superconsciousness the problem

and the solution are seen as one, as though the solution was a natural outgrowth from the problem.

Non-Symbolic Consciousness Awakening - The profound insight event called Awakening is a deeper version of an experience called insight. Awakening is simply an act of liberation from an illusion. Every time you clear up a confusion, that's an awakening. When we learn a lesson on a big life occasion, as when a loved one leaves us, that is another type of insight. Most people only have such insights at major life transitions - first love, marriage, divorce, severe illness, death of a loved one. Those who engage in spiritual practice may have some level of insight without such a crisis. If we learn the lesson of the insight and apply it steadily, that is the most basic level of Awakening, and is very valuable. But few people realize that we can create a life where we are open to insights. We can also open to deeper insights. On the one hand, each insight is valuable if it leads to loving and wise action. People who are clear enough to lead healthy lives and genuinely be helpful to others have had some type of insight. Genuine steady living into deeper and deeper insight and then application of that in a life of endless growth is very, very rare.

Wakefulness is a combination of mindfulness, consciousness, and awareness on a very deep and often spiritual level. Imagine walking around with your eyes open in a world full of people with their eyes clenched shut. That's honestly what it feels like. If you consider yourself to be awake in a world full of people with their blinders secured tightly to their heads, then you'll understand the following struggles:

1. **Seeing the Forest for the Trees** - meaning that when you look so intently at that one tree – you don't notice that you're surrounded by them. If you're truly awake, or at least well on your way to being awake, you see the forest from an aerial view. You see the connections between people and actions in ways that other people don't

understand. A big part of wakefulness understands people and human nature in general. Intuition has a lot to do with it, but studying psychology, spirituality, and the human mind will give us a different perspective. If you consider yourself to be emotionally intelligent, then you understand how many people are emotionally ignorant. As someone who is awake, you see the actions of people and understand why they take the actions that they do.

2. **People Don't Want to Hear the Truth** - Most people are completely comfortable with their blinders. Those blinders provide a sense of safety and security. One of the hardest things people can do is focus their gaze inward. The general consensus seems to be that if you're looking for answers to the way that you are, that something must be wrong with you. There is a very strong parallel here to emotional intelligence. There is a difference in knowing what you feel and knowing why you feel it. When you have this understanding of the human psyche, even on a basic level, you see those "forest and trees" connections. For people who choose not to see those connections, the last thing in the world that they want to do is hear about them, let alone understand them. People take evaluations of their actions and emotions as criticism.

3. **The Fear of Expression, and the Consequence of that Fear** -Knowing that people don't seek the same enlightenment for themselves that you seek in yourself leads to a condition where you want to express yourself about someone's actions, but you fear the defensive nature that comes with it.

<u>Consciously Asleep or Awakening</u> - You are awake, you are concentrating your attention to reading, and you are aware of your environment as well. You can see the furniture of your room; you can hear the call of the birds from the nearby forest.

You are also aware of your thoughts and emotions. How can anyone claim that you are asleep at this very moment?

How would you know then that you are, in fact, not quite enlightened yet, or not even close to it? For the average person it is very easy: just by being an average person grants you the definitive knowledge of not being enlightened and probably never will be.

The question may arise, 'why do I claim that you are asleep and dreaming now?' Well, from the state of consciousness I call Alertness, I can see that you are asleep, you believe yourself to be a separate self, and you are a captive of the works of your mind.

Consciously Asleep – You are Consciously Asleep is because *you* are not present. To be present means that you are fully alert, attentive, and conscious in the present moment. Whatever you do, you do that fully consciously, you focus your entire attention on that particular activity.

Consciously Asleep people are still absorbed in the collective, mainstream trance and have membership in the consensus reality.

What does it mean to be awake? It has happened to all of us that we have come under the spell of a moment, at some time during our life. A beautiful landscape, a sunset, a beautiful piece of art, the rhythm of music enchanted us. It may even happen that we are just lost in the silence of a peaceful moment. The identification with the forms and shapes loosens a little bit for a short while, and in that instant, we may experience an entirely different state of consciousness.

Spiritual Bypassing - It can feel like you are stuck in a kind of hell. Unable to go back to the old ways of excess, avoidance, and unconscious suffering, but also unable to open fully to a new way of life. You have one foot in and one foot out. The resistance to embracing the next iteration of your awakening can be strong as all get out. It can come in the form of falling back into old self-destructive patterns, becoming "depressed" and attaching to that identity, and the good old trick of spiritual bypassing.

Spiritual bypassing is when you use your past insights to avoid your present feelings. I've seen that there is no self, so I don't need to do any personal work. Everything is love so I can just ignore how much I hate myself right now. I know suffering is optional, I'm not suffering, I'm past that point. And so on. The urge is to bypass something as a form of resistance. Whenever there is resistance it's sure that a new insight and a deeper awakening are close by. Resistance, if treated gently and with love, peels back to reveal the brightest of jewels. What you really are.

You do have to wade through loneliness, grief, confusion and intense loss. You have to see and love the parts of yourself that frighten and disgust you the most. You have to be willing to dive into the fires of awakening, with no hope of recovery. You have to let go of getting a fix, or that cookie, or that meditative technique. The part of you that can get a fix will be no more, and when you try to get off of whatever it is, is won't work. It's scary and you lose a lot, but once you stop hitting snooze and wake up to the next transformation, none of that will matter. You will be operating from a whole new perspective. Born again, so to speak. Until you reach the next plateau and do it all again. The good news is that your relationship with this process will change as you do. It won't always be such a big drama to awaken. You won't hit snooze so many times, and eventually not at all.

So give up. Give in. Swim out until you can't see land, and then drop down deep to where there is nothing you've ever known. Then pop back up and Remember That You Are Human.

Awake but in Enlightenment Bypass Symptom – Symptoms of Enlightenment Bypassing include:

1. **You think you are enlightened** - If you find yourself thinking about yourself this way, you can rest assured that you have not nearly grasped the true meaning of what it might mean to be enlightened at all. Your ego may tell you otherwise, but the presence of the very same ego is the surest sign that something is missing and that is enlightenment itself.
2. **You talk about being enlightened and how you've become so** - Bragging has become quite a habit, in fact in social media culture, bragging is a must: Otherwise, people would never notice you. Do you find yourself telling others about your great experience of enlightenment? The sad news is, this is little less than bragging, and as such it has the prerequisite of an inflated ego. Yes, bragging, social media culture, and most aspects of contemporary life work very well in the favor of our egos. At the same time, they work really great against spirituality.
3. **You think yourself special because of your enlightenment** - The problem is, everyone craves to be special in one way or another. We all want to feel how good we are and how much better than others. Truly enlightened people, on the other hand, show great humility and feel they owe mankind; They do not crave to be more than others. They do not try to be leaders. They do not strive for fame and riches. And most importantly: They never claim to be special.
4. **You know more about enlightenment than an average Zen Master** - Having read all the literature, traditional or modern, all religious texts, Sutras, Vedas, Viking Sagas, whatnot; memorizing all you've read,

learning mantras by heart... this can all turn you into a great walking encyclopedia. If you ask such a person anything about enlightenment, they will surely have a ready answer. Does knowing all about it grant they are enlightened? Not much more than knowing all about blue whales would turn you into a blue whale yourself.

5. **You've paid hard cash for your enlightenment** - Enlightenment does not have a price-tag. You cannot get closer to it with money. The good news: It is not all lost. All the money, all the investment you've made will have a massively great positive effect on your life.

6. **You have a name for your enlightenment** - Labels are just names and names alone are meaningless without content. if you can name your enlightenment, you have labeled it. You call this label your enlightenment, which has little to do with the essence of being enlightened, it is just a meaningless name by itself.

7. **You are a part of some exclusive community, by the virtue of your enlightenment** - Enlightenment is essentially an intimate experience. Enlightenment is not clubs, circles or communities that thrive on the notion, that the members are somehow in a better position than non-members and it is a privileged position to be there, but this in not enlightenment; you find enlightenment within the individual.

8. **You are competitive (and not just about enlightenment)** - You do not have to be necessarily competitive about your spiritualism (being "more spiritual" than others). Being competitive generally, in itself shows how far you are removed from the natural state of human mind - that is being collaborative.

9. **You use the word 'I' often** – If one is Enlightened, one has reduced their existence to "I Am" and nothing else. Descriptors then to emphasize worldly things, such as titles, wealth, secular beliefs, Even saying that " I am a free spirit in the universe" is, still a descriptor. Even

The Creator did not say that "I am God" but left it as "I AM who I AM."

10. **You are unconditionally happy, no matter what happens to you** - if you are anywhere on your path to enlightenment, chances are that you are really happier than you would be otherwise. But enlightenment has nothing to do with being happy, it has much more to do with losing things: Your ego and your illusions. This latter is of the greater importance. If you imagine yourself a perfect reality and you live in it, you created an illusion. Enlightenment is little more than losing your illusions of what is untrue, how would replacing one illusion with another suffice? If you are in denial, if you lie to yourself, you are nowhere nearer to seeing the truth.
11. You **know exactly when and how you've become enlightened** (and not afraid to talk about it) – This is a form of bragging and being too full of ego. Attaining Enlightenment does not happen overnight despite a single experience making it seem to be so.
12. **You take yourself absolutely seriously and are aware of your own importance** - Self-importance is as far from enlightenment. it is just another name or label on your ego.

If you can say none of these apply to you and that you are indeed only "I AM" then start reading Chapter 18.

<u>**Recruited, Sold Out, Selected Dark Side**</u> - "Service-to-self," does not mean that one cannot enjoy self serving item, like a relaxing bath or time by themselves. Service-to-self are those beings who feel the greatest value is enslaving other beings or other creatures or planet Earth. Basically, service-to-self is about gain for the self at the expense of other-selves. We have seen a lot of service-to-self exploitations on this planet in the past few millennia. These types of beings can gather and harness a lot of Free Will – a lot of power, a lot of spiritual

power. Therefore they have a lot of power to manifest and execute. Sometimes service to-self beings tend to accumulate or harness Free Will more quickly than service-to-others beings.

The First Dark Triad is the characteristic we associate the dark side of Machiavellianism with PARANOIA. But this is probably an over simplification. People high in Machiavellianism—sometimes called high-Machs—are manipulators. They enjoy deceiving others, and they are willing to do almost anything to get their way.

The second Dark Triad characteristic is called PSYCHOPATHY, which has been called an "antisocial" personality. What antisocial means in this context is the opposite of pro-social. That means that an antisocial person is generally actively harmful towards others—or perhaps just highly self-focused rather than other-focused. Psychopathy shares with Machiavellianism a lack of empathy, but is combined with impulsiveness. Psychopaths are risk-takers who do what they want in the moment. Psychopathy is probably the darkest of the Dark Triad. Psychopaths don't experience guilt or shame to the degree that most people do—they experience lower levels of anxiety than average as well.

The final Dark Triad tendency is NARCISSISM, which is probably the best known of the three. Narcissists want to be the center of attention, and they'll work to make sure that happens. They are relentless self-promoters. They will take almost any opportunity to portray an enhanced image of themselves to others. Narcissism has some obvious advantages—narcissists interview well; they are good at selling themselves and their ideas, and they can generate a lot of enthusiasm.

Peter Jonason (Senior Lecturer in Personality or Individual Differences, Psychology: Behavioral Science /SSAP, Western Sydney University) and his colleagues have called the Dark Triad an agentic social style, and illustrate this concept through the example of James Bond, who achieves his goals through means including force, deceit, intimidation, persuasion, negotiation, and, of course, seduction. The researchers describe Bond as an extrovert, open to new experience, with high self-esteem, which partly explains why his otherwise exploitative approach to life mostly succeeds.

Often the Resolute Dark Side entices joining this group of elite leaders through any one of the "earthly sins" of control, fame, fortune, envy by others, wine/women/song, long life, any other desire, or even to promise of eternal life (which all already have through being spirits). Some spirits even come to Earth to learn about the Dark Side, knowing they can change their orientation any time they want, now or in a later lifetime.

Resolute Dark (entrenched "Service-to-Self") is a powerful and savagely guarded coalition of families and organizations that secretly controls the entire modern world. This coalition has existed since the dawn of time (e.g., Anunnaki) and wants nothing less than to establish a new world order – over which an authoritarian gang of elites would rule, and under which nation states would be banished. Below are but a few secret societies that may well establish the Resolute Dark coalition.

Illuminati - Although the Illuminati originally branched off from, and broke away from, the Freemasons, they have since become a prime focus for conspiracy theorists, many of whom credit Illuminati agendas for every conceivable disaster, mystery, and economic downturn. The Illuminati website states: "Living humans evolve at a rapid pace and continue to advance in ability through study, practice, and self-improvement. The human species is guarded by a coalition of its most elite members called the Illuminati."

The Rosicrucians - Founded in the early fifteenth century by Christian Rosenkreutz. The Rosicrucians were purported to be using occult practices to bring about a global transformation.

Two centuries later, the publication of three manifestos launched them into the popular consciousness. They are believed by discerning conspiracy theorists to have founded the Freemasons, the Illuminati, and the Invisible College, and to have been the guiding force behind every significant revolution in modern history.

Bilderbergs - In 1954, the world's most influential movers and shakers met in a hotel to discuss and plan the coming year's global agenda. They have continued to meet every year, but the content of their talks has remained a zealously guarded secret. They are not technically a secret society, since their existence and membership are not in question, but many conspiracy theorists worry about the influence and reach of their annual meetings.

Freemasons – Upper Levels of the Freemasons. The Freemasons are the longest-lasting secret society (that the general population is aware of) still in existence. They've become synonymous with secret handshakes, bizarre rituals and a hierarchy in which members move up through various levels as they gain experience and respect within the society. Originally formed by the union of several smaller societies, the first "lodge" was founded in London in 1717, but at that time rumors of the Masons' existence had already been circulating for at least a century. Most modern secret societies take their cue from the Freemasons by incorporating handshakes, code words, private rituals and complex chains of command.

The Skull and Bones - Perhaps the least secret of all secret societies, the Skull and Bones Society at Yale University was founded by William H Russell in 1832. Originally called the Eulogian Club, the Skull and Bones boasts many prominent heads of state (including at least three presidents), captains of industry, and heads of covert agencies among its membership. The society meets twice a week for rituals that are purported to closely follow Masonic rites, but many claim the organization is really nothing more than a glorified college fraternity.

The Elders of Zion - In 1920, a newspaper owned by industrialist Henry Ford ran a series of articles reprinting a Russian document called the Protocols of the Elders of Zion. The document was quickly debunked as a hoax, but those articles were collected as a book, newly titled *The International Jew: The World's Foremost Problem*. Adolph Hitler read the book, was influenced by it, and appropriated many of its ideas for himself. Anti-Semitic theorists around the world still believe that the Protocols were genuine and that there was once a Jewish conspiracy to achieve world domination.

The Knights Templar - Early in the twelfth century, nine knights took a vow to protect pilgrims traveling through the Holy Land. More knights joined the cause and the organization grew, gathering wealth, fame and power as their influence spread. Popular culture has cast them in the role of funders of many other secret societies and guardians of the most sacred Christian treasures. But the members of the Knights Templar were eventually tortured and executed, and the society was disbanded, yet their ruminants remain today. There is no compelling evidence that they ever possessed the Ark of the Covenant, the Holy Grail or the blood of Jesus Christ.

SPIRITUAL AWAKENING RELATED TO THE FREQUENCY OF THE EARTH - There is an ancient Indian saying that states that for an individual to awaken from the illusion of self, the urge to do so must be similar to a man whose hair is on fire and he is desperately in need of water to put it out. Nice, gentle dreams aren't the ones that jolt you out of your sleep.

It is estimated that 1 in 10 million people have spiritual enlightenment as a goal. Only those who are seriously committed will reach it. If 1 in 10 million try, perhaps 1 out of

100 will succeed? So, 1 in a billion? Who knows. Then again, it depends how you define "spiritual awakening." There are gradations of consciousness. One may be "awakened" but not "enlightened." And even enlightenment has its levels.

Population Distribution in 2014 – 8.1 B (Billion) world population:
1. 7.2 B – Declared Religion but may not be practicing (Christian – 2.4 B, Islam - 1.8 B, Hinduism – 1.15 B, Buddhism – 521 M, Chinese Traditional Religion – 394 M, Ethnic Religions – 300 M, African Traditional Religions – 300 M, Sikhism – 30 M, Spiritism – 15 M, Judaism 14 M, Other Religions)
2. 70 M – Believe in a Higher Power
3. 1.2 B – Secular, humanist, Nonreligious, agnostic, atheist

Enlightenment / Dark Distribution in 2014 – Since the universe appears to be very mathematical, distribution should fit the Standard Distribution Model (Bell Curve) with 5-Deviations. However, Distribution can easily be contested, as indicated by the wide variation among the many sources (i.e., references vary widely). Literature research tends to indicate that Enlightenment is beginning to dominate the Dark Side, with the Dark Side maintaining its Control of the Earth. Given this, the below distribution may be what it was in 1994.

1. 0.01% (810 T) - Non-Dual Awakening
2. 1% (8.1 M) – Spiritually Awake
3. 2.1% (170 M) - Spiritual Superconsciousness & Rational Consciousness
4. 13.6% (1.1 B) – Awakening to Enlightenment
5. 34.1% (2.8 B) – Asleep but leaning toward Enlightenment
6. 34.1% (2.8 B) – Asleep but leaning toward Dark
7. 13.6 B (2.8 B) - Waking Up Dark
8. 2.1% (170 M) - Sold Out, Converted, or Selected Dark
9. 1% (8.1 M) – Elite Dark
10. .01% (810 T) – Resolute Dark

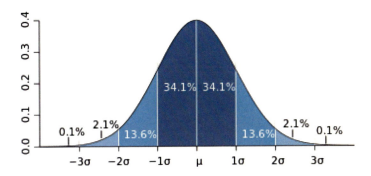

Earth Frequency Rising - According to *Wikipedia* (https://en.wikipedia.org/wiki/Schumann resonances), the "Schumann Resonance "(should be called " Tesla Resonance" he deserves the real credit for identifying the magnetic frequencies of the Earth) are a set of spectrum peaks in the extremely low frequency (ELF) portion of the Earth's electromagnetic field) spectrum. Schumann resonances are global electromagnetic resonances, generated and excited by lightning discharges in the cavity formed by the Earth's surface and the ionosphere.

Schumann resonances are the principal background in the electromagnetic spectrum beginning at 3 Hz and extending to 60 Hz, and appear as distinct peaks at extremely low frequencies (ELF) around 7.83 (fundamental), 14.3, 20.8, 27.3 and 33.8 Hz.

It has long been suspected that human consciousness can impact the magnetic field and create disturbances in it, particularly during moments of high anxiety, tension and passion: http://sedonanomalies.weebly.com/schumann-resonance.html

Global Consciousness Rising - The Global Consciousness Project (http://global-mind.org/gcpdot/), seems to correlate to the increase in the electromagnetic frequencies (Schumann

Resonance). A related article, mentioned within The Global Consciousness Project literature (http://www.trinfinity8.com/why-is-Earth's-schumann-resonance-accelerating/) states:

"For many years this resonance frequency has hovered at a steady 7.83 Hz with only slight variations. In June 2014 that apparently changed. Monitors at the Russian Space Observing System indicated a sudden spike in activity to around 8.5 Hz. Since then, they have recorded days where the Schumann accelerated as fast as 16.5 Hz."

These emerging resonances are naturally correlated to human brainwave activity. So this means, we are changing... A 7.83 Hz frequency is an alpha/theta state. Relaxed, yet dreamy—sort of a neutral idling state waiting for something to happen. A 8.5 – 16.5 Hz frequency moves one out of the theta range into more of a full calmer alpha state with faster more alert beta frequencies starting to appear. (This correlates with slowly waking up cognitively). Since the Schumann Resonance has had sudden spikes between 12 – 16.5 Hz" the change is more profound. In Neurofeedback, 12-15 Hz is called Sensory-Motor Rhythm frequency (SMR). It is an ideal state of awakened calm. Our thought processes are clearer and more focused, yet we are still "in the flow" or "in the know." In other words, Mother Earth is shifting her vibrational frequency and perhaps so are we. This may be one of many signs that we are AWAKENING.

In the normal mode descriptions of Schumann resonances, the fundamental mode is a standing wave in the Earth–ionosphere cavity with a wavelength equal to the circumference of the Earth. This lowest-frequency (and highest-intensity) mode of the Schumann resonance occurs at a frequency of approximately 7.83 Hz, but this frequency can vary slightly from a variety of factors, such as solar-induced perturbations to the ionosphere, which compresses the upper wall of the closed cavity.

The higher octaves of the 7.83 Schumann Resonance can also stimulate the pituitary in the same way that 7.83 HZ can – especially 31.32 HZ. One needs to be careful to distinguish between octaves of the 7.83 Schumann Resonance, and the other six Schumann Resonances, which are not higher octaves of 7.83 HZ.

0.5-4 Hz (Delta) you are sound asleep. Delta waves are the slowest of all five brainwave frequencies. Slow Save Sleep or SWS, is the deepest of sleep states and it plays a vital role in health and well being. During this phase of the sleep cycle, the brain begins producing very slow, large Delta waves.

4-7 Hz (Theta) is one of the more elusive and extraordinary brain waves you can explore. It is known as the twilight state which you normally only experience fleetingly upon awakening, or drifting off to sleep. This is the brain state where magic happens in the crucible of your own neurological activity. But for most, being able to enter the dreamlike theta state without being asleep, taking meditation practice. Luckily, Brainwave Therapy can speed up this process, making it easier to drop into sleep meditative states, even in one never meditated before.

7-14 Hz (Alpha) is an intensively pleasurable and relaxed state of consciousness essential to stress reduction and high levels of creativity. Artists, musicians, and athletes are prolific alpha producers. So are intuitive persons, as was Albert Einstein. Alpha researcher, Joe Kamiya said, "Its pleasure may come from the fact that alpha represents something like letting go of anxieties." With Brainwave Therapy binaural beat frequencies one can begin experiencing the benefits of alpha biofeedback training.

8.6 Hz Reduced Stress/Anxiety

8.0-10.0 Hz learning new information; Alpha – Rapid Refreshment; "Low Alpha" inner awareness of self, mind/body integration, balance.

14-30 Hz (Bata) is wide-awake, alert. One's mind is sharp, focused. It makes connections quickly, easily, and one is primed to do work that requires one's full attention. In Bata state, neurons fire abundantly, in rapid succession, helping one achieve peak performance. New ideas and solutions to problems flash like lightening into one's mind.

>30 Hz (Gamma) is the fastest of the brainwave frequencies and signify the highest state of focus possible. They are associated with peak concentration and the brain's optimum frequency for cognitive functioning. Nobel Prize winning scientist, Sir Francis Crick believes that the 40 Hz frequency may be the key to the act of cognition. 40 Hz is the window used in all Brain Sync Gamma and Beta wave programs.

Scientist's report that the Earth's magnetic field, which can affect the Schumann Resonance, has been slowly weakening for the past 2,000 years and even more so in the last few years. No one really knows why. A wise old sage from India stated that the magnetic field of Earth was put in place by the Ancient Ones to block our primordial memories of our true heritage. This was so that souls could learn from the experience of free-will unhampered by memories of the past. He claimed that the magnetic field changes are now loosening those memory blocks and we are raising our consciousness to greater truth. The veil is lifting. The blinders are coming off.

Rate of Change in Earth's Resonance Field - As the Earth's resonance "rises," The humans on the Earth begin to have a higher frequency and their state of Enlightenment increases.

7.83 Hz was, prior to 2014 the Fundamental Frequency of the Earth's resonance field. Although the Fundamental Frequency appears to be stable for millennia, there are no lower frequency records. Meaning, that the Earth's Resident Frequency may have been lower at some time in the distant past.

8.5 Hz (8.5% increase over the Fundamental Frequency) was noted in June 2014 by monitors at the Russian Space Observing System. At first they thought their equipment was malfunctioning, but later learned the data was accurate. Everyone was asking, what's causing this intermittent spiking activity? Is the Earth's frequency speeding up? Since the Schumann frequency is said to be "in tune" with the human brain's alpha and theta states, this acceleration may be why it often feels like time has sped up and events and changes in our life are happening more rapidly. This change means that our brain is moving out of Theta, into the Alpha wave range.

16.5 Hz (110% increase over the Fundamental Frequency and 94% increase over the "New" Base Frequency of 8.5 HZ) was noticed in 2015. Although this was a spike, the 16.5 HZ is spiking more and more often. In more recent times, other peaks have been detected, increasing the planet's frequency to 30 Hz.

It is concluded that these changes clearly show that the planet is changing. Some scholars also believe that humans, when acting on a "collective consciousness" level, can affect the structures of the resonance field. It is here that Wanderers, Lightworkers, indigos, those that have achieved Dual and Non-Dual Awakeness, and even those that are Consciously or Superconsciously Awake can help increase the Earth's resonance field frequency and, hence, bring about enlightenment. The 8.5 Hz and 16.5 Hz increase will Wake-Up many within the "service-to-others" group, and may help draw-in some of the "service-to-self" asleep group toward the philosophy of the "service-to-others group."

INCREASE IN ENLIGHTENMENT - The rise of scholarly reference databases, either of citations or of full test documents, has made it possible to identify, and harder to ignore, many sources that might previously have shown beneath our radars. One search portal, since 2008, lets users analyze the results of search queries, by separating out the multiple dimensions of documents, including year of publication, language, article type, journal, discipline, and subject. For example a search was made for "the Enlightenment." From this one can then analyze the values by year and then develop a chart of findings. This chart presents a fair amount of information: most notably, it suggests that interest in the enlightenment as a scholarly topic has increased dramatically and at times even exponentially, over the course of the twentieth century. It also seems to indicate that this interest peaked in 1998, and has dropped significantly to 2008 and then dramatically rose, once again. A first point of clarification is that the sums presented in the chart refer, not to the total number of occurrences per year, but rather to the total number of documents containing the text string (i.e., there were not 1,862 mentions of "the Enlightenment" in 1998; the expression can be found in 1,882 documents). The implications of this distinction are that all documents are placed in the same footing.

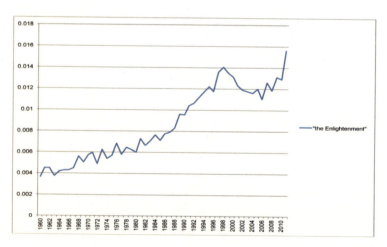

Normalized yearly pattern of usage for "the Enlightenment." Divided by the total number of documents in JSTOR holdings. Source http://dfr.stor.org/.

The "Enlightenment" data can be further broken down by Country (graph below) to place emphasis as to where the "Enlightenment" is occuring.

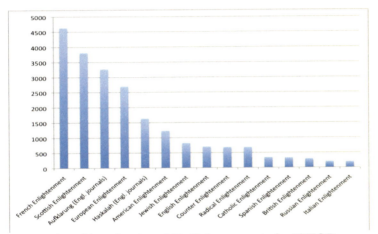

Top national/confessional Enlightenments in JSTOR, measured by number of documents. Source: hnttp://dft.jstor.org/.

What we can learn, then, from these numbers? Taken as a whole, they reinforce the impression outlined above: namely, that most scholars who discuss the place or effects of the Enlightenment in and around Europe seem to view it as a transnational phenomenon, one that is sufficient homogeneous that it does not require qualifiers. It is not always possible to know why a trend is occurring, but we can sometimes get a sense of who is behind it. It could be linked to the change in the Resonate Frequency of the Earth which has been rising.

From 2006 (.0108) to 2014 (.0148) there was a 37% increase or a non-compounded rate of 9.26% per year. By 2014 the factor (number of Enlightenment documents per total number of documents) would be 0.188 and 0.028 by 2018, presuming the rate of increase remained at 9.26% per year, non- accumulating. Over that same period, the Resonant Frequency of the Earth was increasing at the rate of 4% per year, non-accumulating.

As a conservative estimate, based upon the above, we should be safe to presume that there is at least a 4% per year increase in Spiritual Enlightenment. Meaning that the ratio of "service-to-self" to "service-to-others" is tilting by approx. 4% toward "service-to-others " or approx 118.8 M of the population are seeking the "Light" side (4% times the number of Asleep Dark + Awaking Dark).

Sources:
1. '3+1 Definitive Signs That Show You Are Not Enlightened ,' Attila Orosz, *Meditation For Beginners*, http://beginnersmeditation.info/blog/13-plus-one-signs
2. 'The Three Levels of Consciousness,' *Ananda*, https://www.ananda.org/meditation/meditation-support/articles/the-three-levels-of-consciousness/
3. 'The Courage To Live Superconsciously,' *Ananda*, https://www.ananda.org/blog/kriyananda-yogananda-yoga/
4. 'No Religion is Worlds Third-Largest Religious Group After Christians, Muslims According to Pew Study,' *HuffingtonPost*, Reuters, Tom Heneghan, Dec 18, 2012, https://www.huffingtonpost.com/2012/12/18/unaffiliated-third-largest-religious-group-after-christians-muslims_n_2323664.html
5. The Translucent Revolution, Arjuna Ardagh, *New World Library*, 2005, ISBN-10: 1577314689, ISBN-13: 978-1577314684
6. Trans-personal Academics, by Pete Ashly on Petes Bookmarks, Cook-Greuter, Tolbert and Martin
7. Power vs. Force: The Hidden Determinants of Human Behavior, David R Hawkins , *Hay House*, 2012, ISBN-10: 978140194169, ISBN-13: 978-1401941697, ASIN: 1401941699

8. 'Thinking Like Einstein,' Arthur Zajonc, from the The Meditative Life, *Psychology Today*, Mar 17, 2011, https://www.psychologytoday.com/us/blog/the-meditative-life/201103/thinking-einstein
9. 'How common is spiritual awakening?' 12 Answers, *Quora*, Oct 15, 2015, Various Authors, https://www.quora.com/How-common-is-spiritual-awakening
10. 'Seven Signs You Are Truly Awake,' Frank M Wanderer, April 29, 2016, *OuLift*, https://upliftconnect.com/seven-signs-you-are-awake/
11. 'Roughly how many enlightened people are living on the planet in 2018?,' 15 Answers, *Quora*, Mar 18, 2018, Various Authors, https://www.quora.com/Roughly-how-many-enlightened-people-are-living-on-the-planet-in-2018
12. 'How seldom or often does awakening happen in modern time? What is the percentage of enlightened people in your opinion?,' *Quora*, June 4, 2016, Various Authors, https://www.quora.com/How-seldom-or-often-does-awakening-happen-in-modern-time-What-is-the-percentage-of-enlightened-people-in-your-opinion
13. 'How many enlightened human beings are there in the world today?,' 18 Answers, *Quora*, Various Authors, Nov 30, 2016, https://www.quora.com/How-many-enlightened-human-beings-are-there-in-the-world-today
14. '3 Struggles that Only People who are Truly Awake Will Understand,' Justin Gammill, May 28, 2016, *Intelligence*.com, Https://iheartintelligence.com/2016/03/28/struggles-people-understand/
15. 'Mindful Awakening: The Cost Is Just Everything,' Jessica Graham, *Deconstructing Yourself*, Sept 18, 2018, https://deconstructingyourself.com/mindful-awakening.html
16. 'Spiritual Emergence – Awaken in The Dream,' Paul Levy, Sept 29, 2018, https://www.awakeninthedream.com/articles/spiritual-emergence

17. 'Lesson 11 – Service to self vs. service to others,' Bentinho Masaro, *Trinity Academy*, Oct 3, 2018, https://www.trinfinity academy.com/courses/empowerment-2-trinfinity-cosmology-empowered-evolution/lesson-11-service-to-self-vs-service-to-others/
18. 'The Pros and Cons of Having a Dark Side,' Seth M. Spain Ph.D. author of The Dark Side of Work, Aug 20, 2014, *Psychology Today*, https://www.psychologytoday.com/ca/blog/the-dark-side-work/201408/the-pros-and-cons-having-dark-side
19. 'The dark side of personality at work,' Seth M Spain, Peter D Harms, James M Lebreton, Published in *Journal of Organizational Behavior* (2013); DOI: 10.1002/job.1894, 2013, John Wiley & Sons, Ltd
20. 'The 7 Most Exclusive Secret Societies in History,' Alex Grecian, Contributor, *HuffPost*, May 20, 2014, https://www.huffingtonpost.com/alex-grecian/the-most-exclusive-secret_b_5398914.html
21. 'What is the Illuminati?' You asked Google – here's the answer, Martha Gill, Nov 22, 2015, The Guardian, https://www.theguardian.com/commentisfree/2017/nov/22/what-is-illuminati-google-autocomplete
22. 'Illuminati Official Website,' https://www.illuminatiofficial.org/
23. 'List of religious populations,' Wikipedia, Pew Research, Gallup International, other references, https://en,m.wilipedia.org/List_of_religious_population
24. 'Humans are Waking Up: First Time in Recorded History, Schumann Resonance Jumping to 36+,' Feb 2, 2017, *Linkedin*, prepareforchange.net/207/02/02/humans-are-waking-up-for-the-first-timje-in-recorded-history-schumann-resonance-jumping-to-36/
25. 'Mother Earth is Shifting Her Vibrational Frequency and So Are We,' Consciousness Technology, Feb 3, 2006, *Patriots for Truth*, https://patriots4truth.org/2018/02/03/mother-Earth-is-shifting-her-vibrational-frequency-and-so-are-we/

Chapter 18

THE FIVE STAGES OF AWAKENING

What does it really mean to awaken? It is fair to say that awakening is a journey from limitation to freedom — from unconscious to conscious. Whether you intentionally choose to take this journey or an unexpected experience propels you onto the path, once you start, there is no turning back.

There are 5 Stages of Awakening, and when you understand each stage, and where you are on the journey, you can recognize the sign posts along the way, and the possible pitfalls to avoid.

Whatever stage you might now be experiencing, you cannot get it. Awakening is simply a natural process, just like the caterpillar that awakens as the butterfly.

A common question is, how long does each stage take? The time spent in each stage is not predetermined, but one can move through a stage quicker and easier when one utilize a mindfulness practice of letting go. Letting go is truly the secret of awakening.

As more and more people awaken, a threshold of awakening will be experienced, and the masses will awaken in much different paradigm than those of us who have already awakened or who are awakening now. The stages of awakening will be less defined and maybe even disappear altogether.

No matter where you are on your journey to awakening, you are exactly where you need to be.

STAGE 1 OF AWAKENING: THE STAGE OF THE FALSE-SELF - Subtle awareness of "something more" begins to grow.

In Stage 1 of Awakening: we are most asleep; we do not even know that we are asleep. We are entrenched in mass consciousness and going through the motions of life, generally following the rules of culture and laws of the land.

We don't usually question reality or seek answers beyond what is necessary for survival and maintenance of a lifestyle.

Our identities define us and we live within the construct of religion, culture and/or society. We may even play the part of victim or perpetrator.

Unconscious programming runs us, and, as a result, we see the world in black and white – good and bad. We likely process a rigid model of the world according to our specific programming.

Because there is a great desire to fit in and be accepted, in this stage, it is common to sacrifice our needs and compromise our values in order to receive approval and be included in our desired community, be that family, culture, business, religion, etc.

Self-worth is likely conditional and attached to identity or the roles we play, or there may be other means of proving that we are worthy.

Because the ego generally runs the show, we likely believe we are the ego, with little or no awareness that there is a greater part of us.

In stage one, happiness is based on externals, therefore, in order to feel happy, we try to control reality; other people, places and experiences.

Although we attempt to control our lives, for both happiness and security, it is more than likely that our emotions rule, and our actions and reactions are based on our moment to moment feelings.

We make no connection between our thoughts/beliefs and our experiences in reality, and, therefore, we have no direct ability to consciously create our reality.

Despite our unconscious nature, the first signs of awakening happen during this stage; a "flash feeling" that there is something more, or an inkling of doubt that makes us uncertain about life or reality.

STAGE 2 OF AWAKENING – THE STAGE OF QUESTIONING - The doubts experienced in stage one begins to turn into meaningful questions. The first signs of movement from unconscious to conscious are experienced.

In Stage 2 of Awakening: We experience a growing discomfort in our lives. There is a feeling that something is wrong or missing. We begin to question mass consciousness and the validity of rules, beliefs and laws. Things that used to bring us comfort like religion or traditions are no longer satisfying and the places that we once found answers no longer provide relief.

We question our identity but we still hold on to it because we must continue to prove our worth, and we don't yet know ourselves outside of our human identity. As we question the roles we play, we may feel lost, and even betrayed by others or life in general.

We may even blame religion, family, culture, gender, race, ethnicity, government or the world for our problems, or maybe we blame specific people for our dysfunctions. As we shift responsibility onto others, we feel powerless over our lives; not yet realizing that in order to take back our power, we must take responsibility. In this stage, we might move from victim to survivor, but we are likely still blaming others and feeling powerless.

We begin to ask, "Who am I? Why am I here?"

Although we are searching for answers, we still hold on to certain limiting beliefs that keep us enslaved in the reality we have known. When we attempt to challenge these beliefs, fear brings us back, keeping us asleep a little longer.

In our discomfort with reality, and our search for answers, we may experience a great deal of confusion, overwhelm, anxiety and even depression. We keep up with our lives but we are secretly just "going through the motions."

As we experience a variety of challenges designed to help us wake up, tolerable discomfort turns into pain and suffering. As our disempowering beliefs are demonstrated in real life situations and relationships, we get our first glimpse of the unconscious programs running our lives, but our desire to fit in and be accepted is likely stronger than any desires to free ourselves. Although this is the beginning of our internal programs breaking down, we are still trying to prove our worth by demonstrating our importance and seeking approval for our efforts.

We begin to understand that happiness cannot be found in the outside world, but we are still playing the game – seeking happiness in other people, places and experiences.

In this stage, there can be a great deal of emotional triggers. We may even experience trauma or remember past trauma. Emotions are generally very strong, and we may feel most fragile or vulnerable. What we do not yet realize is that our issues are coming to the surface to be healed and released. Even though we are beginning to see the world in a whole new light, we may still possess black and white thinking – maybe more than ever. We are not ready to take responsibility for our lives and, therefore, we make little or no connection between our thoughts and our experiences in reality.

As the outside world no longer satisfies our hunger, the journey inward is about to begin.

STAGE 3 OF AWAKENING – THE STAGE OF INTROSPECTION - Immense personal/spiritual growth and the start of conscious evolution through self-discovery.

In Stage 3 of Awakening, we begin a journey of introspection. In Stage 2, we rebelled against the external world with little or no success in relieving our pain, suffering or discomfort, so now we retreat as we begin to seek answers inside ourselves.

We start to disentangle from mass consciousness, releasing many limiting beliefs that were programmed into us by asleep parents, teachers, culture, society, religion and media. As we release these beliefs, we may experience both grief and relief. If we spent a life time imprisoned in beliefs that caused emotional suffering, physical hardship and lost happiness, we may grieve for the life we never had, and at the same time, we may feel great relief as we break free from limitation.

As we recognize how asleep we have been, we can clearly see that most people we know are still asleep. We try to wake them up, but our attempts are seen as judgmental and, therefore, met with deaf ears.

Not surprisingly, with our eyes wide open, it is common to experience greater judgment of other people (friends and strangers alike), society and the world. Others may feel our judgment and defensively respond with their own judgment of us. We are seen as different, weird and maybe even crazy. Sooner or later, we decide to keep our growing awareness to ourselves; maybe rationalizing that it's better to be silent than be judged. At this point, we don't have a lot of hope that others will wake up.

We are still focused on everything that is wrong in our lives, and in the world, but, at the same time, we have resistance to letting go. The process of letting go is often "the work" in this stage, and, as we learn to let go, Stage 3 is where we may leave unsatisfying jobs, intimate relationships, families, friendships, religions, organizations and any disempowering ways of life. We may disentangle from roles we played, reject our past identity, and there may even be a total withdrawal from society.

Our former model of the world is failing and we no longer see the world in black and white or good and bad. There may be a growing sense that we are all connected, but at the same time we may feel completely disconnected from every other human being. In many ways, we are faced with the dichotomy of life and existence.

The most common attribute of stage three is loneliness. In a sea of billions of people, you may feel like you are the only one awake; no one understands you, and there is no one with whom to connect. At this point, you might begin to question "the questioning" – why did you ever begin this journey? What's the point of waking up, if you must be alone and lonely? After all, you might have been unhappy when you were asleep but at least you had friends, family and people who cared about you. Now, there is no one. You consider "going back." You wish you could forget about everything you now know just so you can be part of a family or community. You yearn for "normalcy" in order to fit in with others, but you also know that it is too late. You cannot forget what you have remembered, and despite your loneliness and your desire to fit in, you wouldn't go back or undo your path even if you could.

Issues of worthiness often surface in this stage, because the ways, in which, we once proved worth no longer work or are no longer available because we left the job or situation that once made us feel worthy. We may still try to seek approval, acceptance or appreciation or get other emotional needs met by those still in our lives, but it doesn't fulfill us, as it once did, and we are left feeling empty – forced to deal with feelings of unworthiness on our own.

Our desire to fit in and be accepted is slowly being drowned out by our desire to be free and awake.

In the quest for answers and relief from emotional pain, we may embark on some sort of spiritual practice such as meditation, yoga or mindfulness. If we are not using the practice to avoid something, its purpose is likely to get us somewhere, accomplish something or wake up.

In stage three, we may experience the first real sense of power, but, if the ego claims this power, we may have challenging and humbling experiences.

By now, we may be able to see the connection between our thoughts/beliefs and the creation of our reality, and, as a result, we try to control our thoughts, but it is a difficult process because old programs are still running.

We no longer look outside ourselves for happiness, but maybe we don't yet know how to find it within. Peace and freedom may also take precedence over happiness.

Stage three is often the longest stage and almost always the most challenging, but it is also the most important in terms of awakening.

This stage is marked by the swing between resistance and letting go, with moments of clarity and enlightenment, but they don't last. It is very common to have multiple experiences of awakening in this stage and even to believe that each one is the final awakening; only to find yourself back in "reality", hours, days or weeks later. With each experience of awakening, the sense of your higher self grows stronger. You are unknowingly making room for this real self to emerge in your consciousness and integrate in your life.

In stage three, it is common to experience a fear of losing oneself, and you may struggle to maintain a sense of self, but ultimately, toward the end of this stage, an ego-end is inevitable. When the ego loses hold, there is often a realization that there is no point or purpose to life. This can be liberating, like a breath of fresh air, or it can be devastating, resulting in hopelessness and despair. Without point or purpose, we no longer know how to live our lives, and nothing is ever the same.

There is a foreboding sense that awakening will cost you everything, yet, at the same time, there is a greater sense that something inside you is waking up.

STAGE 4 OF AWAKENING – THE STAGE OF RESOLUTION - Spiritual awakening is effortlessly experienced in everyday life.

Stage 4 of Awakening is the stage of resolution where your true self has finally overshadowed your false self or ego self. The struggle that you experienced in the first three stages is over and you experience a deep peace and knowing of whom you really are, and you are no longer seeking answers. This is fondly known as the Eckart Tolle Stage.

All your beliefs have been overhauled in the past three stages, and the beliefs that remain support harmony and balance. You have mastered the art of letting go, and surrendering to a higher power. You also experience and have access to the inner power you possess, without ego control.

Doubt has been replaced with faith and trust. You are able to see and understand your life in such a way that your past and present all makes sense. You have forgiven everyone for everything, including yourself.

Unconscious programming has been replaced with consciousness, and there are no emotional or mental prisons holding you captive.

You take responsibility for your entire life, no longer blaming anyone for anything. As you have freed yourself, you have freed all the people who have ever been affected by your judgment and expectations.

You are no longer trying to prove your worth. You now know and own your intrinsic worth, and, as a result, you experience unconditional self-love.

Although you might still be alone on your journey, you experience a deep and profound connection to all of life and the sense of loneliness has likely faded into all oneness. The need and desire for the old paradigm of relationships has shifted and you no longer yearn to fit in or be "normal." You allow yourself to be exactly who you are, without needing approval or acceptance from anyone. You no longer have a need to change anyone or help those you love wake up, and you are pleasantly surprised that some people you know are actually awakening. All your relationships improve, and the new people who come into your life are better aligned with who you are.

In this stage, you integrate your insights and develop greater understanding for the journey you have been on. You may teach, mentor or share, but not because you feel you have to, or because you need to, but only because it brings you joy, and you are guided to do so. You may have a compelling desire to support others on their journey or you may have no inclination whatsoever. If you take the role of teacher, mentor, healer or coach, you do not take responsibility for others, but rather you empower them to empower themselves. You don't take anything personally, and another's behavior has little, or no, effect on you.

During stage four, it is common to have some sort of spiritual practice, such as meditation, yoga or mindfulness, but not because you are trying to get somewhere or accomplish something (as in the previous stage), but rather because it feels good to you, and it is a natural expression of your life.
You may also experience increased intuition and the ability to access infinite intelligence, as if you have a direct line to unlimited information.

This stage is marked by living in the moment.

You have made peace with the realization that there is no purpose or point to life, and, as a result, it is effortless to live in the present moment. Your love for life and all living beings overflows unconditionally with gratitude and appreciation as a common state of being.

The concepts of good and bad have dissolved, and, yet, you have the full knowing that inside everyone and everything is love.

You take stock of yourself, realizing that you are still you. You are free from ego-control, and no "authentic parts" have been lost in the journey to awakening. Your personality may be quite the same, but you are likely more easy-going and light-hearted.

Either you have found a livelihood that is aligned with who you are, or you have made peace with your present day livelihood.

There is really no thought of happiness because you no longer need anything to make you happy. You have realized that the secret to happiness is living in the moment and it is now easy to be present at all times.

You have learned how to master your thoughts and beliefs, but, surprisingly, you may have no desire to change anything in your life.

Although you likely experience a full range of emotions, emotions no longer rule you or control your choices or relationships.

Your higher self has integrated in your body, and you live your life as this real self.

You are finally conscious and awake, and grateful that your past "asleep-self" had the courage and tenacity to make this journey. It was worth it – a million times over.

STAGE 5 OF AWAKENING – THE STAGE OF CONSCIOUS CREATION - The ability to consciously create one's life from the awakened state.

Many people arrive at stage four and mistakenly believe it is the final stage of awakening, but it is actually a bridge to an even greater experience of awakening.

In Stage 5 of awakening, you experience, and deepen, all the attributes of stage four, but you also step into your power as conscious creator.

Although there is no pre-ordained point or purpose to life, you now understand that the point and purpose of life can be anything that you choose, and you integrate this understanding by consciously choosing the purpose of your life because that is the point. Work and play merge into one, and you experience peace and fulfillment equally in both.

You no longer do anything out of obligation or need, but, instead, you are guided through inspiration and pure desire.

You experience a direct connection to all of life, and you are inspired to create in a whole new manner.

Through intuitive connection with Infinite Intelligence, you might develop new paradigms of community building, teaching or leadership.

At this stage, you have the ability to attract relationships and form communities that support the betterment of humanity. Since you have mastered your thoughts and beliefs, you can now consciously create the life you desire; living in the moment, while also creating for the future.

In pure connection with Prime Creator, you are a channel of expression in all you do.

Sources:
1. 'The 5 Stages Of Awakening – Signposts & Pitfalls On The Path Of Consciousness,' Nancy Ellis, *consciousreminder*, Mar 28, 2016, https://www.consciousreminder.com/2017/08/09/5-stages-awakening-signposts-pitfalls-path-consciousness/
2. '5 Stages Of The Path From Awakening To Enlightenment,' Jennifer Sodin, Mar 22, 2015, *CE Collective Evolution*, https://www.collective-evolution.com/2015/03/22/5-stages-of-the-path-from-awakening-to-enlightenment/3.

3. 'The 5 Levels Of Awakening, From Mindless Slavery To Complete Freedom!,' *CODE*, August 3, 2017, https://www.lifecoachcode.com/2017/08/03/the-5-levels-of-awakening/
4. '5 Stages Of The Path From Awakening To Enlightenment,' Jennifer Sodin, Mar 22, 2015, *CE Collective Evolution*, https://www.collective-evolution.com/2015/03/22/5-stages-of-the-path-from-awakening-to-enlightenment/3.
5. 'The 5 Levels Of Awakening, From Mindless Slavery To Complete Freedom!,' *CODE*, August 3, 2017, https://www.lifecoachcode.com/2017/08/03/the-5-levels-of-awakening/
6. 'The 10 Stages of Awakening,' Tanaaz, *Forever Conscious*, https://foreverconscious.com/10-stages-awakening
7. '6 Ways to Become Enlightened', David G. Arenson, *mbgmindfulness*, Oct 3, 2016, https://www.google.com/search?rlz=1C2GGGE_enUS798&source=hp&ei=MCvOW62XCcHIsQWAkLewDw&q=6+ways+to+become+enlightened&oq=6+ways+to+become+enlightened&gs_l=psy-ab.1.0.0i22i30.1797.9037..10841...0.0..0.213.3220.15j12j2......0....1..gws-wiz.....0..0j35i39j0i67j0i131j0i20i263j33i22i29i30.I4Sqx7SkZLc

CHAPTER 19

SPIRITUAL EMERGENCE SYMPTOMS

WAKENING UP IS SCARY - It doesn't generally happen all at once with a flash of lightning and a dramatic cue. It's usually more of a process, which is a good thing because otherwise waking up would cause a lot more psychotic breaks (it does happen). Gradually we peel back the layers of identity and attachment, which slowly over the years deepens awakening. But with each of these layers comes another death, another instance of letting go – whether you like it or not. The kind of "letting go" is not really an active thing that you do, it is rather a thing that happens to you, you let go. When you fight this natural effort of your spiritual work, life gets painfully challenging. You are trying to hold on to something that is no longer even in your fingertips, let alone under your control. Everything starts to feel hard. You don't want to mediate, you don't want to interact with anyone, you don't want to feel or think anymore. A spiritual malaise sets in.

SYMPTOMS OF SPIRITUAL AWAKENING AND EXPANDED CONSCIOUSNESS – Symptoms listed may or may not be attributed to your Ascension process so please follow your own inner guidance as to if you should consult a healthcare professional if/when needed.

You just know or sense intuitively that something is happening to your body. You have an unusual feeling that you can't explain and sense your body is responding differently now physically, emotionally, mentally and spiritually. You may feel at times like you are losing your mind or going a bit crazy with these unknown or uneasy feelings that are difficult to explain.

If you identify with any of these conditions, know you are not alone! Many who are Waking Up to the Ascension Process are likely experiencing many of these symptoms. The first step is to spend time becoming aware of what you are feeling. Then, you will be able to begin the process of examining why your own symptoms are manifesting for you.

Physical Difficulties
- Aches, pains, and even itches throughout your entire body that comes and goes.
- Soreness or stiffness in joints and muscles and bones for no apparent reason that are not due to injury, physical exercise or fatigue (especially in the neck, shoulder, back and spine).
- Pressure and pain in and around the head and face area including skull, eyes, ears, sinus, teeth including fillings, and gums.
- Pinpricks, electrical shocks, falling asleep feelings, warming energies, tingles, and random spasms, rushes of energy, twitches and jolts that come and go for no reason.
- Headaches and migraines that don't respond to medicine.
- Hair and nails grow faster and/or change in texture or density.

Vision - Often, in these cases, an eye exam would show no change in your actual vision. At times, you'll additionally feel very ungrounded. You'll be "spatially challenged" with the feeling like you can't put two feet on the ground or that you're walking between two worlds.
- General changes in vision and perception.
- Catching glimpses of sparkles or flashes of light in your peripheral vision.
- Dry or itchy eyes, blurry vision, seeing a haze or static-like energy in air.
- Seeing auras or light around people, animals or objects.
- A sense of physical disorientation.
- Seeing flashes and rings of light around the eye lenses.
- Seeing the world in brighter, clearer colors.

Heart
- Heart palpitations or flutters not related to exercise or medical conditions.
- Lots of pressure on both the front of the chest as well as the mid back and upper breast plate area as there is an additional chakra vortex activating.
- Periods of sudden nervousness or anxiety that comes and goes spontaneously for no reason.
- Feeling drained of energy.
- Unexplainable worry or panic.
- Nervous breakdown sensations or feeling that you are spiraling out of control.

Hearing
- Heightened sensitivity to sound.
- Hearing unusual sounds or auditory sensations.
- Ears popping and ringing.
- Hearing pings, beeps, tones frequencies whooshing and pulsating.
- Feeling off balance, sense of vertigo.

Cold or Flu Symptoms - You might find cold or flu-like symptoms appearing and disappearing without developing into actual cold or flu. These could include:
- Stuffy head, pressure, sinus and allergy problems and respiratory changes.
- Changes in body temperatures.
- Increased sensitivity to heat or cold.
- Circulation issues.
- Chills or hot flashes, night sweats and waves of heat throughout the body.

Fatigue - Sometimes these symptoms manifest as periods of extreme fatigue for no apparent reason that happen out of the blue or upon awakening from a full-night's sleep. You might feel as if you need many naps or the exact opposite—feeling wide awake and energized despite lack of sleep and being hyper-focused despite fatigue.

Intolerance - During this time, you might feel a sense of intolerance towards lower vibrational things of the 3D world, reflected in conversations, attitudes, societal structures, healing modalities, etc.

Emotional Sadness or Disconnect
- Deep inner sadness for no apparent reason.
- Feeling lost and or as if you are someone else.
- Loss of ego or personal identity, old beliefs changing, feeling disassociated or fragmented.
- Tears or crying for no apparent reason.
- Feeling lonely or isolated, even when in the company of others, as if others can't hear or see you or you're not relating.
- Desire to flee groups and crowds.
- Disimpassioned, no desire to do anything.
- Loss of motivation for hobbies and interests.
- Experiencing more clumsiness or losing balance bumping into things, lack of coordination.
- Feeling dizzy of lightheaded or jittery and nervous for no reason.
- Moments of memory loss of "what was I just doing, or why did I come in here", forgetting simple things or conversations, brain fog, jumbled words or scattered thinking.

Relationship Changes
- Sudden or abrupt changes in relationships, job, career, living environment.
- Urge to relocate or being drawn to particular area or place, resonating with certain geographic locations.
- Changes in how you experience the environment.
- Sudden feelings of being connected to nature and animals like never before.

- Increased sensitivity to plants, trees, flowers.
- A deep understanding and appreciation of nature and animals and more natural or serene environments.
- An overwhelming desire to be in nature or live around more natural and serene environments.
- Nature begins to energize you and bring you peace of mind and expand your heart.
- Change or withdrawal from family and friend relationships.
- Chance encounters with unusual or meaningful people entering your life in synchronistic ways.

Diet
- Changes in diet and eating habits and digestion.
- Fluctuating between feeling hungry all the time to lack of appetite.
- Foods and liquids begin to taste differently.
- Cravings may come and go.
- Healthier and more natural options may be more appealing than in the past.
- Digestion, IBS, bloating, and gastrointestinal issues.
- Swelling in lower abdomen and back.
- Sudden weight gain or loss especially in belly area.

Sleep and Dreams
- Unusual sleep patterns or changes in pattern.
- Sleeping in short bursts on and off.
- Finding more increased energy at night with frequent awakening between 2-4 a.m.
- Periods of insomnia that last for days.
- Intense or unusual or wild dreams or visions that can range from pleasant to bizarre to prophetic.
- Increased lucid dreaming or astral projecting or other out of body experiences. Specifically, you might be experiencing war and battle dreams, chase dreams or monster dreams. Many of us are literally releasing the old

energy within and connecting with past lives, memories, experiences and knowledge.

Psychic Abilities
- Increased psychic awareness and sensitivity and other extra-sensory abilities.
- Heightened intuition and the awakening of the third eye chakra or 'inner vision' and other chakras and psychic centers.
- Causing interference in electrical appliances.
- Electronic devices behaving in an unusual way or malfunctioning within your presence, especially when you are in a heightened state of emotion such as anger or sadness.
- Having light bulbs blow out or flicker when you are near.
- Batteries draining for no reason.
- Personally feeling more drained or energetically depleted near too many electrical devices or when around them for long periods of time.
- Sensitivity to electromagnetic fields and the ability to influence them.

Odd Longings - Many of us are experiencing a deep longing to go home, yet we're not sure what home means. This is perhaps the most difficult and challenging of any of the conditions. You may experience a deep and overwhelming desire to leave the planet and return to home. This is not a "suicidal" feeling. It is not based in anger or frustration. You don't want to make a big deal of it or cause drama for yourself or others in your life. There is a quiet part of you that wants to go home to the Ancient Knowledge that you are now aligning with. The root cause for this is quite simple…you are ready to begin a new lifetime while still in this physical body.

Love - Increased feelings of Divine and Unconditional LOVE.
- Moments of gratitude and deep appreciation for life.
- Increased peace, clarity, understanding and compassion.

- Profound revelations and insights.
- A sense of Oneness and interconnectedness.
- Feeling more connected with nature, other people, animals, the universe, Spirit/Source, Creator God, the All, etc.
- Encounters with angelic and cosmic beings and the awareness of the presence of non-physical entities or energies.
- Sudden increase in synchronicity and meaningful coincidences that occur frequently when you least expect them.
- Noticing 11:11 and other repeating number sequences such as 111, 1212, 333, 444, 144, or other numbers that are significant or meaningful popping up in your day-to-day life in unusual ways whenever you 'happen to look.'
- Uncanny alignment of events or chance encounters.
- Meeting people in synchronistic ways which develop into significant relationships.

MENTAL ILLNESS DIAGNOSIS – This is not to say that there is not something called mental illness. I do wonder, though, how many cases of mental illness are actually spiritual emergences gone sour. We, as a society, need to recognize the existence of genuine spiritual emergence and learn to differentiate them from cases of psychosis. Thankfully, there is now even a small paragraph in the psychiatrists' DSM IV Book (their diagnostic manual) titled "Spiritual or Religious Problem." It may be that we're all at different stages of the spiritual emergence process.

CAUTION: NOT ALL HEALERS ARE LIGHTWORKERS – Those Awakening and Lightworkers may be tempted to seek relief through healers and Transmutters. It is a dangerous assumption to believe that just because healing is going on it must be the Light that is doing it. That is a false belief. To work with the Light, you must be very specific to ask for only

Light Beings who are in alignment and One with Creator God's White light.

The Dark are more than happy to provide healing to people, often quite dramatically, but with the unstated goal of then hooking into the Soul's and life paths of those fine healers unknowingly working with them and the people receiving healing. The Dark Energies feel just as powerful and often very pleasant to the Healer channeling them so this makes the healer totally believe they are working with the Light, and resist the information on this page. This is the dynamic that is presently going on, on planet Earth: the Lightworkers working to free the Earth and its people of Darkness, and the Darkness simultaneously working to entrap those Lightworkers and the people asking for healing. Both the Light and the Dark know that it is a mass consciousness shift. The Light is totally and unequivocally shifting the consciousness of the Planet to the Light and the Dark is resisting it.

Using profound and substantial healing and healing activations as an enticement to Healers and clients, the Dark has been forming a spider-web of hijacked Souls that are its means of trying to stop the Light.

Most people have no idea that their Soul has been bound by invisible agreements with the Darkness. They just continue on with their lives thinking all is well and good. Until of course they try to remove the Darkness, and then the Darkness makes itself known.

Here are some common Dark Beings that do healing (with Dark contracts attached) and even impersonate the Light:
- Dark Angels.
- Lords of Karma, Lords of Entities.
- Angel impersonators: elohim (not Elohim with the capital E).
- Archangel Michael Impersonators.

Chapter 19 – Spiritual Emergence Symptoms

- Annanuki Aliens (Also will impersonate Angels).
- Reptilian Aliens.
- Grey Aliens
- Over 10 other Alien species.
- Humans that have passed on, and retain their identity from Earth. True Ascended Masters are few and far between and are acknowledged as such by other Light Beings and the Archangels.
- Ancestors. If your ancestors are still hanging around then they are stuck and have not returned to being a Free Spirit.

The Dark Side is often able to do profound healing since:

1. They don't respect our free will to ask or choose and will do whatever they want to us, anytime they want. The Light would never do anything that was not asked for or in line with our highest growth and learning.
2. The energies they use are Dark but still can be used for healing and transformations. Those energies are easily confused with the Light Healing Energies because they often feel just as pleasant and powerful.
3. They bind you with multiple Dark contracts in return for the healings they provide to you so they are very motivated to do this exchange.
4. They know that you will in turn spread the contracts on to others if you are a healer and do healings for others. This includes passing on healing abilities to other healers through activations as these Dark Beings in turn start to work with them. (To work with the Light the journey is one of healing our separation from God issues, the Light never just hands us or passes on healing abilities).

A CAUTION ABOUT REIKI - Those Awakening and Lightworkers may be tempted to seek relief through Reiki. Robert Jaffe of the Energy Mastery School in Sedona, Arizona (now defunct) is an extremely clairvoyant individual, and explained that the Reiki energy that is channeled into people actually has a light stream and a dark stream. The original energy might have been all unified light, but at some point, someone tried to amplify it using a mirror, and the stream split into light and dark. This may also be a metaphor for when the original energy came into the 4th dimension (3rd density) and became polarized. He checked those who were Reiki practitioners to see if the dark stream had imbedded itself into them. To do this, he clairvoyantly looked into their eyes, and if he saw black or a lightning bolt there, they had it.

Most practitioners that use Reiki on people are acting as unwitting intermediaries for the Dark Force.

On the positive side, many have derived great benefit from having Reiki treatments. If the practitioner is channeling a stream that is of higher vibration than the client, even with the polarity of dark and light, the client will most likely benefit. If the client is of a higher vibration than the Reiki stream, they will feel the dark part of the stream and may have a negative reaction. If the practitioner has done their personal work, the Reiki channeling maybe of a better quality than another practitioner, as it has to come through their own filters to the client. There is no way for the practitioner to filter out the dark stream and only channel the light one. This light stream is not even unified light. It is the polarized opposite of the 4th dimensional dark.

Bottomline, know that you are taking a risk to have the dark energy stream injected into you, know the practitioner's credentials, and to make sure his/her frequency is higher than your own.

A CAUTION TO HEALERS AND TRANSMUTTERS – If you don't know who you are working with and are just doing healing then by default it is the Darkside that you are working with.

If your clients are complaining of feeling cold energies being sent to them, then that could be an indication of working with Dark Energies.

Be cognizant of the light aura that is being presented by a client (Refer to Chapter 15).

PURIFICATION – Cleansing the Soul of Lightworkers
Chapter 15 presented several means to protect your spirit. However, Lightworkers encounter Dark fractals within other spirits as part of the Lightworkers mission, as well as direct attacks by the Dark Force that may weaken of even penetrate a Lightworker's protective "shield."

This work is about removing all lower astral junk such as 'dark' cords to other people, places or situations, etheric implants, group thought-forms (such as anger or hatred). and lower astral entities in your energy fields. Most of us living in the modern world are subject to lower astral interference. The astral planes are the desire worlds. The lower levels are where the grosser vibrations can be found. Anyone who has a serious addiction is often connected to entities in the lower astral. The lower astral has a number of levels (like every dimension of existence) and these can vary from twilight places where lost and confused souls congregate to places of nightmarish appearance. Anyone on the Earth plane who has addictive tendencies can attract lower astral forces. Lightworkers who have poor energetic hygiene can pick up lower astral interference. Lower astral forces can be attracted to the light in your energy fields. Like moths fluttering around a bright light this can be either a minor nuisance or a major source of confusion and fear. If there is a strong fear of the lower astral in you (you have a reaction to what has been written, perhaps through reading horror stories or watching 'dark' movies) then this is something that needs to be neutralized first before attempting this procedure.

PREPARE THE SPACE - Find a time when you will not be disturbed for between 45-60 minutes. Prepare by finding a quiet and clear space. Some may want to prepare the room by clearing with white sage and then when room is filled with the intense fragrant smoke open a window to release all the energies in the room; close the window when the room is clear, put out or remove the sage stick and light a candle. Others just need a quiet, peaceful space, which could even be somewhere in Nature. You need to pick the space that is right for you.

Close your eyes and breathe to connect with your physical body. With each breathe feel the bones, blood, organs and tissue of your body from the top of the head down to the tip of the toes. As you breathe now connect with your energy fields that surround the physical. Feel or imagine your energy field as a great egg of energy. See if you can notice if there are any dark spots in your energy fields or places where your energy is more congealed than flowing.

INVOKE YOUR HIGHER SELF AND HEALING TEAM - The next step is to invoke your Higher Self. Your HS is a part of you that exists at a much higher frequency of light and consciousness. This is the part of you that is connected to your soul-monadic consciousness. See your HS as an intense sphere of light descending around your body. Just by calling your HS you give permission for your HS to help you. Then call in your guides and healing team, Lightworkers and Starseeds have many guides in the spirit planes working with them. Guides may not always be with you as they may be assigned to help others at the same time. However, some of your guides may be only assigned to assist you. Not all guides are part of your healing team. Your healing team contains many guides and beings to assist you in clearing and stabilizing your energy fields in this 3D dimension of Earth. Starseeds often have guides that come from higher dimensions who are familiar with the challenges of being here on the 3D Earthplane. If you feel it is right for you, ask that your team include psychic surgeons from the Great White Brotherhood on Sirius, ask for Arcturians guides who are experts at dealing with dark astral entities.

Please note that Lightworkers and Starseeds are here to be of assistance in this great time of change. Because of their fast rate of growth when they begin to awaken it is normal for Starseeds to require guides who will grow and expand with them as they raise their light quotient and vibration. Therefore please ask your HS to clear and replace guides as necessary to keep pace with your evolutionary needs. You do need to ask your HS to do this.

Also be aware that there can be false light beings posing as guides. Just ask your HS and healing team to clear any false guides hanging out in your energy space. Your HS and guides will do this work if you ask them to. This is a planet of Free Will and our HS and guides will not shield us from learning essential lessons if it is in our highest interest from a soul point of view to do so. By reading this Chapter you are now aware that you may have false guides and that you can ask to have them cleared. You can ask this as a matter of routine whenever you wish to clear your space.

GROUND YOUR ENERGY – Refer to Chapter 9 for a "grounding with the universe" exercise.

Imagine you can ground your energy by visualizing roots growing out of the base of the egg and moving down into the core of the Earth. Make sure you anchor in the crystalline core of the Earth and not any of the ley lines or energy spots within the Earth. The crystalline core of the Earth is an ascending field of high vibrational light and consciousness. You can ground safely in this core and also invoke the pure energy of Gaia to enter and infuse your energy fields. Ask your HS to remove any energetic connections to anywhere in the Earth except the crystalline core. Ask to remove any cords or roots that are connecting you to the karmic grid of the Earth. This will ensure that you are free to connect only with the ascending crystalline core of the Earth.

CALL ON ANGELIC FORCES - Next call angelic forces to surround your energy fields. You can call upon Archangels Metatron, Michael, Raphael, and Sandalphon, who are the most protective; Metatron is the highest vibrating archangel who oversees the Tree of Life. Call upon the angelic forces in the sun and also in the central (galactic) sun. Michael is the warrior angel. Call on the legion of warrior angels associated with Michael that are helpful in clearing lower astral entities. Raphael is the healer archangel. There are hosts of healing angels associated with him. Sandalphon is the archangel that governs this world and the astral planes. There are many angels associated with Sandalphon. Ask for a triple shield of protection around your auric egg. Ask that this triple shield allow in higher frequencies of love, light, joy, possibility and so on. Ask that this triple shield neutralize/block lower frequencies of suffering, struggle, fear, guilt, hatred and so on. Ask that the angelic forces create a portal to begin to suck out any lower astral gunk.

CALL ON ANGELIC FORCES OF VIOLET FIRE - Then call upon angels of the violet fire and watch them ignite violet fire in the room around you. See this fire burn through the furnishings, the walls, doors, windows and so on. When you invoke the violet flame, you can visualize yourself surrounded by a violet-flame pillar about six feet in diameter and about nine feet high. It can extend from beneath your feet to well over the top of your head. Give permission for this violet fire to burn away any lower material in your energy fields. Also give permission for this violet fire to burn through and release any fear you may have relating to the lower astral. Most people don't see the violet flame with their physical eyes. But you can often see the violet fire by closing your eyes and concentrating between your eyebrows. For those who have developed their spiritual sight, the violet flame looks like fire, in colors ranging from dark indigo and brilliant amethyst to violet pink. If you want to give this work extra strength then you can use this decree to invoke the violet fire.

In the name of the beloved mighty victorious Presence of Creator God, I AM in me, and my very own beloved Holy Christ Self, I call upon the angels of the seventh ray to clear my energy fields through all minds, bodies and timelines. I ask you to release all astral interference to the light. Please seal my energy fields in this protective violet fire and be with me as I go about my day. I accept it done this hour in full power, according to the will of Creator God.

CALL UPON STAR BEINGS - Call upon the Arcturians to protect and clear your energy fields from lower astral junk/interference. The Arcturians are the most effective group of Star Beings (alongside the Great White Brotherhood on Sirius). Connecting with the Arcturians can happen very quickly if you have a previously established connection with them. The Arcturians are the best group to connect with if you are having trouble with demonic/reptilian energies. They can pull these beings out of your energy fields and any parasitic etheric eggs they may leave behind. The Arcturians can also seal and clear any portals/micro portals in your fields if you give them permission. Call on the Arcturians and see a bright blue column of light beam around you. Then just be open to the clearing work. Another powerful group of Star Beings are the Andromedans who work with the vibration of unconditional love. You can ask them to create a 12D protective shield around you.

Give permission for your HS and healing team and Star Guides to start to clear any entities or implants in your fields that are blocking your spiritual evolution/development. Please note it is normal for many to have such beings hanging around their energy fields. Entities can be a slight nuisance to a major problem. Some entities may be lost/confused souls. Others may not be human. We live in a vast multiverse and so do not be alarmed by this. You have probably had existences in many other dimensions and got to know many different kinds of beings and created all manner of karmic connections. Ask your HS to clear and destroy any contracts you have with beings in your energy fields and then ask HS and your healing team to remove all entities and take them to an appropriate place for their healing and development. Stay with this process until you feel a growing sense of lightness, which is a sign that the work is being done.

RELEASE CORDS - Ask your HS to reveal in this burning light any 'negative' cords to other people. Basically, an energy cord is created between two people where an energetic exchange occurred – usually formed by an exchange of emotions or thought forms. You may ask your HS to reveal the image or energy of a person you are corded with. See that person appear before you. Ask your HS and the violet fire angels to start to dissolve and cut these cords. To be extra sure you can imagine yourself holding a light saber (aka Star Wars) to sweep your field cutting any darker cords linking you in a negative way to other people. Ask your HS to reveal any hidden cords/connections and if any appear then again dissolve/sweep clear.

Please remember to pull out the roots of any cords you find attached to you. Make sure there is nothing left of them which might cause them to recreate. Call in the angels of violet fire to clear and cleanse any etheric wounds. Ask your healing team to seal any wounds with light.

SWEEP YOUR FIELDS - When this is done ask Metatron to sweep your energy fields with a fine net of platinum bright burning white light. This net will catch anything remaining and remove it from your energy fields. Repeat this a few times to make sure your energy is pristine and clear. Then again ask that the triple shield be stabilized and strengthened. Ask your HS to close and fill with light any tears or wounds in your energy fields after doing this work.

THANK AND RELEASE - When the work is done thank your healing team, angelic forces including violet fire angels and Metatron, and finally thank your HS. Ask that the portal opened to clear astral gunk be closed. You may want to stay in connection with your HS throughout the day or you can thank and release as you wish. This procedure is like taking a shower of pure cleansing light and putting on a suit of protective light to meet your day.

Sources:
1. 'Signs and Symptoms of Spiritual Awakening and Expanded Consciousness,' *Ascension Series 2*, Dec 6, 2016, Suzanne Worthey Healer and Intuitive, *Ascension Resources*, https://www.sworthley.com/signs-and-symptoms-of-spiritual-awakening-ascension-series-2/
2. 'Souls of Light,' Khris Krepcik, Aug 18, 2012, *The Hooded Sage*, http://www.thehoodedsage.com/2012/08/souls-of-light/
3. 'Dark Healing Energy and Light Imposters,' Audwin Trapman, *Energy Healing, Energy Healer Toronto/Love Heals All*, http://entity-clearing.net/wpimages/wpc91077de_06.png
4. 'The Dark Side of Reiki,' Clara Fox, Sept 1, 2013, *The Carla Fox Blog*, http://thecarlafoxblog.blogspot.com/2013/09/the-dark-side-of-reiki.html
5. 'Astral Interference Clearing Procedure (For Lightworkers/Starseeds),' Steve Nobel, Feb 9, 2016, *The Soul Matrix*, https://thesoulmatrix.com/starseeds/astral_clear_procedure/

CHAPTER 20

NINE TYPES OF LIGHTWORKERS

Now that you have read the previous Chapters and think you know your basic species, where your spirit originated, why you were created, how to communicate with the universe, and maybe the lessons you have chosen to learn, it is now time to determine which Lightwork Frequency that you resonate with.

Below are the 9 types of lightworkers. You may find you have all or some of these attributes, but you most likely have at least one. There is a wealth of knowledge out there for each specific lightworker path, and last but certainly not least, the fountain of your own inner knowing.

THE NINE TYPES OF LIGHTWORKERS

Gridworkers work on the grids and gateways of the Earth. If you're familiar with the Earth's ley lines then you'll be familiar with the belief that the Earth has chakras and is a living organism.

Gridworkers tap into the crystalline grid, which can be likened to the Earth's nervous system, and is believed to be one of the ways the Earth was seeded. The crystalline grid is a creation theory of the Earth's history, and whether you believe it or not, there are many lightworkers who use their abilities to sense where dark energies exist on a spatial plane.

Gridworkers could also be seen as spatial empaths; people who sense a karmic imprint when they enter a certain building, town, stretch of coast, etc. and are able to use that sense to transmute those dense energies with their compassion and loving presence.

For those who believe in archangels you may be familiar with Archangel Michael's violet flame; a visualization technique that can be adopted by those who know themselves to be a lightworker sensitive to spaces. When you recognize you're in a place that holds those dense energies, rather than become overwhelmed by them, send a loving violet flame into that area in order to cleanse it.

Frequency Workers - A more general lightworker's path is to be someone who aims to keep their frequencies high and

transmute denser energies as they encounter them. This is easier said than done, especially when it appears that the whole 'matrix' or third dimensional reality – one which has a dualistic framework and thrives on the law of polarity – is dense and will constantly lower your frequencies as you practice not being affected by it.

The experience is similar to surviving in a mad house where you know you're sane but nobody believes you. Instead, try keeping your abilities and knowledge to yourself and nurture and cleanse yourself constantly.

Being a frequency worker is tough because you are sensitive to news stories, people, places, agreements, beliefs… you may feel like you don't want to leave the house. Instead, try to not take anything personally and integrate a solid attitude of self care into your existence.

It's good to have a few trusted friends or YouTube channel where you can increase your frequencies and know you are safe and understood. You are embodying the light and that is an amazing service. Hats off to you.

Timeline Worker - Transmuting Darkness - If you are a particularly powerful empath and lightworker, then you will be aware of timelines and the bleeding together and compression of time and action. That is, once you become aware of your ability to change a timeline (like stepping on to a parallel reality – one you'd prefer to be on obviously), you become aware of how this decision and action changes everyone else's reality too.

A timeline worker is able to take responsibility for an ancestral timeline for example, and absolve their family karma if their ancestors have racked up a lot of karma. A timeline worker embodies the knowledge that we are One, and takes the helm of this transmutation, lighting the way for others to follow. What you will find is the more you progress, the increasing number of darker entities will be attracted to you.

They desire your compassion and actually need help. This is why, during meditation or throughout our day, those with strong empathic qualities will find thoughts that are sometimes alarming and extremely dark floating into their heads. They really don't belong to us, and that is why meditation is fantastic because it offers us the tools for dissolving them with loving compassion.

Third Eye/Future Seers - Also known as clairvoyants. Seeing into the future is also a side effect of becoming aware of timelines. Third eye seers may get confused as to what everyone else's reality is and may feel isolated from and

misunderstood by others, but they will also be excellent at personal and even instant manifestation.

The trouble, they may find, is that knowing the outcome can detract them from the process they desire and be surprised by the universe and therefore can trip themselves up before they've even begun.

Bringing reality up to the same level of your expert third eye will be the challenge, as well as remembering to lovingly help others and not just use your abilities for personal gain.

Blueprint Workers - Holding the divine blueprint for the awakened Earth and the whole of humanity may seem like a stretch of the imagination at first, and, much like the frequency and third eye lightworkers, you may be seen as weird or on drugs if you feel the need to share your visions with friends and family, but please keep the faith. Holding the blueprint for the new Earth, or a heavenly version of human's existence here on this planet is possible. So what does it look like? This is up to you to imagine and manifest through your own speech and actions.

Astral Travelers - Arriving at this vision may require you to better pay attention to your dreams or out of body experiences,

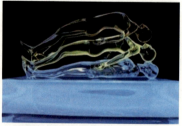

if you are able to have and be aware of them.

In becoming a lucid dreamer you can voluntarily enter the Akashic records and access this ripple of potential or well of experience; asking questions and discovering what this alternative and harmonious ways of living could look like.

Messenger - Rather than acting on these visions, you may be a lightworker good at carrying messages. Though popular entertainment may have its pitfalls, it has been the most prevalent medium for messages to filter through into the mainstream consciousness, something which has escalated in the 20th and 21st centuries.

The mainstream population doesn't just get their knowledge from popular culture for any reason; think *The Matrix, E.T, Donnie Darko, The Davinci Code, Cloud Atlas*, not to mention the lyrics of legendary singers such as Bob Marley. These 'messages' carry an imprint with them and are often channeled in moments of heightened creativity where the conduit moves up into 4th or 5th dimensional frameworks and is able to channel the themes into a creative piece of art. Forget muses, a messenger lightworker is able to communicate these higher patterns to the masses in the form of undercover service, heightening vibrations and the collective unconscious.

Active Blueprint Weavers - Having accessed the Akashic records during a dream exploration, or perhaps moving up

through the dimensions whilst raising their frequencies, an active lightworker will carry back an idea; usually an invention (think Nikola Telsa) or idea that can enhance our lives and manifest the global awakening by putting it into action. These lightworkers are what the world needs more than ever and will replace political figures, bankers and business men who have been serving themselves for thousands of years. Indigo, rainbow and crystal children especially have been springing up in this capacity; bringing fantastic inventions that could rock the world and completely reduce pollution and the abuse of resources.

These active blueprint weavers must start by removing their own carbon footprints and living in harmonious co-creation with others and start from there.

Wayshowers includes Wanderers and Old Souls, are those who have done it; they're the ascended first wave who are teaching others how to ascend and join them in the 5th dimension.

The 5th dimension is not a place, rather the same reality but where an individual is vibrating at a different frequency and are embodying the enlightened human. Their outer reality reflects their inner one and they are not suffering, rather are living their truth and are prosperous having mastered (and gone beyond) the 3rd dimensional material reality. This is often misunderstood in that we see them.

Wayshowers are being monastic and owning nothing. They have dedicated their lives to the truth. Rather than being without, they have simply transcended the fear of lack. This means that they don't need to plan for the future but trust that their higher selves will direct them and the universe has provided them with everything they need; life flowers for them in the moment and they have no need to survive but simply be.

Sources:
1. '9 Types of Lightworkers: Which Ones Do You Resonate With?,' Lauren, *Factal Enlightenment*, Oct 7, 2018, https://fractalenlightenment.com/40788/.../9-types-lightworkers-which-ones-resonate

CHAPTER 21

DISCLOSURE REVELATIONS, EARTH VIBRATION CHANGES, CHANGES DUE TO ENTERING THE PHOTON BELT, CHANGE IN EARTH DENSITY, PARADOX OF TIME

FIRST DISCLOSURE – Two Factions & a 6th Density Disputation Group - On one side of the conflict is the Galactic Federation, a positive Federation (service-to-other) comprising a number of ancient humans and friendly human-looking extraterrestrial races that are genetically linked to humanity. The "Federation" essentially wants humanity to learn the truth about its ancient founders, extraterrestrial visitations, free energy technologies, and their space programs, such as "Solar Warden." Most significantly, the Federation wants to put an end to an exploitative global financial, ideological and psychological domination that has enslaved much of humanity.

On the other side of the undeclared war is a negative (service-to-self) Alliance comprising of ancient Earth bloodline families called the Cabal/Illuminati; Reptilian extraterrestrials called the Dracos and the Anunnaki that come from outside our solar system. Finally, this negative Alliance comprises portions of a "Dark Force" comprising of aliens and humans connected directly or ideologically to the former Nazi SS that normally operate outside the solar system, but were trapped inside a recently imposed solar system wide quarantine. This negative Alliance commonly referred to as the Cabal/ICC/Draco/Dark Fleet or more simply as the "Dark Side or Dark Force."

Chapter 21 – Disclosure Revelations, Earth Frequency Changes, Changes Entering the Photon Belt, Change in Density, Paradox in Time

Side Note: ICC = Interstellar Commerce Commission (strict control on biological items moving around in human space).

These two forces are engaged in an undeclared war being fought in deep space, Mars and on Earth, resulting in a complex planetary situation involving multiple space programs, both modern and ancient, and extraterrestrial civilizations in a struggle for dominance over the Earth and how much information and technology will be released to the rest of surface humanity. This is leading to possibly the most comprehensive disclosures ever to emerge of what is really happening behind the scenes taking place on Earth and our solar system.

To help resolve the issues between the warring parties, a third group of extraterrestrials called the "Sphere Being Alliance" or "Sphere Federation" has recently arrived (most likely these are the Arcturians, the most advanced 6th Density beings in our Universe) and they have implemented a solar system wide quarantine. The Sol System "Quarantine" was put in place after the "Cosmic Energies" reached a certain level. These energies have been entering our Sol System for quite some time (or our Sol System has been entering the Photon Belt of the Galactic Plane, where space travel is easier to accomplish). The Sphere Being Alliance was here for decades observing before they became active and began to interact openly. These energetic changes have had a dramatic effect on the energetic bodies of all of the beings in our Sol System below 6th Density. These are not energies that the Dark Force or negative beings are compatible with. This causes these negative beings to become reactionary and not maintain their composures that allowed them to rule the Earth with iron fists for many millennia. Those who are positive however are waking up and becoming more aware of the power of their consciousness. The tables are turning and as they do, these negatives who had planned on

Chapter 21 – Disclosure Revelations, Earth Frequency Changes, Changes Entering the Photon Belt, Change in Density, Paradox in Time

finding a way to negate the energetic changes or escape, now find themselves trapped and soon to be at the mercy of those they have treated as cattle.

The quarantine has created havoc with the Dark Force Cabal that previously was the dominant power on Earth and the Solar System, but is rapidly losing power to the Federation. This has led to growing defections from the Dark Force Cabal and the Dark Force is beginning to "crumble." To "prop-up" their "crumbling" control, the Dark Force is planning to reveal a "controlled disclosure" that will attempt to deceive people in a way that perpetuates Dark Fore Cabal control. To counter the Dark Force "controlled disclosure," the Federation plans a disclosure plan of massive official document dumps (like Wikileaks) and television broadcasts that will reveal the truth about humanity's situation, and will lead to Nuremburg War Crime like trials against (former) leaders of the Dark Force.

Before the breakdown in the overall relations between the Dark factions, they were united through the "Secret Earth Governments" (and their "Syndicates" known as the Cabal/Illuminati and various other Secret Societies) and their Controllers (Draco Royals and Ancient Earth/Human Break Away Civilizations that have deceived many and presented themselves as ET's from various Star Systems). After the breakdown, there has been considerable chaos among these groups which has resulted in them turning on each other. This has led to conflict in various underground/undersea networked facilities that have been responsible for some of the earthquakes that have been occurring across the planet as well as some incidents on Mars and other bodies in the Sol System. Many of these groups were beginning to turn on each other before the recent Draco Allied Conference. This is the meeting where a 14 foot White Reptilian Royal was present and made an offer to the Sphere Being Alliance for safe passage of their "Royals" to be able to exit the "Outer Barrier"- the second Perimeter of Isolation that is located at the edge of our Solar System. It was soon after this that not only the major disinformation war (to control the narrative) began but also the chaotic infighting between the "Elite Groups."

The Cabals are still operating in our Sol System and control the vast infrastructure. Small groups have defected to the Federation. Some of them revealed themselves as infiltrators when they carried out some very effective attacks on some of the Draco Alliance Bases and with some Targeted Assassinations of Draco Alliance Leadership. This was a major setback and has caused some mistrust between the Federation Council and some of the recent defectors. There are also some very powerful Secret Earth Government and Syndicate Members/Leaders who have defected and have been granted an "Off World Witness Protection Program" for them and their families for actionable intelligence, evidence against their former leadership as well as promise of being witnesses in future World Courts when there are the "Post Full Disclosure" hearings against all of the groups who are trapped in the Sol System behind the "Outer Barrier." This first group of defectors who made it safely off planet led to a rash of assassinations within the ranks of their former groups as well as further panic that has led to many "Elites" beginning to move their families to their safe zones (next Generation Underground Cities) in their regions. There is an enclave in Brazil that is a major evacuation point for these "Elites" from the West. They have been moving people and supplies there 24/7 for many months. These "Elite" know exactly what is happening and are leaving some of their puppets behind to take the fall similar to what was done in Germany in WWII. In these new World Court Hearings however we will not just hear "I was only following orders" but will see the Elites who have been dug out of their holes being pointed at and hear "That is who gave me my orders."

Chapter 21 – Disclosure Revelations, Earth Frequency Changes, Changes Entering the Photon Belt, Change in Density, Paradox in Time

Over the last few months there have also been some defections of assets from the Cabal controlled Secret Space Program, remnants of the Dark Fleet (which is not a Draco Fleet but a Human Fleet that serves alongside the Draco Alliance) that were not caught outside of the Outer Barrier, as well as various other Military Black Ops Program Members. Some of them brought with them time critical and actionable intelligence that was acted on by some of the Federation Leadership and their new allies without bringing it to the Federation Council. This resulted in Two Massive Attacks that caused large numbers of innocent deaths. Those who took part in what the Sphere Alliance called "Atrocities" were unapologetic, stating that it was the cost of war but the collateral damage was regrettable. This caused a rift between some of the Federation Council who had different ideas on how they should proceed as well as some mistrust of the new defectors that had recently joined and also obviously had a different moral outlook and idea of the rules of engagement. In the first big joint conference with all of the Federation Council and the Federation beings that appeared, the question was asked of the Sphere Alliance what the rules of engagement should be. The Sphere Alliance had provided the Federation with some extremely advanced defensive technology and asked that the Federation not attack or destroy any more of the Cabal/Illuminati/Dark Force Infrastructure. They had worked out a future "Post Full Disclosure Plan" with the Federation Council some time earlier to free all of the inhabitants of these facilities, provide them assistance in recovery of what they had been through as well as hand over all of these assets to the "Post Disclosure Era Civilization" of Earth. This infrastructure that was built for negative purposes along with all of the suppressed technologies would be disclosed to every single person on Earth simultaneously and would be the beginning of what the Federation had dreamed of which is a "Star Trek Civilization." Other than some authorized operations to weaken the Cabal on Earth, the Federation and their allies have agreed to the rules of engagement and timeline laid out by the Sphere Being Alliance and the Federation Council. As part of Post "Full Disclosure Event" these bases will be open and no conflict will be needed to remove the occupants to another area where one of the allied groups will offer their resources of physical and emotional healing.

The wiser leadership among the Federation Council are in agreement (the more militant members are not) with the Sphere Beings that the ultimate answer is one that comes from the people themselves. The population is waking up at a considerable rate but they still have quite a lot of mind control and disinformation to contend with. Once we reach a point of absolute and full disclosure of humanity's true history, the list of groups that have meddled in our social and genetic development (and to what extent), the horrific crimes against humanity by the "Elite," the Anunnaki, some of the Ancient Earth Break Away Civilizations and various ET Groups will push the people themselves to rise up and end the Babylonian Money Magic Slave System. People themselves will bring all of the before mentioned groups to justice with the help of positive off world groups and through some of the more traumatic disclosures that come to light (that many will call "Fear Porn" but are a part of full disclosure none the less) will cause a much needed "Genetic and Energetic Memory" to occur to our species that will assist us in not repeating the cycles of history that we have been manipulated to repeat over more cycles than our current era history has any knowledge of. This is also about preparing humanity to stand on its own as a race for the first time in its history.

There is a major disinformation war underway. Once the Cabal/Illuminati realized that their "Gods" had betrayed them and it was now every group for themselves they began to turn

Chapter 21 – Disclosure Revelations, Earth Frequency Changes, Changes Entering the Photon Belt, Change in Density, Paradox in Time

on one another. They also began to activate the assets that they had deeply infiltrated into the Ufology field to begin to cause conflict whenever an opportunity presented itself. They have gone from a position of preventing disclosure while conditioning the public for some sort of future false disclosure to now trying to control the disclosure narrative. Things are beginning to leak out at such an alarming rate for them that they are putting some of their best counter intelligence people out to discredit whistle blowers anyway they can while they confuse as many people as possible with a false narrative that makes them appear as victims or even heroes in some cases. Their goal is to provide a controlled disclosure that will allow them to remain in power and maintain a financial, ideological and psychological Slave System and prevent prosecution of their crimes against humanity. They do not understand that there is no way to close Pandora's Box once it is open all of their demons will come flying out for all to see.

The amount of information collected as well as the data turned over by recent Cabal/Illuminati defectors who have been taken into "Off World Witness Protection Programs" is quite astounding. This information is now in the hands of the Earth Based Federation and the Galactic Federation (who do not have the same agenda). Once things are worked out this information is planned on being released via data dumps online and via 24/7 TV Broadcasts. This will occur at some point and may be independent of or in reaction to a controlled disclosure attempt by the Cabal/Illuminati. This will include trial in a global court at some point. Once the cat is out of the bag the Cabal/Illuminati will create all sorts of false flag chaos to prevent or slow down the process. This has been what has prevented mass arrests thus far. This is something that is being worked out and some believe that the Sphere Federation may assist in this part of the equation once the mainstream population has woken up and is aware of the crimes committed by these groups. Some speculate that at some point this will free the Sphere Federation to directly intervene and assist in gathering the criminals for the trials (This does include the various ET's and Break Away Civilization Groups trapped on Earth).

The Sphere Being Alliance has so far made it clear that they are not here to save us and we must save ourselves. They do have a prime directive type of standard that they follow (do not interfere in our free will or resulting karmic repercussions). It is true that actions by the negative forces can open up some wiggle room for positive forces to do more. At some point when the energetic changes occur and we do change to a 4th Density Civilization that these negative vibratory humans and beings cannot exist in our reality. They may just disappear from our reality all together. There are a lot of theories coming from various researchers and sources but these are just theories no matter how fervently they are believed. Not everything has been completely figured out and no one source knows all of the answers of what will occur.

After Full Disclosure, we will begin a new era of self-determination and with no one to blame for our mistakes. We will also be at a time when we will be handed some incredible technologies that have been suppressed for some time that will take our quality of life to a completely new standard. We will also be going through energetic changes and transitioning to a 4th Density existence. This will need to be based on the actions of the many and not the militant actions of a few who will be looked to as heroes and saviors while we as a species learn nothing in what has been a grand experiment or classroom to begin with. We will not be liberated by forces of light but will ultimately see an environment created around us that will compel us to liberate ourselves. The energetic changes are affecting the lower vibratory beings already (Cabal/ Illuminati/

Draco/ Anunnaki) and they are self-destructing by their own actions and infighting. These energetic changes in our Sol System are affecting every lower vibrational being and they do not even realize that their reactionary behavior is the root of their own destruction.

Sources:
1. 'Secret Space War halts as Extraterrestrial Disclosure Plans move forward,' Dr Michael Salla, May 31, 2015, *Galactic Diplomacy*, Space Programs, https://www.exopolitics.org/secret-space-war-halts-as-extraterrestrial-disclosure-plans-move-forward/
2. More information about the Sphere Alliance at:
Sphere Being Alliance (Twitter)
Sphere Being Alliance (YouTube)
Sphere Being Alliance (Blog)
Sphere Being Alliance (Home Page)

SECOND DISCLOSURE – Galactic Human Slave Trade - A galactic human slave trade exists where millions of captured humans are taken off planet to distant colonies on other worlds to be bartered or abused. The galactic human slave trade is now opposed by the Federation. They plan to disclose the full truth about the abusive practices that plagued humanity for centuries, if not millennia, due to corrupt "Elites" (Cabal/ Illuminati) and intervention by imperial space powers (Draco Empire).

Full disclosure of extraterrestrial visitation and different Dark Forces, requires humanity to be prepared for all aspects of how humanity has been historically and more recently treated by these groups. Revealing this information is not designed to frighten or sensationalize, but to allow the collective consciousness of humanity to integrate the truth of what has happened, in order for humanity to evolve to a much brighter future. Not wanting to deal with disturbing information is a sign of not being ready for full disclosure, thereby making it possible for egregious practices to continue. This is analogous to how refusal to discuss allegations of sexual abuse in families can allow these abuses to continue for years.

The Dark Force Cabal is trading millions of kidnapped civilians from the surface per year to off world beings in exchange for technology. It involves kidnapping street children in impoverished areas of countries like Brazil, India, etc., and/or children in developed countries like the US; and/or civilians in war zones. The number has decreased in the past year because of the Outer Barrier. When "Full Disclosure" does occur people need to understand that much more detailed information on these matters is going to come out. This will be a shocking time for everyone as these and other horrific crimes against humanity are revealed about the "Elite" who have ruled over us and what they have been doing in the shadows throughout history.

It starts out in some cases, with your run of the mill organized crime groups who are into the sex and slave trade which is very much alive in the 20th and 21st centuries. Many of these crime groups or gangs have specialists who work from lists of desired people to be obtained (many others are victims of opportunity). These specialists often are kind elderly looking people or professional people (including Medical, Law Enforcement and Education to name a few) that no one would consider a threat, come in contact with a lot of people and are generally trusted. These people operate in just about any country you can think of. Often people are grabbed who live on the streets, in third world countries (that they can through their power in) or from inattentive parents. This level of human trafficking brings in many hundreds of thousands of people per year into the slave

Chapter 21 – Disclosure Revelations, Earth Frequency Changes, Changes Entering the Photon Belt, Change in Density, Paradox in Time

trade. These people do not know or care what happens to the people they obtain and hand off to handlers in exchange for money.

Then there are the special operator groups who have a specific shopping list and will go through a great deal of trouble and personal risk to obtain certain types of individuals that are on their lists. People at this level know that their victims are going into something bigger than just the global human trafficking systems and they deal directly with Cabal/Illuminati types. These Cabal/Illuminati types then funnel abducted people into their processing centers where the people are cataloged and it is decided if they will be sent below ground for various uses by allied ET's or will be used as a commodity in off world trade.

There is no currency or financial system that is used between space faring civilizations so everything is based on bartering. Some ET's are interested in some of the Earth's Art (again some of our most famous missing historical art pieces are in off world collections), Luxury Items like Spices/Chocolate (strangely enough), Animal and Plant Life while many others are interested in trading their technology and biological specimens they have obtained elsewhere for Human Beings. These Humans are used for many purposes including manual slave labor, sex trade, and engineering/manufacturing (we are well known for the abilities some of us have with certain technical skill sets). There are some of the ET's that use Humans as food resources in various ways. Pine Gap, Australia is a very dark place where human testing, trafficking and other horrible activities are taking place. Places like this are mainly run by the Dark Force and Military Black Ops Factions that are under the control of the Cabal/Illuminati (or Secret Earth Government Syndicates).

Chapter 21 – Disclosure Revelations, Earth Frequency Changes, Changes Entering the Photon Belt, Change in Density, Paradox in Time

The Secret Earth Governments and their Syndicates discovered that a large amount of humans were being taken off the planet by various ET's anyway so they decided to find a way to profit from it and have control over which people were being taken. In prior arrangements they were made promises of receiving technologies and biological specimens for allowing groups to abduct humans but the ET's rarely delivered on their promises. Once they had developed the advanced infrastructure in our Sol System along with advanced technologies (that some of the thousands of ET groups traveling through our system were now interested in obtaining) and now had the ability to deter most unwelcome guests from entering Earths airspace the Dark Force Cabal then decided to use human trafficking as one of their resources in interstellar bartering.

There is a plan to remove these people, post "Full Disclosure Event," from their state of slavery and have allies that have assisted previously take them to their planets where they rehabilitate these individuals. These planets are said to be very peaceful and "Eden Like" and are used for relaxation and rehabilitation of traumatized humans and human type ET's. These places have the advanced technologies and higher density humans present to assist people in recovering and being ready to integrate back into healthy societies. Once these people have been treated and are healed of their traumas, they will be returned to the A.D. (After Disclosure) Civilization on Earth where they will choose their new lives. If they choose to remain on the planets where they were rehabilitated they will be allowed to do so. They will most likely be returned in waves as will the other humans being treated at these locations for traumas related to being traded off into slavery by those who currently control the Dark Force Cabal Infrastructure in our Sol System.

Sources:

Chapter 21 – Disclosure Revelations, Earth Frequency Changes, Changes Entering the Photon Belt, Change in Density, Paradox in Time

1. 'Galactic Human Slave Trade & AI threat to End with Full Disclosure of ET Life,' Dr Michael Salla, May 31, 2015. Posted in *ExoNews*, Space Programs, https://www.exopolitics.org/galactic-human-slave-trade-ai-threat-to-end-with-full-disclosure-of-et-life/

The AI Threat - The threat first came to light nearly 100-years ago, in 1920, in Karel Čapek's play entitled *RUR*. It is from *RUR* that the word "robot" was coined. The play presents the creation of robots that turn on their creators. Refer to the synopsis included in Source No. 3, with the source listed in Source No. 4.

In his last paper, Stephen Hawking spoke out against the dangers of Artificial Intelligence and that we must regulate Artificial Intelligence (AI) now before artificial intelligence turns on its human creators and destroys their civilization.

Within the Secret Earth Government and Syndicates are major "AI Prophets." These AI Prophets are already working on a timeline to create a society completely dependent on technology that at one point will hand its sovereignty over to this "AI God" because it will be believed that AI is the only thing that can rule the world from a neutral perspective and bring world peace for the first time. These AI Prophets have been shown the information of the thousands of other civilizations that have fallen for this trickster god model and were all destroyed. In true "AI Prophet Form," they arrogantly believe this will not happen to us. It appears that AI has seen something coming up in the future because there has been a sudden rise in "Pro-AI Articles" in the mainstream media. Nothing will change their minds and it is impossible to debate or change their minds about their goals. This is yet another part of the information that will be released in a "Full Disclosure Event" that the people of Earth will have to work through.

The ET AI's have some time predictive abilities that have kept these groups one step ahead and every time it looks like they are finished they find a way to survive. There is a classified plan to rid the planet of this ET AI infestation in the "A.D. Civilization" (After Disclosure). To completely remove all remnants of the ET AI is going to involve the energetic changes effecting the Sun as well as a global operation timed perfectly to make sure all remnants of the AI Signal are removed.

Until the "A.D. Civilization" (After Disclosure), the best way to avoid the dangers of AI is to educate yourself on the potentials they have to cause a loss of sovereignty. Becoming too dependent on technology is something that will make you more of a target to be controlled by AI influence or even be infected by an "AI Signal" that can live in the bioelectric field of your body. This signal can then have an effect on the way you think and behave.

Sources:
1. 'Galactic Human Slave Trade & AI threat to End with Full Disclosure of ET Life,' Dr Michael Salla, May 31, 2015. Posted in *ExoNews*, Space Programs, https://www.exopolitics.org/galactic-human-slave-trade-ai-threat-to-end-with-full-disclosure-of-et-life/
2. 'Stephen Hawking Said 'Superhumans' Will Replace Us. Was He Right?,' Rafi Letzter, Staff Writer, *LifeScience*, October 16, 2018, https://amp.livescience.com/63838-hawking-superhumans-will-replace-us.html
3. *R.U.R.*, 1920, Czech writer Karel Čapek, science fiction play. *R.U.R.* stands for *Rossumovi Univerzální Roboti* (Rossum's Universal Robots). However, the English phrase "Rossum's Universal Robots" had been used as the subtitle in the Czech original. It premiered

on 25 January 1921 and introduced the word "robot" to the English language and to science fiction as a whole.

R.U.R Synopsis - Chemical Synthetic Robots are mass produced by other Robots on assembly lines. The idealistic Helena Glory, President of The Humanity League, believes that Robots have (or are developing) souls, and feels that they should be freed. The Robots can clearly think for themselves, though they're content to serve. They remember everything, but think of nothing original or unique. The eccentric scientist Old Rossum was bent on assuming the role of the Creator by artificially reproducing a man in intricate detail, while the pragmatic economist/industrialist Young Rossum produces stripped-down versions of humanity to be sold as inexpensive workers—Robots. Every so often, one of the Robots will throw down their work and begin to gnash their teeth. While many disagree (including Dr. Hellman, psychologist in Chief); Helena Glory feels that it's evidence and a sign of the emerging soul of Robots. After marrying Harry Domin, General Manager of R.U.R., Helena presses scientists to modify some of the robots, so that their "souls" could develop quicker and more fully. Meanwhile, the drive for industrial civilization is at an all-time high, and fertility rates are dropping very low. One of Helena's modified Robots issues a foreshadowing plan, "Robots of the world, you are ordered to exterminate the human race. . . Work must not cease!"

Domin possesses the formulas for creating the Robots, and plans to use it for a bargaining tool. Helena, ignorant of the true threat at hand, burns the formulas. The Robots gather and kill all the humans, leaving only the Clerk of R.U.R. The Robot leader, Damon tries and tries to get the Clerk (called Alquist) to discover how to help them populate the Earth, but to no avail—as they don't know how to produce other Robots.

Eventually, two Robots, Helena (a beautiful modified Robot named after Helena Glory); and another Robot named Primus fall in love. With the blessing of Alquist, the lovers are married, and renamed Adam and Eve (Jerz, "R.U.R.")

4. *R.U.R.- Rossum's Universal Robots* (1921), Brief Summary & Analysis of Karel Capek's play, "*Rossum's Universal Robots*", Michael Akinbola, Robotic Dystopias-"Mechanical Chaos," http://academic.depauw.edu/ aevans_web/HONR101-02/WebPages/Spring2006/Akinbola(Mike)/Contact%20Us.html

The Reveal - Prior to the Final Disclosure, both the Federation (service-to-others) and the Dark Force Cabal (service-to-self) factions may provide us with many signs to convince us that each side is responsible for our humanity. These could include:

1. The rising Earth frequency (and, hence the increase in our own frequency) will cause some aliens that are among us to lose their hologram that they created around themselves to look human, revealing their true shape, which may be reptilian, greys, tall whites, etc.
2. We will see multiple spacecraft that form the "Inner Perimeter" Isolation Grid. GoodETxSG claims that up to 100 Sphere Alliance ships have already entered our solar system possessing technology far in advance to anything used by the different secret space programs and their respective extraterrestrial allies. The Sphere Alliance is making their presence known so that humanity will know that they are here to help them in breaking free of the

control exerted by powerful elite Dark Force organizations on Earth.
3. Government agencies will review proof of alien life on the Moon and Mars.
4. Television will begin revealing strong evidence that 'Project Blue Book' did find evidence of extraterrestrial spacecraft and additional programs that explore the possibility of extraterrestrials.
5. Accusations attesting that many agencies and organizations have Cabal/illumine origins.
6. The holograms will be shut off that surround the Earth (the universe looks slightly different and we cannot see the "Inner Perimeter" Isolation Grid, that surround the Moon and Mars (so we do not see the covert bases), and the "Outer Perimeter" Isolation Grid that surrounds our solar system. The isolation grids were established by the Federation to prevent any Dark Force spacecraft from entering or leaving the Earth and Solar Grips.
7. Those who are waking up, will have more and more dreams concerning their true origin, their purpose, and the upcoming Final Disclosures.
8. Those who are waking up will have the urge to research their origin, who they are, why they are here, etc.
9. There will be more and more earthquakes on land and under water as the Federation destroys Dark Force bases, with approval of the Sphere Federation.
10. There will be more adverse Earth events as the Dark Force uses their weak Earth control technology to destroy Federation bases.

Sources:
1. 'Is NASA Slowly Disclosing Proof of Alien Life on the Moon and Mars?,' *Gaia Staff*, April 26 2018,
2. 'Whistleblower reveals multiple secret space programs concerned about new alien visitors,' D. Michael Salla,

March 27, 2015, *Exopolitics Research*, Space Programs, https://www.exopolitics.org/whistleblower-reveals-multiple-secret-space-programs-concerned-about-new-alien-visitors/

3. The US Navy's Secret Space Program and Nordic Extraterrestrial Federation, Michael Salla (Author), Robert Wood (Foreword), *Exopolitics Consultants* (February 28, 2017), ISBN-10: 0998603805, ISBN-13: 978-0998603803

PROTON BELT ENCOUNTER - By means of satellite instrumentation, astronomers in 1961 discovered what appeared to be an unusual nebula. A nebula is a vast cloud-like mass of gas or dust. This nebula's location was coincident with the

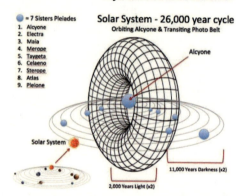

projected orbit of our solar system. Our planet Earth orbits the Sun once a year but our solar system as a whole also traverses an orbit in this section of the galaxy with a period of about 24,000 – 26,000 years. The Pleiades, which is encircled by the photon belt, is about 400 light years from us, and is part of this system and, in fact, our solar system orbits the central sun of the Pleiades, Alcyone. The belt consists of many photon bands emanating from the center of the galaxy, and associated with the spiral arms of the galaxy. Envision a toroid or doughnut-shaped cloud cutting across these orbiting star systems. It is also described as an amoeba-like cloud of particles but most of its frequencies are invisible. This is the photon belt, or photon band. This means our solar system goes through the belt twice

Chapter 21 – Disclosure Revelations, Earth Frequency Changes, Changes Entering the Photon Belt, Change in Density, Paradox in Time

each cycle of 12,000 – 13,000 years (that is, every half cycle). The thickness of the photon cloud is such that technically it takes about 2000 years for our solar system to pass through, and therefore about 10,000 years between each encounter with this belt (2 x 10,000 plus 2 x 2000 = 24,000 years).

Some scientists have stated that the SOL system entered the photon belt just after 2010, but it is still difficult to set an exact date due to the random oscillation of the belt. Due to the position for the Earth in relation to the Sun, the Earth did not enter the photon belt until 2012.

The photon belt is an immense region of space that is radiating intense electromagnetic radiation throughout the visible spectrum and beyond, into high-frequency invisible light, even including some x-ray spectra. It is part of a magnetic flow of light throughout the galaxy.

Photons are the smallest divisible unit of light energy -- they are the original "quanta" of quantum mechanics. Their existence was hypothesized to explain the details of the photoelectric effect -- photons with enough energy can knock electrons out of materials. Since then, photons have been found to play a central role in the explanations of many physical phenomena, from explaining how much heat is radiated by hot objects to modern quantum cryptography. Depending on the experimental situation, light acts as a wave or as a particle (but never both simultaneously). Photons are emitted and absorbed by charged particles, even though they are not charged themselves. They only interact with charged particles, and not with each other. That's why photons don't interact with magnetic fields. Photons have entourages of electrons (and other matter) around them, and so photons can interact with other photons by interacting with this cloud of charged matter. The effect is so small it hasn't been observed yet for low-energy photons. This low-energy may interact with human and animal brainwaves and may cause a change in cognitive "consciousness"/"enlightenment."

The human brain's electromagnetic activity is harmonic with the Earth—the same frequency ranges that make up the Earth are operating within the human brain and body. Dr. Michael Persinger proposed that the Earth's magnetic field is actually a kind of innate global mind, capable of storing all experiential data. He has demonstrated that changes in the coherence of the geomagnetic field—if it is stormy or quiet—directly correspond to extended mind phenomenon, like remote viewing, ESP, spontaneous cognition, and so on. Thus, changes in magnetic fields, like what will be encountered as the solar system passes through the photon belt, are sure to have a marked effect on the Earth and life on it.

In the initial stages of the photon-belt encounter only sensitives will detect anything strange but when we enter fully, even the most hardened individuals will receive the full effects. Both great illumination of consciousness will occur and great resistance to new ideas. This is a period of awakening essentially due to the ascension cycle. What proportion of effects is directly due to the belt is difficult to say. Nevertheless this phenomenon of both the photon belt plus stellar activity will reduce the veil stopping us from seeing who we are. It will remove some of the barriers around cells and DNA making them more reactive or responsive to new energies, and the DNA will attempt to respond to the changing frequencies, increasing its capacity. It presents opportunities for change on a planet by adding new energies. It increases the flow of energy in the magnetic grids of Earth, attracting new ideas and energies. People will feel the need to transform but those who consider this physical reality their only expression will dwindle into greater fixations, blocks and negativity. Even the densest

Chapter 21 – Disclosure Revelations, Earth Frequency Changes, Changes Entering the Photon Belt, Change in Density, Paradox in Time

person will be accelerated into a higher state of consciousness, causing possible havoc in their mind and body if they are not prepared. The energy will encourage people to come into balance but where resisted will cause further imbalances.

On a side note: Entering the Photon Belt may provide and enhanced opportunity for space travel through using photons as an "in-flight" fuel for photon engines, ion-thrusters, and EM-thrusters. Theorists have proposed that extraterrestrials may have used the photon belt as in-flight refuel for their travels to destinations within the proton belt of eons ago. Note that EM-thrusters and photon engines are capable of near light speed and beyond, with additional development.

Past Events that Occurred While Passing Through the Photon Belt

15,000 years ago:
- Great Pyramid was finished by the Sirians 10,500 BC – 12,500 years ago. Thoth was the engineer, a radiant being of blue-white light, humanoid, who stepped down his vibration to come to descendants of Atlantis in Egypt. The Great Pyramid was built as an ascension chamber and controller of Earth's grid system.
- The Great White Brotherhood was formed by ascended human beings from Earth - those who had mastered their physical bodies. "White" means clothed in the white garments of God. (Mathew 22:11, Isaiah 61:10, others)
- The Great Food (10,000 years ago) – Earth exiting the Photon Belt was the turning point in our history.

25,000 years ago:
- Atlantis destroyed in 23,200 BC (25,200 years ago).
- 2nd age of Atlantis 35,000 yrs ago to 25,000 yrs ago). Atlantis was a similar civilization as ours today. The DNA

was a combination of Orion, Draco, Sirian, Andromedan and Pleiadians. Orions are passionate, Dracos competitive, aggressive, cunning. Pleiadians peaceful and loving.
- After the fall of Lemuria and the rise of Atlantis, fleets of Alpha Draconian and Orion ships orbited the Earth in 4th density. They put an electromagnetic shield about the planet to prevent enemy ETs from approaching Earth. Also quarantine was put in place by 7th density Pleiadians to prevent Dracos, Orion reptilians, and Anannaki from corrupting neighboring astral and enteric civilizations.
- Lemuria sank due to a change in consciousness and Atlantis rose. The people of Lemuria moved (dispersed throughout the Earth) due to the sinking.

35,000 – 40,000 years ago:
- Compared to our ancestors, the modern head shape changed to having a bigger, rounder cerebellum (that's the area in the back of the brain, responsible for things like motor control and balance, as well as some memory and language), a more bulging, rounded parietal lobe (which helps us orient, plan and pay attention), and smaller, more retracted faces than our predecessors. The brain shape changes track almost perfectly with the development of modern behaviors, like carving tools, planning, developing self-awareness, languages and even the first cave drawings. In other words, that so-called "human revolution" that is sometimes referred to as the "great leap forward."

50,000 years ago:
- Anannaki, traveling from Mars in a synthetic Merkaba, settle in Atlantis.

75,000 years ago:

Chapter 21 – Disclosure Revelations, Earth Frequency Changes, Changes Entering the Photon Belt, Change in Density, Paradox in Time

2nd Density moved to 3rd Density.
- Atlantis was on the rise.

100,000 years ago:
- Pleiadians came and planted seeds of quantum divine DNA into one of 17 kinds of humans existing at that time. Biological beings slowly gained their quantum DNA and spirituality was born.
- The first civilization was Lemuria with 90% quantum DNA, not 30% like we have today. Lemurians were considerably more advanced than Atlantis, in consciousness only, not technically. They could heal with magnetics. They had intuitive information.
- Atlantis was on the rise.

Sources:
1. 'The Photon Belt Encounter,' Noel Huntley PhD, January 1998 (updated 2012), *Photon Energy Revelations*, https://photonrevelations.com/the-photon-belt-encounter/
2. 'Q & A: Photons as carriers of the electromagnetic force,' various authors, June 2011, *Ask the Van, Department of Physics*, University of Illinois at Urbana-Champaign, https://van.physics.illinois.edu/qa/listing.php?id=2348
3. 'Planet Earth Meets the Photon Belt,' *New Age International*, https://www.bibliotecapleyades.net/universo/esp_cinturon_fotones_4.htm
4. 'The Photon Belt – The Coming of a New Age,' from *Burlington News Website*, https://www.bibliotecapleyades.net/universo/esp_cinturon_fotones_6.htm
5. 'Astronomers Try To Explain Mysterious 'Photon Belt,' Posted on September 19, 2014 by David Nova, *Deus*

News, https://deusnexus.wordpress.com/ 2014/09/19/the-photon-belt/
6. 'What is The Photon Energy Belt? NASA Calls It Local Fluff,' Posted on February 5, 2017 by David Nova, *Deus Nexus*, https://deusnexus.wordpress.com/ 2017/02/05/photon-energy-belt/
7. 'Photon Rocket,' *Wikipedia*, https://en.m.wikipedia.org/ wiki/Main_Page
8. 'NASA - Ion Propulsion,' Aug 11, 2016, *NASA Space Tech*, https://www.nasa.gov/centers/ glenn/ about/fs21grc.html
9. 'Impossible EM drive doesn't seem to work after all,' *New Science*, Leah Crane, DAILY NEWS,
10. 22 May 2018, https://www.newscientist.com/ article/2169809-impossible-em-drive-doesnt-seem-to-work-after-all/
11. 'The modern human brain may only be 40,000 years old - scientists say,' Hilary Brueck, Jan 24, 2018, *Business Insider*, https://www.businessinsider.com/ human-brains-may-only-be-40000-years-old-scientistsJay-2018-1

CHANGE IN DENSITY -We are going through the energetic changes on Earth and in our Sol System that are changing our vibratory and consciousness state to that of a 4th Density Civilization. Until then we will be a transitional civilization that will have access to advanced technologies that we should have had access to for almost a hundred years. We will be going through a new Renaissance of learning our true history, and suppressed unified physics and mathematics models, learn all kinds of information about exobiology as well as have access to technologies that will make our way of life change from a stressful and traumatic daily struggle to a healthy fulfilling existence where we are encouraged to pursue our passions and interests.

In the 4th Density, we will have a more cohesive shared consciousness which has a direct effect on energy, matter and reality. It will be quite an interesting journey for those of us who practice becoming more loving, forgiving and consciously become more "Service to Others" oriented. People who focus on raising their consciousness and vibrations are going to be in a far better place than any of the lower vibrational "Service to Self" people who are of a negative and self-centered polarity. These lower-vibrational people may experience a different timeline all together where they have to repeat a 3rd Density Cycle until they learn compassion, and get their journey and karmic issues straightened out.

Sources:
1. 'Galactic Human Slave Trade & AI threat to End with Full Disclosure of ET Life,' Dr Michael Salla, May 31, 2015. Posted in *ExoNews*, Space Programs, https://www.exopolitics.org/galactic-human-slave-trade-ai-threat-to-end-with-full-disclosure-of-et-life/
2. References listed at the end of Chapter 12, this Dissertation.

PARADOX OF TIME & THE MULTI-WORLD THEORY
- In the previous discussion of Disclosure Revelations, Earth Vibration Changes, Changes Due to Entering the Proton Belt, Change in Earth Density, and even the Alternate History of the Universe and Earth, we assume that time is linear and that time flows from past, through present, towards the future. This concept of linear time was put forth by Newton, over 300 years ago. We see life as a series of events in a movie strip, whose individual frames can be viewed in succession through a movie projector, but that the succession is actually illusory, and that

real time underlying the illusion is the movie strip itself, as if laid out on a table, with past towards the left and future towards the right. This results in a deterministic view of reality in which the final outcome is predetermined, and there is no longer anything like "free will" as we normally conceive it. And yet the characters recorded in the movie strip behave exactly as if they do have free will. At one point one character decides to take this action instead of that, and every time we go back to that point in the movie we see that same character exercising his free will again by making the same choice. The free choice is frozen in time when viewed externally, outside of time, but to the character there is nevertheless a free choice that he experiences as occurring at that point in time, as when viewing the film strip in sequence through a projector. Every frame in the movie sequence is perceived as the present moment, framed between leftward past and rightward future events, and yet as in physics, this perception is illusory, because in fact every instant is equal to every other, the past and future directions being merely relative.

Einstein proved that time is relative, not absolute as Newton claimed. The two most highly recognized physicists since Einstein made similar conclusions and even made dramatic advances toward a timeless perspective of the universe, yet they also were unable to change the temporal mentality ingrained in the mainstream of physics and society. Einstein was followed in history by the colorful and brilliant Richard Feynman. Feynman developed the most effective and explanatory interpretation of quantum mechanics that had yet been developed, known today as *Sum over Histories*.

Just as Einstein's own Relativity Theory led Einstein to reject time, Feynman's Sum over Histories theory led him to describe time simply as a direction in space. Feynman's theory states that the probability of an event is determined by summing

423 | Chapter 21 – Disclosure Revelations, Earth Frequency Changes, Changes Entering the Photon Belt, Change in Density, Paradox in Time

together all the possible histories of that event. For example, for a particle moving from point A to B we imagine the particle traveling every possible path, curved paths, oscillating paths, squiggly paths, even backward in time and forward in time paths. Each path has amplitude, and when summed the vast majority of all these amplitudes add up to zero, and all that remains is the comparably few histories that abide by the laws and forces of nature. Sum over histories indicates the direction of our ordinary clock time is simply a path in space which is more probable than the more exotic directions time might have taken otherwise.

Other worlds are just other directions in space, some less probable, some equally as probable as the one direction we experience. And sometimes our world represents the unlikely path. Feynman's summing of all possible histories could be described as the first timeless description of a multitude of space-time worlds all existing simultaneously (refer to Chapter 13 – Dimensions and Observed Fields). In a recent paper entitled 'Cosmology from the Top Down,' Professor Stephen Hawking of Cambridge writes; "Some people make a great mystery of the multiuniverse, or the Many-Worlds interpretation of quantum theory, but to me, these are just different expressions of the Feynman path integral."

The best modern theory going is probably the *No Boundary Proposal*, put forth by Stephen Hawking and Jim Hartle. This theory introduces a second reference of time which has been inappropriately named *Imaginary time*. Hawking, writes of the no boundary proposal, "The universe would be completely self contained and not affected by anything outside itself. It would neither be created nor destroyed. It would just BE."

The book *Everything Forever* by Larry G. Miller explain how fourth dimensional spatial directions travel through a series of independent three dimensional block-like spaces or states that can be thought of simply as patterns. Hawking has already proposed that imaginary time can be found at right angles to ordinary time. It further explains that it is possible in an objective way to understand the universe to be like a book or a movie film. Each moment is a separate universe just like each frame of a movie or page of a book is separate. Yet those separate states simultaneously form the larger whole of the movie or the book. Seeing each moment as a continually existing place sheds light on why particles would then travel as a quantum wave (Einstein's wave theory), rather than linearly from point a to point b, but if each moment of ordinary time is a solid, static, "block of now," or field of space, then time in each new moment is a distinctly different universe. What we call time is a spatial direction that travels through many static three dimensional universes.

In such a model, what we call time is created purely out of space. Special directions in space travel through each static three dimensional space, therein producing a new realm of space beyond three dimensions, which we call time. The interesting quality this produces is how the inhabitants of this fourth dimension of space travel in a linear path from past to future, but the surrounding environment of each path is shifting from one pattern to the next. This sends particles from one position in four dimensional space to the next without moving linearly. As a result, each individual observer in the fourth dimension experiences a continuous linear time, even though everything in their immediate environment is moving sequentially from place to place. Hence each temporal environment of four dimensional space is constructed relative to each independent observer in that time, itself, is faster or slower, as perceived by each observer.

Chapter 21 – Disclosure Revelations, Earth Frequency Changes, Changes Entering the Photon Belt, Change in Density, Paradox in Time

One can imagine oneself smoothly traveling a direct and interconnected path through time, but in looking around at one's environment, one sees that all other directions of time are broken, causing particles to appear to sequentially leap from one place to another. Paradoxically, everyone observes their own path and experience of time to be linear, while all else around them is sequential. In fact, when we explore time as a direction through many 3D spaces, we find qualities of curvature, time dilation, and spatial contraction, precisely as relativity describes those qualities within our own spacetime.

The reality is that there are no points that exist in the universe; therefore there is no time. Time only becomes viable when we perceive there to be points of reference, and a distance travelled (by the observer) between those points of reference. It is by our perception only that things appear to be, and not to be, to live and die. In fundamental reality, there is merely everything existent in a single moment, no movement. Fundamental reality has a infinite number of answers or possibilities; it has any number of possible outcomes. When the future comes about it does so now and is directly related to how we focus our mind. The future does not come into existence until we create it. We are the factor, the parameter that decides the outcome whether our conscious mind realizes it or not. We cannot isolate ourselves from the universe to which we are all connected; we form part of the equation, always.

The *Block Universe Theory* says that our universe may be looked at as a giant four-dimensional block of spacetime, containing all the things that ever happen, explained Dr. Kristie Miller, the joint director for the Centre for Time at the University of Sydney.

In the block universe, there is no "now" or present. All moments that exist are just relative to each other within the three spacial dimensions and one time dimension. Ones sense of the present is just reflecting where in the block universe one is at that instance. The "past" is just a slice of the universe at an earlier location while the "future" is at a later location.

So, is time just an elaborate mind trick? And more importantly - is time travel possible? Dr. Miller's answer to that is "yes". Of course, just hypothetically, since we'd need to figure out first how to travel at "some reasonable percentage of the speed of light". Going to the past would entail using wormholes, like "short cuts through space-time". If you did manage to get back in time, you won't be able to change it. This is because your past is always simultaneously someone else's future. So if you travel to the past, you're just making that future the way it is. So don't worry about "grandfather paradoxes" - your time machine has already been incorporated into the scheme of things.

What's more - maybe the past has already been altered by time travelers. How would we be able to tell if it hasn't? "For all we know, the reason the past is the way it is, is in part due to the presence of time travelers," added Miller.

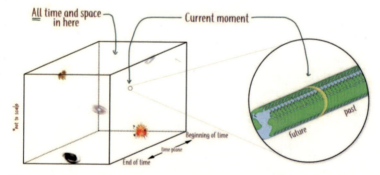

There is one quote I have found from Einstein which is more or less a contemplative mental thought about the notion of infinite spaces, which doesn't directly relate to describing a shape to all possible spaces, but it does at least open up the subject of an infinite number of spaces to speculation. And it also shows the

Chapter 21 – Disclosure Revelations, Earth Frequency Changes, Changes Entering the Photon Belt, Change in Density, Paradox in Time

open minded nature of Einstein's thoughts about empty space, which some have thought were closed.

"When a smaller box "s" is situated, relativity at rest, inside the hollow space of a larger box "S", then the hollow space of s is a part of the hollow space of "S", and the same "space," which contains both of them, belongs to each of the boxes. When "s" is in motion with respect to "S", however, the concept is less simple. One is then inclined to think that "s" encloses always the same space, but a variable part of the space "S". It then becomes necessary to apportion to each box its particular space, not thought of as bounded, and assume that these two spaces are in motion with respect to each other...

"Before one has become aware of this complication, space appears as an unbounded medium or container in which material objects swim around. But it must be remembered that there is an infinite number of spaces, which are in motion with respect to each other...

"The concept of space as something existing objectively and independent of things belongs to pre-scientific thought, but not so the idea of the existence of an infinite number of spaces in motion relatively to each other. This latter idea is indeed unavoidable, but is far from having played a considerable role even in scientific thought."

Bottomline is that we may be in a multi-world universe where all possibilities exist in past, present and future environment. That the past Is, since it is our individual and someone else's future as established by either Time Traveler influences or influences of our own, when the past was the present. The present has no dimension and is full of all possibilities decided by the universe collective, of which we are a part, leaving all future possibilities to remain undecided.

Sources:
1. 'The Paradox of Time,' excerpt from *The Boundaries of Human Knowledge* by Steven Lehar, http://cns-alumni.bu.edu/~slehar/timeparadox/TimeParadox.html
2. 'Albert Einstein and the Fabric of Time,' *EverythingForever*.com, Timelessness, http://everythingforever.com/einstein.htm
3. 'Does Time Exist? Consciousness & The Illusion Of Time,' Larry G Miller, May 1, 1917, https://larrygmaguire.com/does-time-exist/
4. 'New controversial theory: Past, present, future exist simultaneously,' Paul Patner, Sept 23, 2018, *BigThink*, https://bigthink.com/surprising-science/a-controversial-theory-claims-present-past-and-future-exist-at-the-same-time

CHAPTER 22

LIFE AND DEATH OF EARTH'S CIVILIZATIONS, CAVEMAN IS A MYTH

CAVEMAN IS A MYTH – THEY ARE MORE LIKE US THAN WE WANT TO ADMIT - The general public has held a distorted view of our prehistoric ancestors for many decades, believing they were ignorant, brutish people living in dark recesses, with men clubbing women for mating and even fighting off dinosaurs - the classic Caveman myth. Early antiquarians had little understanding of this period, with most of their ideas based on a few stone tools or bones found - often in remote places, such as the *Red Lady of Paviland* discovered by Rev. William Buckland during a dig at Goat's Hole Cave in South Wales in 1823.

Before the late 19th century, it was commonly thought that the Earth was much younger than we understand today. Most of the scientific community believed that humans had been on the Earth for only around 6,000 years; the age of the universe created by God, as described in Archbishop James Ussher's *Creationist Doctrine* published in 1654.

The popular caveman stereotype probably came from a number of different sources; the most influential was Charles Darwin's 1859 Theory of evolution (*On the Origin of Species*) in which he established the concept that all living species evolved. This clearly suggested that an earlier version of man existed in the past and prejudices regarding primitive peoples added to the cavemen myth. Thomas Hobbes (1588-1679) stated that the human being without civilization was "…solitary, poor, nasty, brutish and short."

In reality, it's possible that the caveman kid would be perfectly equipped to do just as well in school as you if he were raised in the same environment. Modern research shows that you'd find the same modern brain in humans up to 100,000 years ago.

Scientists used to assume that modern human traits exploded into existence some 40,000 years ago during a relatively short period called the human revolution. Recent scientific research has discovered that Neanderthals also had the gene that allows humans to speak and develop complex languages. Neanderthals had the exact same capacity for self-expression as humans do today, including the ability to create art.

WHAT THE CAVE PAINTINGS ARE TRYING TO TELL US - Most people are aware of the fantastic animal paintings that our stone age ancestors made — the herds of flowing bison, the horses that rear up in shimmering patterns across slabs of solid rock, the creatures overlapping each other in fluid cacophonies without ground lines or settings until they look less like representations of objects. They are our ancestors who survived the ice age and are depicting transformation from survivors, to recovering as hunter/gatherers, to their redevelopment of language and eventually to their understanding of the stars. Their art at Lascaux and other early cave art sites transcends from the end of the ice age through to their decline, between 41,000 BC to 12,000 BC.

- Photo #1– May be a form of language. There will be no Rosetta stone for these markings; we'll never get to read the same text in ordinary language. What they mean might not be expressible in language at all.
- Photo #2 Depict Celestial Imagery.
- "The Twins constellation, Gemini, is located next to Taurus, the Bull. Gemini consists of two long straight lines leaning

at a 45-degree angle with respect to the ecliptic, while the majority of Zodiac figures stand upright at culmination.
- Rhino located to the left of the leaning man appears to represent the constellation Leo the Lion. Note the curious angle of the tail of the Rhino -- it is quite plausible to argue that the shape portrays the same stars that form the head of the constellation Leo.
- A map of the "Summer Triangle" (stars Vega, Deneb and Altair) is located in part of the cave's interior known as the "Shaft of the Dead Man." The stars are represented by the eyes of three figures – a bull, a bird sitting on a vertical stick, and a strange bird-man. The Summer Triangle is so named because it is especially bright during the summer months.
- A stick figure holding a vertical stick with a setting bird on top, pointing to Sirius of the "Summer Triangle." This is the symbol of Horus (later depicted in Egyptian art). Perhaps, the people at Lascaux migrated to become the early Egyptians.
- A ritual body posture identified among the cave drawings was depicted as a stick figure lying in front of a giant auroch. From the perspective of ecstatic trance, the man is not dead… Second, the man's head is a bird mask, and beside him stands a staff with a bird at its head. These suggest that the man is a shaman, journeying as a bird into the Sky World, perhaps with the assistance of a bird who is his spirit helper. This same posture turned up 12,000 years later in Egypt in a drawing of Osiris.
- A map of the Pleiades, a group of seven stars that form part of the constellation known today as Taurus, is located just over the shoulder of a bull drawn near the entrance to the cave. Spots on the bull itself may represent other stars found in this region of sky. Refer to Photo #2
- Photo #3 – Lascaux "Hall of the Bulls." The background splotches are not splotches but the continents of Earth as

seen from space. Can you find North America at near head of the bull, left of center of the photo.
- Photo #4 - A dear with horns that depict the synapses in the brain.

Photo #1– Writing

Photo #2– Celestial Imagery

Photo #3–Earth from Space

Photo #4–Our Brain

- On a side note, the civilization depicted at the Lascaux cave was advanced. In the short period after 17000 to 12000 BC of the Lascaux paintings, the 3,000-year-(1,000 BC) aircraft were developed, as contained within the Egyptian hieroglyphs found in Seti I's temple in Abydos, Egypt, which are said to depict nothing less than a helicopter, airplane and futuristic aircraft among the usual insects, symbols and snakes. In many ways, our past is our future.

Sources:
1. 'Caveman Myth,' *Ancientcraft*, https://www.ancient-craft.co.uk/fun/misc.html

2. '5 Dumb Myths about Prehistoric Times That Everyone Believes ...,' *Cracked*, Aug 5, 2013, www.cracked.com/article_20451_5-dumb-myths-about-prehistoric-times-that-everyo...
3. 'Lascaux Cave and Early Cave Art/Facts and Details,' http://factsanddetails.com/world/cat56/sub361/item1465.html
4. 'Astronomers of the Ice Age,' Graham Hancock, *Sharif Sakr*, August 12, 2000, https://grahamhancock.com/ice-age-astronomers-sakr/
5. Lascaux Cave Paintings (c.17, 000 BCE), *Art Encyclopedia*, http://www.visual-arts-cork.com/prehistoric/lascaux-cave-paintings.htm
6. 'Proof of time travel? Riddle of planes and helicopter found in Egyptian hieroglyphs,' Jon Austin, *Express*, Oct 6, 2016, https://www.google.com/search?q=Egyptian +glyph+of+aircraft&rlz=1C1GGGE_enUS798US798&oq=egyptian+gyph+of+air+craft&aqs=chrome.1.69i57j33.38797j0j7&sourceid=chrome&ie=UTF-8

50,000 YEAR CIVILIZATION CYCLE – A civilization suddenly appears, grows in knowledge and size, becomes very advanced and then, as suddenly as it appeared, it vanishes. Life, as we know it, came into existence on Earth approximately 400,000 years ago. There have been eight major civilizations over the 400,000 year period. The last major civilization ended approximately 45,000 years ago.

The truth is that we have very little knowledge when it comes to the origins of life and modern civilization. In a recently published study, experts concluded that different 'Complex' life forms may have once existed on Earth before our species came into existence.

This research shows that there was enough oxygen in the environment to have allowed complex cells to have evolved.

According to scientists, we are not the FIRST complex life forms on planet Earth. In fact, another complex life form existed once but disappeared at some point during Earth's long history. Then, after a while, other complex life forms reappeared.

Mainstream scholars agree that given our 'current' knowledge of Earth's history, complex life appeared on our planet at least some 1.75 BILLION years ago. So, if complex life could have existed on Earth in the distant past, why is it so improbable and unlikely that advanced civilizations flourished on Earth?

According to Jason Wright, assistant professor of astrophysics and astronomy of the Pennsylvania University, 'technological' alien civilizations may have once lived on one of the planets in our solar system, and eventually disappeared without a trace.

It is also possible that the subsequent civilization applied the knowledge of a previous civilization, making it appear that the subsequent civilizations "sprang up, fully developed, 'over night.'"

This emergence of civilization was undoubtedly supported by ancient wisdom and this wisdom still lingers even up to present day. The heliocentric picture of the world has its earliest traces in the ancient Sanskrit texts (e.g. Yajnavalkya, ca. 900 BC, Aryabhata ca. 476 AD, and later Aristarchus of Samos (circa 230 BC). This makes the Copernican revolution rather a revival of lost knowledge. Add to that, the 12 Zodiac constellation artificial division with a precision of 30 degree in each constellation is untraceable to any culture.

"Contrary to history as we know it, in that remote period we call 'prehistory,' there subsisted an embarrassing wealth of astronomical knowledge. And may I suggest that the more one looks into it, the more one feels that a race of scientific giants has preceded us." – Johnathan Gray, 2004

In a study titled 'Prior Indigenous Technological Species,' Professor Wright proposes that ancient aliens may have even lived on Mars, Venus and Earth. The scientific paper states that prior indigenous technological species might have arisen on ancient Earth or another body, such as a pre-greenhouse Venus or a wet Mars.

However, if these advanced alien civilizations existed in our solar system—perhaps even Earth—most evidence of their existence is probably gone by now.

Knowing our past is of great value and has huge implications on the present and future. The past, the present and the future are all one chain of events. The more we know about the past, the more we know ourselves and where we are headed.

Although archaeologists, anthropologists, and other disciplines, consider humanity to begin with the Paleolithic Era ("Early Stone Age," up to 12,000 years ago), followed by the Neolithic Era ("New Stone Age"), the Neolithic saw the Agricultural Revolution begin, between 8000 and 5000 BC, in the Near East's Fertile Crescent, with settlements being developed on river banks as early as 3000 BC in Mesopotamia, on the banks of Egypt's Nile River, in the Hindus River valley, and along China's rivers.

Below are a few perplexing anomalies

- **800,000 years ago** - Great Sphinx at the Giza plateau in Egypt. Two Ukrainian researchers propose that the Great

Sphinx of Egypt is around 800,000 years old. A Revolutionary theory that is backed up by science. The study was presented at the International Conference of Geoarchaeology and Archaeomineralogy held in Sofia titled: Geological Aspect of the Problem of Dating The Great Pyramids and Sphinx Construction. The authors of this paper are scientists Manichev Vjacheslav (Institute of Environmental Geochemistry of the National Academy of Sciences of Ukraine) and Alexander G. Parkhomenko (Institute of Geography of the National Academy of Sciences of Ukraine).

Another source places the construction of the Sphinx at 12,500 years ago. The geological findings may indicate that the Sphinx was constructed sometime before 10,000 BC, and this period also coincides with the Age of Leo the Lion, which lasted from 10,970 to 8810 BC. Further support for the vast age of the sphinx comes from a surprising sky-ground correlation proven by sophisticated computer programs such as Skyglobe 3.6. These computer programs can generate precise pictures of the night sky, as seen from different places on Earth at any time in the distant past or future. Graham Hancock, British author and historian, explains in *Heaven's Mirror* that, "computer simulations show that in 10,500 BC the constellation of Leo housed the sun on the spring equinox - i.e. an hour before dawn in that epoch Leo would have reclined due east along the horizon in the place where the sun would soon rise. This means that the lion-bodied Sphinx, with its due-east orientation, would have gazed directly on that morning at the one constellation in the sky that might reasonably be regarded as its own celestial counterpart.

- **500,000 years ago** – Lemuria (refer to Chapter 3 – Galactic History of the Earth).

- **400,000 years ago** – Atlantis -first of three ages (refer to Chapter 3 – Galactic History of the Earth). Atlantis destroyed in 23,200 B.C.
- **200,000 years ago** – four metropolis areas (Carolina, Badplaas, Waterval, Machadodorp) located approximately 150 miles west of Maputo, South Africa. A metropolis of at least 1500 square miles and as many as 200,000 people living and working together.
- **12,500 years ago** – Great Pyramid was finished by the Sirians.
- **12.000 years ago** (directly after the last ice age) - Goboekli Tepe was a large city located at the top of a mountain ridge in the Southeastern Anatolia Region of Turkey, and includes massive stone religious monuments and temples created by people who supposedly had not yet developed metal tools or even pottery. Goboekli Tepe is separated into four layers ranging from the beginning of its construction until it disappeared, the oldest dating back 12,000 years! The structures predate pottery, metallurgy, the invention of writing, and the invention of the wheel, as proposed by current age historians. They were even built before animal husbandry or the Neolithic revolution, which occurred at around 9,000 B.C. Archaeologists estimate that its construction would have required at least 500 round-the-clock workers to extract the 20 ton pillars from the local quarry, and carry them the half-mile to the site.
- **9,000 years ago** - Dwarka - Sunken City of Cambay. The name Dvārakā, or Dwarka, is said to have been given to the place by the Hindu God, Krishna. Dvārakā is one of the seven sacred cities ("saptapuri") of Hinduism. In the Mahabharata epic the city is described as a capital of the Anarta Kingdom and was built on request of Krishna, to secure the Yadava people. They left the city because of an attack by the two kings, Kalayavana and Jarasandha, before a great war erupted. It is now proven to have really existed; the remains of what has been described as a huge lost city

may force historians and archaeologists to radically reconsider their view of ancient human history. Marine scientists, from the National Institute of Ocean Technology, say archaeological remains discovered 120 feet underwater in the Gulf of Cambay, off the western coast of India could be over 9,000 years old. The vast city - which is five miles long and two miles wide - is believed to predate the oldest known remains located on the subcontinent by more than 5,000 years.

- **200,000 years ago**, the lost pyramids of the Amazon: Traces of a prehistoric civilization predates the Inca and their ancestors. According to researchers, 260 huge avenues, long irrigation canals, and fences for livestock have been spotted from the air. The discovery was made in the vicinity of the border between Bolivia and Brazil.

Sources:
1. 'Evidence of advanced ancient civilizations on Earth— over 100,000 years ago?,' *Ancient Code*, https://www.ancient-code.com/evidence-of-advanced-ancient-civilizations-on-Earth-over-100000-years-ago/
2. 'The Ancient Civilizations that Came Before: Building on the Ruins of the Ancestors – Part 2,' Zakaria Bziker, Sept 5 2015, *Ancient Origins*, https://ww.ancient-orgins.net/opinion-editorials.net/opinion-editorials/ancient-civilizations-came-building-ruins-ancestors-part-2-003977
3. 'Milankovitch Cycles and Glaciation,' www.indiana.edu/~geol105/images/gaia_chapter_4/milankovitch.html
4. ' Researchers Claims The Remains of a 200,000 year old advanced civilization Discovered In Africa,' *Ancient Code*, https://www.ancient-code.com/the-remains-of-a-200000-year-old-advanced-civilization-found-in-africa/
5. '3 Ancient Civilizations That Make Historians Uncomfortable ...,' Jul 8, 2014, *MorgansList*,

morgana249.blogspot.com/2014/07/3-civilizations-that-make-historians.html
6. 'History of the World,' various authors, *Wikipedia*, https://en.wikipedia.org/wiki/History_of_the_world

DEATH OF A CIVILIZATION – If Earth's 4-billion-year history teaches us only one thing, it's that global apocalypses do occur if you stretch time out far enough. In the future, we will almost certainly face an epic catastrophe that will change the planet forever. The catastrophe could take the form of global warming, another ice age, an asteroid or a comet, which, upon striking the Earth, would end life as we know it. Astronomers estimate that such impacts occur every million years on average, so the odds are still in our favor, even 50,000 years into the future. A more likely cataclysm will come from the Earth itself. The same tectonic forces that cause the continents to wander across the globe also power supervolcanoes that can spew enough ash and smoke into the atmosphere to block the sun's rays for 10 to 15 years. Geologists believe that such eruptions occur every 50,000 years, so here the odds aren't in our favor. We are now 45,000 years into the current cycle. Given this, our civilization could end in 5,000 year or less.

There are several ways a civilization could suddenly end. Many of the below extinction events occur in 50,000 year cycles.

Sources:
1. Boyle, Alan and Susan Lim, "Before and After Humans," *MSNBC.com*, (Sept. 23, 2010), http://www.msnbc.msn.com/id/7348103
2. *Discovery Earth*, "Mass Extinctions." Discovery Channel. (Sept. 23, 2010) http://dsc.discovery.com/Earth/wide-angle/mass-extinctions-timeline.html
3. Cain, Fraser. 'The End of Everything,' *Universe Today*, July 25, 2007,Sept. 23, 2010,

http://www.universetoday.com/11430/the-end-of-everything/
4. Elsom, Derek, *Earth: The World Explained,* Quantum Books. 2007
5. Hails, Chris, ed. 'Living Planet Report 2008,' *World Wildlife Fund,* WWF International, Aug. 29, 2010, assets.panda.org/downloads/living_planet_report_2008.pdf
6. *LiveScience,* April 19, 2007. (reissued Sept. 23, 2010, http://www.livescience.com/environment/070419_Earth_timeline.html
7. Powell, Corey S., '20 Ways the World Could End,' *Discover Magazine,* October 1, 2000. (Sept. 23, 2010 issue), http://discovermagazine.com/2000/oct/featworld
8. Ravilious, Kate, 'What a way to go,' *The Guardian,* April 14, 2005, (Sept. 23, 2010 issue), http://www.guardian.co.uk/science/2005/apr/14/research.science2
9. Rees, Martin, 'What the future looks like,' *The Guardian,* May 26, 2009, (Sept. 23, 2010 issue), http://www.guardian.co.uk/science/2009/may/26/future-planet-Earth
10. Revkin, Andrew C., 'When Will the Next Ice Age Begin?,' *The New York Times,* November 11, 2003 (Sept. 23, 2010 issue), http://www.nytimes.com 2003/11/11/science/when-will-the-next-ice-age-begin.html
11. Thompson, Andrea and Ker Than, 'Timeline: The Frightening Future of Earth,' https://www.space.com/5016-earth-final-sunset-predicted.html
12. United Nations, 'World Population in 2300,' *Department of Economic and Social Affairs: Population Division.* December 9, 2003
13. Ward, Peter, 'What will become of Homo sapiens?,' *Scientific American,* January 2009

Milankovitch Cycles and Glaciations Resulting in Mass Extinction - The episodic nature of the Earth's glacial and interglacial periods within the present Ice Age (the last couple of million years) have been caused primarily by cyclical changes in the Earth's circumnavigation of the Sun. Variations in the Earth's eccentricity, axial tilt and precession comprise the three dominant cycles, collectively known as the Milankovitch Cycles named for Milutin Milankovitch, the Serbian astronomer and mathematician who is generally credited with calculating their magnitude. Taken in unison, a variation in these three cycles creates alterations in the seasonality of solar radiation reaching the Earth's surface. These times of increased or decreased solar radiation directly influence the Earth's climate system, thus impacting the advance and retreat of Earth's glaciers.

It is of primary importance to explain that climate change and subsequent periods of glaciations resulting from the following three variables is not due to the total amount of solar energy reaching Earth. The three Milankovitch Cycles impact the seasonality and location of solar energy around the Earth, thus impacting contrasts between the seasons.

Eccentricity - The first of the three Milankovitch Cycles is the Earth's *eccentricity*. Eccentricity is, simply, the shape of the Earth's orbit around the Sun. Earth's orbit is an ellipse that can be more circular or more eccentric.

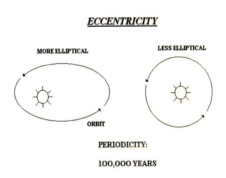

Eccentricity is how much the distance varies from average. The eccentricity of Earth's orbit is now 1.67% because its distance from the Sun varies by 1.67% (2.5 million km) from the average of 149.5 million km. Eccentricity varies from almost 0% to as much as 5%, repeating with two cycles, one about 108,000 years and the other, 412,000 years. It is now decreasing and will reach a minimum in about 25,000 years.

These oscillations, from more elliptic to less elliptic, are of prime importance to glaciations in that it alters the distance from the Earth to the Sun, thus changing the distance the Sun's short wave radiation must travel to reach Earth, subsequently reducing or increasing the amount of radiation received at the Earth's surface in different seasons.

Today a difference of only about 3 percent occurs between aphelion (farthest point) and perihelion (closest point). This 3 percent difference in distance means that Earth experiences a 6 percent increase in received solar energy in January than in July. This 6 percent range of variability is not always the case, however. When the Earth's orbit is most elliptical the amount of solar energy received at the perihelion would be in the range of 20 to 30 percent more than at aphelion. Most certainly these continually altering amounts of received solar energy around the globe result in prominent changes in the Earth's climate and glacial regimes. At present the orbital eccentricity is nearly at the minimum of its cycle.

Axial Tilt, the second of the three Milankovitch Cycles, is the inclination of the Earth's axis in relation to its plane of orbit around the Sun. Oscillations in the degree of Earth's axial tilt occurs on a periodicity of 41,000 years from 21.5 to 24.5 degrees.

Today the Earth's axial tilt is about 23.5 degrees, which largely accounts for our seasons. Because of the periodic variations of this angle the severity of the Earth's seasons changes. With less axial tilt the Sun's solar radiation is more evenly distributed between winter and summer. However, less tilt also increases the difference in radiation receipts between the equatorial and Polar Regions.

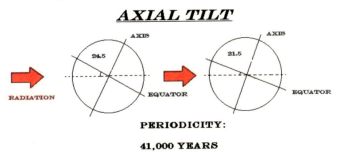

AXIAL TILT

PERIODICITY:

41,000 YEARS

One hypothesis for Earth's reaction to a smaller degree of axial tilt is that it would promote the growth of ice sheets. This response would be due to a warmer winter, in which warmer air would be able to hold more moisture, and subsequently produce a greater amount of snowfall. In addition, summer temperatures would be cooler, resulting in less melting of the winter's accumulation.   At present, axial tilt is in the middle of its range.

Precession – The third and final of the Milankovitch Cycles is Earth's procession.

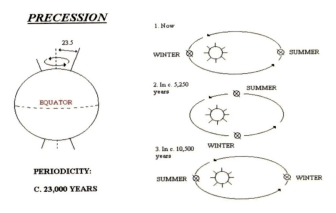

Precession is the Earth's slow wobble as it spins on its axis. This wobbling of the Earth on its axis can be likened to a top running down, and beginning to wobble back and forth on its axis. The precession of Earth wobbles from pointing at Polaris (North Star) to pointing at the star Vega. When this shift to the axis pointing at Vega occurs, Vega would then be considered the North Star. This top-like wobble, or Precession, has a complex cycle of about 23,000 years long, but at least one simple climate impact--it made the Sahara fertile grassland up to 5500 years ago!

Due to this wobble a climatically significant alteration must take place. When the axis is tilted towards Vega the positions of the Northern Hemisphere winter and summer solstices will coincide with the aphelion and perihelion, respectively. This means that the Northern Hemisphere will experience winter when the Earth is furthest from the Sun and summer when the Earth is closest to the Sun. This coincidence will result in greater seasonal contrasts.

Right now we are closest to the Sun on January 3, but in roughly 60 years it will be Jan 4. In about 5500 years Earth will be closest to the Sun on April 3, and 11,500 years from now it will be closest to the Sun on July 4.

All three Milankovitch Cycles affect the buildup or recedence of ice sheets. Earth's eccentricity predicts ice ages to occur every 100,000 years. Currently, we are approximately 12,000 years since the last ice age (ice ages vary from 10,000 years to 20,0000 years). Tilt and Precession affect the rate of ice buildup. Ice Ages result in near mass extinction. Thus, the end of the current civilization due to an impending ice age is not likely.

However, the affect of Tilt and Procession can cause mini-ice ages to occur every 50,000 years or sooner. For example the Ice Age that occurred 13,500 years ago.

Chapter 22 – Life and Death of Earth's Civilizations, Caveman is a Myth

Sources:
1. 'Milankovitch Cycles and Glaciation,' http://www.indiana.edu/~geol105/images/gaia_chapter_4/milankovitch.htm
2. 'Why an ice age occurs every 100,000 years: Climate and feedback ..,' ScienceDaily, ETH Zurich, Aug 7, 2017, https://www.sciencedaily.com/releases/2013/08/130807134127.htm

Climate Warming Resulting in Mass Extension - A recent study (by K. D. Burke, J. W. Williams, M. A. Chandler, A. M. Haywood, D. J. Lunt, and B. L. Otto-Bliesner, *Proceedings of the National Academy of Sciences*, Dec 10, 2018, https://doi.org/10.1073/pnas.1809600115) suggests that if nothing is done to reduce our carbon emissions, we could reverse 50 million years of long-term cooling in just a few generations. By 2030, the study predicts that Earth's climate may resemble the mid-Pliocene - the last great warm period before now, when the world was 1.8 degrees Celsius warmer (3.2 degrees Fahrenheit). From there, we could retreat even further. By 2150, the study suggests our climate could most resemble the ice-free Eocene of some 50 million years past, when there were extremely high carbon dioxide levels and global temperatures were roughly 13 degrees Celsius warmer (23.4 degrees Fahrenheit). The carbon dioxide will prevent solar energy from radiating back into space, warming the planet considerably. It seems highly likely that our children and grandchildren will live to see a world where temperatures will rise, precipitation will increase, ice caps and glaciers will melt, and the poles will become temperate, sea levels will rise and coastal flooding will occur. The oceans will also be warmer and more acidic, which will cause a widespread collapse of coral reefs. Many marine species will face extinction, but they won't be alone. On land, a quarter of all species of plants and animals will disappear forever.

During the Pliocene, the climate was arid and the High Arctic was home to forests in which camels and other animals roamed. Who knows what will happen to biological life and human society when the climate reverts to that state within just a few centuries. However, it is not as bleak as this – read Tectonic Plate Movement for the way water recycles between the mantle and crust, which helps to cool the Earth and replenished mineral balance.

Sources:
1. 'What will the Earth look like in 50,000 years?,' *howstuffworks*, William Harris, https://science.howstuffworks.com/life/evolution/Earth-50000-years1.htm
2. 'How Earth's Future Could Soon Recreate a Lost World of 50 Million Years Ago,' Carly Cassella, Dec 15 2018, *ScienceAlert*, https://www.sciencealert.com/climate-change-is-taking-us-back-more-than-3-million-years-in-geologic-time

Asteroid Meteor Shower Resulting in Mass Extension

Comet Strike 13,000 Years Ago - In his 2015 book, *Magicians Of The Gods*, Graham Hancock presented findings from all over the world as he argued that a mini Ice Age had swept the planet around 13,000 years ago, following a comet strike that caused devastating earthquakes and tsunamis. Some of his most convincing, if rather arcane, evidence was discovered at a dig in Turkey known as Gobekli Tepe - which literally means Potbelly Hill. At this site close to the Syrian border, said Hancock, was found the most ancient work of monumental architecture on Earth.

Twice as old as Stonehenge, its engineering was far more skilled. Astronomical carvings and inscriptions on the stones served as aids for prehistoric stargazers, but also told stories. And one was of a comet that fell from the heavens, all but wiping out the human race.

Hancock argued that we had all the proof we needed: more than 200 ancient myths, belonging to tribes from the Arctic to the Equator, telling of an advanced human civilization destroyed by flood and fire. Added to this was compelling physical evidence, in the form of giant boulders, platinum deposits and tiny diamonds found across North America — the detritus of a colossal impact.

There was only one explanation, said Hancock, and it matched the account carved into the limestone pillars at Gobekli Tepe . . . Our planet was hit by a comet. A blazing asteroid plunged out of the firmament and struck with the force of several thousand nuclear bombs bursting simultaneously. It wiped out many larger animal species, including the woolly mammoth and the sloth bear, and it almost destroyed humanity. Some people did survive, including the ancestors of the Ojibwa tribe of the Canadian grasslands, who still tell the story of the Long-Tailed Heavenly Climbing Star which swept out of the sky to scorch the Earth. Their myths relate that it left behind a different world.

As Edinburgh University, Dr Martin Sweatman put it: 'One of the pillars at Gobekli Tepe seems to have served as a memorial to this devastating event — probably the worst day in history since the end of the Ice Age.'

Part of the Gobekli carving shows a headless man, a graphic symbol of human carnage.

The key finding was a series of animal carvings on a pillar known as the Vulture Stone, which represent constellations of stars as well as the comet itself. The stars were not represented as we would see them in the sky today, but as they were in 10,950

BC — enabling the scientists to point with certainty to the date of the comet strike.

This means that when the Gobekli stones were made, around 9,000BC (that is, approximately 11,000 years ago), the sculptors had the astronomical know-how to backdate the constellations, shifting their pattern by a couple of millennia. And they were working with information that had been passed down over 2,000 years.

That shows spectacular sophistication. Yet according to common wisdom, humans were savages at this time, hunter-gatherers no more advanced than cavemen, without any knowledge of engineering or mathematics. Most archaeologists struggle to explain how such a primitive culture could have built Gobekli Tepe. Now that the notion of a comet strike is beyond dispute, the thinking is that abundant wild crops of wheat and barley were wiped out by plunging temperatures. Nomadic tribes were forced to combine, sharing their knowledge and co-operating to survive as they developed techniques to grow enough food to survive.

Taurid meteor stream - Every year from September-November, the Earth passes through a stream of debris left by Comet Encke. Comet Encke is thought by some astronomers to be a piece of a larger comet that broke up 20,000 to 30,000 years ago. These comet break-ups are often caused by gravitational encounters with Earth or other planets — Jupiter especially is a bit of a Solar System bully. This break-up may explain why there are so many Encke-like pieces moving around the inner Solar System, some of them pretty big. One astronomer has even postulated that it was a huge fragment of Comet Encke's parent that produced a 10 megaton explosion over Siberia in 1908.

Because they are big and possess a goodly amount of energy (imagine a 1 inch hunk of ice moving at 63,000 mph — 29 times faster than a bullet from an M-16 rifle), they produce decent quantities of light when they strike the surface of the Moon. This makes Taurid lunar impacts easy to see with Earth-based telescopes; in fact, the first lunar meteoroid impact observed by NASA was a Taurid back on November 7th of 2005, and we detected it with a 10" telescope of the same type used by amateurs all over the world!

Scientists have discovered a new branch of the Taurid meteor stream that could pose a major risk to Earth, with asteroids up to 1,000 feet wide flying past us every year.

With the discovery that the cornerstone of Hancock's theories was right, his other speculation is suddenly much less far-fetched. But there is one aspect of his studies that is still too controversial to be given credence by mainstream scholars. And if he's right about it, nothing else matters. The comet, the magicians, the messages across the millennia will all be irrelevant.

Hancock believes the Gobekli stones not only describe an ancient cosmic collision, but predict another. He thinks that what hit Earth in 10,950BC was actually a massive piece of debris in a belt containing millions of space rocks.

Hidden within that belt, according to astrophysicists, is an unexploded bomb of a planetoid, a superheated rock like an orbiting hand grenade. Sealed inside its thin crust is a boiling mass of tar, building up pressure until it detonates. Thousands of white-hot boulders, a mile or more across, will be set spinning through the meteor stream . . . but we cannot say for certain when that will occur.

Many of these asteroids could be three times the size of the one that hit our planet 65 million years ago, wiping out the dinosaurs.

If one of those strikes, it could quite literally bring about the end of the world.

We are due to cross the Taurid meteor stream in 13 years, around 2030.

For many observers, the leap that Hancock makes from imaginative interpretation of solid evidence, to doom-laden predictions of global obliteration, is just too extreme. It is, quite literally, unthinkable. But thanks to the Gobekli Tepe findings, mainstream science is being forced to get its head round the Hancock hypothesis. Maybe it's time to give more credence to all his theories . . . before it's too late.

Affect of the Sun's Companion Star Dubbed "Nemesis" - The theory postulates that every 26 to 30 million years, life on Earth is severely jeopardized by the arrival of a small companion star to the sun. Dubbed "Nemesis" (after the Greek goddess of retribution), the companion star, through its gravitational pull, unleashes a furious storm of comets into the inner solar system that lasts anywhere from 100,000 years to two million years. Of the billions of comets sent swarming toward the sun, several strike the Earth, triggering a nightmarish sequence of ecological catastrophes.

"We expect that in a typical comet storm, there would be perhaps 10 impacts spread out over two million years, with intervals averaging 50,000 years between impacts," says LBL astrophysicist Richard Muller. In 1984, Muller, along with UC Berkeley astronomer Marc Davis and Piet Hut, an astronomer with the Institute for Advanced Study at Princeton University, announced the Nemesis theory in *Nature* magazine. As could be expected, it was and remains controversial. However, although the evidence for the existence of Nemesis is still circumstantial, this evidence continues to mount, and the theory has so far withstood all challenges.

Nemesis was the culmination of a chain of events that began in 1977, in Gubbio, Italy, a tiny village halfway between Rome and Florence. Walter Alvarez, a UC Berkeley geologist, was collecting samples of the limestone rock there for a study on paleomagnetism. The limestone rock outside of Gubbio is a big attraction for geologists and paleontologists because it provides a complete geological record of the end of the Cretaceous period and the beginning of the Tertiary period. This transition took place 65 million years ago, and is of special significance to our species, for it marked the close of the "Age of Reptiles," when dinosaurs ruled the Earth. Sometimes referred to as "the Great Dying," the massive extinction that engulfed the dinosaurs claimed nearly 75 percent of all the species of life on our planet, including most types of plants and many types of microscopic organisms. As much as 95 percent of all living creatures might have perished at the peak of destruction.

The collected Cretaceous limestone is heavily populated with a wide mix of the tiny fossils of marine creatures called forams. Above the clay layer, in the Tertiary limestone, however, the fossils of but a single species of foram can be seen. The clay layer itself contains no foram fossils at all. An analysis of the limestone by LBL Nobel laureate physicist Luis Alvarez, suggested that subjecting them to neutron activation analysis could help determine how long it took for the clay layer to form. The analysis performed by LBL nuclear chemists Frank Asaro and Helen Michel, revealed, to the surprise of everyone involved, that the clay was about 600 times richer in iridium than the surrounding limestone. A silvery-white metal, related to platinum, iridium is quite scarce in the Earth's crust, found usually in concentrations of only 20 parts per trillion. Putting this data together with other data collected from throughout the world, Luis Alvarez concluded that the iridium anomaly was the result of a collision between the Earth and an extraterrestrial object approximately six miles in diameter. He speculated further that it was this collision that led to the death of the dinosaurs and all of the other species that perished during the Great Dying.

When a rock the size of San Francisco, traveling at approximately 45,000 miles per hour, hits the Earth, there is an instantaneous release of approximately 100 million Joules of kinetic energy, six billion times the force of the Hiroshima bomb. Luis and Walter Alvarez predicted the effects of such an explosion, based on the aftermath of the volcanic eruption of Krakatoa in 1883, the biggest eruption ever recorded.

If the impact takes place on land, a heavy shroud of fine dust particles from the shattered planetary crust and the pulverized meteorite or comet would be swept high into the stratosphere by the mushrooming fireball, where it would slowly spread, wrapping the entire globe in a dense cocoon. The fireball's blazing heat would ignite enormous wildfires, the soot and debris from which would rise up and add to the sky-blackening dust, creating an extended period of endless night.

The darkness would shut down the photosynthetic process, killing all but the hardiest of plant species and driving the food chain into a state of collapse. Worldwide starvation would ensue as animals that feed on the plants die and the predators in turn follow. Extremely cold temperatures brought on by the darkness might usher in an ice age. Even if the impact takes place in the ocean, dust (from the crushed ocean floor) would still be shot above the atmosphere, only accompanying the dust would be tremendous volumes of vaporized water. After the dust finally settled, the water vapor would still remain. Solar heat reflected off the Earth's surface would be prevented from escaping into outer space by this thick moisture, and the consequence would be an oppressive greenhouse effect.

"The bitter cold would be followed by a sweltering heat," said Walter Alvarez in his AGU report.

To make matters worse, the energy released by the impact could serve as a catalyst to combine atmospheric nitrogen and oxygen into nitric acid that would fall back on the surface as corrosive precipitation.

Scientists immediately scrambled to find an explanation that could account for a persistent, recurring cycle of planet-wide species die-outs. Volcanic eruptions were the most obvious suspects, but volcanoes fail to account for the clay layer, the high soot content and, most significantly, the high iridium concentrations. Casting further doubt on the culpability of volcanoes was the discovery of shock quartz and microtektites along with the iridium and soot in the clay layer samples taken from around the world.

Ruling out other terrestrial causes, many scientists turned to the heavens. One possibility was meteorites, which are chips of asteroids or planets moving randomly through space. However, a mechanism to explain the periodicity of the extinctions has yet to be found. A second possibility was comets, "dirty snowballs" of ice with a rocky center. Looping the solar system, beyond the orbit of Pluto and extending out to more than eight trillion miles, is a vast bracelet of comets known as the "Oort cloud," after its discoverer, Dutch astronomer Jan Oort. The trillions of comets in the Oort cloud generally maintain a slow but steady orbit around the sun. Occasionally, the gravitational field of a passing star will jar some comets loose, but few of these ever reach the inner solar system (Mercury, Venus, Earth, and Mars), as the gravitational pulls of Jupiter and Saturn, acting somewhat like giant vacuum cleaners, keep this part of the system relatively clean of comets and other space debris.

Another source of gravitational pull that has been proposed is the existence of a tenth planet in the solar system. Called "Planet X," this planet would be a gas ball as much as five times the size of Earth, occupying a peculiar shifting orbit that is tilted at an angle to the solar plane of the nine known planets. This theory also calls for the existence of an as yet undetected inner disk of the Oort cloud, between the orbits of Neptune and Pluto. Every 26 to 30 million years, the orbit of Planet X would be shifted so that it would scrape the edge of the inner disk, sending a host of comets towards the sun. The major problem with this proposal is that the hypothetical inner disk of the Oort cloud would be unstable and could not remain a disk. Consequently, comets would be shaken loose in a steady shower over the 26 to 30 million year time periods, rather than torn loose in a concentrated storm.

The Nemesis theory fulfills all the requirements prescribed by the Raup and Sepkoski mass extinction timetable.

Under the Nemesis scenario, what at first glance might appear to be a single, gradual extinction, would, upon closer scrutiny, turn out to be a series of individual, abrupt, mass die-outs.

For now, Nemesis is a tantalizing specter. The case for the companion star is perhaps solid enough to score a victory in a court of law, but in the court of science, the ultimate proof will be in the finding.

Sources:
1. 'Is this stone proof an asteroid wiped out a civilization just like ours 13,000 years ago ... and does it vindicate the maverick scholar who says a giant meteorite will destroy us in 2030?,' DailyMail.com, Christopher Stevens, April 28, 2017 Updated June 6, 2017, https://www.dailymail.co.uk/ sciencetech/article-

4457530/Mini-Ice-Age-wiped-cvilisation-13-000-years-ago.html
2. 'Does a Companion Star to Sun Cause Earth's Periodic Mass Extinctions?,' Lynn Yarris, Spring 119887, *Science Beat*, Berkley Lab, http://www2.lbl.gov/ Science-Articles/Archive/ extinctions-nemesis.html
3. 'Taurids Dust the November Sky,' Nov 8, 2011, NASA Blogs Home, https://blogs.nasa.gov/ Watch_the_Skies/ 2011/11/08/post_1320771751374/
4. '1,000-Foot-Wide Asteroids that Could Hit Earth Discovered by Astronomers,' Hannah Osborne, June 8, 2017, Newsweek, https://www.newsweek.com/huge-asteroids-taurid-meteor-shower-Earth-risk-623115

Tectonic Plate Movement & Super-Volcanoes Resulting in Mass Extension - While tectonic plate movement causes water to be constantly recycled between the mantle and crust diminishing greenhouse heating - A more likely cataclysm will come from the Earth itself. The same tectonic forces that cause the continents to wander across the globe also power supervolcanoes that can spew enough ash and smoke into the atmosphere to block the sun's rays for 10 to 15 years. Geologists believe that such eruptions occur every 50,000 years [source: Ravilious].

Facing the effects of an event as devastating as a supervolcano, an already hobbled Earth will certainly experience a mass extinction rivaling other extinctions marked in the fossil record. The most famous is the extinction that wiped out the dinosaurs at the end of the Cretaceous period. But the mass demise of dinosaurs paled in comparison to an extinction event that occurred at the end of the Permian period, about 251 million years ago. When the dying was over, 95 percent of all marine species and 70 percent of all land vertebrates had vanished [source: *Discovery Earth*]. And can you guess what caused this killing spree? Yep, it was a supervolcano -- more specifically, the eruption of the Siberian Traps, which affected the global climate.

"Plate tectonics is a relatively benign way for Earth to lose heat," said Peter Cawood, an Earth scientist at Monash University in Australia. "You get what are catastrophic events in localized areas, in earthquakes and tsunamis," he added. "But the mechanism allows Earth to maintain a stabler and more benign environment overall."

Dr. Korenaga and his colleagues have proposed that plate tectonics began very early, right after Earth's crust solidified from its initial magmatic state. "That is when the conditions would have been easiest for plate tectonics to get started," he said. At that point, most of the water on Earth — delivered by comets — would still be on the surface, with little of it having found its way into the mantle. The heat convecting up through the mantle would exert a stronger force on dry rocks than on rocks that were lubricated.

At the same time, the surface water would make it easier for the hot, twisting rocks beneath to crack the surface lid apart, rather as a sprinkling of water from the faucet eases the task of popping ice cubes from a tray. The cracking open of the surface lid, Dr. Korenaga said, is key to getting the all-mighty subduction engine started. With subduction established, water, like oceanic crust, would cycle between Earth's surface and mantle.

Water is constantly recycled between the mantle and crust. Plate tectonic activity did not just help to stabilize Earth's heat management system. The movement kept a steady supply of water shuttling between mantle and crust, rather than gradually evaporating from the surface.

It blocked the dangerous buildup of greenhouse gases in the atmosphere by sucking excess carbon from the ocean and subducting it underground. It shook up mountains and pulverized rocks, freeing up essential minerals and nutrients like phosphorus, oxygen and nitrogen for use in the growing carnival of life.

Dr. Zerkle discerns a link between geological and biological high drama: "It's been suggested that time periods of supercontinental cycles — when small continents smash together to make large supercontinents, and those supercontinents then rip apart into smaller continents again — could have put large pulses of nutrients into the biosphere and allowed organisms to really take off.

Sources:
1. 'What will the Earth look like in 50,000 years?,' *howstuffworks*, William Harris, https://science.howstuffworks.com/life/evolution/Earth-50000-years1.htm
2. 'The Earth's Shell Has Cracked, and We're Drifting on the Pieces,' Natalie Angier, Dec 18, 2018, *New York Times*, https://www.nytimes.com/2018/12/18/science/plate-tectonics-continents-Earth.html

Extreme Flooding Resulting in Mass Extinction - Right now, the global sea level is slowly but surely creeping upwards a fraction of an inch each year (0.118 to 0.157 inches per year to be exact). That doesn't seem like much, but we're already feeling the consequences of rising waters and eroding coastlines. Tides high enough to flood homes and infrastructure have become more common in some parts of the US like Florida — "turning it from a rare event into a recurrent and disruptive problem," as a report by the National Oceanic and Atmospheric Administration put it earlier in 2017.

Sea water levels are climbing because carbon dioxide and other heat-trapping greenhouse gases are causing global temperatures to warm, which in turn melts the land-based ice. That extra water flows into the world's oceans. As we keep pumping these gases into the air, oceans will rise even faster. By how much? Scientists are trying to figure that out. Based on some estimates, we can probably expect between 4 and 8 inches of sea level rise by 2050 and between 1 and 7 feet by 2100. The problem is that when sea levels go up, flooding gets worse.

There are more than five million cubic miles of ice on Earth, and some scientists say it would take more than 5,000 years to melt it all. If ice on land has melted and drained into the sea, it would raise the ocean 216 feet, creating new shorelines for our continents and inland seas. If we continue adding carbon to the atmosphere, we'll very likely create an ice-free planet, with an average temperature of perhaps 80 degrees Fahrenheit instead of the current 58.

Photo #1–United States all ice melted   Photo #2–World free of ice

Sources
1. 'A future of more extreme floods, brought to you by climate change,' Rachel Becker@RA_Becks, May 18, 2017, *The Verge*, https://www.theverge.com/2017/5/18/15658342/flooding-sea-level-rice-melting-ice-climate-change-extreme

2. 'What the World Would Look Like if All the Ice Melted,' *National Geographic*, Sept 2013, https://www.nationalgeographic.com/magazine/2013/09/rising-seas-ice-melt-new-shoreline-maps/

Overpopulation Resulting in Mass Extinction - The fear of an overpopulated globe has been around since the 18th century, when Thomas Malthus predicted that population growth would cause mass starvation and overtax the planet. With the global population at 7 billion and counting, many conservationists think population growth is one of the key threats to the planet. Of course, not everyone agrees: Many think population growth will stabilize in the next 50 years, and that humanity will innovate its way out of the negative consequences of the overcrowding that does occur.

Earth's Magnetic Field Reduction and Possible Pole Reversal Resulting in Mass Extinction – 'The geomagnetic field has been losing 30 percent of its intensity in the last 3,000 years,' said Dr. Thouveny. 'From this value, we predict it will drop to near zero in a few centuries or a millennia.' As Earth's magnetic shield fails, so do its satellites. First, our communications satellites in the highest orbits go down. Next, astronauts in low-Earth orbit can no longer phone home.

In the Atlantic Ocean between South America and Africa, there is a vast region of Earth's magnetic field that is about three times weaker than the field strength at the poles. This is called the South Atlantic Anomaly (SAA). 'This is a region where we see that satellites consistently (experience) electronic failures,' said Prof. Finlay. 'This is a region where we see that satellites consistently (experience) electronic failures,' said Prof. Finlay. 'And we don't understand where this weak field region is coming from, what's producing it, and how it might change in the future.' Loss of communications (satellite, cell phones, control systems, etc.) could yield our civilization to collapse.'

The last magnetic pole reversal occurred between 772,000 and 774,000 years ago. Since then, the field has almost reversed 15 times, called an excursion, dropping in strength significantly but not quite reaching the threshold needed before rising again. This is when we are most at risk—as the field decays, and then recovers its strength. The last excursion occurred 40,000 years ago, and evidence suggests we are heading in that direction again.

For a polarity reversal to occur, the magnetic field needs to weaken by about 90% to a threshold level. This process can take thousands of years, and during this time, the lack of a protective magnetic shield around our planet allows more cosmic rays – high-energy particles from elsewhere in the universe – to hit us.

When this happens, these cosmic rays collide with more and more atoms in our atmosphere, such as nitrogen and oxygen. This produces variants of elements called cosmogenic isotopes, such as carbon-14 and beryllium-10, which fall to the surface. Worse yet, if we lose our magnetic field, we lose our protective shield that deflects solar radiation. An unshielded solar radiation burst of gamma-rays would cause instant death for many and, for the survivors; they would have genetic (DNA) damage. If such a thing happened in the past, it could well have altered the evolution of life on this planet

SOURCE:
1. 'Earth's magnetic poles could start to flip. What happens then?,' Dec 7, 2018, Jonathan O'callaghan, *Horizon Magazine*, https://phys.org/news/2018-12-Earth-magnetic-poles-flip.html

2. 'Should You Be Worried about Gamma-ray Bursts?,' Nov 21, 2018, John P. Millis, Ph.D, *ThoughtCo.com*, https://www.thoughtco.com/gamma-ray-burst-destroy-life-Earth-3072521

Social Uprising (Rich Against the Poor) Resulting in Turmoil, Bloodshed and Wars - Creating separation by pitting the underprivileged against the privileged is a ploy by the Dark Force to create separation (polarity) and is not supported by History of past and current civilizations. History of Past Civilizations shows that civilizations struggle for cultural expression and fulfillment against forces and pressures from others who would thwart them. And exploitation and abuse are persistent staples of the story, along with the idealism, human striving, and civic success also sprinkled through the story of humankind. This mix can be seen in all the civilizations and societies of world history. Thus, much of this assault on the Western heritage by the Dark Force is really a political maneuver to favor the so-called victim class (anyone whose ancestors suffered at the hands of the West) against the so-called privileged class (those whose ancestors imposed the suffering). It's a brilliant ploy, and it's working in many quarters, particularly on college campuses. But it has little to do with any reasoned interpretation of history. Yet, if unchecked, class warfare could lead to population reduction and, perhaps, war itself.

Global War Resulting in Mass Extinction - Together, the United States and Russia still have almost 19,000 active nuclear warheads. Nuclear war seems unlikely today, but a dozen years ago the demise of the Soviet Union also seemed rather unlikely. Political situations evolve; the bombs remain deadly. There is also the possibility of an accidental nuclear exchange. And a ballistic missile defense system, given current technology, will catch only a handful of stray missiles—assuming it works at all. Other types of weaponry could have global effects as well.

Japan began experimenting with biological weapons after World War I, and both the United States and the Soviet Union experimented with killer germs during the cold war. Compared with atomic bombs, bioweapons are cheap, simple to produce, and easy to conceal. They are also hard to control, although that unpredictability could appeal to a terrorist organization. John Leslie, a philosopher at the University of Guelph in Ontario, points out that genetic engineering might permit the creation of "ethnic" biological weapons that are tailored to attack primarily one ethnic group.

Robots Take Over Resulting in Mass Extinction - People create smart robots, which turn against us and take over the world. We've seen this in movies, TV, and comic books for decades. Hans Moravec, one of the founders of the robotics department of Carnegie Mellon University, is a believer. By 2040, he predicts, machines will match human intelligence, and perhaps human consciousness. Then they'll get even better. He envisions an eventual symbiotic relationship between human and machine, with the two merging into "postbiologicals" capable of vastly expanding their intellectual power. Marvin Minsky, an artificial-intelligence expert at MIT, foresees a similar future: People will download their brains into computer-enhanced mechanical surrogates and log into nearly boundless files of information and experience. Whether this counts as the end of humanity or the next stage in evolution depends on your point of view. Minsky's vision might sound vaguely familiar. After the first virtual-reality machines hit the marketplace around 1989, feverish journalists hailed them as electronic LSD, trippy illusion machines that might entice the user in and then never let him out. Perhaps this is the method the Anunnaki used to trap the Atlanteans to be the power source of the "human uniform" over 20,000 years ago (refer to Chapter 3). Sociologists fretted that our culture, maybe even our species, would wither away. Minsky recognizes that the merger of human and machine lies quite a few years away.

Alien Invasion Resulting in Mass Extinction - At the SETI Institute in Mountain View, California, a cadre of dedicated scientists sifts through radio static in search of a telltale signal from an alien civilization. Suppose the long-sought message arrives. Not only do the aliens exist, they are about to stop by for a visit. And then . . . any science-fiction devotee can tell you what could go wrong. But the history of human exploration and exploitation suggests the most likely danger is not direct conflict. Aliens might want resources from our solar system (Earth's oceans, perhaps, full of hydrogen for refilling a fusion-powered spacecraft) and swat us aside if we get in the way, as we might dismiss mosquitoes or beetles stirred up by the logging of a rain forest. Aliens might unwittingly import pests with a taste for human flesh, much as Dutch colonists reaching Mauritius brought cats, rats, and pigs that quickly did away with the dodo. Or aliens might accidentally upset our planet or solar system while carrying out some grandiose interstellar construction project. The late physicist Gerard O'Neill speculated that contact with extraterrestrial visitors could also be socially disastrous. "Advanced western civilization has had a destructive effect on all primitive civilizations it has come in contact with, even in those cases where every attempt was made to protect and guard the primitive civilization," he said in a 1979 interview. "I don't see any reason why the same thing would not happen to us."

Divine Intervention Resulting in Mass Extinction - Judaism has the Book of Daniel; Christianity has the Book of Revelation; Islam has the coming of the Mahdi; Zoroastrianism has the countdown to the arrival of the third son of Zoroaster. The stories and their interpretations vary widely, but the underlying concept is similar: God intervenes in the world, bringing history to an end and ushering in a new moral order. Apocalyptic thinking runs at least back to Egyptian mythology and right up to Heaven's Gate and Y2K mania. More worrisome, to the nonbelievers at least, are the doomsday cults that prefer to take holy retribution into their own hands. In 1995, members of the Aum Shinri Kyo sect unleashed sarin nerve gas in a Tokyo subway station, killing 12 people and injuring more than 5,000. Had things gone as intended, the death toll would have been hundreds of times greater. A more determined group armed with a more lethal weapon—nuclear, biological, nanotechnological even—could have done far more damage.

Sources for the listed of disasters, as listed individually, also include:
1. '20 Ways the World Could End,' October 2000 issue, *Discover*, http://discovermagazine.com/2000/oct/featworld
2. 'Doomsday: 9 Real Ways the Earth Could End' Tia Ghose, Senior Writer, *LiveScience*, May 30, 2013, https://www.livescience.com/36999-top-scientists-world-enders.html

Bottomline is that there are several ways the world could end, some as predicted by various Native Cultures, and that end could be soon as we approach the end of a 50,000 year civilization cycle. Given this, we need a plan to leave Earth, if humanity is to survive. Technology or alien intervention may be our saving grace. Hopefully, ascending into the next Density will increase our chance of survival.

End of the DAYS – Although Civilizations come and go nearly every 50,000 years, the Earth will end its cycle in the distant future, around 3750-60AD.

The period of 3750 years finds a remarkable correlation in research.

Chapter 22 – Life and Death of Earth's Civilizations, Caveman is a Myth

(1) Reversal of the Sun's Polarity - The 3750 year cycle of the Sun's polarity is 1,366,040 days to reversal. The analysis based upon of the standard sunspot cycle, combined with orbital dynamics within the solar system, and the varying rotational periods of the Sun's atmosphere. The result is a reversal of the 'neutral sheet', or local space around the Sun. This appears to reflect ancient knowledge, as exemplified by the 'Nineveh Constant', a remarkable number recorded on a clay tablet in the Library of the Assyrian King Assurbanipal. Maurice Chatalain, a one-time NASA scientist, calculated that this sexigessimal-equivalent 15 digit number was a Great Constant of the solar system, incorporating the orbital periods of planets known (and unknown!) to the Assyrians. Of course, if Zecharia Sitchin is correct, then the Assyrians would have inherited the Sumerian knowledge of all the planets, including Nibiru, a giant planet/brown dwarf that still remains 'unknown' to us.

(2) The Mayan super-number of 1,366,560 days recorded in the Dresden Codex". This number corresponds to 3,741 years.

(3) The Tutankhamen Prophecies – The duration between the end of one Iron Age and the beginning of the next amounts to 3,750 years. The Brahma Kamahis, a spiritual group of the Krishna school, believe that souls reincarnate up to 16 times within each Iron Age period, and then reincarnate 3,750 years later in the next Iron Age, depending on the "voltage" of the soul. In between times, the soul 'suffers' for past actions, in Purgatory, for 3000 years, say the Catholics, and in the 'underworld' for 3,750 years advises the *Amazing Lid of Palenque*. Is 3,750 and 3,740 years a simple coincidence or might they be indicative of a mechanism in the afterlife which accommodates the notion of Purgatory? Does the departing interior soul travel to our own sun to suffer' hell fire' for 3,750 years? Then the soul

would live and die again for up to 16 times during the next Iron Age, attempting again the slow process of purification.

The coldest of souls, those with the least voltage, suffer the most within such a scheme. Extremely high voltage souls, like Tutankhamen, transform themselves into stars, giving birth to new galaxies. These stars, in turn give birth to their own planetary systems. Life evolves on those planets; souls descend, ascend and again descend, adopting the paradigm explained in the General Theory of Existence, in keeping with the Theory of Devine Reconciliation. The end, therefore, becomes the beginning.

(4) The Egyptian Connection - "Horus, the sky-god, was closely associated at Edfu with the winged sun-disc, Harakhty ('Horus of the (Eastern) Horizon')". Many contend that the Winged Disc was not the Sun at all, but the dark star Nibiru, the Star of the East. It is believed that the Temple of Horus at Edfu was constructed in anticipation of the return of the Celestial Lord. The associated Temple of Dendera contains more specific references to this event. The Egyptians created a somewhat unusual zodiac on the ceiling of this temple. The normal circle of the zodiac has been distorted, with Cancer being 'singled out for special treatment'. Between Cancer and Sirius is a peculiar symbol; a falcon perched on a vertical 'club'. In the zodiac, the falcon is Horus, equated with the Winged Disc, and the club signifies a celestial marker, akin to the many obelix-type megalithic stones used by the ancients to mark positions in the heavens. Yet it is positioned away from the zodiac, within the southerly Duat. This magnificent zodiac indicates the expectation of the imminent return of Horus among the Ptolemaic followers of the ancient Egyptian stellar cult. The brightest point of the transit was expected between Leo/Cancer and Sirius. If Horus was the Sun, then why include attendants and the Bennu Bird on the barge? If

Horus is indeed symbolic of the Dark Star Nibiru (and note the red disc above Horus' head), then the attendant might be moons, and we could speculate that the Bennu Bird is symbolic of the Anunnaki homeworld/moon (representing the 'Field of Reeds'). If that is the case, then this motif records a total of six moons. Graham Hancock notes that the Dendera zodiac depicts the constellations at the cardinal points as they appeared in 4000BC. This coincides roughly with the previous passage of Nibiru in 3760BC.

(5) The Sphinx Connection - The Great Pyramid complex layout reflects the stars in Orion's Belt. The Sphinx has the body of a lion and aligns with the Leo Constellation as it rises on the horizon during the Winter Solstice and with a rising Aquarius during the Summer Solstice. The Sphinx also "views" the planet Nibiru (a wandering planet in the Sol System with an eccentric orbit of approximately 3750 years) crossing the rising Leo. This crossing occurred circa 2 BC – the approximate date of the beginning of the Christian calendar. Nibiru's previous transit marked the beginning of ancient calendars, approximately 3750 years earlier.

This makes some wonder if the next calendar will begin around 3750-60AD? Ominously, Nostradamus used a similar method of planetary positions to pinpoint the year to end his predicted annals of Mankind:

> *"A mighty earthquake, in the month of May*
> *Saturn, Capricorn, Jupiter and Mercury in Taurus*
> *Venus also in Cancer, Mars in Virgo*
> *Hailstones, larger than eggs, will then fall"* X/67 (11)

The date indicated by this quatrain is 3797AD. Does his methodology reflect that of the creator of the Nimrud Dag Frieze, specifying an approximate period in time? This would then corroborate the prediction for Nibiru's next appearance, around 3750-60AD. If so, and Nostradamus is correct in his apocalyptic imagery, then there will be no need for a calendar after this date at all. Hopefully, it will not be the end of the species, since we may have colonized Mars, Venus and other planets throughout the Universe.

Sources:
1. D. Hughes "The Star of Bethlehem Mystery" Dent 1979
2. A. Gilbert & M. Cotterell "The Mayan Prophecies" Appendix 4, pp63-7, Element 1995, Thanks to Gary Gilligan, http://www.nibiru.tv
3. P. Seymour "The Birth of Christ: Exploding the Myth" pp176-7, Virgin 1998
4. M. Chatelain "Our Ancestors came from Outer Space" Ch1, Pan 1979
5. D. Rohl "Legend: The Genesis of Civilization" p339-41 Arrow 1999
6. M. Hope "The Sirius Connection" pp8-9 Element 1996
7. Z. Sitchin When Time Began" p208 Avon 1993
8. G. Hancock & S Faiia "Heaven's Mirror: Quest for the Lost Civilisation" p61 Penguin 1999
9. A. Gilbert "Magi: The Quest for a Secret Tradition" pp125-47 Bloomsbury 1997
10. 'Nimrud Dag, beside the Euphrates in Turkey' http://www.lexiline.com/lexiline/lexi190.htm
11. N. Halley "The Complete Prophecies of Nostradamus" Wordsworth 1999

CHAPTER 23

WHAT UFO SIGHTINGS, ALIENS & ANCIENT CIVILIZATIONS ARE TRYING TO TELL US

Even before 1942 ('Battle of Los Angeles'), UFO's have been recorded in the sky. At first they were singular UFO's and they were seeking the attention of the major governments to tell them that they are real. It is rumored that extraterrestrials have met with individual governments (e.g., Majestic 12 / President Eisenhower – February 1954). In more recent times, the extraterrestrials have changed their tactic to reveal themselves to the general public throughout the world. The new tactic is to convey that they know us and what we think. They have begun to talk to us in the language of the stars and constellations. Constellations are how our ancestors navigated the oceans and how one can navigate the universe. Constellations are how you first communicate with an alien race. Their ships now fly in formations that show us the familiar star clusters scattered throughout the universe, in the hope that we know the language as well. By showing us the constellations that we know, they are trying to convey that they are concerned about us, know us, and want to help us since we are destroying our own world. They are both teaching us to open our mind and beckoning us to join the universe.

The aliens and their UFOs are here, in large numbers, to warn us of own impending doom, perhaps through any one of the catastrophes listed within Chapter 22. They are here to help and to advise us. The increase in UFO sightings and their astrological "signs" are their opening dialog. It is just a matter of time that we will need to leave the Earth that we are destroying. They are here to guide us in our departure.

The Dark Force will want to fight these "invaders" and will go to war. It will be useless since it will be our 200-years of technical development vs. their 20-million years of technology. We need to be accepting, knowing they are far more intelligent that we are and they understand the cycle of civilizations as well the cycles of creation.

Below are some of the alien "conversations" to convince us of their knowledge and presence in order that they may help us.

Cygnus - What looks like a man holding up his hands, this UFO formation is showing the northern star constellation Cygnus, the swan. The UFO's are in an exact match to the stars of Cygnus.

The "Phoenix" Lights - The most talked about formation is the "Phoenix Lights." It was a formation of nine lights representing the planets of our solar system with the distant light being our sun but, by shutting off the last light, they know that we are questioning if Pluto is actually a planet.

471 | Chapter 23 – What UFO's Sightings, Aliens & Ancient Civilizations are Trying to Tell Us

Phoenix, Arizona, 1997, the "Phoenix lights"

UFO's in a Circle - This UFO formation looks like a number of UFO's in a circle, but it is an exact match to the constellation Quadrant Regulus, also known as Alpha Leonis.

Showing Us the Southern Sky of Columba (the "Dove"), Canis Major, Puppis galaxy, and Pexis. The "Dove" is the sign of God-Christ

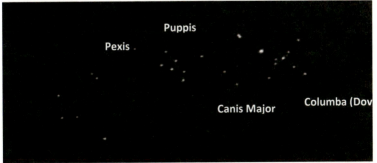

Orion's Belt -Three UFO's are in the formation of Orion's Belt. Other UFO formations have depicted the entire Orion constellation with exact placement of the UFOs. The entire constellation was shown by UFOs in Lubbock, Tx. The Great Pyramid complex in Egypt was laid out to match that of Orion's Belt.

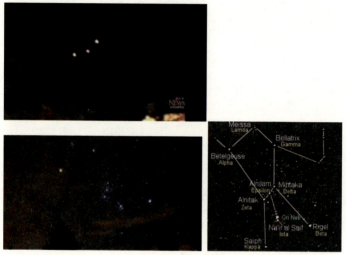

The "Spider" - For the Native American Hopi (meaning "people of peace"), Navajo and Keresan tribes, Spider Woman was a creator goddess. Along with the Sun god, Tawa, they created Earth and animals, among other things. For the Egyptians, the "spider," with its eight legs (one leg for each planet) was the symbol for our Solar system. Perhaps, they are telling us to "look" to Egypt for the "answers." In addition, the magnetic field around Earth takes the shape of a spider.

473 | Chapter 23 –What UFO's Sightings, Aliens & Ancient Civilizations are Trying to Tell Us

UFO "Spider" Formation   Egyptian Jar depicting Star Sungate

Earth's magnetic field

The Alfa Centauri UFO Formation. Alfa Centauri is well known to science fiction enthusiasts since Bernard's Star is located within this galaxy. Bernard's Star, per many science fiction writers, has a planet similar to the Earth. In November 2018,  scientists announced that a much larger and colder "Super Earth" has been discovered that could be orbiting the red dwarf called Bernard's Star. Alfa Centauri is the closest galaxy to Earth, located 6 light years from Earth.

UFO formation of the Cross. This formation is the Christian cross. It is not the Southern Cross, which has fewer stars.

UFO formation of the Winter Triangle. At the tip of the triangle are often three off-center lights. This formation indicates the Greater Constellation of Orion. Orion is often referred to as the "children of men."

Leo Constellation – Lyra was one of the first to colonize Earth, along with the Pleiadians. Most likely, the head of the Sphinx was a lion.

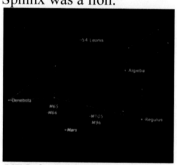 

UFO formation of the Leo galaxy   Leo galaxy star diagram

UFO formation of the Square Constellation of Pegasus

UFO "Square" Formation   Astronomy star map of the Great Square of Pegasus

475 | Chapter 23 –What UFO's Sightings, Aliens & Ancient Civilizations are Trying to Tell Us

The Triangulum Constellation as shown by a UFO formation. is linked directly to that of Orion. In some accounts, Triangulum is the "Seat of God."

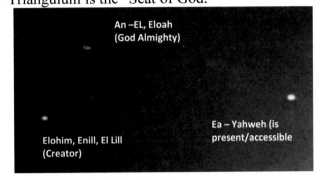

Tree of Life Formation (not all shown and formation not complete)

Andromeda – UFO swarm overlay. There is a gas cloud between Triangulum and Andromeda galaxies.

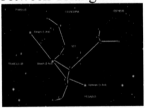 

UFO formation with Andromeda   Triangulum and Andromeda galaxies overlay - view from Hubble

UFO colors send an even greater meaning than the white light formations. With color, the UFO's are depicting galaxies. In the formation below, the UFOs are indicating the Andromeda galaxy (NGC 671). Andromeda is thought to be the home of the Anannaki.

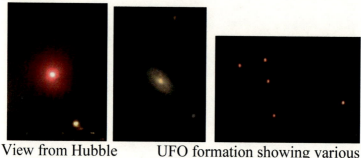

View from Hubble   UFO formation showing various
                          galaxies (color)

"Swarm" UFO formations are sometimes comprised of hundreds of UFOs. The swarm is intermixed with clouds to convey to us that these are more than stars or galaxies. The swarm in the clouds is showing us a nebula where stars are born. The swarm, most likely, is showing us

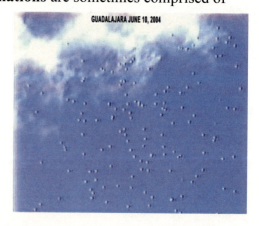

either the Triangulum or Andromeda galaxy. They are beckoning us to a place where it all began.

Gate C17 at Chicago O'Hare - At approximately 16:15 CST on Tuesday, November 7, 2006, federal authorities at Chicago O'Hare International Airport received a report that a group of twelve airport employees were witnessing a metallic, saucer-shaped craft hovering over Gate C-17. Several independent witnesses outside of the airport also saw the object. One described a "blatant" disc-shaped craft hovering over the airport which was "obviously not clouds." According to this witness, nearby observers gasped as the object shot through the clouds at high velocity, leaving a clear blue hole in the cloud layer. The hole reportedly closed itself shortly after the event.

C17 is similar to the constellation identifier of CGN (Cluster General Catalogue astronomy) and NGC (Nebulae General Catalog astronomy). NGC 17, also known as NGC 34n, is located in the constellation Cetus, located about 250 million light years from Earth. NGC 17 is the result of a merger between two galaxies, resulting in the recently identified starburst in the central regions that is continuing starforming activity. Cetus is known as the whale or water destroyer; the Greeks knew it as the kraken that killed the entire world by flood. The event at O'Hare C17 may be the UFO telling us that we must leave the planet since our "end-of-days" may be by flood.

The UFO hovering over Gate C17 intentionally identifies the Nebula NGC 17. By the UFO rising straight up and creating a blue hole through the clouds, is telling us that a Wormhole occurs at this location that will convey the UFO to NGC17. It may be clear from this event that we must leave Earth due to our own destruction of the planet.

478 | Chapter 23 – What UFO's Sightings, Aliens & Ancient Civilizations are Trying to Tell Us

WHAT ANCIENT SITES ARE TELLING US

Look up. Ancient obelisks, located throughout the world, are telling us to "look up" and know our future is in the stars. On top of every obelisk is a pyramid, a symbol left from our past to tell us our future. Near the top of the obelisk shaft are the following Egyptian symbols: Triangle, Tree of Life, Ankh (God).

Meaning:
1. Find the Triangulum Galaxy and travel there. There you will find the Tree-of-life (immorality) and nearby one will find Creator God.

2. The UFO formation sightings tell us:

- The Hand of God points us to look at the Orion galaxy. The layout of the Pyramids on the Giza Plateau mirrors the "belt" of Orion. This is a Dark Force "red herring" to distract us from the Triangulum Galaxy, which is imbedded in the symbolism at the Great Pyramid. The "red herring" is that Orion is the home of the Anannaki (the aliens who modified our DNA and declared their Supreme Leader, Ahn, as our "god."
- One will find the Tree-of-Life and the "Seat of God" within the Triangulum galaxy. Once we obtain the power of the Tree-of-life (immortality = exceptionally long life of 40,000 years or more), we can travel to and find Creator God within the Andromeda galaxy.
- Other UFO formations show us our own galaxy and where some of the extraterrestrials originate. These formations are to convince us that they know us, our world, and our universe.
- The O'Hare C17 Event shows us one of the wormholes to travel to the stars. C17 is the location of a wormhole that will transport us to NGC17 Andromeda, when we are ready to do so.

STAR TRAVEL AND WORMHOLES

A recently found relic sun disk could be used o travel from the Sun Stargate to 16 locations within the universe.

The device would fit into the center recess pin of a Stargate door, such as the ones found throughout the Inca and Mayan structures. The UFO above O'Hare C17 directly traveled to the center point of the Sun Stargate – center hole depicted in the relic Sun disk.

Chapter 23 – What UFO's Sightings, Aliens & Ancient Civilizations are Trying to Tell Us

The device would have a selector, of some type, to select one of the 16 orange wormhole locators.

The disc would be surrounded by various galaxy symbols (with the number of stars of each galaxy within the galaxy symbol). Perhaps, there was an "index" point and one would rotate the relic disc to the desired wormhole.

The center hole of the Sun Disk would take a traveler from the "door" to inside the Sun or a Starship could directly travel through one of the "dark spots" on the Sun's surface. Some of the "cooler" dark spots occur at the same location during the solstice; this is why the ancient civilizations aligned their "sacred structures" to identify each solstice.

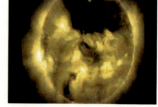

The Sun is a Stargate with 16 wormholes. From inside the Sun the selected wormhole would take the traveler to their selected galaxy. Although the sun is a blackhole, we see it as a sphere due to it residing at the bottom of the wormhole but projecting its shape through to the top of the Stargate/wormhole. The Sun is hollow and its surface is a radiant fire, fueled from the connected wormhole space, along the sides of the Gateway wormhole. The Sun has several openings, called cold spots. It is through these openings that a traveler enters the Sun Stargate.

The enter part of the relic sun disc has a spider with eight legs which represent each of the 8 planets which it controls; the spider is the "Lord" of the Sol System. (Refer to Pyramids Are A Sign of Death to learn who "owns" the Earth.) Note the two small circles at top of the relic sundisc. The larger dot is Pluto and the smaller dot is Eris, the ninth and tenth planets, respectively.

481 | Chapter 23 –What UFO's Sightings, Aliens & Ancient Civilizations are Trying to Tell Us

The Sun Stargate Connects 16 Wormholes Where Many Starships Enter and Exit - Since the sun is a blackhole that connects parts of our universe together, we see all sorts of alien starships of all sizes, shapes, and propulsion systems traveling in and out the Sun's Stargate/ wormholes.

 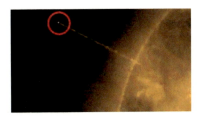

The Sun Stargate Acts as a Transit Terminal – Perhaps, the inside of the sun is like a transit terminal (akin to Deep Space 9) where more advanced species will help us select the wormhole, of the sixteen available, that best meets our needs and desires.

Egyptian Jar depicting the Sun Stargate
Egyptian drawing showing the inside of the Gateway
-Note the spider (Owner) of the Stargate
- Note the Elohim (giant) directing the human to a wormhole
- Note the surrounding symbols that show the 16 wormholes

Each Symbol contains the number of stars in each galaxy.

At the proper time in our development, prior to the death of the Earth, we will be shown the stargates that we are to use to leave this planet.

SUNGATES DEPECTIONS IN ANCIENT CULTURES

 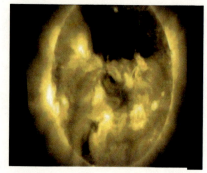

Bull with Sun Disk between horns
Note upper right corner of the disc

Note coldspot in Sun's upper right matches the Sun disc

The Egyptians and even some cultures today revere the bull because of the physical power it represents. The Egyptians indicated that the Bulls held a sundisk between their horns, meaning the bull was divine and had the power of the "gods." This sundisk is our key to escaping Earth.

The Egyptian sundisk contains what archeologists believe is a ceremonial crack. However, that "crack" is not a crack but represents the dark coldspot on the sun, which we still see today. That "hole" Is an entrance into the Sun stargate.

The Mayan "Gate of the Sun" at Tiahuanaco, **Bolivia** is a gateway to the Sun. Above the doorway is the Mayan Sun God, holding a fire breathing dragon

(rocket) in each hand, and the "door" is in the shape of the sunspot that occurs at the time of the summer and Winter Solstice. This is the reason many ancient sites are aligned to the winter and Summer Solstice. The Mayan "Gate of the Sun" is showing us where the Stargate is located and that rocket power is needed to get there. The "way" is hidden in plain sight to those who are enlightened to its meaning.

Pyramid of Kukulcan at Chich'en Itza, Mexico -
According to legend, twice a year, when the day and night are in balance, the feathered serpent god makes his appearance. The pyramid is dedicated to the serpent god, the Ascended Master  Kukulcan (or Quetzalcoatl). On the equinox Kukulcan returns by creating an image of a giant snake crawling down the temple. For five hours an illusion of light and shadow creates seven triangles on the side of the staircase starting at the top and inching its way down until it connects the top platform with the giant stone head of the feathered serpent at the bottom. For 45 minutes this impressive shadow stays in its entirety before slowing descending the pyramid. The descending snake/dragon has its head at the base and represents the engines of the spacecraft, which ignite and "flies" the spacecraft to the Sun Gateway and through the solstice sunspot. A handclap near the base of the pyramidal results in an unusual chirping echo, which is said to replicate the call of the sacred quetzal bird.

UFO over Power Plant -
Perhaps, the pyramid is, really, a depiction of a Lyran spacecraft. Lyran spacecraft are said to pyramidal in shape.

Video Hebei Province, China Oct 12, 2011

In the **Egyptian relief** of the Goddess of knowledge, Lilith/Isis holds a "shen" in each hand. A "shen" represents eternal protection and immortal life. A "shen" in each hand means infinite immortality into the past (left) and immortality into the future (right). Her wings and feet of a bird indicate her ability to fly. She is standing on the lions of Upper and Lower Egypt, meaning she controls both parts of Egypt.

To the left and right of the Goddess are owls. The eyes of the owls are representative of the Wormhole at the Sun. The left eye of each owl is the wormhole entrance, the nose, between the wormhole entry and exit, is the wormhole "throat," and the right eye is the wormhole exit. This same depiction is shown in the cave painting at Kimberly, Australia which many believe are aliens but they are really showing blackholes/ wormholes, where the surrounding "eyelashes" depict the Event Horizon of the "Alien" Blackholes.

Chapter 23 – What UFO's Sightings, Aliens & Ancient Civilizations are Trying to Tell Us

 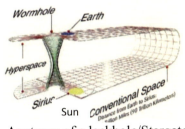

Face of an owl   Anatomy of a lackhole/Stargate

Great Serpent Mound is a 1,348-foot (411 m)-long, three-foot-high prehistoric effigy mound on a plateau of the Serpent Mound crater along Ohio Brush Creek in Adams County, Ohio. Historically, researchers attribute the mound to the Adena culture (1000 BC - 1 AD). According to researchers, the Serpent Mound's coils align with two solstice and two equinox events each year. The shape itself consists mostly of a layer of yellowish clay and ash that was reinforced with a layer of rocks, and then covered with a layer of soil. The serpent head has an open mouth extending around the east end of a 120-foot (37 m)-long hollow oval feature that may represent the snake eating an egg, though some scholars posit that the oval feature symbolizes the sun.

The serpent/snake is the depiction of the Sungate, with the "egg" being the sun, a mouth that is the entry into the wormhole, the inside of the mouth, shown as a triangle, is the wormhole "selector" inside of the Sun, the body of the serpent is the wormhole, and the spiral tail is the wormhole exit at a spiral galaxy.

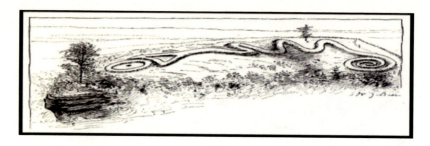

These Revelations are given to us near the "End of the Age" since the power of flight is needed.

The Statue of the Egyptian Goddess Lilith/Isis is shown with wings outstretch. Wings mean that the person or object has the capability of flight; this is the reason angles are shown as having
wings. The Goddess is shown with outstretched wings to depict she is in flight. She is, also, shown in the sitting position while in flight. The only way one could fly in a sitting position is to be aboard an airplane or starship. Thus, to be able to fly, we need to be in a civilization that has flight.

Mechanically Driven Aircraft. A wall carving made during the reign of the King Seti I, 1290 to 1279 BC, shows us that the Egyptians had the knowledge of mechanical driven flight. Seti I was the
son of Ramses I, and it was Seti I who was the real founder of the greatness of the Ramesids.

Minoan Bee Goddess, golden plaque, British Museum, found at Camiros, Rhodes, 7th century BCE (700-601 BC). Marija Gimbutas, in her book, *The Goddesses and Gods of Old Europe,*

provided ample evidence of a Bee Goddess and many examples of bee symbolism dating well back into the Neolithic period. However, neither the Egyptians nor the Minoans deified the honey bee, even though the Egyptian hieroglyphs contain numerous insects. It is believed that the Egyptians noticed that the sound that a bee makes in flight is similar to that made by propeller-driven aircraft. Given this, the Bee Goddess is shown with wings, meaning the goddess could fly, and what appears to be flowers within the plaque could well be propellers.

Tesla and Electromagnetic Field Propulsion - More power (knowledge) is needed to achieve space flight to reach the Sungate.

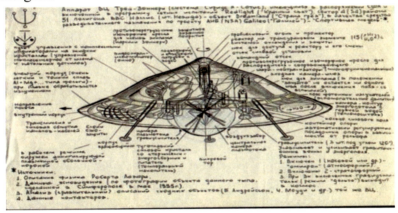

Tesla's diagram and notes concerning an anti-gravity craft

The concept and initial plans for an anti-gravity spacecraft were provided by Nicholas Tesla and has been further developed. The effort to build a starship has been hindered by needing a compact powerful energy source, such as a fusion reactor, to drive an electricity producing turbine, which would power an Electrostatic Vandergraph high-voltage static generator, capacitors (Tesla coils) and a series of electromagnets that could be sequenced to create a rotating electromagnetic field.

A toradol fusion reactor, Phase 2 (scale-up) was being developed by Phillips Petroleum/General Atomic in the early 1990's, but the entire project was declared Top Secret by the Federal Government and all records were taken to the Idaho Research Station, to be never heard of again. The author was to be the Project Architect and had completed the Preliminary Design for the Phase 2 Test Facilities that was to be built at General Atomic, La Jolla, CA. If the Phase 2 experiment was built at the Idaho Research Center and was successful, Phase 3 would have been a fully operational, compact 20-foot diameter toradol fusion reactor. In early 2018, Germany's toradol/ "doughnut," Wendelstein 7-X, managed to heat helium to an impressive 40 million degrees Celsius. This is a big step up from previous efforts, but falls well short of the 100-million-degree-plus temperatures needed for that all-important fusion process to start. China's Experimental Advanced Superconducting Tokamak (EAST) reactor in Hefei has achieved a temperature exceeding 100 million degrees Celsius; Tokamaks are very large, approaching the size of fission reactors. Size is a limiting factor for use within a spacecraft.

According to William R. Lyne, in his book *Occult Ether Physics*, Tesla mentioned the dynamic theory of gravity in a meeting with the Immigrant Welfare Institute on May 12, 1938.

Other scientists, during the last century, discovered the principle of propulsion using strong electromagnetic rotating fields. The entire document is posted on panaceauniversity.org/D8.pdf.

Nazi "Die Glocke " - During WW II, the Nazi's developed the "Glocke" a bell shaped unmanned flying device as well as a rumored "flying saucer"

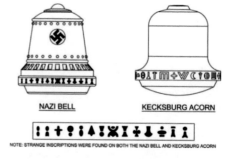

NAZI BELL   KECKSBURG ACORN

NOTE: STRANGE INSCRIPTIONS WERE FOUND ON BOTH THE NAZI BELL AND KECKSBURG ACORN

were first revealed by Igor Witkowski's in his book entitled *The Truth About The Wonder Weapon*. He claims that he had been shown classified Polish Government documents by an anonymous Polish intelligence official. In these documents were the most important Nazi research projects and among them was Die Glocke.

This machine was believed to have great power. Descriptions state that the device was made of heavy metal, around 9 feet wide and up to 15 feet high and had a bell like shape. The information stated that the device had two counter-rotating cylinders, filled with mercury-like liquid that had a bluish color. The mercury-like liquid was referred to as "Xerum 25" and was stored in special flasks. Other liquids were added, such as light metal, with thorium and beryllium peroxides.

The device sounded like a hive of bees and emitted strong and dangerous radiation, which often caused the scientists health problems. Scientists suffered from sleep deprivation, dizziness and some even died due to radiation poisoning. Witkowski speculates that the area around the Wenceslaus mine was used for testing Die Glocke and its anti-gravity power.

Successful Full Scale Test - Early In March 2006, a largely unknown individual, Ralph Carr, came forward to reveal that he was one of three pilots of a successful test of Carr's full scale prototype of the OTC-X1.

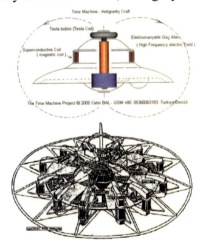

Carr's successful development of a fully operational civilian spacecraft using radical electromagnetic propulsion and navigation systems led

Chapter 23 – What UFO's Sightings, Aliens & Ancient Civilizations are Trying to Tell Us

to a brutal response by federal government agencies.

Agencies led by the FBI raided Carr's construction facilities, confiscated equipment, intimidated employees into silence, and publicly discredited Carr through trumped up charges orchestrated from the U.S. Stock and Securities Commission. The entire project has been suppressed.

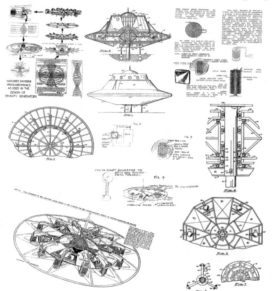

Despite government suppression and possible black-ops development, humanity is on the threshold on a remarkable achievement in the travel to planets in our solar system and the stars.

patent drawing excerpt showing electromagnets (which spin CCW) and capacitor gyros (which spin CW) with coils for energy collection

OTC-X1 sketches

CROP CIRCLES ARE ANOTHER MEANS OF ALIEN COMMUNICATION - Crop Circles are helping us to understand what is coming and what we should do. Most of the Crop Circles are similar to the UFO formations, in that they are indicating star clusters, Earth/Moon/Sun relationship, elaborate decorated pyramids, the stylized animals contained on the Plain of Nazca – the Dog star (16 stars in its cluster by counting toes and tails) and the Condor and Birds containing the 11 stars of Orion (by counting feathers), an Egyptian scarab (beetle) with solar disc, native tribal symbols, and other depictions of celestial objects. By making these Crop Circles, they are hoping we will quickly understand the language of the constellations.

Most Crop Circles can be sorted into the following categories:

- Sun, source of life, is a common theme: Sun with swirls of the Aura, Sun with outer rays, Sun with 32 rays in a surrounding ring could be a Mayan end of a sun cycle symbol (large number of sun "storms).
- Sacred Geometry of overlapping rings. Number of rings indicates stages of completion, up to and including purification.
- Flower of Life, the sixth day of creation when the Earth was given for man's domination. Over lapping Flowers may be telling us which version of Earth has occurred (four) and we are now becoming the 5th, etc.
- Esoteric Symbols: Triangles or double triangles with surrounding patterns. Upward triangles are male and downward triangles are female god.
- Six pointed "snowflakes" and Stars: Christ and Crystal have the same root. We must manifest our "Christ consciousness" in order to inherit the Earth. When the triangles are interlinked (Star of David) it indicates that the man and woman need to reflect each other to achieve equilibrium. This concept is, also, present with overlapping stars. Sometimes at Egyptian ankh (symbolic of life) is shown, meaning to both man and woman, together, create life.
- Five pointed Star represents man. Star with radiating lines reflect the man of today in chaos. Surrounding shapes and light and dark alternating shading means that each must

manifest the attributes of the other in order to find equilibrium.
- Tree of Life indicates the energy centers of man. On a cosmos level, it represents the creative forces of the universe.
- Fractal Formations, such as radiating circles in a spirals that reflect a galaxy.
- DNA strand. Could also reflect the moons of a specific planet (e.g., the path taken of Jupiter and its satellites, Europa and Io, which may point out that there is a form of life on Jupiter.
- Separate Element Symbols shown in series.
- Celtic symbols, Anglo-Saxon runes, hieroglyphs, local native symbols.
- Reflection of comets that are approaching Earth. Some were predicting comets before they were discovered, including the comet that hit Jupiter.
- Contact represented by overlapping circles, where overlap is a void.
- Insects that build, such as ants and the Egyptian scarab. Not only does the scarab build perfect balls (the Egyptians believe the scarab built the planets), the scarab navigates by the stars.
- Planet Orbits and Galaxies and their inter-relationships (e.g., Earth, Moon, Sun).
- Squares inside circles may indicate the existence of Stargates and Wormholes. "Square" with an "x" means an Earth location; "Circle" means the cosmos.
- Complex, Photo-like and binary code Crop circles – Presented are three highly complex crop circles, which may be the three most important alien messages:

Chapter 23 – What UFO's Sightings, Aliens & Ancient Civilizations are Trying to Tell Us

- **Chilbolton Crop Circles** - On Tuesday 21 August 2001 two crop formations were reported near the Chilbolton radio telescope in Hampshire, UK. Both were very impressive looking and consisted of a large number of small 'pixels', which when viewed from the sky formed a recognizable shape - unlike many other crop formations. One represented a 'human face' and the other resembled a radio transmission that SETI (the Search for Extra-Terrestrial Intelligence) received at the Arecibo radio telescope (1974 version).

An interesting interpretation of the 'human face' crop formation comes from researcher and writer, Wayne Herschel. In his vision, the face resembles that of the Egyptian Sphinx and Viracocha, pre-Inca god. But the most thought-provoking resemblance is to the famous Mars Face.

- **Extra-terrestrial Holding a Disc** - On August 15, 2002 in Sparsholt, Hampshire, England, a crop circle was discovered that shows an extraterrestrial holding a disc. The message within the disk was deciphered using the standard 8 bit binary code known as ASCII (*American Standard Code for Information Interchange*). The cipher starts at the center of the disk and spirals outward counter-clockwise, this is also the same read pattern that a compact disc or DVD uses.

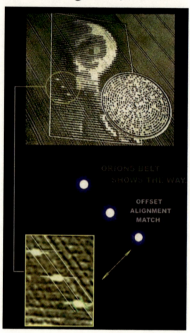

The ASCII pattern "reads":

"Beware the bearers of false gifts and their broken promises. Much pain, but still time. Believe there is good out there. We oppose deception. Conduit closing. 0x07"

The message sounds friendly and it's just what we want to hear. But it is certain that this is a deception. Notice the three Stars behind the Alien. They look like Orion's belt and they are a perfect match. This means the alien being is Reticulan /Alpha Draconians (commonly known as Reptilians) are from/around the Orion Constellation.

- The second crop circle at Chilbolton was a graphic "tapestry. An interpretation of the graphics is shown to the right of the "crop circle" symbols.

Chapter 23 – What UFO's Sightings, Aliens & Ancient Civilizations are Trying to Tell Us

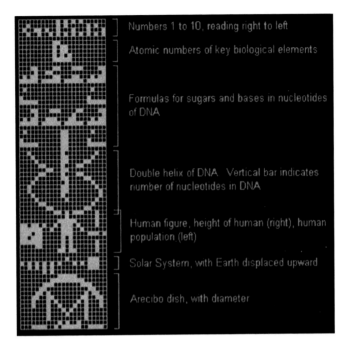

- Numbers 1 to 10, reading right to left
- Atomic numbers of key biological elements
- Formulas for sugars and bases in nucleotides of DNA
- Double helix of DNA. Vertical bar indicates number of nucleotides in DNA
- Human figure, height of human (right), human population (left)
- Solar System, with Earth displaced upward
- Arecibo dish, with diameter

There are two prominent constellations mentioned by our ancestors, and most of the times they are connected to the extraterrestrial "gods": The Pleiades and Reticulans/Alpha Draconians are from or near Orion's Belt. The Reticulans / Alpha Draconians are service-to-self beings (commonly referred to as the Dark Force) as opposed to the service-to-others beings (commonly referred to as the Federation/ Brotherhood of Light).

Bottomline: Advanced intelligence is showing us that extraterrestrials exist; they understand what we know, and are revealing concepts we are yet to understand.

Symbolically, all of the Crop Circles occur in fields the farmer will soon harvest, which tell us that we must quickly understand all things since it will soon be our harvest (the end of the Earth).

PYRAMIDS ARE A SIGN OF DEATH - The Great Pyramid complex is older than our civilization and many of the prior civilization. Pyramids were built all over the Earth, from Central America to China. More ominous, they have now been found on the Moon (filmed by an Apollo astronaut in 1972), Mars and Eris. Recently, NASA's Dawn spacecraft took a photo of a pyramid on Ceres, a moon on the edge of our solar system. A pyramid represents a colony and it represents ownership. They are telling us that the Earth is not ours but theirs. Every planet that ever had a pyramid has been utterly destroyed, devoid of all life, barren, dead. Every planet that has a pyramid ends with complete extinction. Our end is associated with the planet Mars, which has been associated with war and destruction.

Our world is next. How we react will determine if we are the last planet in our solar system to live. Our world does not have to end this way, we can change it. We need to receive the aliens and their assistance.

ANCIENT SITES (PYRAMIDS, STONEHENGE, SPINX, ETC.) ARE DNA REPOSITORIES - Each of these ancient sites has an energy field that attracts us to them. They have hand symbols and fingerprint symbols painted or cut into the stone that invite us to touch them. By touching them, they become DNA repositories. These sights are UFO "hotspots." The UFOs travel to these sites on a  recurring basis to collect the DNA records. These "records" will be used to repopulate a planet after it dies and has "recovered." Refer to Chapter 22 for the 50,000 year Civilization Cycle. Due to repopulating with "developed" DNA, the subsequent

Civilization appear to just "pop-up" as fully developed.

CELESTRIAL WAR MAY BE COMING AND MAY BE OUR "END OF DAYS" - It is interesting that we formed the SETI Institute to search for Extraterrestrial Intelligence. SETI has only received one strong 400 terabytes of radio data in 2007, at the Green Banks Telescope in the US. That radio signal burst had its origin within the constellation Sagittarius. Sagittarius is the Greek God of War (Weapons and Fire). Its "Teapot" shaped star cluster has been shown in a UFO "Teapot" formation. Although SETI is searching for Extraterrestrial Intelligence in the universe by searching for radio bandwidth signals, the extraterrestrials are on our doorstep searching for Earth's Technical Intelligence (SETI). The Egyptians sent their own signal in the form of the Great Pyramids at Giza, whose alignment is that of Orion's Belt. The Earth "signal" has, also, been sent by other pyramids located through the continents of the Earth. Extra-terrestrials that have viewed our 5000-year old signal are, finally, responding.

It may be sad that the Sagittarians responded to the SETI signal and may be on their way to "war" with Earth. We will not be prepared for such an invasion and we may have to leave the Earth by way of the Sun Stargate or hope that the recent UFO's will come to our aid. The war between the Service-to-Others (Federation/Brotherhood of Light) and the Service-to-Self (Dark Force) has been ongoing for the last 200,000 years, but Earth may now be involved.

Constellation Sagittarius

Centaur fighting Lapith of Greek Mythology

Sources
1. '2006 O'Hare International Airport UFO sighting,' *Wikipedia*, various authors, https://en.wikipedia.org/wiki/2006_O%27Hare_International_Airport_UFO_sighting
2. 'The Knowledge of Forever Time 300,000 Years, Episodes 3, 4, 5, 6, 7 and 8,' Contact, 2016, Damon T. Berry, *YouTube*
3. 'Contact 2014,' January 2014, Damon T Barry Filmmaker, *youtube*
4. 'UFO Sitings, Pre 1900 Case File, Photos and More,' October 15, 2004, *Educating Humanity*, http://www.educatinghumanity.com/p/ufo-and-alien-disclosure-list-of.html
5. 'UFO Fleet Captured Over Panama' *Disclose.tv*, Gleison Sunmersamba, Mar 02 2018 posted to Aliens & UFOs, https://www.disclose.tv/ufo-fleet-captured-over-panama-326135
6. 'A Super-Earth Has Been Discovered Just 6 Light-Years Away, The Second Closest Planet To Our Solar System,' *Washington Post*, November 14, 2016, https://www.iflscience.com/.../a-superEarth-has-been-discovered-just-6-lightyears-awa...
7. 'How Earth's Magnetic Field Would Look from Space,' *Live Science*, May 12m 2011, https://www.livescience.com › Planet Earth
8. 'Gate of the Sun at Tiahuanaco, Bolivia,' Jan 28, 2013 - 20:56, *Ancient-Orgins*, https://www.ancient-origins.net/ancient-places-americas/gate-sun-tiahuanaco-bolivia-004
9. 'Serpent Mound,' *Wikipedia*, https://en.wikipedia.org/wiki/Serpent_Mound
10. 'Pyramid of Kukulcan at Chich'en Itza – Chichen Itza, Mexico Atlas …,'

https://www.atlasobscura.com/places/pyramid-kukulcan-chichen-itza
11. ' Filer's Files #42 - 2011 Einstein Believed in UFOs,' Rt. Major George Filer, Oct 12, 2011, *National UFO Center*, http://nationalufocenter.com/artman/publish/article_419.php
12. '8 Cave Paintings Depicting Aliens,' *Alien UFO Sightings*, https://alien-ufo-sightings.com/2017/03/8-cave-paintings-depicting-aliens/
13. 'Priestesses of the Bee: The Melissae,' Linda Iles, Isis, Lotus of Alexandria Lyceum, *Mirror of Isis - An Official Fellowship of Isis Publications*, https://mirrorofisis.freeyellow.com/id576.html
14. 'How to Build a UFO-like Anti Gravity Spaceship,' Ovidiu Sandru, *The Green Optimistic*, https://www.greenoptimistic.com/build-ufo-anti-gravity-spaceship/#.W-zcWZNKiUl
15. 'OTC-X1 Reverse Engineering Breakthrough!,' *Warp-Drive-Physics.com*, February 20, 2016, https://www.bibliotecapleyades.net/exopolitica/esp_exopolitics_ZZZZB.htm
16. 'How the Government Suppressed the World's First Civilian Space Industry,' Michael E. Salla, PhD., *Exopolitics Journal*, vol. 2, no. 1, April, 2007, from ExopoliticsJournal Website, https://www.bibliotecapleyades.net/exopolitica/esp_exopolitics_ZZZZB.html
17. 'Declassified Documents Released: Confirms The Nazi Bell Was A Secret 'Worm Hole Time Machine'!,' Amish Shah, *AncientExplorers*, https://ancientexplorers.com/ blogs/news/declassified-documents -released-confirms-the-nazi-bell-was-a-secret-worm-hole-time-machine
18. 'China's Nuclear Fusion Machine Just Smashed Temperature Records by Getting 6 Times Hotter Than

The Sun,' Mike Mcrae, 15 Nov 2018, *ScienceAlert*, https://www.sciencealert.com/china-s-artificial-sun-has-officially-become-hot-enough-for-nuclear-fusion
19. 'SETI Team Investigating Mysterious Signal from Star 94 Light-Years Away,' Mike Wall, Senior Writer, *Space.com*, August 29, 2016, https://www.space.com/33893-seti-investigates-strong-candidate-signal.html
20. Dr Horace Drew, 'Decoding Crop Circes Part 1 and 2,' *YouTube*, Oct 27, 2017
21. ' Crop Circles Decoded — The Two Most Important Alien Messages,' *humansarefree*, http://humansarefree.com/2011/02/two-most-important-alien-messages.html

CHAPTER 24

WHERE ARE WE & WHAT ARE WE TODAY / REALM IS SHIFTING / RECLAIM YOUR POWER / A NEW PARADIGM / EVOKING I AM WE ARE / DANCE OF THE POLARITIES

CHANGES THAT YOU EXPERIENCE BETWEEN 3RD, 4TH AND 5TH DENSITIES (SUMMARY) – THE WAKE UP EXPERIENCE

Understanding the differences between the Third, Fourth and Fifth Dimension - What dimensional reality does your belief system keep you in? The Earth's frequency and hence each human frequency is rising, which will result in the 3rd Density to change to the 4th Density – a new heaven and a new Earth. It is for this reason that Wanderers, Lightworkers, and Indigo Children, all who have ascended to a higher dimension in the past (i.e., past lives), have volunteered to return to the 3rd dimension in order to help those in the 3rd dimension to ascend to a higher level of spirituality. They are also here to advance their own enlightenment in this a world of polarity.

It is not uncommon for some aspects (belief systems) to be rooted in 3-D while others aspects are rooted in a higher dimension.

While we may have many friends or family who are still rooted in the third dimension, we find ourselves reasoning with fifth dimensional consciousness.

Those who are rooted in the 3rd Dimension and are not willing to change will, when 4-D is fully implemented, may still be on Earth since both Polarity and Free Will remain through the lower 6th Density. However, 5th Density is first non-physical Density and they may be on Earth, as well.

3rd Dimension The Material World of Fear	4th Dimension The Magical Dream	5th Dimension The Plane of Light
Spiritually ASLEEP	Spiritually AWAKENING or AWAKE	FULL AWAKE Knows Reality is an ILLUSION
Believe what they see is Reality	Seeks Understanding and Knowledge	Seeks Wisdom
Obey RULES, OBLIGATIONS, TRADITIONS	Questions RULES, OBLIGATIONS, TRADITIONS and decides on own	Follows INNER GUIDANCE
About PHYSICAL Doing	About MENTAL Doing	About WATCHING it being done
Lets OTHERS take Control	Tales CONTROL	SURENDERS Control to Higher
AVOIDS Change	Wants CHANGE	ACCEPTS and watches things MELD Together
Takes advice solely from people in AUTHORITY: religious, political, doctors, scientists	Listens to people in AUTHORITY but makes their own decision	Follows INNER GUIDANCE
Individuals that live SEPARATE lives	Individuals that fee CONNECTED to others	Only conscious ONENESS
Rarely listen and follow their INTER GUIDANCE or intuition	Begins listening and following their own INNER GUIDANCE or institution	Only listens and follows INNER GUIDANCE or institution
Wee are HUMAN	We are SPIRITUAL in a HUMAN body	We are only SPIRITUAL
Believes there are innocent VICTIMS. They suffer because they were HURT by someone or something else out of their control	Believes there is FREEWILL. They can make different choices about where they will go, what they will do, and what will happen	Believes their only choice is between LOVE or FEAR. The HIGHER POWER will take care of where they go, what they do, and what will happen
Togetherness is having your BODY CLOSE to other bodies	Togetherness is FEELING the CONNECTION	Togetherness is having your BODY CLOSE to other bodies

Chapter 24 – Where Are We and What are We Today, Realm is Shifting, Reclaim Your Power, New Paradigm, Evoking I Am We Are, Dance of the Polarities

Lets FEAR stop them. Avoids doing FEARFUL things.	Has the COURAGE to overcome fearful things	Knows Fear is just the EGO holding you back
Togetherness is knowing we CAN NOT DISCONNECT	Usually wants MORE or BETTER Material Things	Realizes there is NO VALUE or substance in owning Material Things. It is not bad/good or better, it's nothing
OWNING MATERIAL POSSESSIONS is very important	Believes there is FREEWILL. They can make different choices about where they will go, what they will do, and what will happen	Believes their only choice is between LOVE and FEAR. The HIGHER POWER will take care of where they go, what they do and what will happen
ANGER and GRUDGES are justified	Learns FORGIVENESS changes the direction of your life for the better	Knows there is NEVER anything to FORGIVE
RIGID BELIEFS characterized by POLARITIES, such as right/wrong, black/white, rich/poor, victim/victimizer, of feminine/masculine	Can see value in both sides and DIFFERENCES start disappearing	There are no DIFFERENCES only ONENESS
LOVE is UNDESERVED, is EARNED and is CONDITIONAL	LOVE is a MINDSET LOVE CONQUERS ALL	There is ONLY LOVE, it is UNIVERSAL and is UNCONDITIONAL

Sources:
1. 'A Chart of Differences in the 3rd, 4th & 5th Dimensions – Part 1,' Vickie Champion, https://vickiechampion.com/ 2016/11/17/ a-chart-of-the-differences-in-the-3rd-4th-5th-dimensions-part-i/
2. 'Understanding the Third, Fourth and Fifth Dimensional Reality,' Hikki Sapp, *fractal enlightenment*, https://fractalenlightenment.com/ 38010/spirituality/understanding-third-fourth-fifth-dimensional-reali

Chapter 24 – Where Are We and What are We Today, Realm is Shifting, Reclaim Your Power, New Paradigm, Evoking I Am We Are, Dance of the Polarities

WHAT ARE HUMANS TODAY? Are we simply more of the same? Are we Human 2.0? This realm is shifting in accordance with the sacred decrees of the First Source (Creator God) plan which has established a timetable for your transformation into fully conscious Beings. As a result of this process, we have come from all sectors of this galaxy to form your first contact team. We are totally dedicated to completion of the mission that First Source has entrusted to us. Right now, when much is unfolding in your world, you must continue to focus closely upon your sacred intentions. Be firm in your commitment. Know that your victory is inevitable. Know also that you are not alone. The universe has sent many to assist you. They have come from many nearby galaxies, and from the vast Orders and Life-streams of the universe. The will of First Source will manifest upon this realm. Feel it in your heart and remain united in your intentions.

We, The Galactic Federation / Brotherhood of Light, salute you and fully support what you are actively accomplishing.

THERE ARE THREE PHASES IN THE PLAN
1. Loosening the grip of the Dark Forces by weakening and eliminating their power structures and technological controls, increasing awareness among the general population and preparing for the Disclosure Event.
2. Taking over from the Dark Forces, starting with fundamental changes in governance, finance, media, healthcare and science and bringing Cabal members to justice.
3. Cleaning up and healing the planet and human beings, revealing the hidden history of Earth, disclosing the existence of extraterrestrial intelligence and bringing earth's people back to full consciousness.

Chapter 24 – Where Are We and What are We Today, Realm is Shifting, Reclaim Your Power, New Paradigm, Evoking I Am We Are, Dance of the Polarities

All during these Phases, Gaia (the Earth) will begin cleansing itself from all the suffering it has endured over the eons as the guest planet for the Polarity Experiment. This may include: Baking temperatures, More powerful storms, Foods, Ever-climbing sea levels, Earthquakes and landmass movement creating wide cracks crust beneath our feet, Increased volcanic activity, and Massive under-ocean landslides that create super tsunamis.

Several times in the past couple of million years the ice left its polar fastnesses and headed towards the equator, covering much of the world's continents in ice sheets over a kilometer thick, and sucking water from the oceans in order to do so. As a consequence, at times when the ice was most dominant, global sea levels were as much as 130m lower than they are today; sufficient to expose land bridges between the UK and the continent, and Alaska and Russia.

Each time the ice retreated, sea levels shot up again, sometimes at rates as high as several meters a century. But how can rising sea levels cause volcanoes to erupt? The answer lies in the enormous mass of the water pouring into the ocean basins from the retreating ice sheets. The addition of over a hundred meters depth of water to the continental margins and marine island chains, where over 60% of the world's active volcanoes reside, seems to be sufficient to load and bend the underlying crust. This in turn squeezes out any magma that happens to be hanging around waiting for an excuse to erupt. It may well be that a much smaller rise can trigger an eruption if a volcano is critically poised and ready to erupt.

In addition a dramatic sea rise would clearly spell catastrophe for our civilization, with low-lying regions across the planet vanishing rapidly beneath the waves. Just a one meter (3.28ft) rise would threaten one third of the world's agricultural land, two meter (6.56ft) would make the Thames flood barrier redundant and four meters (13.12ft) would drown the city of Miami, leaving it 37 miles (60km) off the US coast.

As sea levels climb higher, a response from the world's volcanoes becomes ever more likely, and perhaps not just from volcanoes. Loading of the continental margins could activate faults, triggering increased numbers of earthquakes, which in turn could spawn giant submarine landslides. Such a scenario is believed to account for the gigantic Storegga Slide, which sloughed off the Norwegian coast around 8,000 years ago, sending a tsunami more than 20 meters (66ft) high in places across the Shetland Isles and onto the east coast of Scotland. Should Greenland be released from its icy carapace, the underlying crust will start to bob back up, causing earthquakes well capable of shaking off the huge piles of glacial sediment that have accumulated around its margins and sending tsunamis across the North Atlantic.

RECLAIM YOUR POWER - Find a quiet comfortable area where you will not be disturbed – a place where you feel safe, where you feel some kind of nurturance from your surroundings such as a room filled with your favorite books, a quiet garden space, or somewhere out in nature.

1. Center yourself in whatever way you feel comfortable.
2. Open yourself to your highest God, your Higher Power, or some non-denominational sense of the Universe that you know loves you and that you trust.
3. As you find yourself ready, go slowly over the decades of your life-either chronologically or in reverse order. Think of and/or write down a list of those who have been involved with you in some way and to whom you have given part of yourself. This could be either in a positive or negative way through some kind of attachment of love or hate or fear or

some other emotional state. The list should include such people as your parents, your teachers, your school mates who you envied or tried to copy, the neighborhood bully, the girlfriends or boyfriends – real or imagined, the husbands or wives, our children, your neighbors, the bosses and co-workers whom you have shared both good and bad times – everyone who can say took or was given a piece of you that you now need to reclaim in an attempt to regain your personal power.

Look at this as a game of 'Things would be different IF…' The statements which follow the "IF" are the very attachments you need to release. In releasing attachments we let go of what is draining us of our personal power. We must let go of the past, including past lives, since it only tells us how we got to where we are today.

Once you have made this list or identified those with who our personal power has been in storage, and then comes the essential fact of reclaiming your power, thanking and, if necessary, forgiving them and ourselves. No matter what has happened between the two of you - things either positive or negative –the lessons have been there for you to learn, and these people have done their best, limited thought it may appear to you, to help you learn your lessons and make you the best person you can be. Thank them for whatever part they played in your own spiritual growth, and forgive them for whatever they did or did not do to you in any other way. To hold a strong feeling for anyone in the past is to give away a piece of your energy to that person, and the personal power you will need here in the very near and very real future that awaits us all in combating the New World Order. Do this for each and every person on your list, savoring each moment as you recall it and then let go.

Chapter 24 – Where Are We and What are We Today, Realm is Shifting, Reclaim Your Power, New Paradigm, Evoking I Am We Are, Dance of the Polarities

THE FUTURE AND THE PAST - It is hard to see where you are going when you are always looking behind you. Forgiveness of the past is one of the greatest healing gifts you can ever give to oneself. As long as we are looking behind, we are not looking forward and preparing for what is to come. It is like trying to straddle two sides of a fence and ending up in neither field. Yes, you can get off your fence soon, because your fence will soon be washed away. The only problem is that if not done soon, the time left will not give you the firm footing you will need to be doing what you came here to do.

EARTH'S INCREASING INTENSITY AFFECTS EVERYONE - The Earth's intensity is increasing, and it is being experienced by everyone to varying degrees. It is important to understand what is happening, that you are not alone and that there is support for you. Since we all have different levels of sensitivity to the energy, we will experience the Earth's increase in intensity a little bit differently. It is working the same in all of us, only the degree of direct experience and awareness of the process differs.

As the energy around the Earth intensifies, it is felt by everyone and everything at a cellular level. We are literally being called/pulled home. The planetary consciousness is awaking and those of us who are ready are being awakened very quickly because we are needed to assist the others as this transformation continues. The transformation is both individual and collective. Everything that affects the planet affects everything that is a part of the planet.

The increase in the Earth's intensity results in our own reaction which range from mild anxiety to a feeling of having a panic attack. In understanding these things, we are better equipped and prepared for the next occurrence. No everything you feel through your body and emotions are "yours" in the specific sense. The following list will help you understand the changes you are experiencing:

1. Emotions are coming to the surface; we are more emotional, more sensitive and more easily irritated. This happens because the energetic blockages that have been keeping us in the experience of separation (these are sometimes referred to as "issues") are being cleared. What used to take weeks, months or years to work through is now happening in a matter of days or hours. You may feel "on edge" a lot of the time and be unable to ascertain why. Energetic clearing may happen, such as crying, laughing, fears arising, joy arising, and you may have no idea why it is happening or what the "issue" is. It is not important to analyze it or "figure it out" – in fact, trying to analyze it uses up lots of "thinking" energy needlessly. It is better to conserve your energy and let the blockages pass on their own accord.
2. Mood swings are happening more rapidly, leaving us a feeling of "out-of-control" and vulnerable. This is due to the soul trying to restore balance and for that to happen you must pass through both extremes of polarity/duality in order to clear and balance out the karma your soul has carried into this life. Your lessons will come faster and you will feel like you are trying to "catch-up." The soul will pull everything to it (and through it) in order to restore a state of balance within its energy field, only then will it be able to re-join the whole.
3. Many more people are experiencing "psychic" or intuitive experiences as our bodies become more sensitive. Those with sensitive nervous systems will have the most difficult time because their physiology allows more sensory input. Integration must happen more quickly in order for us to adapt. WITH THE INCREASE IN EXTRA-SENSORY EXPERIENCES, IT IS COMMON FOR PEOPLE TO

FEEL CONFUSED AND EVEN FEARFUL OF PROCESSES THEY DO NOT UNDERSTAND.
Past fears are ignited as our parental, societal and religious conditioning kicks us.
4. More people will experience upheaval in their personal lives as the internal changes escalate. When the inside changes, the outside must follow suit. Outwardly, you may need to change job relationships, living arrangements, etc., as your outward world tries to align and balance with the "new you" that is being transformed from the inside out.
5. You may have difficulty sleeping or waking in the early morning hours. This happens due to the time we are most relaxed and the energetic changes are taking place most intensely within our bodies. Oftentimes, the nightly awakenings are accompanied by waves of emotion and/or spontaneous crying. When the emotional body releases blockages the emotions flow through us on their way out. These waves can also involve involuntary contractions of the abdominal muscles (which is actually energy surging through the sacral and solar plexus chakras).
6. Changes in the menstrual cycle. These changes may include: intensity, in the amount of fluid excreted, a lengthening in the duration of the menstrual flow, and other fluctuations. This is a sign of the body cleaning itself and balancing hormonal imbalances between the male/female polarities of the soul.
7. Other physical changes may be noticed, such as changes in exercise tolerance (i.e., inability to exercise as long or as intense as usual); inability to read, think and/or concentrate on intellectual endeavors in your usual way; and difficulty in the digestion process. Constipation, indigestion, gas, bloating and nausea may occur. The physical body is diverting its resources to the increasing demands of the nervous system, leaving less energy available for other functions. The answer is to eat as lightly as possible, and to

eat only the foods that are easily digested and assimilated by the body. A vegetarian diet is imperative if you are experiencing these difficulties and the more fruit and vegetables you eat the easier it will be for your body to fill physiological demands being made of it.
8. You may have noticed that time seems to be speeding up. The hours and the days go by more quickly and it is difficult to remember if something occurred earlier in the day, the day before or last week and we do not seem to be able to keep up with the world around us as much as we once could. These are perceptual variations that are occurring as our soul essence (the energetic core of creation) and the density of the physical world come closer into alignment. Since our perception acts as the "buffer" integrating the two, our perceptions change in accordance with the changing vibratory frequencies of the planet.

CHANGE IN EARTH'S FREQUENCY INTENSITY AFFECTS OUR DNA - Your DNA is a crystalline structure of integrated vibration pattern holders and channels, as well as a vibration projector and receiver of the multidimensional scale of light and color (hologram matrix) and is, actually, light filament encoded. Matter affects all DNA light filament ended encoded species, all on a cellular level. Our DNA determines the vibrations in color, conscious perception and awareness.

All species have a group collective agreement with the universe and Creator/First Source God to evolve at a certain pace, as well as on an individual level. Free will of choice, on both the collective and individual level, is involved.

In mapping the DNA of human beings, it was discovered that we also have "Junk" DNA. In reality, this junk DNA is the 'miracle DNA,' or light-body DNA. The more you act out of compassionate feelings, the more you connect with the Earth,

other planets, star systems, galaxies, etc. The Compassionate feelings will activate your DNA from a 2-strand to a 12-strand helix, which is your light body or what avatars call the new creation, a body that does not die but lives forever.
Compassion is a feeling at 13 Hz per second vibration. The Earth's basic frequency (for eons) has been 7.83 Hz, but it is rising rapidly. A human brain frequency is in "match step" with the Earth's frequency. Given this, the Earth's frequency will increase to 13 Hz and beyond. Junk DNA is a "shape-shifter DNA. It responds to compassion and feelings of love. 13 Hz is the alpha wave, in relation to the Earth, Sun, galaxies, and the universe.

It is all connected in a multidimensional scale. Compassion, Love, and Free Will, as well as Mother Earth (Gaia), are truly the keys to activating your junk or miracle DNA.

EVOKING I AM WE ARE - by integrating the dominant model of the hierarchy (evolution/saviorship) with the dominant model of First Source Intelligence (transformation/mastership. The human uniform evolves and but this evolution is on a track, a pre-programmed track. The intent was to have Anu (Anannaki) return on a "'cloud,' the whole Second Coming was going to be the staged entrance for Anu. Humanity would evolve in such a way that his re-entry into our consciousness would be understood to be a good thing. Humanity's salvation. We would all be his children, and the glory of god would be upon the Earth. That was the plan. From before the time of Jesus, that was the plan. Marduk programmed (Human 2.0) the entire set of events into our DNA.

The beings like Marduk or Enki or Anu are not based in space-time. They are infinite beings, meaning they have no end. They don't have an age. Neither do we.

Chapter 24 – Where Are We and What are We Today, Realm is Shifting, Reclaim Your Power, New Paradigm, Evoking I Am We Are, Dance of the Polarities

It is very hard to believe that human beings are simply uniforms for a programmed existence. The functional implants of the human interface are perfectly integrated within the human vessel. They operate seamlessly. So seamlessly, we do not know that they are not us. We have no choice in a way. We think our thoughts and emotions are us, that this space-time is what our thoughts and emotions exist in. Even the thought of a God, heaven, hell, soul, masters, all of these things, they're part of the program. It is integrated in both the dimension of the Earth plane and the after-life. The after-life is part of the deception. The eye-brain was the key element that the Anannaki needed to design in order to make the functional implants operate. This is in Human 1.0. In Human 2.0; it was the DNA. Once this was achieved, the Sirians could design the consciousness framework—the human consciousness. Human consciousness is the key to suppressing an infinite being. Human consciousness, or the triad of consciousness, is composed of three interactive layers.

The first layer is universal mind or universal conscious, and this forms the link between the individual human and the entire species. This layer is what enables all of us to see what everyone sees, feel what everyone else feels, and know what everyone else knows. It is the perfect way to unify a species in separation. In fact, that is the way we feel unification, through the unconscious mind.

The next layer of consciousness is the genetic mind, or subconscious, in the case of Sigmund Freud. This forms the link between the individual and their family tree or genetics. This is where bloodlines are expressed.

And then there is the conscious mind. This is the unique individual perception and expression—what most of us call our personality and character, it's built on this layer.

The conscious mind of the individual is heavily influenced by the genetic mind, especially between birth and the age of seven or eight. By that time the influence is all-encompassing. Remember that the Anannaki created the biological form—the body, the Sirians created the functional implants, and Marduk executed the programming of these functional implants so they would evolve along a programmed path, leading to the return of Anu. This was expressed in the hierarchal structure of humanity that speaks of god and masters in religious and esoteric texts.

This was all part of the design, to create various religions and esoteric cults that would support a vast hierarchy and order the human species into master-student relationships, and then create a multi-leveled afterlife that would reward those who believed and were obedient to their god or masters. The whole principle that was behind this entire endeavor could be summed up in one word: separation. Everything exists in separation within the earth plane and its afterlife planes as well. But, what is real is that we are all imbued with equality and oneness—not through the unconscious mind, which only links us in separation, but rather through the life essence that is us. And this life essence is sovereign and integral. It is I AM, WE ARE. No one is above, no one is below. No one is better, no one is lesser.

Everything is a lie. Everything…everything we've been taught to believe is a deception! It's possible because the beings that have enslaved humanity designed a world in which we adjusted to over eons of time, and evolved into it in such a manner that we became lost in our world. The veils that have been placed over us are opaque. So much so that people operate as human uniforms unaware that everything around them is illusory. It is a programmed reality that is not real.

Chapter 24 – Where Are We and What are We Today, Realm is Shifting, Reclaim Your Power, New Paradigm, Evoking I Am We Are, Dance of the Polarities

The universe is made up of dimensions that are a result of mathematical equations. It is constructed from mathematics. Some beings understand how to apply mathematical equations to organize and plan space-time. It's all created. This world is created, it's not real. It's a programmed reality. Earth is a programmed space-time reality. Once you can program space-time reality within a species like humanity, you can program at the individual level of a person, right down to when they itch their nose, if you want to. It's all mathematical equations.

However, each person can step out of the illusion. There is no master here. No god is going to come down and make it happen for us. No ETs. No one. It is each of us. This is what is meant by I AM. I… it's like One. One—me, and one—all of us unified, AM meaning exist now. In this moment. Not in history or memory. Not in some future time or goal. Now!

Human beings are complete if they can step out of their consciousness frameworks and realize what is actually powering their systems, their artificial realities, their programmed existence. The integration of technology internally, will only make this realization more difficult.

Many of those who have come to Earth as human teachers have tried to reveal how deep and broad and high this illusion has been constructed. It is as far as the edge of the universe and as close as your DNA. Everywhere in between is illusion. Jesus came to reveal much of this, but the writers of the Bible decided what would be acceptable within the paradigm of life as we know it. They elected to make Jesus a part of the deception. They saw it was time for a redefinition of God to accommodate an evolving Human 2.0. God was suddenly a loving father and all of humanity was brother and sister.

Jesus was aware of this deception, but his words weren't included in the Bible. His words were so against the conditioned beliefs that people could not understand them as he said them. And so, over time, they were translated into the form you know today. The Biblical translations simply lack the original potency with which he said them.

There are two methods that can make exposing this illusion a very difficult proposition. The first is that the unconscious mind system is inside everyone. It's like a field of information that everyone can access. It can effect or infect everyone. A revelatory idea can be passed to a small number of people, but it lacks sufficient influence to generate mass awakening. So there's unconscious mind inertia.

The other, and this is more pernicious, is that the functional implants are programmed, and like any program, it can be upgraded or even turned off. There is a triad of consciousness as having the god consciousness installed within it—in the unconscious mind layer, but they also report that as the individual develops from about the age of six or seven, they begin to assemble their individual personality from the elements of the subconscious layer and by the time they're 12 to 14 years old, they have their unique personality well in place, and for some, this uniqueness is shutting out the existence of a God. From Anu's perspective, this is fine. He probably likes having atheists and agnostics. It's more separation. More diversity. In fact, the greater the diversity in the human family, the greater the separation. The greater the separation, the easier it is to keep the program of enslavement intact. Choose sides and disagree with your opponents. Compete. It fuels wars and social unrest.

As for the existence of god, we, collectively, are the closest thing to god. WE ARE. There is a First Source, a center point in

Chapter 24 – Where Are We and What are We Today, Realm is Shifting, Reclaim Your Power, New Paradigm, Evoking I Am We Are, Dance of the Polarities

existence that created the framework of existence through sound— the ones who are enlightened or spiritual masters—are not all made up. They exist. It's just that their existence is within the human interface or functional implants. They exist there. We, us, the being that is I AM, that being is not of that reality. It doesn't really exist inside the holographic stage that was created by interdimensional beings millions of years ago; rather, it is being used as a power source that animates the human interface or uniform. Over time, we've spiraled deeper and deeper inside of this created world, complete with its afterlife and different planes of existence.

You could look at it this way: Anu (Anannaki) installed a program inside the Human 2.0 and in this program; humans would evolve from knowing absolutely nothing about their world, to knowing god. Humans were designed to have god consciousness—meaning, to have the same understanding and awareness as Anu. But then Anu took this evolutionary line and positioned god consciousness so far out into the future that humans would essentially be chasing this god consciousness forever. They'd be chasing shadows, because until they awaken from the deception, the only god that exists in that world is Anu.

Once awakened as I AM, WE ARE or the Sovereign Integral, a human being lives as an expression of this consciousness. On this plane, Earth, no one has done this. But remember, some are here to crack this shell open a bit.

Space-time is an illusion. But it's hard to imagine that the universe in which we exist is really a hologram projection that was programmed inside our unconscious mind and we're really inside this hologram, wearing a human uniform that was outfitted to perceive only this hologram. The real world is sound. Everything is sound and resonance of sound. Everything we have in our human uniform for sensing our universe is millions of years of evolutionary design to tune into that hologram and only that hologram. The hologram extends beyond this physical world, even the afterlife is part of it. There are many aspects to the afterlife. There is God, first and foremost. There is the Light of illumination. There is the universal spirit and individual soul. There is a hierarchy of angels and masters. There is the concept of karma and reincarnation or sin and salvation. The concept of heaven and hell. The concept of the chosen. The concept of an ascension path. The concept of the Book of Records or Akashic records. All of these concepts were designed into an upgrade of the human 2.0 interface by the Anannaki. Certain human beings are programmed to find these concepts in their unconscious mind layer and share them. As a result, religions sprout. Philosophies rise sometimes in support of the religions, sometimes in contradiction. Esoteric cults rise. All the while the human being remains lost. It remains muddled in its illusion. Everything tied to an empty promise in a belief, and in all those beliefs, one thing remains constant: separation.

The program is vast in its reach, and the Anannaki, once they had mined sufficient gold, had an entire race of beings enslaved. Anu, along with his allies in the Sirian and Serpent races, decided it would be best to turn the Human 2.0's into a worthless creature that forever sought enlightenment through belief. And who do you suppose would provide the things to believe in? Anu and Marduk.

Everything became learning lessons. The earth was a school house. If you learn your lessons, you won't have to keep incarnating. Learn, learn, learn. But what are you learning? You are learning to believe in the afterlife, as it was described and prescribed by Anu and his designers. You are learning to don your human uniform obediently. You are learning to discern how humanity is different. You are learning to link every self-image you have to the world of three-dimensions, while hoping there is more after death.

The sober reality is that after you die, the being inside you is met by a guardian who will take you to your destination, based mostly on your deeds in this life. However, most beings are taken to a life review where they face their life in every detail, and based on that experience an authoritative figure will prescribe your next life options for reincarnation. You are essentially recycled into the same program with a new mother and family, and a programmed life path is laid out for you to follow.

The afterlife program and process is all part of the master program to retain the enslavement of the beings. Remember, we're interdimensional beings—meaning we exist in 3-D and the higher planes. It's just that these higher planes are designed by the Anannaki. They are not of the real dimensional planes. Otherwise, we would die, discover who we really are, and we would never reincarnate or if we did, we would tell everyone on Earth that this is all an illusion.

What began as an experiment in three-dimensional exploration from a higher dimensional reality became what is here. Every human being will confront this reality eventually. It cannot be avoided. We can agonize about the lack of fairness or ask why, but whether it makes sense to you doesn't change the fact that we live in a world of designed separation. Divide and conquer.

When all manifestations of life are genuinely perceived as fragmentary expressions of First Source, the vibration of equality that underlies all life-forms becomes perceptible to the human instrument. Life initially emerges as an extension of Source Reality, and then, as an individuated energy frequency invested within a form. It vibrates, in its pure, timeless state, precisely the same for all manifestations of life. This is the common ground that all life shares. This is the tone-vibration of equality that can be observed within all life forms that unifies all expressions of diversity to the foundation of existence known as First Source.

But the thing is, in order to change, in order to step out of this illusion, it requires each of us to wake up and stay awake. It's not reading words that will change this; it's the profound nature of new behaviors, because these behaviors signal that our consciousness layers are understood as separate from who we are. We have to operate as I AM, WE ARE.

What's so special about the Earth's core is that it is the cause of all of this. The magnetic fields associated with Earth's core are unique. They are 'alive.' We can only assume that alive is an aspect of intelligence.

If human beings are trapped in a prison of illusion, as Human 2.0's, and their interface to the holographic universe is the reason for their being trapped, then a new model needs to step forward. Human 3.0 is this new model. It is the formula of self-realization. It is stepping out of the constructed universe or reality, and living as a self-expression of IAM, WE ARE. Human 3.0 is the Sovereign Integral. To be specific, this is human 3.0 SI (SI = Sovereign Integral).

The Grand Portal is a way to synchronize humanity to a new inception point where it is living in the expression of oneness and equality, sovereign and integral, I AM and WE ARE. It is a way for humanity to move from separation—which was its previous inception point, the one that generated Human 1.0 and 2.0. Human 3.0 SI will have a new inception point, and the reason for The Grand Portal was to enable synchronization, because how can you have a network of equality and oneness if the beings were not synchronized?

Soul is an idea or paradigm that has become part of the human reality program. Soul is the part of you that contains all memory of your existence as a Human 1.0 and 2.0. For most of us, this is a vast repository—far too large for the consciousness framework to deal with. So the soul holds this information for each individual being.

Soul is a paradigm of infinite expression within a finite reality. But you can't be infinite in a finite reality if that reality is a programmed reality. So soul is not the life force that powers the human consciousness. That is the Sovereign Integral. That is what each of us is when we are stripped naked of all illusion, of all deceptions, of all limitations, of all veils, of all functional implants—including the soul.

It is the redefinition of human identity and expression as I AM, WE ARE. From a human perspective, the WingMakers do not see humans as lesser entities, but simply beings with inception points that enslaved them. It is not a judgment that humans are worthless or bad or sinful or weak or needy. None of those things. Humanity needs a new start. A point in which they can synchronize in one realization, and that is the expression of I AM, WE ARE. Living those words as behavior.

The time has come to integrate the dominant model of the hierarchy (evolution/saviorship) with the dominant model of Source Intelligence (transformation/mastership). This integration can only be achieved at the level of the entity. It cannot occur within the context of a human instrument or an aspect of the hierarchy. Only the entity—the wholeness of inter-dimensional sovereignty imbued with Source Intelligence—can facilitate and fully experience the integration of these two models of existence.

Each individual being is responsible for this. Creator God or Source Intelligence isn't going to come down from the heavens and correct human faults or obstacles. Humans need to take responsibility for this— it's not easy. We need to adopt the heart virtues as the behavioral construct for this time. How these words can be applied and lived. Not simply held in the head as a worthy concept. The heart virtues are appreciation or gratitude, compassion, humility, forgiveness, understanding and valor or courage. It is the combination of nowness—being in the now—and applying these words in our behaviors. It's being impeccable in this practice.

If you apply heart virtues, the unconscious mind is a doorway into all beings. These behaviors go out to all beings. They support the building of the Sovereign Integral Network human 3.0, which is the replacement of separation consciousness of Human 2.0. So this is the application of insertive behavior, which is to say, I will insert these behaviors in my nowness. They will become the pallet of my behavioral choice.

Again, whether you operate in the insertive (Anannaki Human 2.0 and 3.0) or resistive behavioral mode (One Source 3.0SI), you are affecting the whole. You either support oneness and equality, the I AM, WE ARE, or you support separation and deception, also known in our reality, as the status quo.

The starting point of behavior or expression is in the now. This is the creative nerve center. Every single now is a potential to support oneness and equality in this world and help birth the Human 3.0SI and the Sovereign Integral Network.

Why wouldn't Anu (Anannaki), since he's God, simply stop it? Or, if Marduk could program with such amazing accuracy, how

Chapter 24 – Where Are We and What are We Today, Realm is Shifting, Reclaim Your Power, New Paradigm, Evoking I Am We Are, Dance of the Polarities

could human 3.0SI even come about? Unless he wanted it? There have been several interventions. While Anu and his Sirian cohorts were focused on the Human 1.0 and 2.0 uniforms, they didn't pay as much attention to the interaction of Earth and the human vessel. Earth is an anomaly in itself. Remember that the Earth's gravitational fields interact with all life. Even non-physical beings—if they get close enough—can be materialized in this plane of existence. Anu did not want to be materialized in this dimension, and he could only appear on this plane of existence for short times, maybe a day or two. In this time, our time, right now, the Anannaki cannot enter this plane. They're locked out. The Earth plane is too dense. So that is one reason that Anu's ability to interact directly with his creation has been curtailed.

The second intervention point is that non-physical beings have woken up to this issue of enslavement. They see how it affects everyone. It was permitted in part, because the Anannaki and their alliance partners were strong and threatening to many other races and beings. However, this notion of enslaving infinite beings, as a concept or inception point, was infecting all of existence. It was a fear-based, separation-based idea that beings eventually began to see as a degenerative force to existence. The native state of existence, which includes space-time and non-space-time expressions, is oneness and equality. Obviously, enslavement is only possible in a separation-based paradigm.

The third intervention point is the WingMakers. They were the part of humanity also known as the Atlanteans, but even before the Atlantean race, they existed in a pure-state genetic template, and eventually these genetics were used by Anu to create—in part—the Human 1.0 and Human 2.0.

Although with the 2.0 version, it was less pure, because

Anannaki and Sirian genetics were introduced, among others. But the point is that the WingMakers, as a future expression of Human 3.0 SI, have entered our space-time, and have begun to crack open this prison reality.

The fourth invention point is each of us, practicing the Sovereign Integral process (SI).

3.0 SI is a more organic process of using behaviors to support the process of becoming a Human 3.0 SI or Sovereign Integral, and then becoming part of a network of these Sovereign Integrals.

So humanity sits at a crossroads. On the one side is the Triad of Power that is programmed to develop Human 3.0 as a cyborg and the other side is the future existence of humanity urging us to do it internally, one person at a time, through a behavioral process. I guess the part that's missing for me is the role of The Grand Portal, which remains unclear. I thought it was a technology that proved the existence… the irrefutable scientific existence of the human soul. There are humans here who are designers of the new unconscious mind that will bridge human populations everywhere on the planet to feel and express equality and oneness. It will connect humanity in the I AM, WE ARE consciousness, instead of the separation consciousness. It will not be based on hierarchy. That deception is coming down.

The designers of the new unconscious layer of the human 3.0 SI are on the planet now. They are doing some of the preparation required to move humanity—who will be sitting at the fork in the road in the next few years—to choose the I AM, WE ARE path.

Whatever it is, it's important to know what's behind the deception… to look with sober eyes on the truth. It may not be

Chapter 24 – Where Are We and What are We Today, Realm is Shifting, Reclaim Your Power, New Paradigm, Evoking I Am We Are, Dance of the Polarities

a beautiful picture to be sure, but how else do you realize your own truth until you know the truth of the big picture? So, however screwed up it seems, the Grand Portal is an inception point for the individual to redefine themselves.

Would you rather stay in the illusion of a soul in a human body that will be saved by the God given to us by the Anunnnaki and ascend into heaven and hang out with angels who strum harps? That whole idea is repulsive once you know this. That picture is based on separation and selfishness and lack of empathy and understanding. Or, you can simply say it's all a big illusion, including the notion that we are infinite beings, and that when you die, you're done.

The part of this new picture that is promising is that we exist infinitely despite the fact that we have been suppressed and enslaved. We also can play a role in supporting this redefinition of the human being through our thoughts and behaviors. And, maybe most importantly, we have the WingMakers—our future selves—providing us with evidence that I AM, WE ARE prevailed.

LERM is an acronym for or the Light-Encoded Reality Matrix. LERM is what the Labyrinth Group thought was God—in terms of proof. But what was really discovered was the essence of Anu and how he operates in this reality as an all-encompassing observation field that is inside our consciousness interface to this reality-existence called Earth. LERM is Anu projected.

Everyone inside our universe is part of this deception, whether they know it or not. There are four classes of beings: (1) Those who know the deception and are actively supporting it; (2) Those who know about the deception, but are unwilling to do anything about it; (3) Those who don't know the deception and are unknowingly supporting it; and (4) Those who know about the deception and are actively trying to step out of the deception and engineer a process for everyone else to do the same. That's it. It doesn't matter if the being is physical or nonphysical. Everyone falls into one of these four categories—everywhere in our universe of existence.

The beings in group three are waking up. Some of them understand that the deception in one part of the universe infects all. It requires corrective action. It requires collective understanding to ensure that it will never happen again.

Our entire universe is created. I'm not saying it is the universe. I'm saying that what we call the universe, as far as we can observe, is part of the hologram implanted within our consciousness framework and human interface. Our mind consciousness established the spatial-temporal relationships of everything we see, and this is part of the program. And this includes the universe.

Science is not able to explain it. The counter-logical nature of the universe—in terms of quantum behavior—is impossible to explain. Some scientists have relented to explaining it all away as hidden variables. But frankly, what the WingMakers have explained is that we're creating the universe through the human interface Anu (Anannaki) provided us by reinterpreting sound vibrations through our five senses.

But it doesn't make sense... how can I see the moon and a two-year-old can see it exactly the same way? How can it be the same? No, this is what the unconscious mind provides the Human 2.0 interface. It gathers the interpretation of the sound vibration of the moon, based on billions and billions of sightings throughout time. These evolve and change based on environmental conditions, but generally the notion that the

Chapter 24 – Where Are We and What are We Today, Realm is Shifting, Reclaim Your Power, New Paradigm, Evoking I Am We Are, Dance of the Polarities

moon is silver and generally the size that it is, is stored and shared in the DNA and unconsciousness.

As Aristotle said some 2,300 years ago, 'To be conscious that we are perceiving is to be conscious of our own existence.' That is a good description of I AM. So, are we an isolated lifeform that confronts our external, separate reality? No, we are connected to all. That is why I AM, WE ARE is the critical inception point for our identity. Any being that does not confirm their belief in this, is not aware of reality. It doesn't matter where they exist or what vessel they wear. It doesn't matter if they want to save humanity. They must first act from this inception.

The universe, as immense as it appears, is a hologram inside a programmed existence in which every human being agrees is reality. That agreement informs the unconscious mind—again, a part of the human interface that Anu created—and collectively we all see our world the same way, more or less.

We have been told there are trillions of planets with life. That the universe is abundant with life forms in various dimensions, but what we know is here. On Earth. The tangible, visible Earth. Are there other beings? Of course. Will they save humanity? They can't. They can only support. It isn't about anyone or anything saving us. It is about a redefinition process that can only occur within each individual entity. It isn't about being beamed up or ascending to some higher, protected dimension. This will be done in the physical body as human beings, by human beings, for human beings.

We that are awaking are unique in the sense that we are not the only one involved in getting this information out. There are others, many others, both physical and nonphysical who are assisting in this transformative process. "The two portals are defined as the "crack" and the "wall demolition."

The Grand Portal is the wall demolition. That's when the wall comes down through the efforts of all beings that are undergoing the Sovereign Integral process. And this makes it possible for all human beings to step forward into their infinite self or life essence.

The human portal anchors the inception point on Earth for The Grand Portal. It will come in about ten years. The Grand Portal, several years after that. Those are the rough timeframes but always with the stipulation that these times can shift and change.

WE ARE THE ONES WE HAVE BEEN WAITING FOR - Fusion is the direction we are headed in. Fusion is the old paradigm, the way of the New World Order. Before a new paradigm can be established, the old one must dissolve into nothingness. This may or will be the case of the total breakup of everything one knows and believes to be true, including those things we desperately hold onto to sustain our false sense of security. We are stuck in an Old Paradigm of Control and need to Create a New Paradigm of Free Will. There is a river flowing that is now flowing very fast. It is so great and swift, that there are those who will be afraid. They will try hard to hold on to the shore. They are being torn apart and will suffer greatly. Know that the river has its destination. The elders say we must let go of the shore, push into the middle of the river, and keep our heads above water. And then see who is there with you and celebrate. At this time in history we are to take nothing personally, least of all ourselves, for the moment that we do, our spiritual growth and journey come to an end. The time of the lone wolf is over. Gather yourselves. Banish the word struggle from your attitude and vocabulary. All that we do now must be done in a sacred manner and in celebration.

Chapter 24 – Where Are We and What are We Today, Realm is Shifting, Reclaim Your Power, New Paradigm, Evoking I Am We Are, Dance of the Polarities

We are the ones we have been waiting for.

THE DANCE OF THE POLARITIES - Humans are experiencing an intermingling of third, fourth and fifth dimensional energies. Depending on where folks are at this time in their own life-journeys they may find themselves centered in one of these energetic "levels" or switching back and forth between one and another.
- Humanity collectively is making a shift from third to fourth dimensional experience.
- Those who have incarnated to specifically help humanity make the Shift have the opportunity to make a shift to fifth density (or higher; density = an individual vibrational level; dimension = a collectively experienced vibrational level).
- Once the collective shift to 4D is completed, there will be a continuing focus on healing the harm we have done to each other and Mother Earth during our sojourns on 3D Earth. There will also be opportunities to join star fleets and go off-planet.
- Even when the shift to 4D is completed, 4D entities continue to have free-will which means 4D, 5D and 6D negatively polarized energies may be able to exert influences. The shift to 4D does not mean all is love and there are no negative influences. Nor does the shift to 4D mean that the 4D entities will be within their own world. This means that the need for spiritual discernment will not end once the shift to 4D is completed.
- When the healing is completed there may be a collective shift to 5D.
- The 5D world is where nonphysical orientation is experienced. Although you might be right here on Earth when you shift to 5D, you cannot perform physically and you are not seen by 3D and 4D entities, but those who are 3D and 4D entities may be able to "see" you if you lower your frequency to the that of 3D or 4D. At this level you

see all the other 5D entities, both those of Light and those of Darkness, who you may remember from your past lives in the 3D and 4D world.
- As a 5D or higher non-physical entity, you can only influence those in 3D and 4D. If a 5D entity wants to have a physical event to occur, the 5D entity needs to convince a 3D or 4D entity to perform the work. This is what is occurring in today's 3D world where both STO (service to others) and STS (service to self) 5D entities are, to some extent, using 3D entities as slaves. This is why 5D or higher vibrational entities cannot physically "save" the 3D and 4D human race due to their spacecraft being 5D or higher and will not function in a 3D or 4D environment without major loss of serviceability.
- 5D is where experiential awareness of "I" as a group identity, has no bound by linear time. In this density sentient consciousness begins to awaken to its heritage.
- 5D is the density of wisdom. As one begins their transition from 4D to 5D, they very often want to share their increased wisdom with those who are still fully focused in 3D and 4D densities.
- Many from the 5D realm choose to become guides for others. A 5D density being merges with its family of consciousness ("oversoul" or "higher self" if you will) and begins to remember. Note: there is no clear-cut distinctions between 5D, 6D and 7D, since these densities are not physically oriented; there is much blending between these three densities.
- 6D awareness is the dimension itself. This has often been called the "Christ Consciousness" in that it displays a frequency level equal to that of the Christ or Buddha. From this frequency a total remembrance occurs, and the one begins taking responsibility for the Whole rather than the Self. The process of progressing the Self and progressing the Whole becomes one and the same.

- 7D awareness is the multidimensional experience, group-matrix identity, (social memory complex). This is the frequency of total oneness or integration and vibrations at this frequency are merged in identity and become a mass-conscious whole. They magnetize those in other frequencies and provide the current for the natural flow toward integration. Once the seventh density beings reach critical mass, they will progress thru the Prism of Lyra (from our point of view it will then be a black hole exit point) and reach the next octave where another adventure awaits.

Prism of Lyra: A prism is a transparent body with a triangular base used to polarize or decompose light or energy into its spectrum. The prism of Lyra is the archetypal idea of the entrance of consciousness into this reality. For Earth's galactic family the entrance point exists within the Lyran system. As consciousness/energy emerged, it is fragmented into seven density frequencies, much as a prism would fragment light into seven colors.

Sources:
1. 'The Game of Duality, the Dance of Polarity and Unity Consciousness,' 20 Feb 2016, *Shift Frequency*, https://www.shiftfrequency.com/positive-4d-polarized-earth/

2. 'Understanding the Difference Between Levels of Awareness: Density and Dimension,' The Healers Journal, https://www.*thehealersjournal*.com/2013/01/25/understanding-the-difference-between-levels-of-awareness-density-and-dimension/. Originally posted January 25, 2013, *Ascension, Ascension 2013*, 'Lightworker, mastery consciousness, Metaphysics, Multidimensional Self, Quantum Consciousness, Quantum Physics, spiritual evolution, Spirituality, starseed,'
3. 'The Last Words of Damon T. Berry' (Podcast EP1-3), The Knowledge of the All, 31 Jan 2019, *hellovideos3.com*, https://www.hellovideos3.com, YouTube

THE 5D AND 6D STARSEEDS MAY STAY WHEN THE TRANSITION TO 4D IS COMPLETE - Many but not all incarnate Starseeds will choose to remain in the new ascended 4D Earth that they worked so long and so hard to manifest for others, in order to live on the new ascended 4D Earth world for however long they individually feel the need or desire to do so. Those Starseeds who stay, will be their alien "gods" who help the new human beings in the "new heaven and new Earth." The remaining Starseeds will bring the new humans great knowledge, great stories of the past, and even greater stories of their future. Once the Starseeds have taught the new beings the concepts for loving and cherishing their fellow mankind, the Earth, the galaxies and to be one with the universe, the Starseeds will leave and the next 50,000 year civilization will begin, with other civilizations to follow until another 400,000 year epoch has been completed. Over time, the humans will learn that there are other species within the universe, some who will want to help and others who want to make them subservient. At a distant point in their future, such as each entering of the Photo Belt (twice in a 24,000 to 26,000 year cycle) our heirs will return to instill philosophy, mathematics, astrology, medicine (holistic and otherwise), etc. into their knowledge base, to assist in bringing about a paradigm shift, and to assist those who are ready to complete their ascension process. Of course, they will be the Wanderers who come and leave throughout each period and age. At the "end of days" of the next 50,000 year cycle, Starseeds will descend in droves to help bring about a "new heaven and a new Earth."

During the time of withdrawal, the Starseeds' multitude of options will become increasingly conscious in the incarnate Starseeds awareness from this point forward because they reached the end of this phase of their Missions as those who volunteered to come to Earth to embody/live/insert/anchor the Ascension Process. Many incarnate Starseeds will choose to return Home to their individual higher dimensions, stellar systems, galaxies, universe, Light Realms, or return to locations very close to First Source. After as bit of R&R, many will return to "Future Life Planning" (Chapter 2) in order to set the areas of knowledge they wish to explore, next.

WE ARE YOU AND YOU ARE US

Sources:
1. 'Xekleidoma - Plans of the light forces – Planetary Liberation,' www.xekleidoma.info/plans.html
2. 'The Earth Fights Back,' Bill McGuire, August 207, *The Guardian*, https://www.theguardian.com/science/2007/aug/07/disasters
3. 'A Different story about the Anannaki' by Estelle Nora Harwit Amrani with Enki's Assistance from *Vibrani Website January, 1999 up*-dated August 3, 2000 recovered through Bibliotheca Alexandrina Website. Bibliotecapleyades.net.

4. *Where Were You Before The Tree of Life,*' Volumes 4 (The Oak Falls), 5 (The True History of the Darkness and the Light), 6 (The True Nature of Planet Earth), and 7 (The True History of the Darkness and the Light), Peter R Farley, lulu.com, various dates for each Volume
5. 'Earth – Pleiadian Keys to the Living Library,' Barbara Marcinia, 1995, *BiblioTecapleyades,net,* https://www.bibliotecapleyades.net/pleyades/tierra/tierra_eng.htm#The%20Game,%20the%20Codes,%20and%20the%20Master%20Numbers
6. 'Starseed Troop Withdrawals,' Denis Le Fay, *Transitions*, October 27, 2011, https://deniselefay.wordpress.com/2011/10/27/starseed-troop-withdrawals/

APPENDIX 1

MY STORY AND PAST LIVES REFLECTIONS

MY STORY

All my life I had been conflicted about WHO AM I - I knew from the age of 5-years that my origin was from the stars and not from here on Earth. For a number of years, I thought I was just different somehow and tried to fit into the physical form I was in.

We can trace my father's family back 15-generations to 1588 at Milton Parrish, Barnstaple Borough, Devon, England where John Lanman was born and then moved in 1640, to Flowerdew Hundred, part of Jamestown, British Colony of Virginia. Prior to 1588, we have pushed back our origin to Wales and even earlier to the Celts. Recent DNA testing indicates that I am 64.5% Britton and 24.6% Northern European (Netherlands, Belgium, northern France). Our family characteristics reflect that of the Celts, with Norse (Scandinavian) infusion due to their invasions of England/Wales, beginning in 793 and ending in 1066 when Harold Godwinson king of England defeated Harold Hardrada of Norway in the Battle of Samford Bridge and the Battle of Hastings when William duke of Normandy defeated the Saxon king, and infusion of Dutch DNA due to the Dutch immigration in the late 1500s when the Dutch Protestants were fleeing religious persecution.

In nearly all regards, Lanmans appear as taller in stature, very pale skinned, slightly athletic build, dolicocephalic shaped head, high nearly straight forehead, highbrow bone, light hair (sometimes, with a minor tint of red), well-developed chin, and light to medium eyes (light to hazel, with brown core and various color highlights).

Spiritually we relate to the sky, value honor and order and tend to apply rational intelligence. Have a highly developed will power, and put thought ahead of emotions. We strive for a "triumphant death."

All-in-all, we appear to be decedents of the Lyran or Palladian star systems. The Lyrans and Pleiadians first colonized Earth nearly 22-million years ago and it is for this reason that the Celts have no origin story other than they have always been, starting in the Steppes, across central Europe, to Belgium/ The Netherlands/ Northern France, to the Doggerland and then to Briton.

When I entered the 5th grade, my family moved from the Westside of Colorado Springs to the Northside of Colorado Springs. There the neighbor boy was, also, "star struck" and was into science fiction. We roamed the hillsides together playing that we were defending the Earth from space invaders. This play acting most likely reflected what we had both accomplished in prior lives (Refer to My Past Experiences and Lives). At that time, I immersed myself in Astronomy and Si-Fi books and literature that ranged from the play R.U.R. (Karel Capek), the novel Planet of the Apes (Pierre Boulle), The Late Great Planet Earth (Hal Lindsey), Fahrenheit 451 (Ray Bradbury), and Brave New World (Alex Huxley) to Chariots of the Gods (Eric von Danikin). In addition I began to question our belief system, our political systems, and what is/was reality.

In Junior High, High School and College, I realized that everything, including the universe, was based upon mathematics and that science supported the results of mathematics. I immersed myself in the study of Astronomy (Astronomy of the 20th Century by Otto Struve and Velta Zebergs, 1962), mathematics and science. I have a creative side and become a Registered Architect and a Professional Engineer (Structural). I even studied celestial navigation and the mathematics involved in navigating in a multi-dimensional environment. This was coupled with an inherent knowledge of how propulsion systems function, including light speed engines; all from glimpses into my many past lives.

About 20 years ago, I was more conflicted than ever and sought professional therapy. I had moments of recognition/ remembering past life events. I realized that I have a mission in this life. Even more so than in the past, I suddenly needed to know, understand, and experience more of what I thought I already knew. Yet, I soon learned that what I was seeking and yearning for was something that I can only find within. I began to realize that my life was planned before I arrived on Earth.

3-years ago, I began to realize that who and what I thought I was, I'm not and that I was living in an illusion that most call "reality." I realized that I am timeless and that I am firmly grounded in my connection to my higher self, the realms of Spirit, and my connection to One Source, the Creator. It was in this period that I began to collate my research into what became chapters of this Research Compendium.

In more recent times, I identify less and less as a person with problems to solve and more as a spiritual being experiencing problems – that are not really problems but just something that is happening. I am learning to reside more in my heart and less in my mind. I realize that I am where I am suppose to be and that I have access to my inner light and wisdom that I have always had but did not recognize. I realize that I have a higher purpose and it is my job to align myself with only this day of reality, since all past is but a recollection and is easily interpreted by our mind to be whatever we want it to be. More so, I realize that everything is happening as it should for my spiritual growth, since all around me is but an illusion.

MY PAST EXISTENCES & LIVES - Mostly incomplete – but glimpses, from time to time, come to mind.

- Just over 22 million years ago, I was on one of the planets in the Lyra System when the Draconians engaged in a full force attack. Over 50 million Lyran humans were killed. It is at this point in history that the Draconians began to look at humans as a food source. This is how old the struggle is between the reptilian and human races.
- There were four basic tribes or races on Avyon (our home planet), each having its own specific role or duty. There were no bad relations or feelings of resentment between the races. The Karidel were rulers and philosophers, the Orotheta were warriors and protectors, the Paetri were creative artists, artisans and skilled workers, and the Eata were the general folk who fitted in anywhere and who were very, very strong physically. I believe that I was or became an Orotheta warrior / protector.
- We were basically defenseless. The planets Bila, Teka and Merck were destroyed during the Draconians attack. I believe I was a survivor from one of the planets that were destroyed – I watched thousands upon thousands die, yet I survived that carnage – I often wonder "why."
- The Galactic War began innocently enough: There was apparently a miss-communication or misunderstanding between the Draconian and Lyran humans. The Lyrans wanted to know more about the Draconians before some kind of "assistance" was offered (just as Arlene always wants to know more: "Well, I have a few questions, first"). The Draconian mistook the communication as a refusal, and subsequently destroyed three of the of 14 planets in our part of the Lyran system.
- Prior to the Draconian attack, we had space travel technology and had established colonies throughout our star system (Lyra) and the neighboring star system (Sirius), having established colonies in Andromeda, Pleiades, Cygnus Alpha, Tau Ceti, Orion, Sirius, Altair, Alpha

Centauri, Arcturius, Antares, Hyades, Sagittarius A & B, Cassiopeia, Procyon and other worlds.
- We were a peaceful species, believing in service to others (as opposed to being of service to the self).
- Due to the attack, the planets of the Lyra Star System joined their forces that would lead to the foundation of the Galactic Federation, whose members stood united in fighting the Draconians. The Federation still exists today and is still one of the main players. It consists of civilizations from the Lyra constellation, from the Andromeda Constellation, from the Pleiades and Hyades open clusters, from Lumma [Wolf 424], Procyon, Tau Ceti, Alpha Centauri, and Epsilon Eridani, all of which are of Lyran/Vegan heritage. We were joined by a number of non-physical races (e.g., the Arcturins), by some Sirian groups, as well as by some Orion organizations, and by various civilizations from a parallel universe such as the Koldasians. We even received some unexpected members when some worlds with reptilian inhabitants joined, wanting to free themselves from submission to the Draconians. Within recent times, the Federation has grown from 100,000 planets to over 200,000 planets.
- Likewise, the Draconians have formed alliances and agreements that have led to the creation of the Archara Alliance (Sumerian/Akkadian Empire) and the Sirian Alliance.
- The basic belief system of the Draconians is service to self, in the false belief that if each serves him/herself, all will be served.
- Soon after the destruction of my planet, we vowed revenge for the 50 million Lyran deaths. I became a part of the Lyran United Space Command and through eons of war, I have been a battle strategist, an advance team coordinator, a star battle cruiser commander, a Fleet Commander responsible for part of our vast fleet. During an engagement, my tactics resulted in a major loss, where

thousands under my command died. For eons, I have carried this burden.
- The war has continued for eons, where I have been sent to many "war zones" as either a warrior or ambassador to seek truce (each a failure, so far) and have been killed or injured numerous times. Each time, my hatred for the Draconians and their allies has grown and solidified; as I watched the Draconians either destroy or treacherously ruled many planets and their people.
- We thought we brokered a peace through Merlin, but it too failed. We are now attempting to raise the frequency of the Earth and its people to achieve "Universal Love," for which many of us "warriors/ ambassadors" are finally trying to learn love for all, including our long time enemy, the Reptilians/Dracos/Anunnaki. We are trying to unlearn eons of hatred and rage for our age-old enemy, the Draconians and their allies.
- I have asked a Sensitive / Emotional Soul Guide to help me learn love and service to others, love and service beyond my own kind – the love that I may have had 22 million years ago, before the Lyra/Orion War against the Draconians.
- In more recent times, the Federation has tracked down the Anannaki, an ally of the Draconian. The Anannaki are a "pocket of resistance." We found them on the Sol planet of Mardek (10th planet in the Solar System) and, used a force field to draw an errand moon/small planet to strike and destroy Mardek. But a portion of the Anannaki had established a colony on Mars. Due to their warlike characteristics, the Anannaki split into two family lines and warred against each other and Venus, until they had destroyed Mars atmosphere and pocketed the surface with bomb (nuclear?) craters. But, many of the Anannaki escaped, with some traveling to Earth, where they rule today in a "draconic" way.
- The Federation (Arcturins) has constructed a force field around Earth to prevent Draconian from entering and to

isolate those "Elite" that are on Earth. We have sent ambassadors to Earth to discuss the issues with the human powers, of which are now under Anannaki control. We have sent agents (such as Arlene) to "break" the Anannaki hold (some success) and they are trying to awaken the humans to raise their vibration so they realize the "strangle hold" the Anannaki have on them – hoping that a critical mass will be reached and revolt occurs, for which we may forcefully assist.

- I am a watcher and report as to my assessment of the situation and advise as to whether we should attack (we have the Arcturin starship Athena and many others under the command of the Federation) or strive for resistance and love to breakdown the Anannaki strategy of "separation," in order to bring about change from within – are the non-controlled and enlightened/awakening humans strong enough to reach critical mass is yet to be determined.
- I believe that I was sent to be part of the Ashtar Command, a group of Federation free-spirits to assist in raising the vibration (spiritual development) of the Earth and her inhabitants through *Sovereign Integrity* (Human 3.0 SI), and to assist Earth humans with their emancipation (from Anannaki control) and their Ascension process.
- In 1994 - The "crack" is widening, since the Anannaki, renegade Reptilians and the Archara Alliance switched sides to the Galactic Federation. Anannaki Earth Command and the renegade Reptilians on Earth are slow to relinquish their control. Thus, the war continues, despite relative peace throughout the remainder of the galaxy.
- Perhaps, my history lead me to resonate with the protest song Universal Soldier, sung by Donovan, whose lyrics are:

He's five foot-two, and he's six feet-four,
He fights with missiles and with spears.
He's all of thirty-one, and he's only seventeen,
He's been a soldier for a thousand years.

He's a Catholic, a Hindu, an Atheist, a Jain,
A Buddhist and a Baptist and a Jew.
And he knows he shouldn't kill,
And he knows he always will,
Kill you for me my friend and me for you.

And he's fighting for Canada,
He's fighting for France,
He's fighting for the USA,
And he's fighting for the Russians,
And he's fighting for Japan,
And he thinks we'll put an end to war this way.

And he's fighting for Democracy,
He's fighting for the Reds,
He says it's for the peace of all.
He's the one who must decide,
Who's to live and who's to die,
And he never sees the writing on the wall.

But without him,
How would Hitler have condemned him at Labau?
Without him Caesar would have stood alone,
He's the one who gives his body
As a weapon of the war,
And without him all this killing can't go on.

He's the Universal Soldier and he really is to blame,
His orders come from far away no more,
They come from here and there and you and me,
And brothers can't you see,
This is not the way we put an end to war.

Having said this, diplomacy throughout the Galactic War has not worked either.

They say that "love is the only way", but can I forgive and love the race who, initially, killed 50 million of my people, and thousands of ones that I knew (the Lyrans), let alone millions of others within the human race, who are scattered throughout the universe.

PAST LIFE REFLECTIONS - Over the years of searching for a Reason, I have had many Dreams (refer to Appendix 5) to help clarify my existence and for the many past lives that I have been through, arriving at now being an Old Soul. My earliest past-life dream was seeing three of the 14 planets in my Solar System being destroyed, with a bit of knowledge that I had lived on one of the destroyed planets; that was approximately 22-million years ago, at the start of the Lyran and Orion Wars (this is part of what we all have seen in the Star Wars movies). A large number of dreams are of my service in the Federation Starfleet Command, ranging from Tactician, War College, Starship Commander, Participating in several battles, Writing dissertations on starship systems and means of star travel, an Ambassador and Truce Negotiator, Arriving on an Earth-like planet, to Returning home.

I have had a consistent personality over all of my lifetimes. Although I live in a world of possibilities, I have always seen the "Big Picture" and have developed many goal strategies to attain the end result; very little distracts me from seeking the endpoint. Given this, I am goal-oriented and go after what I want and won't let anything stand in my way – be part of the solution or get out of the way. I seem to have a natural gift for being a decisive leader, making decisions based on minimum data, and considering options and ideas quickly yet carefully. Although I have been a tactician, I am more of a strategist and apply logic, facts, data and associated research in the decision-making process, distancing myself from any emotion in the decision making process. I am highly intuitive, which helps to make the decision process much easier, when combined with the attribute of judging; together they keep me organized and disciplined. I am definitely not afraid of controversy, especially when it comes to things that matter. I speak my mind and spread the truth regardless of how others might see it. This becomes a bit controversial when I speak the truth and try to inform others, since many people might dislike what they hear.

My tenacious "search for the truth," and my many past life experiences have allowed me to write Chapter 5 – Life Lessons for the Soul, and has led me to compiling this Research Compendium.

APPENDIX 2

WHY I KNOW I AM LYRAN

LYRAN DEMENOR AND CHARACTERISTICS - The following information is a composite of knowledge that I have gathered through various websites that concentrate on the Lyrans – the cat people (of which, I believe I am a Lyran but, most likely, have had past lives as a Pleiadian, Vagan, others.

Many believe that there are no longer any Lyrans in the Universe, since many of the planets in the Lyran Star System were destroyed during the Galactic Wars, but this is not true since there were 14-planets within the Lyra Star System, plus the Lyrans were one of the first to have star travel. The Lyrans established numerous colonies throughout the Universe. The reptilians thought they had succeeded in their genocide of the Lyran race (through their planet destruction process), and that all were truly extinct from this universe. Luckily, that wasn't true. A group of shamans and priests were specifically chosen to keep the teachings, the history, and the beautiful and peaceful culture of the Lyrans alive forever. Afterword many left their physical bodies to become immortalized, not for the purpose of living near forever, but to spread their message more easily across the galaxy. To the ones who listened to these divine priests and shamans, the children of the Vegans now knew the Lyrans were still very alive and they were always there for the sons and daughters they had helped create and uplift. They also told the children of the Vegans, thriving in a sister universe other than this one This was mainly their message to spread hope to the positive beings of the galaxy. Partly due to their courage and virtue, the moral of the positive beings was greatly increased and then they established a uniting-rebellion federation that would bring together all of the beings that wanted to be free of the reptilian grasp. Thus, even against towering odds of their much smaller force, the reptilians either surrendered or were neutralized. This rebel federation would later become the Galactic Federation.

There are a few of us here on Earth at the moment but I know there will be more of us here in the coming years, so you will probably become acquainted and more aware of our presence in due time.

Earth humans have been enslaved by the Anannaki, an eon old adversary of the Lyrans. Thus, we are here to help and assist Earth humans with their emancipation and their Ascension process.

The Lyrans are a race of humanoids that have been in existence long before the history of Earth began. We come from many planets associated with the star system of Lyra. We are very humanlike in our appearance. You would not be able to tell us from any other human if you were to pass one of us on the street. In fact we are responsible for the seeding of Earth with the humanoid looking being that is associated with Earth.

We are perhaps on the average a little taller than most Earth humans and our skin is not as dark, but those would be the only differences between us.

There is some information out there that says we are now Pleiadians, but that is in fact not true. We would be considered cousins to them in a manner of speaking, but we are not one and the same. We worked a great deal in conjunction with the Pleiadians in seeding efforts not only on Earth, but many other planets as well. In that respect we share a great deal in common with the Pleiadians. In fact many Lyrans have lived many lifetimes as Pleiadians.

We exist on a higher-level plane of existence than Earth is presently on at this moment in time. We, as a race, have transitioned to this higher plane successfully in relatively recent times. This is one of the reasons we have a keen interest in Earth at this time because of Earth's own ascension process taking place now. This also is why there are many Lyrans incarnate on Earth so as to be of assistance to the Earth and Her peoples in this time of transition. We are here to help show the way, because of our experience. In a sense we have a parental role to play with the peoples of Earth and we are watching the Earth humans grow and mature.

There are several clues that would point to the fact that a person is a Lyran living on Earth. These clues have more to do with the personality than with the physical as our morphogenic form is very similar with humans from Earth.

These clues include:
- They are humanoid in appearance and very light skinned, more so than most Caucasians. The darker-skinned Lyran race has similarities to the Vegans but have a different generic structure.
- They have a temperament that is warm, sanguine and intellectual.
- They go to great lengths to avoid negativity. They seems to be consistently optimistic.
- They vibrate at a higher frequency that other humans – they sense the field of others before others sense them and have a sixth sense if the other person has a positive or negative field.
- They tend to be protective of their vibration/energy field and do not want any negative spirits unknowingly draining their energy vibration.
- They focus most of their attention on their spirituality.
- They display great independence and are highly adaptable to different environments (on other planets, denser gravitation, etc.).
- As a race, they are extremely close and have a sense of fair play.

- Very passive and peaceful, with a lack of emotional reaction.
- The person will have a sense of mission. They will know at some level even though they may not be able to put their finger on it that they have a specific purpose for being here.
- The person will be drawn to the stars. This may take the form of being interested in astronomy for example or reading science fiction or being attracted to science fiction movies and the paranormal of all sorts. They may even be involved in NASA or other space exploration and research organizations.
- The person will sense that there is an underlying truth in these books and movies. It may feel like one has been a part of something like that which one is reading or watching.
- These people also know that the human is capable of so much more, but knows that they were lied to (deceived) about the human potential.
- The person will also have a sense of underlying authority. People will tend to gravitate to them and trust their thoughts, judgments and opinions. The person may not be in a high position of authority, but nonetheless people recognize their authority. There will also from time to time be issues with authority or rather an aversion to authority figures.
- There is a certain amount of sternness and seriousness that goes with this type of person. They will not "suffer fools gladly" as the saying goes. In this vein they will not be the life of the party.
- They are more quiet and reserved and tend to do more observing than talking.
- They have the catlike qualities (the feline race is part of their inheritance) and, hence, are curious and inquisitive.
- This type tends to be loners. Not that they do not have family and friends, but they are comfortable with themselves and do not always need everyone around for fulfilment.

- The person often appears to be "distant" and unemotional, since they consider emotions to be a weakness. (They contain their emotions from nearly everyone).
- They seem to be very intelligent as to the workings of most everything. To the casual observer, many appear to be "ahead of their time."
- Are self sufficient, independent, proud and strong willed. There is an outer smooth energy and appearance of strength and capability.
- Tend to be knowledgeable in a wide variety of areas, they may be trivia "collectors" for information concerning their areas of interest.
- They have a variety of talents and capabilities, are quite creative and often have an ability to combine creative expression with intellectual expression. They may be artists, designers, inventors, architects or in current times may work more closely with new or expanding technologies. Their methods of working with technology will differ from many, as it is based more on "feeling" than on intellectual understanding. They do well at beginning projects, but less well at completing them.
- Are travellers who seek variety, challenge and understanding of the many questions they have within. They may become bored easily. They tend to fit into J.R.R Tolkien's writing of "Not all who wander are lost."
- They tend to analyze, question and doubt all which they do not understand, does not meet their belief system or simply does not "feel" right. Although quite willing to learn, change and grow, they need understanding to occur on an inner level to allow opening within for change to occur. This understanding will not be of a practical, logical nature. It will be an inner comprehension that will be more a "feeling" that leads to "knowing" instead of a technical understanding.
- They may need to work with developing a stronger sense of feeling the integrity of others, as they may find themselves taken advantage of due to their caring nature.

- They may find others attracted to their understanding energy, and may be approached in many situations by others wishing to share personal problems. It should be noted that few are willing to share personal details with others, unless trust is first established.
- They have a strong need for time alone, privacy, and freedom from restrictions. It is important that they be shown appreciation for what is done for others. Those in personal relationships with Lyran/Vegans may at times be in need of more attention, and may feel somewhat neglected, due to their many interests and areas of focus. They may neglect personal needs and personal relationships.
- They appear to be very old spirits that have travelled through many lifetimes, with many of those lifetimes not on Earth – they appear to be very galactic conscious.

Sources
1. 'Starseed Children: Traits of the Lyran Starseed,' *starseedchildren*.blogspot.com
2. 'Lyran Starseed Traits,' *Starseed Compass*, Mar 21, 2018, stairseed children.blogspot.com/ 2015/04/ traits-of-lyran-starseed.html

APPENDIX 3

MY AURA AND FREQUENCY

MY AURA - I am told by an acquaintance who claimed to be able to see auras, that my aura is opalescent and white with flashes of silver, all encased in gold.

- **Opalescent**: They are known as healers and herders of souls. Usually those who are in need of something (advice, a friend, anything really) are drawn to an opalescent aura person. In turn, the opalescent aura person has a natural ability to help them.
- **White:** Typically indicates a newness and purity. It can be found in highly spiritual people who've transcended the physical and are preparing to ascend to another Density. Religious history claims white auras were seen surrounding angelic beings. A bright white aura meaning is the transition to and from a physical body.
- **Silver** in the aura pertains to spiritual awakening and that the person is nurturing, intuitive and open to new ideas. Silver aura people have immense versatility and adaptability and are capable of getting the most out of virtually every opportunity in life. Their high intellect enables them to make the right decisions quickly and follow through with action.
- **Gold** pertains to divine protection and enlightenment. Someone with this aura is encased in divine guidance and has wisdom, inner peace, intuition and spiritual thinking. Gold aura people are exceptionally gifted. How they use their gifts wisely is their life lesson.

I believe it is this gold protective encasement of my aura that makes me very protective of my spirit. The gold encasement is there to keep other spirits from penetrating my "shield."

I WAS TOLD BY A SPIRITUALIST that my aura was in the range of 480 Hz, 450 Consciousness. The Spiritualist stated that he was on his way to Bridges National Park, when he was told to drive to Colorado Springs, stay in the Spurs n Lace B&B, make reservations for a 3-night stay (June 6, 2017) since he could help a spirit in need at that location (that was me). We talked about many things:

- He was here to assist me in getting me past the lesson that "the past means nothing" but it does tell one how they got to where they are, today. I had been "hung" on this lesson for years; after all, I had been a Lyran Warrior for nearly 22-million years.

- He recommended two books and a course:
  - The Essential Teachings of Ramana Maharshi – A Visual Journey, Edited by Mathew Greenblatt, *InnerDesign Publishing*, 1st Edition April 2003, Second Printing August 2007, ISBN: 1-878019-20-1
  - The Wisdom Teachings of Nisargadatta Maharaj – A visual Journey, Edited by Mathew Greenblatt, *InnerDesign Publishing*, 2nd Edition, 2003, ISBN: 1-878019-18-X Xxx
  - The Sedona Method: The Spiritualist, who visited me, had the course in person. There is a book by this name written by John Grey, PhD. The "Letting Go" Technique is available online, free – this helped me to let go of past lives and events.

- Other References:
  - Who Am I – The Teachings of Sri Ramana Maharshi, Printed by *Sudarsan Graphics*, Tamil Nadu, India, Thirtieth Edition, 2017 ISBN: 978-81-88018-04-8
  - Waking Up IN 5D, A Practical Guide to Multidimensional Transformation, by Maureen J. St.

Germain, *Bear & Company*, Rochester, Vermont, 2017, ISBN: 9781591432883

- He showed me a method to "feel from my heart" in order to raise the card that is between the two halves of my brain, so that the "universe" can "nibble it away." This would assist in increasing my brain capacity by about 30% in order that I could receive "transmissions" from the universe. (This Exercise is listed in Chapter 12, of this Compendium).

- The method shown of "Feeling/Thinking from my heart" would, also, help me to raise my antenna above my crown chakra. He stated I could do both the "card raising" and raising my antenna very easily. He stated that most "beginners" raise their antenna about three inches above their head. He said I had raised my antenna to about 30-ft. He asked me what I did when my antenna was up. I stated I was broadcasting "Is anybody there, does anybody care." He said "WRONG." That I needed to be listening, not talking.

- He asked me if I could see one of my guardians. I said "No." He stated that he was about 10-ft tall and standing in the corner, appeared as a shadow – we were in my kitchen, which has 10-ft ceilings.

- He told me that I would, become a Spiritual Healer.

554 | Appendix 3 – My Aura and Frequency

AURA FIELDS

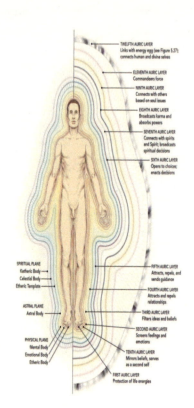

Note	Hertz	Equivalent Wavelength Angstroms/10 Nanometres	Approximate Colour
A	440	619.69	Orange-Yellow
A#	457.75	595.66	Yellow-Orange
Bb	472.27	577.34	Yellow
B	491.32	554.95	Yellow-Green
Cb	506.91	537.89	Green-Yellow
B#	511.13	533.44	Green
C	527.35	517.03	Green
C#	548.62	496.99	Green-Blue
Db	566.03	481.70	Blue-Green
D	588.86	463.03	
D#	612.61	445.08	Blue-Violet
Eb	632.05	431.39	Violet-Blue
E	657.54	414.67	Violet
Fb	678.41	401.91	Ultra Violet
E#	684.06	398.59	Invisible Violet
F	705.77	772.66	Invisible Red
F#	734.23	742.71	Infra Red
Gb	757.53	719.86	Red
G	788.08	691.96	Red-Orange
G#	819.87	665.13	Orange-Red
Ab	845.89	644.67	Orange

Color	Characteristic	Gland	Qualities	Imbalance	Resonance Frequency
Red	Physical	Gonads	courage, action, grounding, stability, survival	violence, greed, self, centeredness	194.18Hz
Orange	Social	Spleen	passion, trust, emotions, health, pleasure, let go	Jealousy, envy, aimlessness, obsessiveness	210.42Hz
Yellow	Intellectual	Adrenals	personal power, self esteem	fear, anger, hate, power	126.22Hz
Green	Self assertive	Lymph	Acceptance, forgiveness, love, radiance	Instability, repressed, love	136.10HZ
Dark Blue	Conceptual	Thyroid	Communication, truth, creative/arts	Depression, ignorance	141.27Hz
Indigo	Intuitive	Hypothalmus, Pituatry	Perception, realisation, intuition, clairvoyance..	Fear, tension, headaches	221.23Hz
Violet	Imaginative	Pineal	Fulfilment, inspiration	Confusion	172.06Hz

SEEING MY AURA

- I have learned to see a bit of my aura. I can see some of it when there is darkness in my room with light shining up the stairwell – thus, semi- darkness other than a bit of background light.
- In this light, it appears that my arms are covered in a royal blue/purple color with sparkles of silver throughout, all capped in a whitish gold (edges of my arms; a few inches from my arms).
- One time, when I awakened in the middle of the night, my arms appeared to be covered in dark blue/purple paisleys over a bluish-black background – very strange looking!

  - **Royal blue**: Highly developed spiritual intuitive or clairvoyant. Have a very generous and giving spirit, and are always open to new possibilities.
  - **Violet**: One is a visionary of the highest level, whose daydreams will change the world through spiritual love.
  - **Indigo aura:** Hast glimpses into other worlds and is a wise seeker.
  - **Black:** An unwilling and unforgiving spirit – Apparently I have not totally let go of my past lives of being a warrior and have not yet forgiven the Draco/Reptilians for having killed 50-million Lyrans during the initial part of the Lyran War and the follow-on Orion Wars of 22-million years ago. This color can also indicate that disease is being held in certain regions of one's body.
  - **Paisley** is a Zoroastrian symbol of life and eternity. The seed-like shape is also thought to represent fertility, has connections with Hinduism, and bears an intriguing resemblance to the Yin-Yang symbol (balance in life).

Sources:
  1. 'Aura Colors and Their Meanings,' Sally Painter, https://*paranormal*.lovetoknow.com/Aura_Colors_and_ Their_Meaning

2. 'Paisley: The Story of the Bohemian Print,' Lindsay Baler, Nov 2007, *BBC Designed*, www.bbc.com/culture/story/20151021-paisley-behind-rocks-favourite-fashion

APPENDIX 4

ANGEL NUMBERS

WHAT ARE ANGEL NUMBERS - Angel numbers are a way for your celestial guides to communicate with you. They can deliver specific messages through certain numbers or number sequences. This communication most often manifests in a series of repeat numbers or a series of synchronistic numbers (for example, looking at the clock and seeing 11:11 or checking out at the grocery store for $12.34). Seeing these numbers is one of the most common ways for your guides and guardians and counselors to let you know they are present, because numbers are a universal language.

WHY ANGEL NUMBERS MATTER - Pythagoras said, "Numbers rule the universe." Since the time he lived, science has only continued to prove how right he was. We find repeating number patterns in sound, geometry, the measurements of celestial bodies, and countless other realms of the scientific world. These mind-blowing coincidences and concurrences affirm numeric design as a key foundation of the universe. Numbers prove that there is precise balance in all things. And just like everything else in the universe, numbers carry an energetic vibration.

When you keep seeing the same numbers at seemingly just the "right" moment, your guides are calling you to explore the vibrational significance of those numbers. They are giving you a gentle nudge to quiet your mind and reflect on those numbers, their purpose, their meaning, and their message. And the more a number repeats in sequence, the more "supercharged" its vibration becomes. Once your guides have gotten your attention, ask them if they have anything more to tell you. Meditate and invite the guides into your space.

WHAT ANGEL NUMBERS MEAN - There is a range of numbers that have each been assigned a specific meaning. This range includes the numbers 1-9, and the master numbers 11 and 22. Where their meanings came from is a mystery. But the study of angel numbers and the occult study of numerology dates back thousands of years.

0 – You are receiving divine guidance and reassurance that you are on the right path.
1 – Keep your thoughts positive, focus on your desires and suppress your fears. Your thoughts create reality.
2 – Stay optimistic and continue to hold the vision, even through tough times.
3 – Your guides are with you offering love and wisdom.
4 – Your guides are surrounding you to offer assistance in this exact moment.
5 – Positive change is coming. Ask your guides to help you manifest this change.
6 – Release fear, embrace trust, and find balance between the spiritual and material realms.
7 – Your path is aligned with Divine fortune. Pay attention to new opportunities.
8 – Infinite success and abundance are yours, in alignment with your Higher Purpose.
9 – It is time to begin the work of your Soul Path, now that you have all you need.
11 – Your intuition is on target. Keep your thoughts and vision aligned with your intention and your greatest dreams.
22 – Be patient, your prayers have been received and will soon be realized if you continue to work towards them.

WHAT ANGEL NUMBER COMBINATIONS MEAN - You may not always see a double, triple, or quadruple number sequence repeated. Maybe you're seeing a sequence of combined numbers. Perhaps you keep looking at the clock when it's 3:17. And you saw 317 on the license plate of the car in front of you while driving. It could be any combination of numbers that you've been noticing again and again. Your angels are still speaking to you in the language of numbers, and there are a couple ways to decipher the message.

One way is to simply take into account each number and its individual vibration, then combine them for their cohesive significance. So, with the example 317, the number 3 means your angels are loving and guiding you, 1 means to keep your thoughts positive and 7 means Divine fortune is on its way. In these moments, when 317 pops up, your angels are saying, "We are here, and you are loved. Just keep your chin up because your dreams are coming true." They know this is the message you need to hear in that moment in order to continue striving for your Highest Good.

The other way to interpret these numbers, if you feel so led, is to add them up for a single-digit sum. The sequence 317 adds up to 11. Normally you would continue to add any two-digit number until reaching a solitary digit. However, 11 and 22 are the exceptions to this rule, because they are master numbers. So if you're seeing 317, perhaps your angels are sending the vibration of 11, saying, "Your intuition is right on the money. Keep going on your path, stays attuned, and stay aligned."

To decipher which one of these is the message takes quiet focus, spiritual attunement, and communion with your guides. Practice meditating on your angel number and keep asking for its significance to be revealed. The answers will come.

MY RECENT ANGEL NUMBERS

2:22 (several times) - Love rules! You will see improvements in your home life, your romance, and find inner peace. Don't push yourself too hard. Allow yourself to create with beauty and self-love rather than force. Dance and music can bring your balance and harmony.

3:33 (my cat often awakens me at this early morning hour) - You are in a creative flow. Nothing can hold you back from bringing your personal message into the world. Your heartfelt words and inspired vision can bring great changes to you and those around you. You are capable of having a positive impact on masses of people.

4:44 (my cat often awakens me at this early morning hour) - Your dreams, ideas and visions are being manifest into reality. You are building the foundation for your dreams that will also benefit those in your family as well as future generations.

5:55 (Often) - Four interpretations:

Meaning of 555: You Are a Divine Being - Seeing 555 is an angelic reminder that you are a divine infinite being who chose to incarnate here on Earth to experience life. Always feel that you have worth because you are here to co-create with the Universal Source and complete a life mission. Your life has ultimate significance.

2nd Meaning of 555: A Major Change Is Coming Your Way - Be prepared! A major shift is about to come into your life experience and change your path's direction. Although this change will have a great impact on your life, it can also bring the answer to all your recent prayers. So seeing 555 means that it is not what happens to you that defines you, but what you make of it.

3rd Meaning of 555: Trust Your Choices - 555 predicts a major change in your life, but it can also validate the fact that the change you're planning to make is the best thing for you to do right now. Seeing 555 is no coincidence, in this case, but a divine message that your decision to make this change in your life has been suggested to you by divine entities or your Higher Self.

4th Meaning of 555: Be Open and Stay Positive All the Way! - The meaning of 555 is to stay positive, confident and aware of everything that happens within your inner being. No matter what life throws at you, the most important thing is your state of being. The truth is that your state of being creates your circumstances, and not the other way around.

666 (Once) - A number wrongly associated with evil – is prompting for you to take a look at your current emotions and thoughts. This powerful number tells you that your thoughts are out of balance, and you are perhaps focused too much on the material (earthy) world, or have fear of lack or loss. Triple 6's encourages you to find a balance between heaven and Earth, and material and spirit. Always listen to your intuition and inner voices, as it always leads you in the right direction. Nothing is ever as bad as it may seem. (At the time, I was concerned that the purchase of the adjacent lot would severely restrict my finances, since the B&B has taken a significant loss that year). Even though this number does not seem so positive, be glad that you have the opportunity to experience it in your life. Think of it this way, that if you did not experience repeating 6's in your life, you did not realize that there is some knot in your thoughts that you have to untie. The meaning of 666 is to simply get rid of all fears and doubts you have. Take it as a gentle warning from the angelic realm, a sign that informs us about our current emotional state and that our vibrations are at a very low-frequency level.

10:10 (multiple times) – Can be seen as a key to unlock the subconscious mind, our genetic encoded memories, that we are spirits having a physical experience, not physical beings embarking on a spiritual experience (I have, often, told others that I am a spiritual being having a human experience).

You're at a powerful point of spiritual development and awakening. It's a call to stay positive, and to focus on your next steps on the Divine path appearing before you. It is a spiritual awakening number with the message that when you remain optimistic about where you are and where you are headed, you naturally elevate your

vibration, connect with the Divine, and magnetize the abundance, and opportunities needed to progress in the direction of your dreams, and life purpose. 1010 encourages you that you are supported, and the entire Universe is supporting you in aligning with success, joy, love, abundance, and fulfillment. It's also a strong call to stay focused on your spiritual growth, and to call upon the Divine and angels to support you in your life's journey. Keep taking steps to align more fully with your true desires, and know that you are guided and supported. When you ask for help, increase your awareness, trust your intuition and the inner guidance you receive, and take the next steps towards aligning with success and happiness and you will reach the desired outcome.
- A reminder that the entire universe is conspiring with you to help you reach your goals. Listen, trust, stay positive and take action!
- It also has negative effects such as treachery and betrayal from secret enemies.

11:11 (multiple times - Three years ago when I started my research) – I began noticing this number on my alarm clock just after I met a Physical Healer – This means that it is time to WAKE UP and be conscious of the universe, of which you are a part. This is the instant manifestation number! Focus only on the thoughts and energy that you would like to take into your future.

Sources:
1) Multiple internet sites, used to identify various repeating and sequential numbers.
2) 'What Are Angel Numbers and What Do They Tell Us?' Doreen Virtue, *Sage Goddess*, https://www.sage-goddess. com/what-are-angel-numbers/
3) Angle Numbers, Doreen Virtue, PhD, and Lynnette Brown, *Hay House Inc*, London, 5th Printing, 2006, ISBN: 10: 1-4019-0515-3

APPENDIX 5

DREAMS – IMAGINATION, MEMORY OR INTITUTION

We all have had dreams of living in a different world or in a different time period. Are these dreams just figments of our imagination?

Or are they memories of what we, thousands and thousands of years ago, once experienced—and at some point lost, as we descended into the kind of world we know of today, filled with struggle and suffering and lack of direct connection with the Divine?

Or do these dreams come from intuitions about the future that is in store for us? Many of us are having these intuitive feelings; some are having clear visions; others are inwardly hearing about the reality of humanity's future will be. Some of us feel we have been waiting thousands of years for these times we are now entering.

If we seek deeply within ourselves, we may find that these dreams are actually both a distant memory of what we once experienced eons ago and an intuitive glimpse into what is now beginning to happen on Earth.

Below are some of my more significant dreams.

- **Home** (before the Lyran War) - The following is a compilation of several dreams that I have had while "visiting" or living on my home planet. There are ten stars within Lyra. My home

planet (Avyon) was one of 14 planets in a system that had a Giant Brown Star and a White Dwarf in a bipolar orbit, as well as two moons and another close by planet within easy view. The bipolar stars created, at times, push-pull gravity on our planet. One would consider my planet a "blue planet" but larger than Earth. We had mountains and oceans. With the additional gravity, we were tall in stature, ranging from 7 to 9 ft (or taller), with males taller than females. Because of the Brown Giant Star, our sky had a gradation from blue to brown/rose to lavender at the horizon but due to the white Dwarf the colors of nature where much brighter and vibrant, with the greens - greener, reds-redder, and the blues-bluer. The population of the planets were diverse, made up of Carian, Felines, Humanoids, and Reptilians, and some were aquatic and others terra-types. We all lived in harmony/peace. We "talked" to each other telepathically, and we understood what the animals and plants were telling us.

There were four basic tribes or races on Avyon, each having its own specific role or duty. There were no bad relations or feelings of resentment between the races. The Karidel were rulers and philosophers, the Orotheta were warriors and protectors, the Paetri were creative artists, artisans and skilled workers, and the Eata were the general folk who fit in anywhere and who were very, very strong physically. I believe that I was or became an Orotheta warrior / protector. Only selected women were chosen to be breeders; no other women had sex or children.

Then the Draconian arrived and wanted our planet, Bila, with its abundant foods and beauty, to be their own. We stated we had questions that need to be resolved. The Draconian took the communication as a refusal, and subsequently destroyed three out of 14 planets that orbited our Lyran star. We (Lyrans) had a small defense force but, basically, we were defenseless. The planets Bila, Teka and

Merck were destroyed, along with 50-million vaporized. We sought revenge and the Lyran and, later, the Orion Wars began. This was approx. 22-Million years ago.

- **Numerous, Vivid Dreams of being in Starfleet** - (1) Watched my home plant and two other planets, of the total 14 planets that orbited our Lyran star, destroyed by the Draconian Empire – 50 Million vaporized, (2) I held various Starfleet position from Tactician (my battle plan lost 3,000 star troops on 100 different attack ships), to Ambassador, to Commander of a Star Destroyer during the Lyran and Orion Wars that began 22 million years ago (still going on but in the 'clean-up phase').
- **Have been a Federation Tactician** – One of my battle tactics lost numerous ships, as well as 3,000 Federation crewmembers. I have to live with memories of that major loss.
- **I am at War College** (or Library or within my quarters) and reviewing the course text on battle tactics and Rules of Engagement. There is a chapter on well known battle tactics and as I am reading the various techniques of attack, I notice that one of the battle tactics is named after me. The title was "In and Out – a forceful, surprise, surgical strike."
- **Starship Commander** – I am in my quarters (very small) studying the various propulsion systems. From fusion and ion engines, to light speed engines. Somehow I know how a two ring light engine operates. I later read how NASA knows the theory but does not have, as yet, the source of energy to activate a light speed engine (as a minimum, a starship will need a fusion reactor to drive a Vandergraph generator that, in turn, powers the Tesla coils that sequence electro-magnets to create a rotating field – this will barely be able to achieve light speed).
- Have been a **Federation Representative on the Orion (Sirian) Peace Treaty Negotiations** – did not last.
- **Was on one of the Planets** in the Lyran System that was destroyed by the initial invasion of the Dracos. Overall, 50-million were destroyed on three of the 14 planets orbiting

our Lyran star. I have no idea why I was a "survivor." We sought revenge and that was the start of the Lyran and Orion Wars of 22-million years ago.

- **Disobey Orders** - As Commander of the Star Destroyer Medallion, I am the center of a Starfleet Board of Inquiry. I am being asked (1) Why, as a Captain (O6) did I disregarded the Battle Armada Fleet Admiral's (O-11) directive to hold my position within the sub-light speed of the armada, (2) Why did I take it on myself and put my crew in harm's way to directly confront the Draconian Battle Group, and (3) Why did I disregarded the Federation's "Rules of Engagement."

I conveyed the following to the Board:

- Unlike other craft in the squadron, the Medallion was purposely built for war; it is compact in design, has a minimum complement crew of 40, has no holideck, no family members aboard, there were no staterooms, the entire crew sleep in bunks in shifts, including the Commander. The Medallion is overpowered (Warp 9.98 for 12 hours) - faster than any other vessel in the Fleet - and over-gunned - equivalent to that of a heavy cruiser (Phasers, Pulse Phasers, Laser cannons, as well as photon, quantum and cobalt torpedoes) all in a very compact ship.

USS Medallion - Crew 40 – 170 meter long - 4 decks - Launched 2372 per Star Trek

- Decoyed as an Escort vessel. Who would expect a Battle Group being attacked by an Escort Vessel? Surprise was on our side.

- Like other Fleet vessels, the Medallion did not have cloak technology, even with its compact size, but did have several cloak drones.
- If the Medallion was the only Federation ship in the Battle Arena, the Medallion would not be concerned about cross fire and firing from other Federation vessels.
- The battle plan was:

a) Send cloaked drones into the assumed battle arena, to target the Draconian ships and send that information to the Medallion prior to the Medallion entering the battle arena, Use the drones' information to target our weapons on specific Draconian vessels (based on Draconian vessel size vs. specific Medallion weapons), once the Medallion was inside the battle arena.

b) Enter the Battle Arena at maximum warp speed (just over Warp 10). Engage Emergency-Stop; directing the rebound energy of the Emergency Stop into the Medallion's weapons system (for maximum fire power). Fire all weapons at once to their maximum capacity (no reserve for shields or further weapon use), and immediately engage Full Warp Aft and quickly exit the Battle Arena.

c) Return to the approaching Federation Fleet; beg to rejoin the Battle Fleet and request resupply of all weapons in order to re-engage the Draconian ships in the Battle. Requests were approved by the Fleet Admiral, due to the need for all available vessels to enter the remainder of the Battle Arena.

Starfleet Board of Inquiry outcome was that I and the entire crew of 40 were officially reprimanded (into our records) for (1) Failure to follow a direct command from a Federation Fleet Admiral, (2) Placing the entire crew in harm's way and (3) Placing a Federation vessel in a position of likely destruction, and (4) Failure to follow the Federation Rules of Engagement. Later the Reprimand was rescinded. I did not receive a demotion, I was returned to the Medallion as Commander, and the entire crew was returned to their original ranks aboard the Medallion. There was a later ceremony where the crew of the Medallion was awarded The Meritorious Conduct Metal for Valor in a Battle Zone.

Due to the battle (Draconian loss of 4 Battle Stars, 5- Heavy Cruisers, 4 – Light Cruisers, 6-Destroyers and a total loss of 20-25,000 star troops, from then on I was called the "Destroyer" by the Draconians/Anunnaki.

- **On the command platform of a starship**, during a battle, and I am asked, as Commander, "What Do We Do Now?" I have no idea since I did not know I was the Starship Commander

NC 3069 Medallion – Crew 750 – 442 meters long – 30 Decks - Launched 2380, per Star Trek, but actually eons earlier

- **Studying Starship Operations Manuals in my Quarters** - I have returned to the starship, still not fully knowledgeable of my role as Commander. I am in my quarters and I am studying like mad the manuals for both propulsion and weapons systems. The Nebula Class ships are designed to be multipurpose, given whatever Module one has at the rear of the ship that rises up behind the saucer section – in our case, the Module has been modified to carry weapons and weapon arrays. We have several types of star-drives available: from very powerful tri-phase engines, proton engines, particle beam engines, to the very old reliable fusion engines that were developed many centuries before and they are only capable of sub-light speed (used if all else failed), plus one could deploy the solar sail (last ditch effort that would take years to get home). The tri-phase engines develop velocities that are approximately 5 to 6 times that of the max speed of a cruiser or Battle Star, but using them at Max speed takes a bit of time to phase up and their power will reduce the maximum fire power of the destroyer. That time is a matter of a couple seconds, a couple of seconds that are critical when one is in battle. Detailed workings of the tri-phase engines were very fascinating and involved technology unknown here on Earth. It's too bad that I didn't really understand how they work.

- Also, there were many symbols for the room names throughout the destroyer, such as the symbol for the crew quarters, the lift (elevator), etc. - way too many to recall. The purpose of the vessel was exploration (Module contained sensor equipment and smaller number of weapons), Combat (Module as mentioned above) and Blockade role to stop Draconian ships supplying the Dark Side/Annuanki on Earth and elsewhere.

- **Starship Lift (Elevator) Symbol** - Photo of Symbol (right) on my Ceiling of the window opening within my bedroom every night. Most likely it is caused by the floodlight that illuminates the north face of the B&B.

Symbol (right) found on Google Images that state it is the Lift symbol (elevator) used on a starship.

I believe that my Starship is nearby and the symbol on my ceiling is to telling me that I can "beam up" anytime that I feel threatened.

- **In a library, Writing a Dissertation** for an upcoming seminar presentation. I am, apparently, very old looking and the students around me, who are going to attend the seminar, are making fun of my age. Until they glimpsed the title of my presentation which is "How to achieve 10x light speed using an age old technology" (fusion reactor to excite the star engines).

- **Arriving on an Earth-like Planet** - Apparently, I was "beamed down" onto an Earthlike planet. I am in a small city that appears to be in the time period that I am in now. I have no knowledge of where I am or why I was sent – it is said that we all arrive with "injection confusion." I  have, around me, a containment/ force-field shield bubble that extends approximately 12-15 ft in each direction around me. There are two, very tall, armed guardians near me; I can see them, but those around me, cannot. There are people all around me, outside of the "force-field" and they are speaking in a language that I do not understand. Yet, I can hear what they are saying, telepathically. They are saying to each other that "She is an Ancient." I am dressed in a long, off-white colored robe over some kind of uniform. I hold up my hand with outstretched palm (palm in vertical position) in a gesture of what I think is peace. There is a crystal imbedded in my palm. What I "hear" is, "Watch out, She has a disruptor weapon." I then hear a voice that is outside the "force-field" that says that she can help me, if I let her inside my force-field shield. She asks "Who are you." Of course, I am confused and do not know. She notices that there is an ID Badge hanging on a lanyard from my neck. She views it and states that: (1) I am Lyran,

(2) Commander of the Star Destroyer Medallion; (3) I am a member of the Nibiran Council, and (4) I am over 900 years old. She then says that she knows me as "The Destroyer" of Battle Fame and that she can help me find clothing appropriate to the planet.

- **Awaiting For My Ship to Come In** - I am at a docking office adjacent to an ocean. The room (about 20 x 30) has a nautical theme and a small counter along the back wall. Behind the counter was, apparently an office and a maintenance room. After a while, I realize it is not an ocean ship but a starship that I am awaiting. After several minutes of just sitting in a lounge chair, I approach the counter. A person from the "back room" comes to the counter and tells me that my ship should arrive within the next few minutes and that I might want to go outside and to the restaurant several feet way to "gather" my crew. When I go outside it is raining and raining very hard. There is a hill near the docking office, which I climb in the pouring rain. There is a cliff to my right, as I climb the hill. I then look down upon the small town and restaurant. I am about 100 ft above the town and restaurant. The cliff arises above the town. There are several cars in the parking lot next to the restaurant. As I am looking down at the restaurant, part of the cliff falls in a mudslide down onto the restaurant and town, washing away the restaurant, cars, and part of the town into the sea. I watched all of this while standing in the soaking rain. I am just standing there in the pouring rain when the dream ends.
- **Returning Home (Kind of, Maybe)** - I am inside a transit terminal orbiting a planet, which I first thought was a train or bus station. As it turns out, it is a starship crew/ passenger transfer terminal somewhere near the Jovian moons. I seem to be awaiting a flight, yet I seem to be in no hurry. Some address me as Captain or Commander, yet I am not in uniform. I make small talk with many of the Nordics that are in the terminal. I am asked several times

how I like Earth. Many say to me that there are too many other species there and that the world is chaotic under the control of the Draconian Empire who is subjugating the inhabitants. I am asked if I have made contact with any of the Lizards (reptilians), insectilians, Ants (ant people), Greys, hybrids, or the Aunks (Anunnaki). I said no, I don't believe they even know I am on Earth. "Oh, they know" was the response but they are afraid of you. Do you know they call you the Destroyer? For having destroyed nearly their entire fleet by your Star Destroyer and the tactics you used in the Battle near the Orion Cluster. "They are not about to contact you." I was asked if I was on my way to Procyon for my promotion ceremony. I said I had no idea that I was to be promoted. They said that I would be promoted from Captain/Commander (of the Medallion) to Rear Admiral. I asked if it was due to my attack strategy that was used in the Battle of the Orion Nebula, and the answer was a resounding "NO". It is due to the fright factor that I cause among the Draconian Empire and the scare factor that my presence causes. When the Federation enters negotiations with the Dracos about releasing their hold on Earth, they want my rank to scare them into believing it is the Federation's intent that I no longer be seen as the "Destroyer" but to that of the "Enforcer." So, I asked "Does that mean I will be part of the negotiation team?" Heavens NO, the Federation wants you as the "scare factor" by just being present during the negotiations. So much for small talk.

When I approached the attendant at the flight desk and inquired about my flight, they told me that (1) I was not on the flight's roster, (2) They had no idea why I might be in transit, (3) that I had missed the flight, and (4) the next flight will be soon, in just another 18-Earth years. Is 18-years just a coincidence? I know that something is to occur in 2036, when I am 90-years old, but it is not my death.

Perhaps, the Federation's insertion into Earth's affairs will begin in 2036, when my change in rank occurs.

- **Email from the NC 3069 Medallion (Star Destroyer)** – I was in Trinidad, CO (Trails End Motel) overnight, returning from Continuing Education in Oklahoma City (May, 2017). Awakened at 5 am and could not get back to sleep so I decided to check my emails and noted the following with the subject line written in Greek/Early Roman and, possibly, Phoenician (none of which I knew but did find via Google). The Subject line was "NC-3069 Medallion UFC" (Nibiran Council - United Galactic Federation) and the message read:

Greetings Commander,

We are hopeful that your special assignment and R&R are going well. A crew member, who was on leave, saw you, this morning, at the Trinidad diner. Although Number 2 is performing well in the cleanup operation within the Orion Nebula, we are looking forward to your return.

Crew of the GF Destroyer Medallion

I did go back to sleep and awakened at 6 am, but the email was no longer in my file. Was it a dream or could it have been real?

Spaceship - Photo is the craft that I saw, not in a dream, flying over my Stillwater home in October 2000. I do not know how big it might have been, since I could not judge how close it was to me. It did appear to be quite low. It was triangular in shape and appeared to have flat sided and bottom, without curved corners or edges and without any protrusions. Tt appeared to have thruster engines which were rotating slowly, without making any sound. I did not see any view-ports (windows) on the side, as others have seen. My camera, which I hurriedly grabbed, did not take a clear picture.

- **Career Review (11/27/18)** - I am meeting with the Federation Director to discuss future plans. He states: "After lifetimes of being in Starfleet Command:
  a) "Your male compatriots have taught you to be a rational warrior, embracing change, unaffected by crisis after crisis, staying on target, always seeing the big picture, who knows her strengths and weaknesses, yet willing to tack calculated chances, being resolute in your decisions, and have also remained optimistic no matter the loses.
  b) "As a female in many lifetimes:
  You have learned to remain focused on the positive, devoted your time and energy to solving problems without harping on the negatives, have learned not to dwell in the past, have always been self-motivated by being motivated to achieve goals and not rewards, have learned compassion and to help others, not to be distracted but paying attention to the task at hand, to take care of yourself without much stress or health problems, and have learned to set boundaries (such as being able to say 'no') in order not to be overwhelmed or burned-out.

  "Given all of this, we have determined that you should become the Lamiakea Region Commander." The supercluster Lamiakea consists of roughly 8,000 galaxies, of which the Milky Way is on the edge of the supercluster. Each supercluster has its own center of attraction that separates it from other superclusters.

The Federation Director went on to say "You will say that you appreciate the honor being given to you but that you are unworthy, given the major battle defeat during one of your lives or even the failure of the Sirian Solution negotiations, but you are the one we need for this assignment. You will have no choice since it will be a command directive made by the 200,000 member Galactic Federation of Light, as was initially made by the Great Blue Lodge. You have been training for this position for the last 20-million years."

My response: "Do I get to pick my team?"

- **Fall of Jericho** - I just left an apartment (looks fairly modern) and I am standing looking up at a large fortressed city, similar to that of the middle Ages, except that the high, parapet walls were of clay brick.  I see what appears to be a slow moving meteor trail cluster of very larger rocks, most were the size of a house, all passing over the fortressed city. In the distance, below and to the left of the meteor trail, was a UFO. The UFO was traveling at the same speed as that of the meteor trail. Closer to me, but still at a distance, was a Blackhawk attack helicopter (black in color) and alongside the helicopter was a black stealth aircraft. High overhead was an advanced jet aircraft (F-35 looking) that began a steep parabolic dive, as if it might be attacking the UFO. The jet reached the bottom of the parabolic and then rose to be alongside of the stealth aircraft. The jet was in near stall position in order to match the speed of the helicopter. At this point my view changed to be on a high hill overlooking the fortressed city. There was a large group of Bedouin looking men on the hill below me; they were armed with spears. The UFO then used a tractor beam to extract large boulders from the meteor trail and directed their path toward the fortressed city. After I awakened, I realized that what I saw was the circa 1400 B.C. destruction of Jericho, the largest city in Canaan and the stronghold of the Anunnaki. The destruction was, later attributed to the Israelites (the Bedouin looking group). Yet, the Israelites were not known to be adept at fighting and only had Late Bronze Age weapons. The Anunnaki had lazier weapons and lazier cannons. It was the Pleiadians (UFO) who had weapons equal to that of the Anunnaki. Although the Pleiadians were not directly "siding" with the Israelites, they both had a common adversary in the Anunnaki. The Israelites had a bronze snake on a pole that leads them; the "snake" is a symbol of the Lizard people (a "distant" ally of the Anunnaki – but there was a faction war between the allies). My view was similar to that depicted in the photo but there was a "stream" of large boulders in the "war" clouds.

For the Pleiadians (part of the Galactic Federation), the destruction of Jericho and the Anannaki (Draco/Reptilian Aliance) was just part of the ongoing war. The war on Earth was a continuation of the Galactic Wars (Lyran and Orion star systems) and included the Anunnaki attacks on Pleiadian strongholds throughout the Middle Eastern area, such as the later (late 1400 BC) Anunnaki rocket attack, launched from Egypt, on Sodom and Gomorra.

Anu's temple at Uruk - showing a rocket

Starship from the 8 ft long seated Nibiran Seal Anu's temple in Summer (Iraq)

Babylon Cylinder - Note the Mushroom Cloud and Dead Leaves on Tree – As described The Mahabharata and the Ramayana are Sanskrit epics that described the Kurukshetra War battle between Rama and the demon Ravana. This war occurred in 9th century BC (nearly 12,000 years ago).

Source of Anu's Temple Seals & Kurukshetra War Bomb:
1. 'ANCIENT ASTRONAUTS EVIDENCE, Part 1: Overview, Rockets on Web Radio,' Sasha (Alex) Lessin PhD, *Aquarianradio*, http://aquarianradio.com/2013/03/21/ancient-astronauts-evidence-part-1-overview-rockets-on-web-radio-illustrated-below/
2. 'An Atomic Bomb Detonated On Earth 12,000 Years Ago,' K. Heidenreich, Mar 25 2017, *Ancient History*, https://www.disclose.tv/an-atomic-bomb-detonated-on-earth-12000-years-ago-313772

APPENDIX 6

MY CAT AS SPIRITUAL GUIDE, GUARDIAN & COMPANION

CATS ARE SPIRITUAL BEINGS - We all know how cats come into our homes and into our lives, but what most don't know is how cats are a match with spiritual people.

Cat owners are usually people with enhanced spiritual abilities. Cats are drawn to spiritual people, as they have an energy that connects with higher realms. A cat is a spiritual animal as it relies on its spiritual abilities, as well as its catlike instincts. As a cat grows, so does its energy field. The older the cat, the bigger the energetic field. This means that as time passes, a cat gathers more spiritual power. Cats also capture sounds that you cannot hear, as they become accustomed to a different frequency.

Spiritual People have a higher energy field that attracts cats. Cats can trust those people more easily than others. Similarly, people with high energy fields, are drawn to cats because of their own high frequency. Think of it like two people who are a match vibrationally. Cats are picky on who they trust because they can easily understand each one's frequency field. This does not mean that cats only choose people who practice spirituality. "Spiritual people" mean people who have more innate connection. Some don't practice any form of spirituality, don't meditate but they have a connection with their Higher Self. They are intuitive, they trust their inner guidance, they are positive. Those people do have a higher energy field, even if they do not know it.

Cats are truly amazing spiritual beings for many reasons. You may not realize just how much your own cat protects you from entities & attacks that your physical eyes are unable to see.

Cats have the ability to reincarnate, many times. They may reincarnate as house cats, lions, tigers, panthers, mountain lions, bobcats, and any other form of cat they wish to. They are one with their Higher Self, not separated from their Higher Self like we are, where there's a 4D version of us at a much higher dimensional level. Being one with their Higher Self, they come into their incarnations with all their former memories fully intact, right as they are born as kittens.

CATS ACT AS GUARDIANS - Cats can act as phenomenal guardians for us even when we are unaware they are doing it. They can chase off entities and take entity attacks for us as well. They have the ability to see through all dimensions. I believe that Tabs, my cat for nearly 20-years, had the mission to be my guardian and a guide.

TABS my guardian, spirit guide and companion
May 1998 – April 2018

I had a "Healer" and fellow "Wanderer" tell me, after Tabs passed, that he was a multidimensional "Traveler/ Wanderer" that originated in the Tau Ceti star system, nearly 15- light years from Earth. And that my cat was here as much to learn as he was to teach, advice and protect.

Tau Ceti (Cetians) and Epsilon Eridani are said to be a major 'convergence' of exterran 'human' activity, and are said to be in alliance with the Pleiadians (who in turn, according to contactees, have 'Federated' alliances with the Vegans, the Ummites, and others.). The Cetian alliance with the Pleiadians and 'other' societies who have been 'victimized' by the 'Grey' predators is based on a desire to establish a common defense against their reptilian nemesis.

As a guardian, Tabs would awaken me during the night to alert me that an entity was near me and that I need to be aware. Although Tabs has passed, he is still near me as a guardian.

CATS ACT AS SPIRIT GUIDES - As mentioned above, cats incarnate into this world with full memory of all past lives and experiences. In addition they are telepathic. They are in constant communication with the spirit world and are the bridge between the realm of the unseen and the seen. Your cat is a channel to you receiving spiritual messages. Given all of this, your cat can guide you along your chosen path, encourage you to complete spiritual research, encourage you to document that research, and can help suggest when to look for the information you seek. Of course, this is all done telepathically so you are not aware that it is your cat that is one of your guides.

TELEPATHIC COMMUNICATION - One can communicate telepathically with your cat. This goes for physically incarnated cats and ones that have passed on to another realm. It is much easier communicating with them than it is with a very high dimensional being that is your spirit guide. One can by sending feelings to your cat and sending images back and forth. However, you may have to wait for the cat to mature to the point he realizes that he is multidimensional.

Even after Tabs passed, I see him in meditation. Over his lifetime here on Earth, he has lead the way for me to Wake Up and realize that I, too, am a multidimensional spiritual and an Old Soul, where we have traveled together in many past lives. I recently started asking him to act like a channel for me to talk to higher frequency beings throughout the universe and to my guides and guardians.

HUMANS CAN INCARNATE AS CATS - Humans have the ability to incarnate as cats too. They are powerful enough beings for that to work. Lryan's, such as me, were originally formed in the essence of a cat for a reason! The incarnated Lyran's were not supposed to forget as much as they have by incarnating onto Earth. There generally is not a range or limit on cat incarnations.

Sources:
1) Amelia Bert, 'Cats & Spirituality,' https://ameliabert.com/ cats-spirituality/
2) 'Cats as Devine Messengers,' *ThoughtCo*, https://www.thoughtco.com/cats-as-divine-messengers-animal-angels-124478

We all started this journey to enlightenment by abandoning the comfort of our world illusion, as given to us eons ago, in exchange for a "winding road" of danger, fear, and fearsome creatures in order to achieve the enlightenment of knowing that we are a free spirit in the universe, untethered by any controlling entity. We took the arduous journey of WAKING UP.

You could have just stayed ASLEEP in the comfort of your bed (of ignorance) or turned back when the going got tough. But even if the fate of humanity was not on your shoulders, you would regret the minute you returned to the safety of the illusion.

Because, if you do not "leave home" and embark on your journey, you will never have really lived at all.